Build Your Own Frame House

S. Blackwell Duncan

TAB BOOKS

Blue Ridge Summit, PA

FIRST EDITION
FIRST PRINTING

© 1991 by **TAB Books**.
TAB Books is a division of McGraw-Hill, Inc.

Library of Congress Cataloging-in-Publication Data

Duncan, S. Blackwell.
    Build your own frame house / by S. Blackwell Duncan.
        p.   cm.
    Includes index.
    ISBN 0-8306-8453-0 (hard)   ISBN 0-8306-3453-3 (pbk.)
    1. Wooden-frame houses—Design and construction—Amateurs'
manuals.   I. Title.
    TH4818.W6D86   1991   90-24056
    690′.837—dc20   CIP

TAB Books offers software for sale. For information and a catalog, please contact TAB Software Department, Blue Ridge Summit, PA 17294-0850.

Questions regarding the content of this book should be addressed to:

Reader Inquiry Branch
TAB Books
Blue Ridge Summit, PA 17294-0850

Acquisitions Editor: Kimberly Tabor
Book Editor: Cherie R. Blazer
Production: Katherine G. Brown
Book Design: Jaclyn J. Boone

Contents

Introduction

One of the goals of every family has been to have a home of their own. It is part of the American Dream. A home has always been a symbol of security, of happiness, of success, of love and warmth. It is a place of refuge from the rest of the world. The English statesman William Pitt once remarked, "The poorest man may in his cottage bid defiance to all the force of the Crown."

In the early days of this country even the "poorest man" could have his own cottage, or cabin, especially in the rural areas that were mostly on the edge of an untracked wilderness. People usually built their own houses, sometimes several of them, during the course of a lifetime. As the country grew, so too did available funds, and the building and associated trades. Especially in the populated areas, house building was relegated to commercial builders. Those who could afford to have their homes built did so, while they followed other pursuits. But there were still many owner-builders around.

As the decades passed, house construction became more complex, more expensive, and more regulated. New materials, new methods, new techniques, new systems, new rules and regulations proliferated. At the same time the population became more involved in specialized areas of work, so for the most part house building was left to those who made a career of building houses. The skills of the carpenter, builder, mason, and similar artisans were lost to most of the population.

Today most houses are still being built by professionals, but unfortunately their cost is unconscionably high. And the price tag on a preowned house, even a small one, is hardly less than a new one. It has been decades since any but the most affluent could purchase a house outright, for cash—financial aid has long been a requirement for nearly all homebuyers. However, the amounts needed and the costs of borrowing are so high that the average wage earner finds it difficult at best to qualify for a home loan, or even scrape up a down payment. For many people, purchasing a home is impossible.

There is hope. Some folks have concluded that if they're ever going to have a home of their own, they must follow in the footsteps of their forefathers and build it themselves. More and more people are realizing that in order to attain that goal of home ownership they're going to have to scheme, plan, scrounge, cut costs, maximize every possible advantage, overcome the potential problems, invest their own energy and sweat and tears, and become owner-builders.

One factor that holds many would-be owner-builders back from building themselves is a lack of specific house construction knowledge, together with the impression that a house is an awfully intricate, complex structure that is beyond their ken and capability. It is true that there are many, many components in a house, and you do have to know which ones go where and how to tie them all together. On the other hand, you don't have to be a rocket scientist to get the job done. Once you reduce a house to its various subassemblies, then to the various parts of each of these, it's not nearly as complicated as its completed appearance suggests. For example, you can actually build a complete house shell (not including foundation) with just three piles of materials—one of 2×4s, one of 2×10s, and one of 1/2-inch plywood panels. Plus a few boxes of nails.

If you are holding back from starting your own home planning/building project because of a lack of specific information on how to construct a wood frame house, this is just the manual you need. It will show you in detail how a platform-framed house is put together. The text presupposes that you have some knowledge of and skills in basic carpentry and can hang onto the right end of a hammer, make measurements, do the simple math that all such construction requires, and can sort out the details shown on sketches, drawings, and blueprints. That's all you need, except for some time, ambition, courage, and cash, to get rolling on a home of your own using this book as a guide. From preparation and planning; through siting, choosing and building a foundation; through framing and sheathing the shell and applying the finishing touches, it's all here. There are no mysteries nor any magical processes, just straightforward, commonsensical, hard work that ends in one of the most satisfying and rewarding results imaginable: a home of your own.

Chapter **1**

Preliminaries

*P*erhaps you already have completed the plans for your house, or purchased ready-made plans from an architectural firm or a plans publisher. The problem here is that the plans might not be complete or suit your particular circumstances. New house plans should always be completely reviewed prior to the start of construction. This double check will often save everybody time, effort, and money, and maybe some grief as well.

For example, as a result of reading this book, you might determine that some alterations in your plans are necessary or advisable. You might also discover some ideas that appeal to you, leading to some changes or additions. A last check can turn up items that have been forgotten or set aside, or an error, or some previously unknown factor that will mean changes. And even if nothing appears to be out of order, the exercise is a good one if only from the standpoint of peace of mind.

Before construction or even lot clearing can properly begin, there are a good many preliminary matters that should be checked out. The paperwork must be complete and the bureaucracy must be served; having your project stopped by the local building department before you barely get rolling is discouraging to say the least. Following are the items that you *must* investigate:

- Clear title—It would seem obvious that you should have clear title to a building lot or a tract of land when you purchase it, much less before building a house, but many people do not. If the property has liens or encumbrances, or if there is any hint that some other person or entity might have a claim to the property or can show color of title, or if the metes and bounds are fouled up, or if there are any legal questions of any kind about the property, there could be trouble in the future. If a title company will issue title insurance to you, that is a good indication that the title is probably clear, subject to whatever exceptions are written into the policy. But it does not give you 100 percent assurance that the title actually *is* clear, only that there is nothing in the public records to indicate otherwise. The more straightforward and unfettered the property, the better.

- Deed restrictions—Many people purchase property that is conveyed by a deed containing restrictions of one sort or another. They may pay little attention to them, or think perhaps after enough time passes the restrictions won't apply, or they don't understand the full import of them. Deed restrictions, whatever they might be, can remain in force forever. They can range from disallowing persons of a certain race or faith to purchase the property, to restricting use of the property for certain things, to ensuring that there is a vegetable garden kept in perpetuity—any cockeyed notion that someone else will agree to. Be wary of any restrictions.

- Legal access—This is a grand trap that lots of folks fall into. A property can be free and clear with a solid title, but have no legal access at all. A property can appear to have legal access but actually have none. An access route may be provided by means of a verbal agreement, a letter of permission from another landowner, or through public lands, or by means of a purported easement, or in some other questionable way. Any of these might eventually evaporate for any number of reasons. Note too that a property might have a road or trail onto part or all of it that is supposed to be private and a part of that property—but which in fact is a legal right-of-way to other property. This can cause all manner of problems. Make sure of your access situation.

- Water availability—Water is an absolute necessity at a building site, but not automatically present. This is not a factor with urban and suburban properties, because a municipal potable water main passes close to the property. Residential subdivisions also almost always pipe water to each lot. For exurban and rural sites, however, you need some assurance that water is available, at least potentially. Surface water supplies are sometimes used. In this case, make sure they do not seasonally dry up, and check to see what claims or restrictions are on the water. If a well must be dug or drilled, make certain that there are others producing a sufficient year-round quantity of usable water.

- Well permit—In many areas of the country you must get a permit to drill a water well; it is not automatically granted. Usually, domestic and agricultural water uses are separated; in some areas only domestic permits can be obtained. Issuance can take several months, and there is often a fee. Permits usually come from the state level, but administration might be at a local level. Check with your county or city health or building department.

- Percolation test—Building sites that are not served by a municipal sewage system must have a septic system installed. This requires that the soil at the site of the septic leach field be capable of absorbing a minimum amount of fluid. And that, in turn, requires that a percolation test be made on the soil to determine the rate of absorption. If the rate is unsatisfactory a system cannot be built, nor can the house. Often the sale of a property is contractually contingent upon a satisfactory "perc" rate. Make sure that this requirement is satisfactorily filled, if necessary. Note, however, that in some areas there are newer types of septic systems in use that can be installed in soils unacceptable for conventional systems.

- Septic system permit—In almost every part of the country a permit is required to install a septic system. A satisfactory soil percolation rate is one requirement for obtaining one, and an approved system design and inspections of the installation are others. The process is governed usually at state level but administered by town, city, or county building or health officials. There is a fee.

- Electrical service—Having electricity provided by a public utility at the building site is not an absolute essential, because there are ways to get around this potential problem. However, few houses are built where line power is not available—and there are plenty of places where it is not. The cost of bringing in electricity can be enormous—thousands of dollars per mile in some cases—and sometimes it is not obtainable at all.

- Telephone service—If this is important to you, as it is to most folks, make sure that service is available. If not, determine what the cost might be to bring a line in to your property. As with power lines, the cost of obtaining service in rural areas has escalated greatly in the past few years and sometimes is a practical impossibility. There are communication alternatives to an ordinary telephone, but they are expensive.

- Zoning—These laws are in effect in most parts of the country, especially in population centers. If in your area there are no laws, you can build anything you want to, any way you want to. If zoning is a fact of life, make sure that your plans comply. The regulations can be far-reaching, and can include such items as minimum or maximum square footage of the house, maximum square footage of the building lot that the building can cover, height restrictions, property line setbacks, and plenty of other constraints. Zoning also governs the kind of buildings that can be constructed in certain areas. Check for any indications that the zone where you intend to build could later be changed to allow other uses. Such zoning changes could lower your property value or desirability, or affect your lifestyle.

- Land-use laws—Numerous kinds of land-use laws are in effect across the country. They govern what can be built in certain areas and what the land can be used for. If any are in effect where you propose to build, make sure you are either in compliance or unaffected by them.

- Wildlife review—In some rural areas a prospective home builder must submit a complete plot plan to state wildlife authorities, showing the exact location of all buildings and improvements on the property. The plan is reviewed to ensure that wildlife in the area will not be adversely affected by either the construction of a building or its continued presence.

- Covenants—These are common in housing subdivisions and are used even in a few cities and towns. They consist of a lengthy and complex list of regulations covering a host of matters. Typically they govern the placement of houses, height of fences, location of clotheslines and trash containers, colors of paint and kinds of exterior materials used on houses, traffic speeds on internal roads, and the number of vehicles permitted per family. These rules usually have the force of law and are a part of the property deed. Be wary, for often a set of covenants, especially if they are particularly restrictive and disputatious, does not accompany the paperwork given to a purchaser. Many people find many covenants difficult to live with. Covenants are recorded documents, so you can find out if any exist and what they are at the town, city, or county clerk's or assessor's office.

- Building codes—These are the most commonly used sets of rules and regulations, along with zoning, to govern the construction of residences. They address the methods, design, engineering, materials, and safety aspects of the construction itself. There are four model building codes in widespread use today: the Uniform Building Code (UBC), the Southern Standard Building Code (SSBC), the Basic Building Code (BBC), and the National Building Code (NBC). They are not identical but have a similar thrust. Several auxiliary codes are used in conjunction with the model codes, such as the Standard Plumbing Code, the Uniform Fire Code, and the Basic Mechanical Code. The National Electrical Code is almost universally employed to govern electrical installations of all kinds. Check locally to determine which, if any, codes are in effect, and go over your plans to make sure you are in compliance. Code copies are usually readily available.

- Variances—If something in your plans runs afoul of a zoning regulation, land-use law, or local building code provision, and you are refused permission to build, you can appeal the decision. By taking your case before a local board and explaining why the decision was wrong or unfair, or that is a proven hardship, you might be able to get a variance that will allow you to go ahead. Otherwise, you will have to change your plans. The local building department will give you the details on this process.

- Building permit—In most places a building permit is required before any work whatsoever, even groundbreaking, can start. The permit often applies whether or not zoning is in effect, and regardless of how strictly any building codes are enforced. It covers all the general aspects of construction, except the mechanical trades and a few specialty items. The usual requirement is to submit a full set of plans and specifications to the local building department. They check if everything is in compliance with local regulations. If everything is in order the permit is issued; if not, changes must be made until compliance is assured. A fee is charged, often based upon the estimated value of the completed project. Inspections of the work in progress are required—phase by phase at the discretion of the building department—and the inspector has the power to stop the work at any point for code violations. You can get full details from your local city or county building department.
- Electrical permit—This might be required even in the absence of a building permit, and covers the entire electrical installation. Issuance is often at state level, and inspections made by state personnel. Your local building department or other town offices will have the necessary information.
- Plumbing permit—This covers the installation of the cold and hot water systems, the drain-waste-vent (DWV) system, and the water supply lines. This permit might also be required even though a building permit is not; check with local authorities.
- Sewer tap—Where a municipal sewer system is involved, you must make application to the appropriate office for a sewer tap, which is a hookup of your main house drain to the system. The tap is usually made by sanitation department employees or their contractor, for a fee.
- Water tap—This is the same situation as the sewer tap. Make application at the local water department; for a fee they will make the tap.
- Soil survey—It is a good idea (and sometimes required by local authorities or lenders), to have the soil at the building site examined. This is done by a soils engineer, to ascertain the composition of the soil at the points where the house foundation will be constructed. By determining the soil classification, the engineer will determine how much weight per square foot it can hold up with-

out subsidence, and assess other factors that have to do with designing a stable foundation. The local building department might have a list of contractors, or you can check the Yellow Pages.

- Fireplace permit—More and more often, permits and accompanying inspections are being required for fireplace and wood stove installations. In some areas only approved units are allowed, in others only gas-burning units can be installed. A fee is charged for the permit. Check with the local building department.

- Satellite dish permit—Because of the proliferation of satellite dishes on the landscape, many cities and counties now require a permit, location approval, and final inspection for a dish installation, for which they charge a fee.

- Certificate of occupancy—In many places you cannot just move into your house after it's finished. You must first obtain a certificate of occupancy from the local building department stating that the premises have been inspected and found to be safe and habitable. Also, you might not be able to move into a partly completed house, with the thought that you will finish up while living there. This is up to the discretion of the inspector.

- Licenses—In most places, and under all the model codes, you can do whatever work you wish to on your own house or outbuildings without having a license. Local authorities in a few areas, especially urban ones, do not agree, and require appropriate licenses for various aspects of the construction process. In many cases you can do the actual work under the supervision of a licensed contractor. Situations vary; check with the building department or a local materials dealer.

- Improvement survey—Before you can start work, you might be required by one authority or another to have an improvement survey made. You select the surveyor and pay the bill. The surveyor surveys your entire property, noting all improvements, and submits a survey map and report to the requester, and forwards copies to you.

- Financing—Before you start, make doubly sure that all of your financial arrangements are rock solid, especially if they happen to be made with noncommercial sources. Understand the fine print, be aware of the contingencies, know your part in the arrangement, and be prepared to faithfully carry it out. Obtain legal advice if you feel uncomfortable or unsure about any part of any financial agreement, no matter how minor. Financing problems account for a lot of unfinished houses.

Chapter **2**

Site preparation

*T*he first step in the construction of a house is to prepare the building site so that work on the structure can begin. At this stage owner involvement is important—and the larger and more complex the structure and the overall plan, the more important this becomes. An owner who actively participates can be reasonably assured that the maximum potential of the building site will be realized. This can mean savings that range from modest to huge in terms of time, effort, and money expended later on. Further, a relatively minor effort at the beginning helps avoid hassles and disappointments and makes for a smoother, more satisfactory construction program.

If a 25-by-50-foot house is to be built on a 75-by-125-foot town lot with the topography of a billiard table, there isn't a whole lot to do in the way of site preparation. A pad must be prepared for a slab foundation, a shallow hole for a crawl space foundation, a deeper hole for a full basement. Spoil dirt must usually be trucked away and gravel or sand hauled in. This work should be monitored if anything on the site must be protected or preserved. Some recontouring might be possible or desirable, and continuous owner input on the exact shaping is valuable there. Make sure the excavating contractor understands beforehand what is required. Existing trees or shrubs might be saved, especially if the site has been previously built upon. Otherwise, there is not much for the homeowner or owner-builder to do except keep an eye on things.

As the building site gets up toward half-acre size (roughly 100 by 200 feet), there is more for the owner to do and watch over. This increases considerably with the size of the land. Now owner involvement is crucial if the site amenities are to be protected and site disturbance minimized.

7

Regardless of the degree in which you as owner will engage in the construction of your house, supervise as much as possible. You are the only one who knows exactly what you want. Do as much of the actual work as you can yourself, and hire capable people who can understand directions to help as necessary.

PLOT PLAN

If you don't already have one, this is a good time to prepare a plot plan. This shows in outline form the entire property, with the house and any outbuildings drawn to scale and located in proper relationship with one another and with the property boundaries (FIG. 2-1). The house should be oriented in the desired compass direction (with north at the top of the plan, like a map). Include on this plan the approximate routes of the power, telephone, and water lines; the driveway or approach road; parking area or pad; septic system or sewer line; water well if present; and any other pertinent items. Note the major dimensions and distances as well.

Depending upon the size of the map, it is a good idea to note all of the major topographical and natural features in the vicinity of the house and in any other areas of the property that will be improved. If the property is a large one, you can make a smaller landscaping plan that details all such existing features that you plan to retain, plus those that will eventually be added, in the area that constitutes the immediate house grounds (FIG. 2-2). With all of this, there is less chance of forgetting something or making mistakes.

Usually the first step in site preparation is to locate the house footprint or envelope. This is an area, somewhat larger than the house, to allow room for orienting the structure to the most desirable direction. You can stake out the envelope and flag it with surveyor's tape. Next, orientate the structure within the envelope, so that you will know within a few feet where the outline of the structure will lie. This will also give you an idea of the lie of the access route. Perhaps only a short driveway is needed, perhaps a long one. In some cases providing the access amounts to a road-building project.

DRIVEWAY

Stake out the driveway or access road line with care. Consider minimum grades and curves while preserving a pleasing aspect. Make sure you have ample width. If you are in winter country, make the drive easy to plow with plenty of room at the sides for snow piles. If you can avoid cut-and-fill work you will keep earth moving expenses down, but the degree of difficulty of navigating the driveway may escalate. This is often a compromise situation. Clear brush and cut down trees by hand; save the wood for firewood and chip the brush and branches for mulch and compost. Save as much natural vegetation as you can, to the extent of skirting around mature trees and shrubbery clumps. This is especially worthwhile if vegetation is sparse and/or the growing season is short or dry, or both.

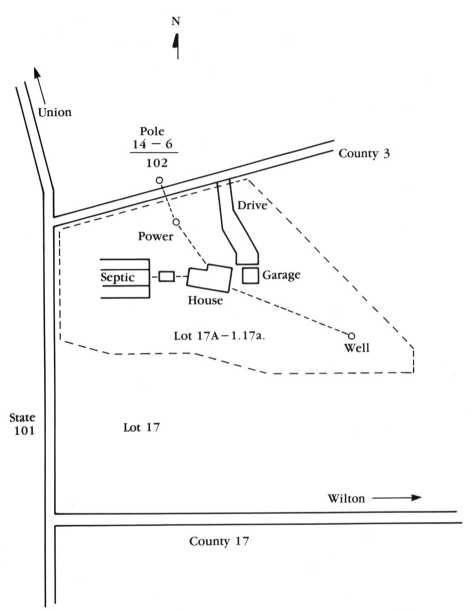

2-1 A typical general plot plan for a large tract, showing the basic proposed layout.

Have the driveway bulldozed or scraped with a small machine that won't tear everything up, but make it wide enough for easy driving. The turnout onto the public roadway should be extra wide to allow turning room with no danger of dropping into a ditch or cutting into the side banks. Dig down deep enough to remove all live roots; take up all the wood and dispose of it. Small amounts of spoil can simply be spread

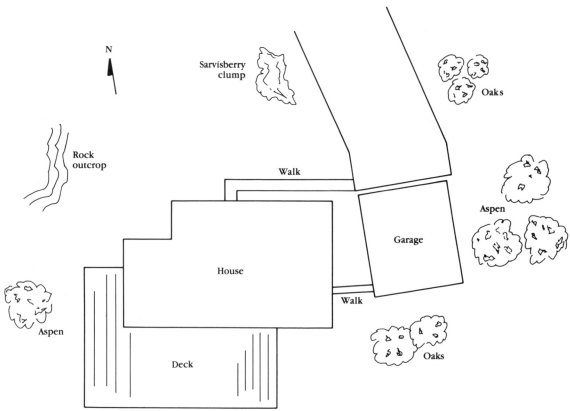

2-2 A smaller, more localized plot plan including landscaping details is often helpful.

around; large quantities might have to be dumped elsewhere as fill or for recontouring, or trucked away entirely. This operation needs to be undertaken with care to avoid unnecessary damage by thoughtless equipment operators.

As soon as the driveway base is established, have it covered with a material usually called roadbase, or crushed bank run. This is a fairly coarse, sandy gravel makes an excellent base for graveling or paving later on, and meanwhile will keep you and your workers and the delivery trucks out of the mud. A couple of inches deep is enough on fairly solid, sandy/gravelly soil, but use 4 to 6 inches on clay or soft soil, especially in rainy country.

Provide a large area for vehicle parking, handy to the construction site but not in the way. Make sure there is plenty of room for lumber trucks, concrete trucks, and similar vehicles to maneuver. If you can roadbase the parking and/or delivery area, so much the better, but this is not always advisable. The site of a future detached garage, driveway turnaround, or parking pad all make good spots for parking.

UTILITIES

Consider the utilities. Electric and telephone lines can come in overhead or underground. The latter is aesthetically preferable and less susceptible to damage, but also might be more expensive. A trench is required, although both telephone and electric lines can be put in the same trench, if properly done and if the point of origination at the street is the same. Although overhead lines are usually considered unsightly and are more damage-prone, you do avoid the costly trench digging that tears up the landscape. However, you might need to have poles installed to carry the lines, which involves substantial cost and site disruption. The choice is yours.

If you do go underground, chart out a route that causes the least damage, even if a bit longer. Usually trenches must be dug by a backhoe. Employ the smallest machine that's practical, for the least amount of site disturbance. Or, consider having the cables laid with a trenching machine, which cuts a slit in the earth, sets the cable, and covers it over in one continuous operation, leaving hardly a sign of its passage. Often, depending upon the nature of the soil and ground cover, this creates less disturbance than hand-digging a narrow trench.

A water supply line must be buried, from either a well or a water main in the street. In some areas a shallow trench can be hand dug, but usually a backhoe is required, especially in cold-weather areas where the pipe must be laid 6 or 8 feet deep to prevent freezing. Again, a small hoe with a narrow bucket can be used to minimize site disturbance. You can backfill by hand and dispose of any remaining spoil dirt unobtrusively. The same is true of a main house drain leading to a municipal sewer line. Whenever possible choose a path that is not necessarily the straightest line between two points, but rather the course that causes the least amount of disturbance to the vegetation and that requires the least amount of digging. Note, however, that drain lines have to be properly pitched and in a relatively straight line.

SEPTIC SYSTEM

A septic system installation inevitably causes a lot of disruption (FIG. 2-3). Much digging is required, considerable spoil must be hauled off, and gravel must be trucked in. Also, a large tank, sometimes two, must be machine set. You can minimize site damage by locating the system in an area easy to work on where digging will do the least amount of damage. Haul spoil away promptly and backfill as soon as possible, to uncover vegetation where dirt was piled. It is also possible to hand dig leach line trenches—which are usually only about 18 inches deep. Use a wheelbarrow to gravel them from a gravel stockpile, then backfill by hand.

PRESERVATION OF NATURAL RESOURCES

Before heavy machinery starts charging around the place, determine which natural resources you want to preserve. Trees are by far the most

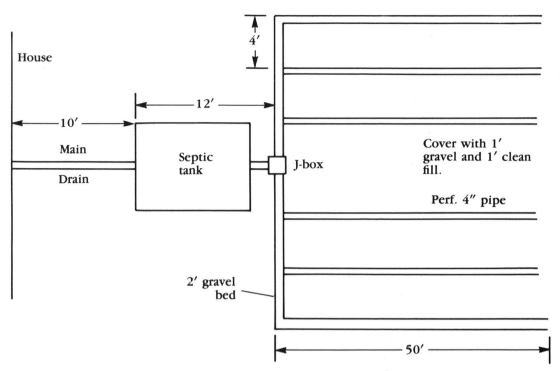

2-3 A typical septic system arrangement. There are many variations, depending upon local conditions and regulations.

valuable assets, large shrub clumps are second, and smaller shrub vegetation next. You might also wish to protect other features like ravines or gullies, certain rocks or rock outcrops, hillocks or knolls, or a spring or rivulet. All of these can be made to work for you and become a part of the final landscaping scheme. It is better to leave such elements in place so you have a chance to live with them and decide, piece by piece, what to do with them. Flag or mechanically protect with barriers anything worth saving that might be in harm's way.

Trees and large shrub clumps need special attention. Trees, even mature ones, are especially susceptible to both stress and mechanical damage. It takes many years for a tree to grow, but only a few moments to kill one. And apart from being visually pleasing, trees add considerably to the value of your property.

One way to protect trees is to ring them with old tires wired or roped in a ring around the trunk. Another is to build a cylinder of boards or 2×4s wired together around the trunk. Even wrapping with burlap is effective in some cases. Bundling the sprawling branches of a shrub clump together with rope into a tight upright cylinder will help protect them, and fencing them off will help further. In addition, tie streamers of colored plastic survey tape to everything you want to be saved. Often just advertising the fact of their existence and that they are not to be damaged is enough to keep them from harm.

A common and often unrecognized danger to existing trees is a change in their surrounding grade level. Filling around a tree trunk to a depth of more than just a few inches, or cutting the soil down to a lower grade level around a tree trunk, is likely to cause its demise. When this occurs, whether accidentally or purposefully, there is a procedure that might save the tree. It is called *cribbing*. Follow this procedure as soon as possible after a change in grade level.

Cribbing involves raising the grade level around a tree. Build a crib around the trunk to create a free, open well with at least 3 feet between the cribbing and the tree trunk at all points (FIG. 2-4). When the grade level must be lowered, stop digging at least 3 feet away from the trunk and crib up from the new grade level to the old (FIG. 2-5). The cribbing can be laid in any outline, but the original grade level should be left intact around the tree.

Fieldstone makes an excellent natural material for the cribbing. It should be dry-laid like a stone wall. You can also use masonry units like brick or concrete landscaping block, railroad ties or preservative-treated gardening timbers, or natural redwood or cedar dimension stock in heartwood. Ordinary lumber treated with preservatives can be used, but these should be kept well back from the tree; even so the preservatives might leach into the soil and harm the tree. Wood treated to 0.40 pounds of preservative salts per cubic foot of wood is adequate, but wood treated to 0.60—such as is used in permanent wood foundation (PWF) systems— will last indefinitely. And new on the horizon, possibly available by the

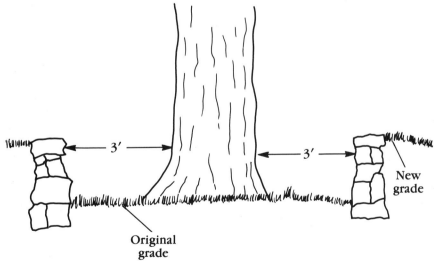

2-4 When raising the finish grade around a tree, build a large well around it and preserve the original grade.

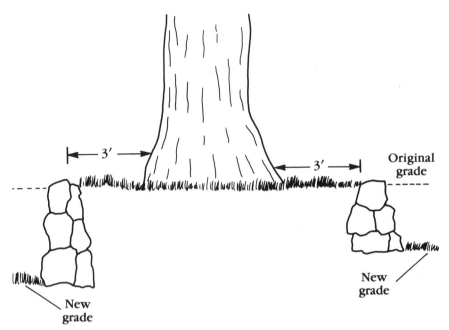

2-5 When lowering the grade around a tree, keep the original grade for a distance of at least 3 feet around the tree and install cribbing or a wall to the new, lower grade.

time you read this, is wood treated with the nontoxic preservative sodium borate. This material might be the answer to a lot of problems.

The procedure most disruptive to the building site and surrounding territory, and often the most destructive as well, is digging a cellar hole. Even more problematic is a full basement that has difficult access. The soil must be stripped away and chopped out, maybe even with access ramps and haulways, in a wide swath around the structure location. This can create a real mess on the lot. However, if the excavator is careful and is well aware that you will be sitting on his shoulder watching, the mess can be minimized. Although the cost might well be higher and the time required longer, sometimes picking away at the job with small machines rather than behemoths results in a better, cleaner excavation.

The least problematical arrangement is a pier foundation; this usually requires very little soil removal. The removal that is required can often be done by hand or with a portable power auger.

The bottom line is to save as much as possible and to cause the least disruption to the site and immediate vicinity. The less cleanup, rebuilding, replanting, repairing, and recontouring you will have to do around the grounds after the house is built, the more time and money and effort you will save. And, your estate will look better.

Chapter **3**

Initial layout and orientation

As site preparation proceeds, or immediately after its completion, you can orient the house within the building envelope. On a small building lot this isn't much of a chore, but it still deserves attention, if only to ensure that there are no conflicts. Consider a solar room or sunspace that is to be located at the back of the building. For such a room to be effective, the rear of the house must face close to south. If your town lot faces south, however, you'll have to place the back of the house facing the street—an odd situation—or move the sunspace to the front, or do away with it entirely.

NATURAL FEATURES

If you have a sizable lot or a building site on a parcel of land you should have several options, and therefore several compromises to make. The object is to make the most of whatever advantages are offered by the natural features, while at the same time minimizing any disadvantages. Often a good first approach is to make up a sketch map as an aid. Use your plot plan, or your landscaping plan if that seems more complete, as a starting point. Add to it the elements that will affect you (FIG. 3-1).

Using the building envelope as the viewpoint, make sure that you have the compass direction north located at the top of the sketch. Note where the views are, and in what direction. Then add the directions from which the sunshine will come at sunrise, midday, and sunset—and the beginning of summer and the beginning of winter. You can indicate the directions of moonrise and set, too, if that's of interest. More importantly, note the prevailing wind directions. There will likely be two or more:

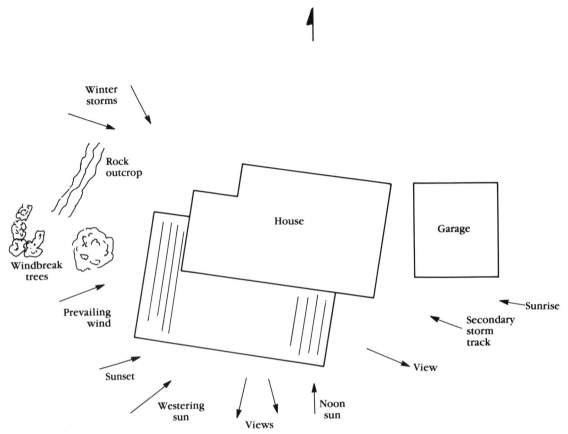

3-1 A landscaping or a plot plan can also serve as an orientation guide for the house.

One will be a year-round, fair-weather wind, and there will probably be a secondary summer breeze direction. And there will be a storm track direction, too; make note of these.

Add in any other items that you feel are important, such as short-range outlooks from various site points, tree stands or ridges that provide a windbreak, or whatever. Then you are ready to make some judgements. They will permanently affect your house and the way you live in it, so give them plenty of consideration. Here's what you have to think about.

View

No matter where your house is located, there is a view. Some are a lot better than others, of course, and often there are several good views on a lot. They might be short range—just a matter of a few feet into a garden, or long range—several miles off to a mountain range. Whatever the case at your building site, you will want to select the best views and orient the house, and/or arrange the decks, windows, porches, or patio so as to take the greatest advantage of them. At the same time, you might want to be able to see a sunrise from the kitchen deck, or a moonrise from a master bedroom window. Short-range views might include such items as a grove of trees, a garden area, a clump of shrubs, or a rock outcrop that you'll want to be able to see from various vantage points. Don't forget to include them in your plans.

Weather patterns

The weather is an important factor, too. By knowing the prevailing and secondary wind directions, the primary and secondary storm tracks, and the fair-weather breeze patterns, you can more advantageously position the house. The goal is to diminish the impact of the prevailing winds and the principal storm track as much as possible. Usually this means that the narrowest part of the building, that which has the smallest area and thus the least exposure of both wall and roof, should be set facing into the wind/storm flow (FIG. 3-2). This affords the current relatively less structure area to impact, breaks its force, and deflects the force around the building. If this facing area happens to be rounded or wedge shaped, or perhaps three faces of an octagon, so much the better; the aerodynamics are thereby improved. All of this reduces wind pressures and the possibility of consequent damage to the structure, reduces heat loss during cold and windy weather, and diminishes the total weathering of the house exterior.

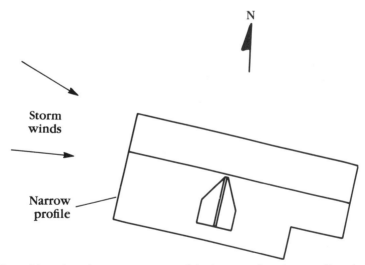

3-2 If possible, orient the narrowest part of the house to face the prevailing wind/storm tracks to lessen their impact.

You can also use your knowledge of the wind/weather patterns to position the windows and doors in your house (FIG. 3-3). For example, the exterior doors should be located out of the winter storm and prevailing wind track if possible, to minimize heat loss in cold weather, lower the

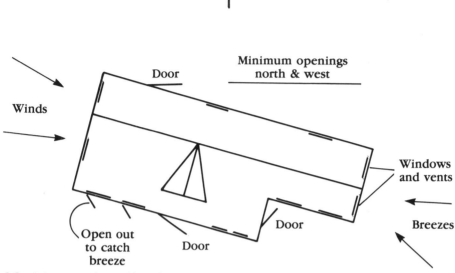

N

3-3 A house can be positioned to take maximum advantage of fair weather and breezes for ventilation, and to minimize the effects of cold winds.

amount of dust and dirt that can whip in on the breeze, and reduce the possibility of damage from gusts. Storm doors should be set to open against the wind for the same reasons, and to help protect the user against the icy blast. Little or no glass, either as door lights or as windows, should be placed in the wind/weather track; this helps with heat conservation and lowers damage possibilities from storm-tossed debris.

Using the wind/weather tracks and taking special note of the fair-weather and summer breeze directions, you can set your windows for the best possible cross ventilation coupled with minimum storm impact. You can also suit the type of window to the particular location. For example, a casement window can be placed to open out into the fair-weather wind to act as a scoop that will direct the air into the house. An awning type of window can be set directly across the breeze direction; it will afford excellent ventilation without admitting a great blast of air.

Sunlight

Ample sunshine, of course, is one of the greatest assets a home can have. Except in locales that are hot all the time, the more sunshine the better. If you don't have sunshine, you can't get it, but if you do, you can control and use it to great advantage through the design of your house and the way you position it on the building site. Within limits, you can arrange for as much or as little light/shade and heat/coolness as you wish; there are methods and technologies for all manner of solar control.

A maximum of daily sunshine all year is a great plus. It provides excellent light inside the house, as well as a substantial amount of free heat during the cold winter months. With a specific solar design and with the requisite passive or active aids, you can avail yourself of solar heating and cooling.

Knowing how, when, and where the sun strikes at your building site will tell you how it will fall upon the house if it is positioned in various ways. This in turn will allow you to determine where the shade will be at any given time. Thus, you can determine which house position will give you both sun and shade at various locations at the same time (FIG. 3-4). You can decide where your decks and patios might be best located for

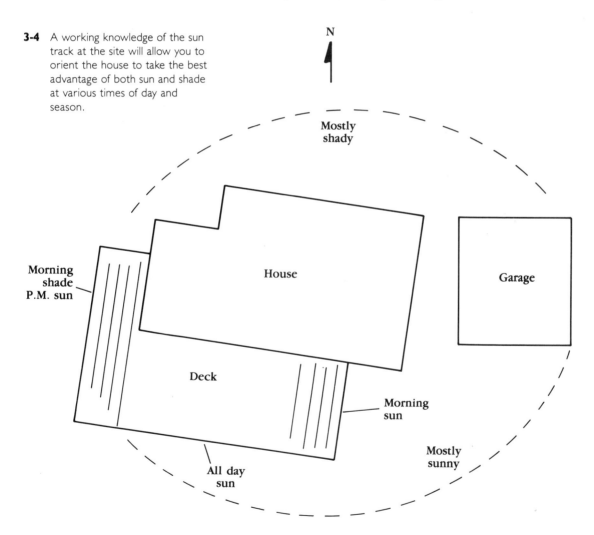

3-4 A working knowledge of the sun track at the site will allow you to orient the house to take the best advantage of both sun and shade at various times of day and season.

sunbathing or relaxing in the shade, depending on the time of day and season. These details also will affect the placement of certain windows, garage doors, horse stalls or loafing shed, gardens, different species of plantings, tennis court, or a swimming pool. For example, in snow country garage doors should not be located beneath north-side eaves.

SITING THE HOUSE

With all this information gathered and sorted out, you can make any changes in your plans that seem appropriate, even though they might be tentative at this point. Then start siting the house. The first step is to double check and make sure that the building envelope is actually positioned where it should be. This is particularly important in situations where that envelope was established by authority of a building department or architectural control committee as being the only place on the lot where a house can be constructed. This is common practice in some residential subdivisions.

Next, orient yourself with a compass and stake the cardinal compass points for reference. Using them, establish the sun, wind, and storm tracks. Take note of your various view opportunities. Then lay out one axis or perhaps one long wall of the house, oriented so that the entire structure faces in exactly the direction you've chosen as being the most desirable. For a solar design, or for maximum gains for a conventional design, this should be within an arc of about 15 degrees to either side of due south (FIG. 3-5).

Next, locate all the corners of the house by measuring out with a 50- or 100-foot tape, keeping everything pretty much in square. Drive stakes at the corners, and check for squareness by measuring the diagonals. Most house layouts can be broken into a number of squares and rectangles for this purpose; if the diagonals of each are equal, the layout will be in square. Check angled lines with a protractor or similar device and run string from stake to stake. You'll end up with a reasonably accurate full-sized outline of your house. Add a few more stakes and strings and you can draw in the first-floor rooms as well—the rest you'll just have to imagine.

Now you can relate your sketches and plans to the full-sized outline, and to your surroundings and the compass directions of the winds and storms and such. How does it all fit? Maybe you need to reposition a door or two, or make some windows larger or smaller, or change the shape or extension of a deck. Perhaps the entire house should be shifted back or sideways a few feet or rotated a bit, to take advantage of some unnoticed or underestimated site asset. Maybe there isn't as much room for the paddock as you thought, or the winter storm track slams right against the great room windows.

This orientation and preliminary layout is usually your last chance before construction to make changes on paper—changes that don't cost anything except a bit of your time. Shift the outline stakes around as nec-

3-5 For maximum solar benefits, a house or its major windows or solar collectors should face within 15 degrees either way of due south.

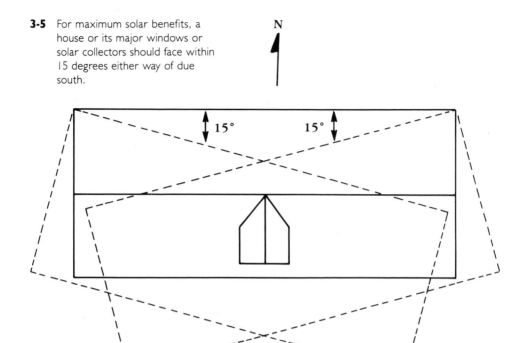

essary, amend the plans and specifications to suit the new reality of the site. Take as much time as you need to become comfortable with your plans. If possible, allow this process to extend over the better part of a full year. Then you can visit the site and make observations and assessments during all the seasons and in all kinds of weather. When you are satisfied, set all the stakes in their approximate final locations and leave them. They will serve as preliminary reference points a bit later when the time comes to lay out the house foundation.

Chapter **4**

Foundation choices

When it comes to foundations, you have several styles and types of materials from which to choose. All can be used beneath a wood frame house. Frequently a house design features a single style and one material; in other instances there are reasons to combine styles and materials. Specific construction details of the different styles are covered in later chapters, but here is an introduction to basic foundations.

FOUNDATION

There are three foundation arrangements that can provide the main support for a structure.

Grade level

The grade-level foundation (FIG. 4-1) is a concrete slab type, of which there are several variations. The foundation actually is set slightly above the surrounding finished grade, rather than on the existing building site grade, which usually requires some leveling and recontouring. The finished grade surrounding the house must be at least several inches lower than and slope down and away from the foundation. All utilities, including domestic water supply, house main drain, and sometimes electrical, telephone, and heating must be in place before the slab is poured. This type of foundation is advantageous in certain types of soil that are not capable of holding heavy loads, because of the great flotation it provides for the house mass.

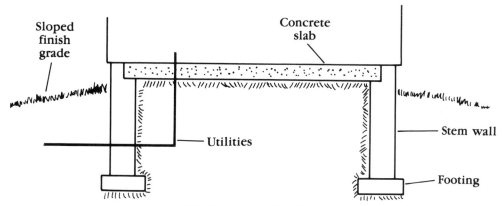

4-1   A grade-level foundation.

Crawl space

A crawl space foundation arrangement supports the house above both the surrounding and the interior grades, occasionally by as little as a foot (not recommended) but usually at least 3 feet and sometimes as much as 5 or 6 feet (FIG. 4-2). This allows working room beneath the structure, making the installation of utilities easier and affording later access for repairs or storage. In a few designs the space may also be employed as a part of a heating system, especially of the solar variety. The arrangement works well on uneven ground, and it is usually (but not always) the least expensive method.

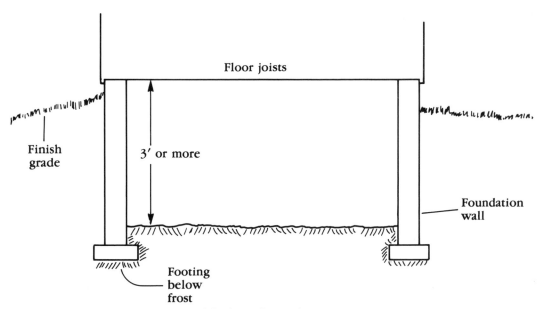

4-2   A crawl space foundation.

Full basement

The full basement (FIG. 4-3) includes a full-height space beneath the first floor of the frame structure, completely enclosed and essentially another floor of the house. Headroom may be as little as 7 feet, but is usually the conventional 8 feet and sometimes more. Construction of a full basement requires considerable excavation and causes more site disruption than other arrangements. It also can result in a damp, dark, underground space with poor access, and if not well built can be problematical.

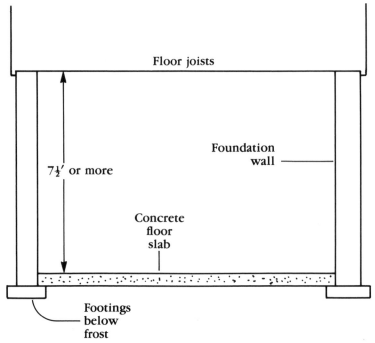

Floor joists

Foundation wall

$7\frac{1}{2}'$ or more

Concrete floor slab

Footings below frost

4-3 A full basement foundation.

On the other hand, if properly constructed, a full basement can be the least expensive space in the house per square foot of living space. A variation is a daylight or garden basement, which has at least part of one wall (usually a good deal more) fully exposed to the outside and containing a door and windows (FIG. 4-4). At least part of the basement thus becomes an added living level of the house.

Any two or all three of the above arrangements can be combined to support a single structure (FIG. 4-5). Depending upon the design, various building materials can be employed in their construction. These include stone of numerous kinds, brick, concrete block, poured concrete, and treated wood. Exactly what can be used, and how, depends upon the type of foundation. Consider the following types for house support purposes.

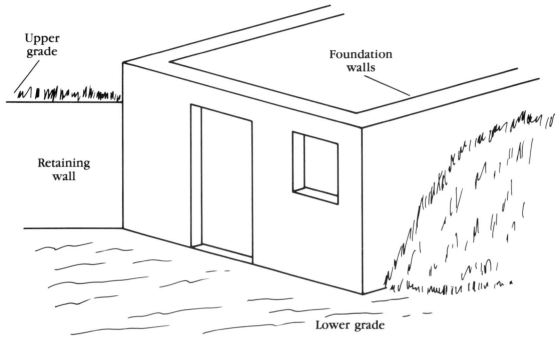

4-4 A popular variation of the full basement is the walk-out, garden, or daylight basement, with direct access to an exterior grade level.

FOUNDATION TYPES

Slab-on-grade

The slab-on-grade foundation can only be constructed of poured concrete. This consists of a flat pad several inches thick, whose upper surface is usually a minimum of several inches above the surrounding finished grade. This becomes the first floor of the structure. Usually it is on one level, but in some house designs there can be two or more separated levels. Part of the house might be additionally supported by other means. There are three fundamental kinds of slab-on-grade. The first is a monolithic slab. The slab, the perimeter footings, and any intermediate footings, are all poured and finished at one time. The second is a three-part job, consisting of poured concrete footings, poured concrete stem walls, and poured concrete slab. The third is a minor variation using concrete block for the stem walls rather than poured concrete.

Pier

The pier foundation is an extremely useful type, especially for smaller, one-story houses. It consists of a series of piers set into the ground under

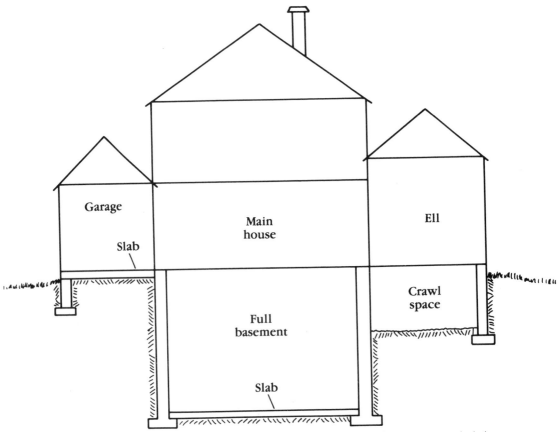

4-5 Two or more types of foundations can be, and frequently are, built to support a single house.

the perimeter of the building and at certain intermediate points as well. The structure is then built in the usual fashion upon sills or sill beams, with intermediate girders as required. The piers can be made of treated wood posts, round or square; concrete poured into square wood forms or special tubular cardboard forms; concrete blocks stacked in any of several configurations; concrete block and brick combinations; and in certain circumstances (usually in combination with other types), steel posts.

The pier is an excellent foundation for uneven or sloping sites. It causes virtually no site disruption, is the least expensive type of foundation, requires little experience or equipment, and lends itself admirably to do-it-yourself installation. It is not a good choice, though, in soft soils or under large, unusually heavy, and/or multistory houses. Only a crawl space arrangement can be used, and the average above-grade height of the piers should be kept in the 4- to 5-foot range or less for best results.

Poured concrete wall

Poured concrete wall foundations are probably the most common of all types, and are considered by many to be the best. They can be made in either full basement or crawl space arrangements, and are endlessly flexible in configuration; anything that can be formed can be poured and cured. They can also be made extremely strong with steel reinforcing. Poured concrete wall foundations can be designed to suit any soil or topographic conditions, and to accommodate any house design.

The usual arrangement is to employ the concrete in perimeter walls based upon a poured concrete footing, with support provided at interior points by piers and/or girders. There are potential disadvantages, depending upon circumstances. These include: inability to obtain ready-mix concrete, no access at the site for concrete mixer trucks, high cost, difficulty of forming for the pour, adverse weather conditions affecting the concrete quality or interfering with the pouring schedule, hydroscopic character requiring excellent dampproofing or waterproofing, and the extreme weight of the material. Also, concrete is not a particularly manageable material, especially in large quantities, for a do-it-yourselfer.

Concrete block wall

The concrete block wall foundation probably ranks second in popularity to the poured concrete type. The arrangement is the same, a continuous perimeter wall with interior support handled by piers and/or girders. Concrete block can be employed for either a full basement or a crawl space foundation. The block assembly must be based upon a poured concrete footing. There are three systems that can be used for this purpose. The first is the conventional system, in which standard blocks are mortared together at the joints. The second is the surface-bonded system: standard concrete blocks are stacked up dry and then thickly plastered inside and out with a special bonding material. The third is the stack-block or interlocking blocks system, where the special interlocking blocks are stacked dry, and certain cores are then filled with grout and tied with reinforcing bar.

These three systems are roughly similar in strength and perfectly adequate for house foundations. The surface bonding system requires the least amount of concrete/mortar/grout work, the stack block system is perhaps the simplest to build, and the conventional system uses readily available materials. All are suitable for do-it-yourself work, with the latter two being the easiest. Again, there can be disadvantages: the length of time and amount of physical effort needed to erect a large foundation, the need for a poured concrete footing, the porosity of the block requiring a particularly good waterproofing, and a lack of strength by comparison with poured concrete walls (although reinforcing can be added). All blocks, especially lightweights and those made with cinder, slag, and other less common aggregates, must be of suitably high strength for foundation construction.

Grade beam

A grade beam foundation is a grade-level type, similar to a slab-on-grade but with somewhat different characteristics. It is made up of three parts in combination. A series of below-grade, poured concrete piers actually support the weight of the structure. The grade beam, a continuous, poured concrete perimeter stem wall with a sloped inner side rests atop and is tied to the piers, and extends a minimum of several inches above grade. This acts as a containment for the third element, a relatively thin poured concrete pad resting upon a gravel cushion. The pad serves as the first floor of the house. This type of foundation is only moderately expensive, and is a good choice where the site soils are weak or unstable. The piers can extend as far below grade as desirable, or driven pilings can be substituted for them. Other advantages and disadvantages are about the same as for a slab-on-grade foundation.

Permanent wood

The permanent wood foundation is a system that has been developed over the past few decades under the auspices of the American Plywood Association and others, and has proven very successful. The materials can be employed to construct on-grade, crawl space, and full basement foundations. Construction procedures are just about the same as for building any ordinary stud frame wall. The materials used are specially preservative-treated dimension stock and plywood, stainless steel or zinc-coated fasteners, a small amount of standard construction lumber, and special adhesives or caulks and polyethylene sheeting as required.

No concrete or mortar of any kind is needed in this type of foundation, and the walls are based on wood footings set upon, or in, fine gravel. An entire foundation can be shop-built in panels, transported to the building site, and erected in short order once the footing trenches have been prepared. No unusual expertise or equipment is needed. This type of foundation should not be considered where Type IV soils exist—marshy, boggy organic silts and peat—but are satisfactory everywhere else and will support any kind of frame house or outbuilding. This is an ideal foundation type for do-it-yourselfers, and where weather conditions are adverse. It is also a good choice when building in remote locations where access is difficult, and where poured concrete or perhaps even electricity are unavailable.

Stone

Stone foundations were common many years ago but are seldom built today, at least in the old way. Both cut stone and random fieldstone were frequently used for both crawl space and full basement walls, and often the stone was dry-laid, without benefit of mortar. Such foundations held up well, although occasional repair was needed. They still could be used with certain types of structures, but are not approved by the model building codes. However, some kinds of houses are especially suited for stone foundations, and there are three variations that will work.

The first is a continuous perimeter wall of either poured concrete or concrete block that is shelved back just below grade level. A stone veneer is then built up on that shelf and securely mortared in place. The stonework can be cobbles, fieldstone, cut stone, or brick. A second method must be achieved with a poured concrete wall. It consists of placing preselected stones in the upper part of the form, against the inside of the outer wall, and pouring the concrete around them. When the form is removed, there is the appearance of a stone wall. The third method requires a pier foundation, and the stonework can be done at any time. A shallow trench is dug between the piers and aligned with them, and a thin concrete footing is poured. Then the stonework is built up, using mortared joints, to fill the open spaces between piers. It provides no support and carries no load except itself. The stonework could also be dry-laid and set in the earth instead of on a footing.

Chapter 5

Excavation

Building a modern house without doing any excavating is an impossibility. And unfortunately, this is where a lot of early problems arise that are difficult, expensive, and time consuming to correct. In some instances the homeowner can take care of a few or maybe even all of the excavating chores. This is certainly the best situation. However, usually an earthmoving or excavating contractor must be hired.

When hiring a contractor for this kind of work, your best bet is a local concern with a good reputation, decent equipment, and capable operators. The contractor should also have trucks for hauling away spoil dirt if necessary, and the capability of furnishing you with whatever is required in the way of roadbase, gravel, sand, and clean fill or topsoil. It is usually best to have one contractor take care of all the various excavating, grading, dirt hauling, and similar chores throughout the course of a project than to have two or three different ones in and out.

PERC TEST

The soil percolation test is often the first call for heavy equipment (although hand digging is a reasonable alternative). Usually the two or three holes for the perc test need be neither large nor deep (FIG. 5-1), but the locations should be carefully spotted. One or more of the spots will probably be dug where the leach field for the septic system will be located.

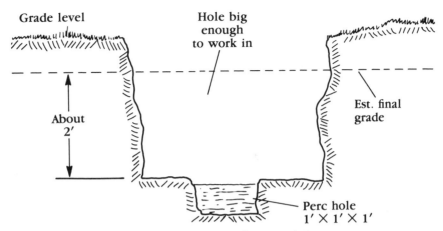

5-1 A typical arrangement for a percolation test.

DRIVEWAY

The driveway, if short and simple, will probably only require scraping down to subsoil, removing any roots and similar debris, and basing up with roadbase and/or gravel. Save any topsoil for future use. Usually a small machine is most suitable for this purpose, and is less likely to cause damage. A long driveway, access road, extensive parking area, cut-and-fill requirements, brush and tree removal, rocky soil, marsh or other watery problems—these are all a different story.

First lay out the course. Consider what will be easiest to build now, but also what will be easiest to navigate and maintain later on. Try to avoid rock, especially blasting, and keep cut-and-fill work to a minimum. All of this gets expensive. If possible, trim out vegetation and trees yourself, or closely supervise a worker or two. Cut out just the bare minimum to allow construction now; more can be trimmed away later as the need becomes obvious. Swampy, marshy areas—even if the problem is only seasonal—are best avoided. These are expensive to properly base and problems are nearly always recurrent. When having the road or drive cut through, specify use of the smallest equipment that is practical for the job, even if the cost is a bit higher. This will mean less damage to be repaired later.

FOUNDATION PREPARATION

The excavating project that often causes the greatest site disruption—sometimes practically destroying the immediate area—is preparation for the foundation. The degree of damage depends on both the kind and size of the foundation and the topography of the site.

Pier foundation

A pier foundation usually causes the least problem. On a flat or moderately sloping or uneven site, with proper planning the grade can be left intact. Pier holes can be dug by hand, either with a posthole bar and shovel or with a power auger. The latter can be a portable one-man rig in clean, light soil; a two-man auger if the soil is tight or a bit rocky; or an auger mounted on a special truck or a farm tractor if access is suitable. Failing these methods, usual practice is to employ a backhoe fitted with a relatively small bucket. Part of the soil that is removed will be used later as backfill around the piers. The small remaining amount of soil can be spread about until it disappears, or it can be hauled off.

With a pier foundation, total apparent site disruption, if the work is done carefully, is practically none. There should be little or no damage to repair later. If the site topography is such that some leveling must be done, remove the spoil dirt as it is generated, using the same track for each load and staying within the foundation outline entirely, or at least as much as possible. A small, maneuverable front-loader or loader/backhoe combination, perhaps together with a small crawler bulldozer, usually is enough to get the job done.

Slab foundation

Preparation for a slab foundation requires that a flat pad somewhat larger than the slab be cleared. Even on a flat site there will be considerable disruption. All vegetation must be completely removed, and topsoil either scraped to one side or picked up and dumped elsewhere, for later use. On uneven ground, the site will have to be recontoured, and if very uneven it might have to be rebuilt to a greater or lesser extent. About all that can be done is to minimize the impact as much as possible. Plan spoil and topsoil storage sites and haul routes ahead of time and stick to them, keeping random movement of big machinery about the site to a minimum. Here, big machines might be more advantageous than small, if their use can be confined to the immediate site area.

Crawl space foundation

If the foundation is to be a crawl space, a large amount of spoil dirt must be removed. If a full basement, more than twice as much as for a crawl space must usually be taken out. Only about a quarter or less of that amount might be used for backfill later on. Again, select appropriate storage spots for spoil and topsoil ahead of time, or dumping/recontouring locations if that is appropriate. Haul away as much as is possible as it is generated. Position backfill material handy to where it will be needed. Use the same haulway for inbound and outbound materials, and keep random machinery movements under control. Make sure that the foundation area is accurately laid out, and that no more area than is absolutely necessary for access to and reasonable working space around the building is dug up.

TRENCHING

There is a certain amount of trenching that must be done in any house construction project. The domestic water supply line from either a well or a street main requires a trench that can be anywhere from 1 or 2 to 7 or 8 feet deep. Typically this is accomplished by a backhoe, preferably fitted with as narrow a bucket as is available. A pipe trenching machine is better because it lays the pipe in a deep slit rather than a trench, which causes less disturbance. However, such a rig might not be suitable for local conditions, or even available in the first place. In some areas where the weather is always benign and the soil soft and rock-free, the water line trench can be dug by hand.

A trench for the main drain to a municipal sewer line is a necessity in many projects. This too must be cut below frost line. Usually the trench is made wide enough for a person to work in, and is made with a backhoe or power shovel. If no sewer system is available, a septic system must be installed. A large, fairly deep hole is needed for the tank. Depending upon the system design, another deep hole might be needed for a deep bed, a secondary tank, or a drywell. A short trench is required for the line from the house to the tank, and another 100 feet or more of trench for the leach field, if necessary. The deep holes must be dug with a backhoe or power shovel, the trenches usually with a backhoe. Sometimes, though, it is possible to dig these trenches by hand, because they need only be about 18−24 inches deep.

Much of the spoil produced by all this digging will be replaced by piping, tanks, and gravel, so the spoil must be hauled away and the gravel hauled in. Plan this along the most logical routes, keeping in mind that trucks cannot cross the trench lines even after they are filled. The cleanest spoil dirt should be kept for backfill. Gravel placement and backfill can be done by a small front-loader like a Bobcat—or better yet, for minimum damage, with a wheelbarrow and shovel.

UTILITY LINES

Telephone and electrical power lines can be brought in overhead, from a pole to the house. Thus, there is no site disturbance unless a pole or two must be installed, and this usually does not create major problems. However, aesthetics and local regulations sometimes require that the lines be placed underground. Telephone cable presents no problems; it can be set with a slit trencher in all but the worst of soil conditions. Bringing power in underground can sometimes be done with a trencher, but more often a backhoe fitted with a narrow bucket is used. Both the telephone and electric lines can be placed in the same trench (unless local regulations forbid it), if the two are separated by a certain minimum distance (FIG. 5-2).

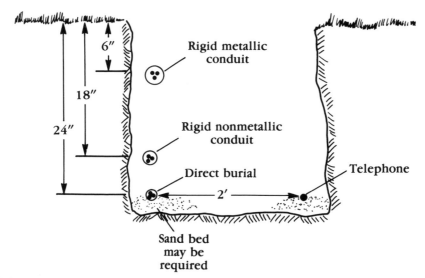

5-2 Given the right conditions and depending upon local building codes, telephone and electrical cables sometimes can be buried in the same trench.

All of the same material removed from the trench will be put back in it, so little or no spoil need be hauled away. The exception is when the soil is rocky, and/or the lines are required to be bedded in a substantial amount of sand and much of the rocky spoil has to be replaced with clean fill. In this case, hauling in both directions might be required. Again, the traffic pattern should be laid out for minimum problems, and as much of the work as possible done with a small Bobcat type of machine, or by hand.

There are occasions when, because of problems with topography, house design, type of soil, or underground springs, the building site resembles a war zone. Complete recontouring, rebuilding, and revegetating of the whole area could be required. This might or might not be apparent ahead of time, so work out a complete plan for all excavating, earthmoving, and general landscaping in as much detail as seems practical. This will save everybody a lot of time, work, and aggravation later on, and certainly will result in a better job. Despite careful planning, sometimes you will have to work out many details as the need arises, sometimes you'll have to make quick decisions. The results might turn out well, and they might not. Expect some of that. But it is always true that the more you preplan, the better off you will be in the long run.

Chapter **6**

Foundation design fundamentals

*T*he foundation is the base upon which your house rests, and the interface between the structure and the earth. Its functions are to evenly support the weight of the structure; elevate the above-ground portion a suitable distance above the finished grade; keep the building from settling, shifting, and sinking into the ground; and provide a solid platform for the house that is impervious to the elements and has an indefinite lifespan. In addition, the foundation might also enclose a service/access area beneath the main structure (crawl space), or provide additional living space (daylight basement). The foundation is a crucial element upon which the entire remainder of the construction project rests, both figuratively and literally. Even if you don't build your own foundation, a knowledge of foundation fundamentals is worthwhile in terms of understanding the overall concept of the structural integrity of a house.

The principal concern in foundation design is the total weight of the structure that will rest upon it. This is determined by three elements: The first is the weight of the structure itself and all the furnishings contained therein, the total of which is called the *dead load*. The second element is the *live load*, a variable number that includes the occupants of the house plus the wind and snow loads that will be imposed upon it. The third element is the dead weight of the foundation itself.

A secondary concern in house foundation design is the height of the foundation walls or columns. The higher these must be, the less weight can be imposed upon them and the more susceptible they are to lateral forces. These lateral forces are another secondary concern. They can occur variably, such as wind pressure driving against the side of the house, or steadily, such as the force of backfill earth pushing against a foundation wall. All of these elements must be considered as a foundation is designed.

There are several ways in which the strength and rigidity of a foundation can be adjusted to suit particular conditions. One is to select an appropriate thickness for a continuous-wall foundation. Foundation height can often be altered by changing finished grade levels. Footings can be made more or less wide or thick. Reinforcing steel can be added. Piers can be varied in size, number, or depth, and the size of their footings varied. Piers, girders, columns, or walls can be added at interior locations to help support the load. And depending upon the overall makeup of the foundation, there are other, more sophisticated design devices that can also be employed.

GROUND LOADS

The big consideration in most house foundations is the ground loading factor. All of this weight—the live and dead loads—will rest upon the foundation. That plus the weight of the foundation itself must rest upon the ground. If the foundation is a slab type, the weight will be well spread out. If any other type of foundation, the weight will rest entirely upon a few relatively small strips and patches of earth. But the earth will hold only so much weight before it gives way and mushes down—*subsides* is the technical term. Different kinds of soils have different load-carrying capacities; a given load will subside to varying degrees on various kinds of soils. But that load can be made to "float" on almost any kind of soil by increasing the area over which it is spread. If you provide insufficient flotation at the footings so that the load is too concentrated at those points, subsidence to one degree or another is inevitable.

You can prove this to yourself easily enough. Set the point of a knitting needle on the ground and lower a 50-pound weight gently onto it. The needle will drive down into the ground for a substantial distance. Park that same weight on top of a chunk of 2×4 rested endwise on the ground, and not much is likely to happen. You have increased the flotation from the tiny, conical area at the point of the needle to a flat, 8-inch pad. Put another way, you have decreased the ground loading from perhaps 500 pounds of pressure per square inch to around 10 pounds per square inch. The reduced pressure, by virtue of added area, provides flotation and reduces *subsidence* or sinking. This is the same principal behind using fat tires on dune buggies and snowshoes on deep snow.

So to begin with, you need to know two things. First, how much will your house weigh? Second, how much weight will the soil at your building site carry? Complete accuracy here is impossible; approximations must be used.

Calculating live and dead loads

There are two ways to figure the dead load or the weight of your house. One is to add up the weights of all its individual parts, which is not as difficult as it sounds. TABLE 6-1 shows weights of the most common building

**Table 6-1 Average Weights of Common
Building Materials and Sections**

Brick, pressed, solid	150	Lbs./Cu. Ft.
Brick, common	125	Lbs./Cu. Ft.
Cedar	22	Lbs./Cu. Ft.
Ceiling, 1/2-inch gypsum wallboard	2	Lbs./Sq. Ft.
Ceiling, gypsum lath and plaster	6	Lbs./Sq. Ft.
Ceiling, metal lath and plaster	10	Lbs./Sq. Ft.
Cement, portland, loose	92	Lbs./Cu. Ft.
Clay, wet	130	Lbs./Cu. Ft.
Concrete, stone aggregate	150	Lbs./Cu. Ft.
Concrete, lightweight	100	Lbs./Cu. Ft.
Fill dirt	90–110	Lbs./Cu. Ft.
Fir, Douglas	36	Lbs./Cu. Ft.
Firebrick	150	Lbs./Cu. Ft.
Floor, concrete, per 1-inch thickness	12	Lbs./Sq. Ft.
Floor, vinyl on underlayment	2–3	Lbs./Sq. Ft.
Floor, wood on plywood	3–5	Lbs./Sq. Ft.
Glass	160	Lbs./Cu. Ft.
Granite	170	Lbs./Cu. Ft.
Gravel	90–110	Lbs./Cu. Ft.
Insulation, loose-fill	10	Lbs./Cu. Ft.
Insulation, blanket mineral wool	12	Lbs./Cu. Ft.
Maple	48	Lbs./Cu. Ft.
Oak, red	40	Lbs./Cu. Ft.
Pine, white	20	Lbs./Cu. Ft.
Plaster	96	Lbs./Cu. Ft.
Roof, asphalt felt and gravel	5–7	Lbs./Sq. Ft.
Roof, clay tile	10–15	Lbs./Sq. Ft.
Roof, plywood and asphalt shingles	3–5	Lbs./Sq. Ft.
Roof, plywood and sheet metal	2–5	Lbs./Sq. Ft.
Sand, dry	100	Lbs./Cu. Ft.
Sandstone	145	Lbs./Cu. Ft.
Slate	175	Lbs./Cu. Ft.
Steel	490	Lbs./Cu. Ft.
Stone masonry	160	Lbs./Cu. Ft.
Wall, concrete	144	Lbs./Cu. Ft.
Wall, 1/2-inch gypsum board and stud	6	Lbs./Sq. Ft.
Wall, lath and plaster	18	Lbs./Sq. Ft.
Wall, ordinary brick	120	Lbs./Cu. Ft.

materials and sections. More complex and complete tables exist in various construction and engineering reference and data manuals. Go through your plans section by section and determine the square footage, volume, or other appropriate amounts of the different materials or sections that will go into your structure. Then add them all together.

Another way to calculate structure weight is to use commonly accepted and reasonably accurate round figures. Allow 100 pounds per square foot of total floor area, as measured by outside dimensions, for standard wood frame house construction. Twenty-one hundred square feet of house would equal 210,000 pounds. If your house will have some exceptionally heavy feature, make an allowance for this.

Now you need to calculate the live load. The figures commonly used for human occupancy are usually taken from construction tables set up for the purpose, and they differ from locale to locale. One favorite number for single-family residences is 40 pounds per square foot of living area, usually calculated on the basis of inside dimensions of habitable areas only. So, 1800 square feet of net living space equals 72,000 pounds of live load. To this you must add the roof loading. This includes the weight of the roof itself—the dead load—which can run anywhere from 1 or 2 pounds per square foot to as much as 15-18 pounds, plus the live load. That is the wind/snow load, which is highly variable and usually established by local building departments. In big-snow or high-wind country, this can be 100 pounds or more. Add all the figures up, and you have the total structure load.

SOIL TYPING

Determining the soil-loading capacity can be tricky. Soils are formally classified according to types, depending upon their composition. Each type has a different load-carrying capacity (TABLE 6-2). Keep in mind, however, that soil types can vary widely from spot to spot, even in areas that are only a few feet apart. Also, determining the exact soil type is difficult because they are not always as clear-cut as TABLE 6-2 suggests, but rather are a mixture. And, there is a spread in capacity from one type to another that makes accuracy difficult. Any determination of soil type must be made not at the surface, but rather at the depth where the bottom of the foundation footings will lie, plus a short distance below that. Finally, the soil must be undisturbed native soil, not fill of any kind.

The most satisfactory method of determining soil type is to hire the services of a qualified engineering firm that can take core samples, make the necessary analyses, then give you a full written report. The cost of this is not great, and you can get some valuable data as well as some peace of mind from it, especially if there is any question about the nature of the soils underlying the surface of the building site.

You may sometimes bypass this whole matter. There are two instances in which this is possible. First, check to see what kind of foundations the neighboring structures are built upon, or what kinds are in common use throughout the local area. If those have been successful, chances are that yours will be too. Second, follow a common rule of thumb that is useful so long as the soil is not obviously unstable, boggy, marshy, or periodically swampy: Keep the total weight of the building and its foundation to 1000 pounds or less per square foot of ground bearing area. This allows an ample margin of safety in all soils except those classed as organic clays or silts, highly organic soils, or peat.

Note that model building codes typically do not allow ground loading that corresponds to the maximum carrying capacity figures shown in TABLE 6-2. A large safety factor is built in, as shown in TABLE 6-3. The 1000-pound rule is not that far off the typical code-enforced figures, and at worst can result in some harmless overbuilding and a small extra expense.

To work out an example, assume a 30-by-50-foot, one-story, single-family residence with a gross area of 1500 square feet and a net living area of 1200 square feet. The dead load would be 150,000 pounds at 100 pounds per square foot, the live load 48,000 pounds at 40 pounds per square foot. The roof loads at 50 pounds per square foot for 1700 square feet of roof equal 85,000 square feet. The total is 283,000 pounds, without the foundation. In order to stay within the 1000-pound limit, 283 square feet of bearing area will have to be provided, plus enough extra to include the weight of the foundation. A continuous-wall foundation with a footing 18 inches wide would probably be sufficient, assuming that part of the load would be taken by intermediate supports such as a girder and columns positioned along the longitudinal centerline of the structure. Of course, much depends upon the specific design of the house; the weight is seldom distributed equally just around the perimeter of the building.

BEARING AREA

The foundation walls that do carry the weight of the structure, or any substantial amount of weight other than their own mass, are called *bearing walls*. Model building codes specify certain minimum specifications for continuous-wall foundations (TABLE 6-4). Poured concrete walls can be formed to any thickness if need be, but in practice are usually 8 or 12 inches. The height can be whatever is desired. Masonry units, which are invariably concrete blocks in foundation work, are nearly always 8 or 12 inches thick, and the wall height is calculated in accord with a 4-inch module. The foundation depth below the finished grade level is usually deeper than the minimum, as a practical matter. Foundation walls of these thicknesses are actually oversized for most average-sized houses.

If the foundation is to be a series of piers, the same amount of square footage of bearing area must be provided. In this case it will be divided up among a group of individual footings. If the footings were 36 inches square, 32 piers would be needed for the example house, set out equally around the perimeter and at some intermediate points. In practice, a logical number of piers set in logical spacing on footings of conventionally calculated size comprises a foundation that can hold up considerably

Table 6-2   Soils: Types and Design Properties

Soil Group	Unified Soil Classification Symbol	Soil Description	Allowable Bearing in Pounds/Square Foot with Medium Compaction or Stiffness[1]	Drainage Characteristics[2]	Frost Heave Potential	Volume Change Potential Expansion[3]
Group I Excellent	GS	Well-graded gravels, gravel-sand mixtures, little or no fines.	8000	Good	Low	Low
	GP	Poorly graded gravels or gravel-sand mixtures, little or no fines.	8000	Good	Low	Low
	SW	Well-graded sands, gravelly sands, little or no fines.	6000	Good	Low	Low
	SP	Poorly graded sands or gravelly sands, little or no fines.	5000	Good	Low	Low
	GM	Silty gravels, gravel-sand-silt mixtures.	4000	Good	Medium	Low
	SM	Silty sand, sand-silt mixtures.	4000	Good	Medium	Low
Group II Fair to Good	GC	Clayey gravels, gravel-sand-clay mixtures.	4000	Medium	Medium	Low
	SC	Clayey sands, sand-clay mixtures.	4000	Medium	Medium	Low

Table 6-2 Continued

	ML	Inorganic silts and very fine sands, rock flour, silty or clayey fine sands or clayey silts with slight plasticity.	2000	Medium	High	Low
	CL	Inorganic clays of low to medium plasticity; gravelly clays, sandy clays, silty clays, lean clays.	2000	Medium	Medium	Medium[1]
	CH	Inorganic clays of high plasticity, fat clays.	2000	Poor	Medium	High[1]
Group III Poor	MH	Inorganic silts, micaceous or diato-maceous fine sandy or silty soils, elastic silts.	2000	Poor	High	High
	OL	Organic silts and organic silty clays of low plasticity	400	Poor	Medium	Medium
Group IV Unsatisfactory	OH	Organic clays of medium to high plasticity, organic silts.	—0—	Unsatisfactory	Medium	High
	Pt	Peat and other highly organic soils.	—0—	Unsatisfactory	Medium	High

[1] Allowable bearing value may be increased 25 percent for very compact, coarse grained gravelly or sandy soils, or very stiff fine-grained clayey or silty soils.

Allowable bearing value shall be decreased 25 percent for loose, coarse-grained gravelly or sandy soils, or soft, fine-grained clayey or silty soils.

[2] The percolation rate for good drainage is over 4 inches per hour, medium drainage is 2 to 4 inches per hour, and poor is less than 2 inches per hour.

[3] For expansive soils, contact local soils engineer for verification of design assumptions.

[4] Dangerous expansion might occur if these soil types are dry but subject to future wetting.

Table 6-3 Typical Allowable Foundation Loading

Material	Load (Lbs./Sq. Ft.)
Massive crystalline bedrock	4000
Sedimentary and foliated rock	2000
Sandy gravel and/or gravel (GS, GP)	2000
Sand, silty sand, clayey sand, silty gravel, and clayey gravel (SW, SP, SM, SC, GM, GC)	1500
Clay, sandy clay, silty clay, clayey silt (CL, ML, MH, CH)	1000

Noted values are for a footing 12 inches wide set 12 inches into natural undisturbed soil. For each additional 12 inches of depth and/or width, add 20 percent, up to a maximum of three times the noted value, except that there is no increase for added width for the last category.

Table 6-4 Typical Required Thicknesses for Foundation Walls Under Stud Walls

| Stories | Wall Thickness (Inches) | |
	Concrete	Block
1	6	6
2	8	8
3	10	10

more house than is likely to be placed upon it. Piers, especially if short and properly based, can hold up an enormous amount of weight. The number actually employed to support a given house could depend largely upon its first-floor configuration and obvious support points.

Chapter **7**

Footings

*T*he footings, also sometimes called footers, comprise the base upon which foundation walls, columns, or piers are erected. The footings are always wider than the foundation walls, and their purpose is to form a platform for the foundation and provide whatever flotation is required to support the weight of the building. Footings are placed beneath construction elements that are on or in the earth, whether they are actually load bearing or not.

There are two instances in which footings are not used in this way. One is when relatively lightweight, nonload-bearing, poured concrete walls have bases that are wide enough to give them sufficient flotation without footings. The other is when posts or solid columns are used in a situation where the loading is not enough to cause subsidence. Footings are almost always made of poured concrete and usually contain reinforcing steel bars, also called *rebar*. Again there is an exception. Large, flat stones may be set as footings for posts, and they work quite well; they are often called *punch pads*.

FOOTING SIZES

TABLE 7-1 shows the typical minimum sizes of footings, required by model building codes, that must be set beneath minimum-size poured concrete or concrete masonry foundation walls. This applies to all continuous-wall types of foundations, which are primarily perimeter walls but often include some interior walls as well. No differentiation is made between footings beneath load-bearing and nonload-bearing walls. The tops of the footings should lie at least 12 inches below finished grade or natural

**Table 7-1 Typical Required Footing
Sizes Under Stud Wall Foundations**

Stories	Width (Inches)	Thickness (Inches)	Depth* (Inches)
1	12	6	12
2	15	7	18
3	18	8	24

*The depth is measured from the surface of natural undisturbed soil and finish grade to the bottom of the footing.

ground surface. The exception is that in an enclosed area, such as a base-ment or crawl space, that has a higher exterior grade line, the interior grade may be level with the footing top (FIG. 7-1). Footings should always be set below frost line, which can be 5−6 feet in many areas; check the local code or usual practice.

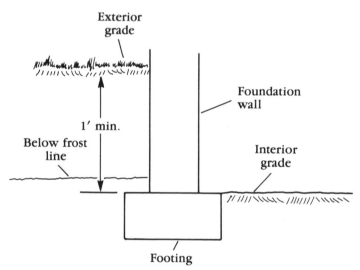

7-1 In a crawl space the interior grade level can be even with the footing top, but no lower.

In practice, a somewhat different arrangement is frequently fol-lowed. As FIG. 7-2 shows, the footing is sized in a direct relationship to the foundation wall size. Its thickness, or height, equals the thickness of the wall. Its width equals twice the wall thickness. As you can see, the foun-dation wall is always centered upon the footing. Because the 4-inch/8-inch building module is so common, in residential construction where the foundation does not need to be engineered and designed for special

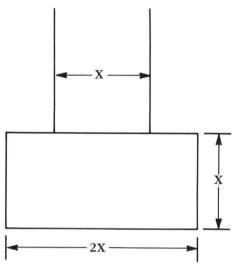

7-2 A poured concrete footing is usually the same thickness as the wall it supports, and twice as wide as the wall thickness.

conditions, the footings are often 8 inches thick and 16 inches wide to support 8-inch-thick walls, or 12 inches thick and 24 inches wide for 12-inch walls. Again, often there is no distinction made between nonload-bearing and load-bearing walls; it is simply easier to make everything alike. However, if the nonload-bearing walls are extensive enough that money can be saved by making them thinner and their footings smaller, this procedure becomes worthwhile. Such walls may shrink to 6 inches thick in poured concrete or 4 inches in concrete block, with commensurately smaller footings.

REINFORCING ROD

Usual practice is to include reinforcing rod or rebar in footings. One arrangement is to set them as shown in FIG. 7-3, with one No. 4 (¹/₂-inch

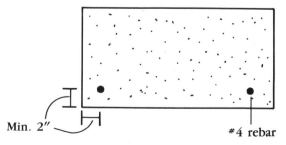

7-3 A poured concrete footing typically is reinforced with a pair of continuous steel reinforcing rods placed in the lower corners.

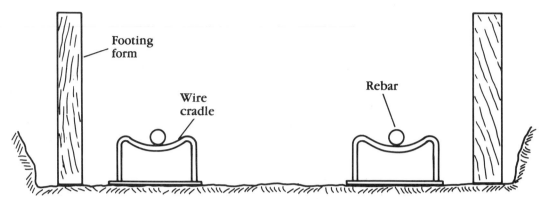

7-4 The cleanest way to support reinforcing rods in footings prior to pouring the concrete is to lay them on special wire chairs or cradles.

diameter) rod toward each lower corner and covered by at least 2 inches of concrete. They can be supported in place before the pour with clean stones or chunks of concrete block or brick, or they can be placed by hand as the concrete is poured. A preferable arrangement is to set special wire chairs in the bottom of the footing and lay the rods on them (FIG. 7-4). This will position and hold the rods accurately. However, requirements vary: three rods might be needed, or four, or perhaps No. 5 (⁵⁄₈-inch diameter) rod instead of No. 4, or the positioning might be different. Check local building codes.

CONTINUOUS-WALL FOOTINGS

Continuous-wall footings are made in one of two ways. The first is the flat-topped style shown in FIG. 7-3. The upper surface is screeded off cleanly as the forms are filled, with the top surface kept rough and slightly irregular. This style is usually employed when the foundation wall will be made of concrete block. The second style includes a keyway, which can be made with slanted or with straight sides (FIG. 7-5); the difference is immaterial. This arrangement is commonly used where the walls are to be poured concrete. The concrete fills the groove in the footing and becomes keyed immovably to it. If concrete blocks are used, the results are the same, but keying is more important for poured concrete than for block.

Keyways

You can make straight-sided keyways easily enough. As the footing forms are topped up with fresh concrete and screeded off, lay 2×4s flatwise and end to end along the centerline of the footings. Press them down so their top surfaces are level with the form tops, or a tad below, and rescreed. After the concrete has started to cure, but before it is completely hard, pull them up carefully. It helps if you coat the 2×4s first with oil, but this

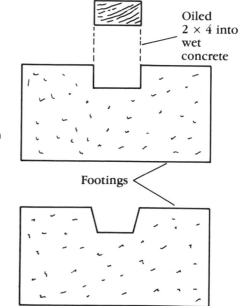

Oiled
2 × 4 into
wet
concrete

7-5 Footing keyways can be made with slanted or straight sides.

Footings

isn't essential. You can brush on motor oil, either new or used, or you can buy a special product (which is preferable) called form release oil.

PAD FOOTINGS

Pad-type footings are relatively small—usually square or rectangular—noncontinuous bases for piers, columns, and posts. The area they cover depends upon the amount of weight they must individually support, or their allotted share of the total weight to be supported. Their thickness may be selected upon the basis of engineering data, but often as not it is an arbitrary figure—commonly 8 or 12 inches. It is good practice to include some No. 4 rod. Use a pattern like the one in FIG. 7-6, tying the lengths at the joints using black iron mechanic's wire. Set the grid so that at least 2 inches of concrete, or preferably a bit more, surrounds all of the

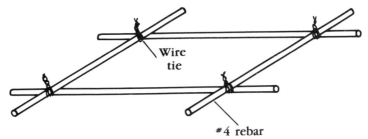

Wire
tie

#4 rebar

7-6 A four-piece grid tied with soft iron wire makes a good reinforcing arrangement for a pad footing.

rod, including the cut ends. If desired, an upward stub or two of bar can be set to key either poured concrete or concrete blocks to the footing (FIG. 7-7). Never use heat when bending rebar; always cold-bend it with as little deformation as possible.

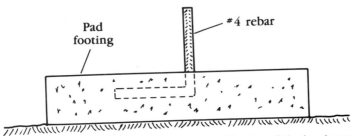

7-7 A right-angled length of reinforcing rod set in a pad footing will tie the pier or column securely to it.

FOOTING FORMS

Making forms for footings is a simple matter. The easiest method, provided the soil is tight and stable, is to cut square-sided trenches directly into the soil (FIG. 7-8). Small variations in width or depth don't matter as long as they are on the plus side, but the trenches must be accurately positioned relative to one another. Just before pouring, clean loose dirt out of the trenches, then dampen the soil thoroughly, almost to the point of puddling. Pour concrete carefully to avoid dislodging soil into the fresh concrete. Screed the tops of the pour with a short length of 2×4 or something similar. Keep the footing tops level; check this often as you go along.

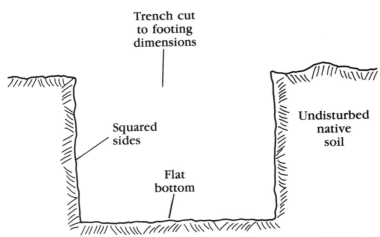

7-8 A continuous concrete footing can be poured directly into a square-sided trench if the native soil is solid enough.

A more common method of forming uses plans and stakes, usually an easier and more satisfactory arrangement (FIG. 7-9). Set 2-inch-thick (nominal) planks of the same approximate width as the footing thickness up on edge, properly aligned, and anchor them in place with wood stakes. You can make your own stakes out of short lengths of 1×2, or you can buy them all cut and pointed and packed in bundles as survey stakes. Every few feet, nail a 1-×-2 tie across the form sides, and keep the top edges of the two sides level and even with one another. Place spreaders (also called spacers) across the bottom of the forms every few feet to keep them aligned; remove these as the concrete is being poured. Make sure you have plenty of stakes and ties. The fresh concrete is very heavy, plus you'll be shoving it into the forms, which tends to open and collapse weak forms. This is a disaster.

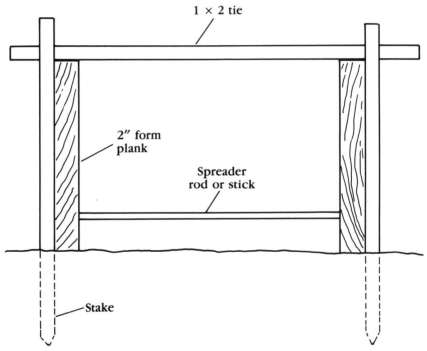

7-9 A continuous footing form is easy to make with planks, stakes, spreaders, and ties.

Pad footings

Forms for pad-type footings are made in just the same way. Dig an appropriate hole in undisturbed native soil, which is a practical method for underfloor support points in slabs, or pier supports in a crawl space. Alternatively, create a box form from planks, position it accurately, and stake it in place firmly enough that it can neither come apart nor scoot out of position when the concrete is poured and screeded (FIG. 7-10). As mentioned earlier, reinforcing bars can be set so as to tie poured concrete or

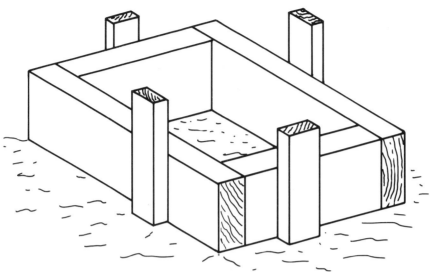

7-10   A typical pad footing form made of planks or boards.

concrete block to the footing. If a wood post or column is to be set on the footing, you can bed one or two anchor pins in the fresh footing concrete, or an appropriate post anchor can be similarly set. Details for this vary with the kind of post and the anchoring product used. In the case of a wall sole plate, set anchor bolts in the concrete in the same way as they are set in a foundation wall top for a sill plate.

When the forms are done, check them over to make sure that all the alignments are correct. In particular, check the elevation of the form top edges to make sure that they are the correct distance below the finish grade—or the control elevation selected for that purpose—and that the top edges are all level and even with one another. Clear the area and make sure that the concrete mixer truck will have good access. It is best if the truck chutes will reach the footings (ascertain this ahead of time). If they do not, have wheelbarrows and a crew ready, with walkway planks laid out—or hire the services of a concrete pumper.

Pour the forms full of concrete; a typical mix is a ratio of 1 part portland cement, $2^3/4$ parts sand, and 4 parts gravel. Other mixes are used, however, and you can be guided by local practice or the recommendations of the concrete company. Jiggle the wet mix into all the crevices and corners in the forms, smoothing the excess forward into empty areas as you go. As the forms fill, screed the excess with a short length of 2×4 by running it along the form tops, leaving a fairly smooth surface. If a keyway is needed, set the key forms and screed again as necessary. Cover the concrete with plastic film snugged down and held in place with weights, and allow it to cure. The plastic is often removed and the forms stripped off in three days to speed up construction, but a five-day curing time results in stronger concrete and a better job.

Chapter **8**

Foundation layout

*L*aying out a foundation is not a difficult chore, but the job needs to be done with care and attention to detail. Accuracy is important, because the integrity of the remainder of the project rests upon this first step. If the foundation ends up a little short, oversized, or cockeyed because it wasn't laid out correctly, you could be in big trouble. If the site topography is tricky or the foundation complex, or if you just don't feel comfortable in doing the layout yourself, by all means hire a competent professional to do the job for you. (Your excavating contractor might be a good choice.) However, on a straightforward layout there's probably no reason why you can't do a satisfactory job yourself.

ROUGH GRADING

First double check the siting and orientation of the structure, as discussed in Chapter 3, just to make sure nothing's awry. Presumably any trees and brush have already been cleared from the site, as necessary. If the site is sloped or irregular, usual procedure for most foundation installations is to rough-grade the immediate area before laying out the foundation.

To prepare for rough grading, set additional stakes out around the original house orientation stakes to mark out another perimeter a specific distance (several feet) beyond, in whatever configuration seems logical (FIG. 8-1). These stakes are best tall and flagged with bright surveyor's tape so they can be easily seen; they will serve as guides for the rough grading. Remove the original house orientation stakes, after referencing a couple or more of them to the new stakes.

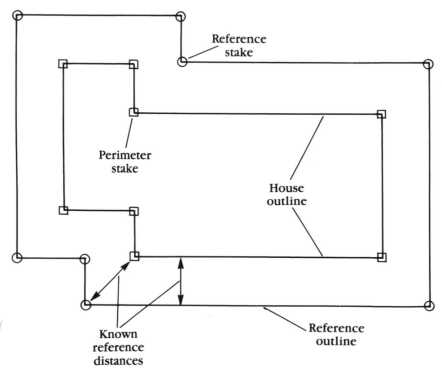

Reference
stake

Perimeter
stake

House
outline

Known
reference
distances

Reference
outline

8-1   Reference stakes and a reference outline can be set up at known distances from the true layout, to permit accurate foundation excavation and relocation of the original stakes.

Proceed with the grading. Depending upon the roughness or the amount of slope of the site, quite a bit of grading, then checking, then grading again might be needed to establish a final, reasonably flat and level site area upon which the final foundation layout can be made.

ASSURING ACCURACY OF LAYOUT

When the rough grading has been completed, reset at least two of the original orientation stakes that mark the corners of one of the principal house walls. If no rough grading was needed and the site is suitably flat to begin with, pick one of the wall lines from the original layout. Check to make sure that this line, or wall, is facing in exactly the direction you want it to, and that it is positioned on the site exactly where you want it. If it needs to be adjusted, now is the time. Drive a short 2×2 stake firmly into the ground, straight up. Cross-hatch the top of the stake and drive a 4d or 6d finish nail straight into the center, leaving about 1 inch sticking up. This is Corner 1 (FIG. 8-2). Another method, useful when the soil is tight and solid, is to drive a spike directly into the ground. A patch of bright survey tape beneath the head makes it easy to spot.

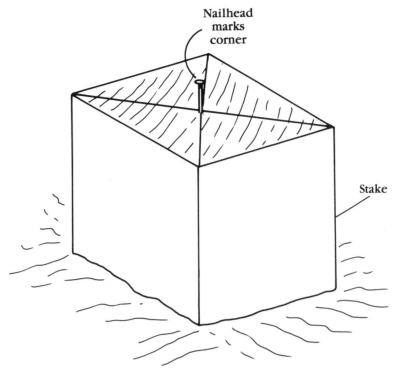

8-2 A finish nail driven in a corner stake marks the precise corner location.

Using the nailhead as a center point, measure along the line the necessary distance (equal to the length of the wall) to Corner 2. Drive another
2×2 stake, set another nail, and continue to Corner 3. Keep going this
way until you have all of the corners staked. By making continual checks
and adjustments with a carpenter's square and your measuring tape, you
can in due course get the layout set to an accuracy of less than 1 inch of
variation.

Checking the angles

You can check your right angles by dividing the overall layout into
squares and rectangles, then measuring the diagonals of each. When they
are equal, the angles are at 90 degrees (FIG. 8-3). Another method is the 3-
4-5 system. If you measure from a corner point A along one line 3 feet to
point B, along the other line 4 feet to point C, the distance along imagi-
nary line BC will be 5 feet when the corner angle is 90 degrees (FIG. 8-4).
You can make up a wood triangle to do these measurements, with sides 3,
4, and 5 feet long, or 6, 8, and 10 feet—or even 9, 12, and 15 feet if you
have a helper working with you. Incidentally, having a helper makes layout work easier and a lot less dull.

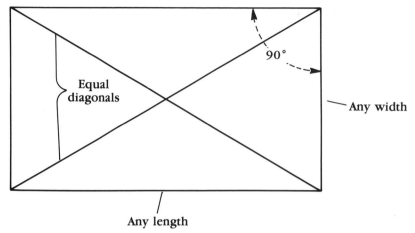

8-3 When the diagonals of squares or rectangles are equal, the corner angles are exactly 90 degrees.

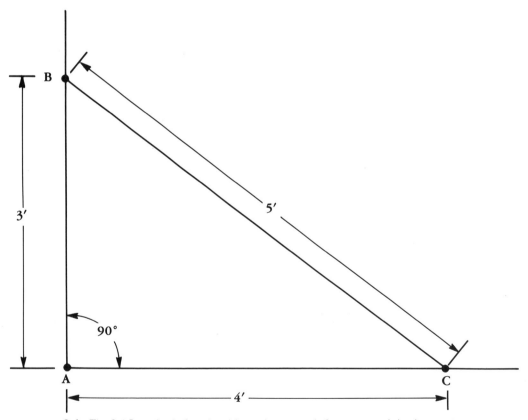

8-4 The 3-4-5 method of setting right-angle corners is fast, easy, and dead accurate.

When measuring between corner points, make sure that you make them all on-level, in the same horizontal plane. If one end of the tape is higher or lower than the other, or the tape wanders up and down over humps in the ground, your measurements will not be accurate. You can use a line level on your taut line to keep it horizontal and measure along it, or transfer your measurements from point to point with a rod held vertical with the aid of a carpenter's spirit level.

Instruments

The business of laying out with spirit levels, squares, tapes, and lines works, but it takes time and patience, and after you go around the circuit for the seventeenth time, causes some frustrations. Consider using a surveyor's level or a transit to get the job done faster and easier, and probably more accurately as well. Either instrument is simple enough to use for this kind of work, and can be rented at any well-stocked equipment rental shop.

Laying out the corners

To lay out the corners, just set the instrument on its tripod and center it directly over your Corner 1 stake, with the plumb bob centered exactly on the nailhead. Level the scope on its base, then sight through the scope toward a rod positioned at Corner 2, measure out the required distance, and set a Corner 2 stake (FIG. 8-5). Swing the instrument 90 degrees and

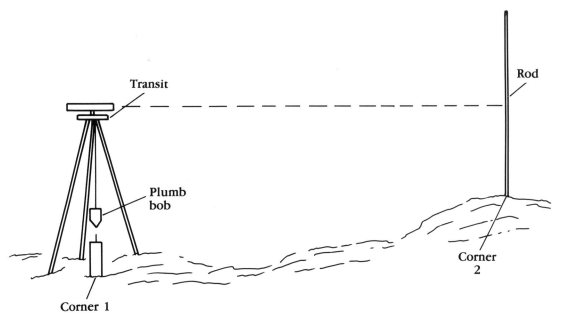

8-5 A surveyor's level or transit makes accurately ''shooting'' corners an easy chore.

repeat the performance for Corner 3. Then move the instrument to Corner 2 or Corner 3, set it up again, and repeat for Corner 4. Keep this up for as many corner stakes as required, meanwhile repeatedly sighting back to previous corners to double check for accuracy. If your layout includes some odd angles, the instrument makes layout a good deal easier. With right angles, you don't have to fuss with a 3-4-5 template or a carpenter's square. Just swing the scope to the required angle as indicated on the instrument.

Setting up batter boards

You now have an accurate perimeter layout of the house as represented by a set of corner stakes. The next step is to set up batter boards, one right angle (or other appropriate angle) set for each outside corner, and straight ones as needed for inside corners. Make these out of pointed lengths of 2×4 for stakes and a 1×6 or more 2×4s for cross pieces. The ends should extend well to the inside of each wall line, and the whole affair should be set back about 4 feet from them, as shown in FIG. 8-6. Drive the stakes well into the ground and nail the cross pieces on solidly, because they'll take

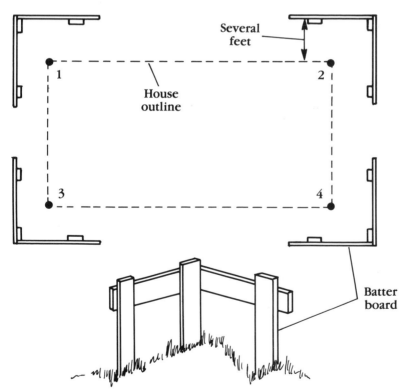

8-6 This typical batter board setup for locating the foundation lines can be altered to suit different shapes and angles.

some strain and probably some bumps, and you don't want them moving around or coming apart.

Spotting corner points

Now you can run the taut lines that will position the foundation. Mason's line or any fairly heavy nylon cord works well. Tie a brick or some other heavy weight around one end, hang it over a batter board, and run it along a wall line. Then hang it over the opposite batter board, also weighted so that the line stretches tight. Repeat so that you have crossing taut lines at all corners. Keep adjusting the lines so that when you dangle a plumb bob from each line intersection it falls directly on a corner point (FIG. 8-7). Fiddle with the alignment until you are certain of complete accuracy; double check all your measurements if necessary.

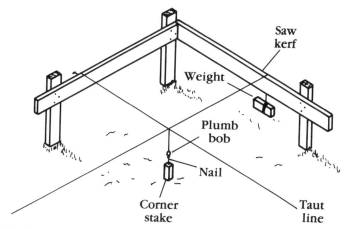

8-7   The taut lines and plumb lines are adjusted to spot the corner points.

When you are satisfied, cut a shallow kerf in each cross piece directly under each taut line, making grooves about 1/8 inch deep for the lines to rest in. Then shift all the lines outward so they form a perimeter line about 1 foot outside the house perimeter lines. Using these as a guide, sprinkle stripes of lime on the ground (like marking a football field) to make footing trench excavation guidelines. Note: Keep the lime off your hands—it burns. Then remove all of the taut lines and set them aside for future use, and proceed with the excavation.

EXCAVATION

The depth of the excavation must be controlled as work goes along so that it remains relatively level and plane, and so it does not get too deep at any one point. Also make sure the footing areas, especially trench bottoms, are cut to the correct depth. This is important because the grade elevation at the bottoms of the footings governs the top elevation of a given foundation. Footings should always be poured on undisturbed native soil. If the excavation is too deep, the grade has to be built up with gravel or sand, which has to be hauled in, placed, and compacted, then tested. All of this is expensive, time consuming, and generally unsatisfactory, and might cause settling of the foundation.

Presumably the height of the foundations have been calculated, including specific amounts above and below the finish grade around the house. In order for this to work out properly, the bottoms of the footings must be set at a particular depth. This is especially crucial for a series of piers, whose tops must all be even with one another (although sometimes they can be set and then trimmed later). On a perfectly flat site, this depth would be a certain distance below grade all around. However, usually the grade varies, so you must select a reference point.

The highest convenient point above and just outside the excavation is a good reference. Then, compare this point with numerous others in

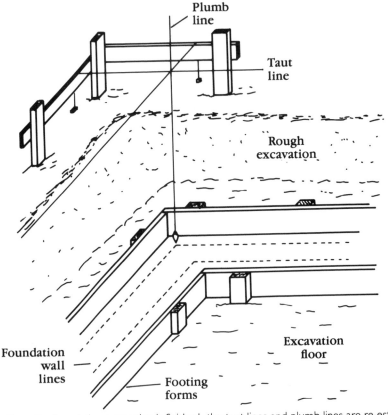

8-8 Once the foundation excavation is finished, the taut lines and plumb lines are re-established to locate the footing corners.

the excavation area, using taut lines, line and carpenter's levels, measuring tape, and a sighting rod or transit and rod. In this way the footing areas of the excavation can be cut straight and to a uniform level in accord with the required finished grade elevation.

Once the excavating is finished, reset the taut lines across the batter boards. Dropping a plumb bob at each intersection will give you the corner locations once more, which you can mark with a stake and finish nail or a 20d nail driven into the ground over a scrap of survey tape. From those points, you can go ahead and calculate exactly where the inner and outer edges of the footings or foundation wall must lie (FIG. 8-8), or begin to line out the piers.

Chapter **9**

Slab foundation

There are several ways to build a slab foundation, no one of which is necessarily better than another. Three basic slab foundation types are: the monolithic slab, in which the entire assembly is cast in one pour; the three-part slab, which is constructed in three principal steps and has several variations; and the PWF system, which is entirely different and has several steps. In all cases the supporting perimeter walls/footings should extend at least 12 inches below grade, and typically they are deeper than that. In cold country they are usually required to go below average frost depth. There are variations and exceptions, however; check local building codes and practices.

MONOLITHIC SLAB

A cross section of a typical monolithic slab construction is shown in FIG. 9-1. The squared outer edge is for a standard wood exterior siding arrangement, while the notched edge accommodates a stone or brick veneer. This is also known as a floating slab or a thickened-edge slab, and is a good design for unstable soil conditions. No discrete footings are used. The advantages of this construction are that minimal forming is needed, and the entire pour can be done at once, which saves time.

Trenches can be cut with squared sides and flat bottoms (or, the entire outside face can be formed) in undisturbed native soil for the perimeter wall. Any disturbed soil beneath the slab proper should be thoroughly compacted in shallow, successive layers. The cushion should be at least 4 inches thick. Use either compacted sand, road base or crushed bank run, or crushed rock or gravel to about a 3/4 inch size. The

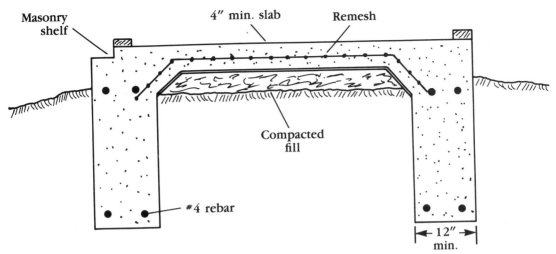

Masonry shelf

4″ min. slab

Remesh

Compacted fill

#4 rebar

← 12″ → min.

9-1 Typical monolithic or thickened-edge slab-on-grade foundation construction.

rigid insulation is optional depending upon climatic conditions. Whatever is used must be thermally adequate, moisture- and vermin-proof, and strong enough to withstand the pressure of the concrete without crushing. The vapor barrier should always be used, and can be 6-mil polyethylene sheet, 55-pound roll roofing, or any special material made for the purpose.

THREE-PART SLAB

Figure 9-2 shows a typical three-part slab foundation made entirely of poured concrete. Reinforced footings are poured first, either in square-cut trenches or in forms. The soil bed that will lie beneath the slab is disturbed as little as possible. After the footings have cured for at least three days and preferably five, the stem walls can be formed up.

There are three ways to finish the tops of the stem walls. The method illustrated in FIG. 9-2 is a common practice, and affords good edge support for the slab and expansion/contraction space. Another possibility is shown in FIG. 9-3. This one gives full edge support and does away with having to form a notch. A keyway could also be used here, to tie the slab to the walls. Sometimes a full-floating slab is used (FIG. 9-4), but is probably more common to retrofits than new construction. The cushion, insulation, and vapor barrier details are the same as for a monolithic slab.

The three-part slab foundation can also be made with concrete block stem walls (FIG. 9-5). This arrangement is for a full-block construction, but again there are variations. If the masonry wall is to be continued upward, a floating slab is commonly used (FIG. 9-6). A stone or brick veneer can be added to the above-grade portion of the foundation. Cap the top course with solid half-height blocks on edge to the inside of the wall, and bond

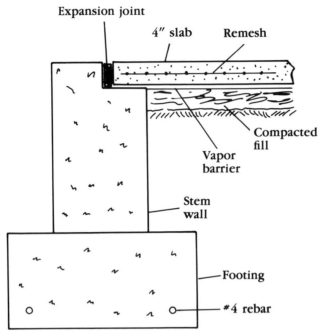

9-2   A common method of constructing a three-part slab-on-grade foundation.

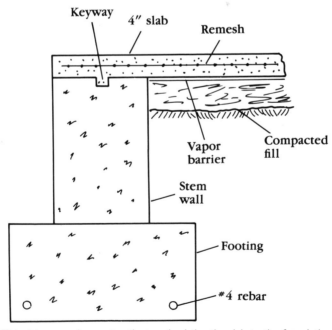

9-3   This slab-on-grade construction method ties the slab to the foundation walls.

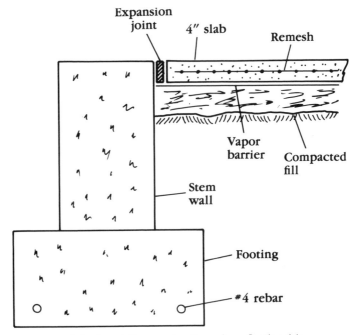

9-4 Foundation construction using a floating slab.

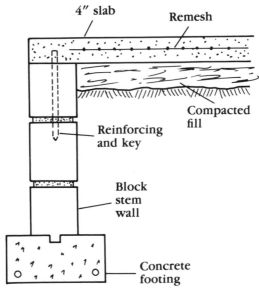

9-5 The poured concrete slab is tied to a concrete block foundation wall in this construction, common in frame buildings.

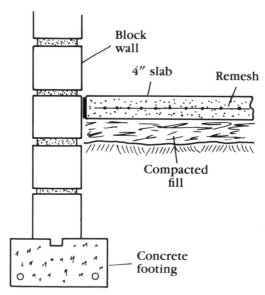

9-6   When a masonry wall is to be continued upward past a poured concrete slab, the slab may be a floating type.

the veneer to the outside. Note that the anchor bolts in this case extend down through the entire veneered section into the first full-block course. This arrangement can also be used with poured concrete walls simply by forming in the appropriate notch at the outside wall tops. (See also Chapter 16.) The cushion, insulation, and vapor barrier details are the same as for a monolithic slab.

PWF SLAB

The PWF or permanent wood foundation construction for a slab foundation is different. This system is not recommended for wet or unstable soils (Group IV). There are two basic versions.

The first version is a typical stem wall setup (FIG. 9-7). For example, construction might consist of a 2-×-12 footing plate set on the gravel bed with a 2-×-6 conventionally built stud stem wall attached to it. The outside of the wall is sheathed with 3/8- or 1/2-inch plywood and rigid insulation is set between the studs as required. The framing is fastened together with hot-dipped galvanized nails, and the sheathing is attached with stainless steel nails or staples. Note that the backfill on the inside is gravel or crushed rock, a continuation of the under-slab cushion, while ordinary fill is used on the outside. The slab is keyed by pouring it between the studs and also by 16d nails driven down through the lower top plate to extend into the concrete.

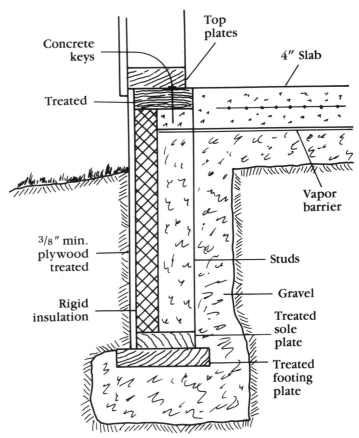

Concrete keys

Top plates

4" Slab

Treated

Vapor barrier

3/8" min. plywood treated

Studs

Gravel

Rigid insulation

Treated sole plate

Treated footing plate

9-7 A typical arrangement for a combination permanent wood foundation (PWF) stem wall and slab-on-grade house foundation.

Construction of the second version (FIG. 9-8) is similar, but intended for an unheated garage, outbuilding, or similar structure. Note the different configuration of the gravel fill area, lack of rigid insulation, and different grade levels and top plate placement. Here the slab is keyed between the wall studs and with 16d nails. The nails are driven into the faces of the wall studs at the half-depth point in the slab. The studs could be 2×4 and the footing plate 2×8 in most cases. (See Chapter 14 for more details on PWF construction.)

INSTALLATION

Installation procedures vary with the three types of slab foundations mentioned here. With the three-part and PWF types, much of the work can be accomplished by the average do-it-yourselfer. The monolithic version is a job for a professional crew.

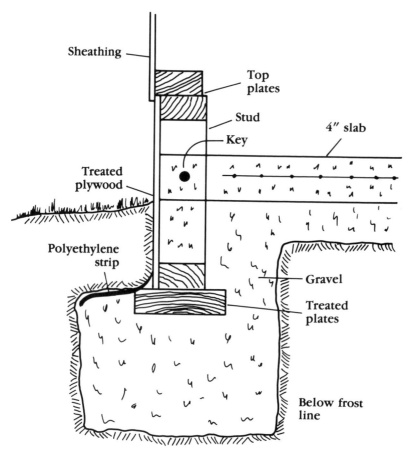

Sheathing

Top plates

Stud

Key

4" slab

Treated plywood

Polyethylene strip

Gravel

Treated plates

Below frost line

9-8   The PWF arrangement for a slab-on-grade outbuilding foundation is simple and effective.

Monolithic

Once the foundation is laid out, perimeter trenches must be cut. All utility lines such as water supply, electrical lines, and sewer lines, must be trenched in. These lines are run to their exact locations and stubbed up above finished slab level. Usually they are protected with sleeves. Any items that extend up through the floor must be placed early on and accurately positioned. Then the perimeter forms can be built. In some cases there are interior footings that have to be located and trenched, as for interior load-bearing walls or support columns. Then the gravel cushion is placed and leveled. Compaction by mechanical tamping is recommended. The soil and cushion should be "carved" around the perimeter to provide for the thickened slab edges.

The next step is to lay the vapor barrier, with sheet laps of at least 6 inches all around. The rigid insulation goes on top of the vapor barrier.

This sometimes extends inward from the walls only a matter of 2 feet or so. However, in very cold climates or if the structure is narrow, the insulation might be continuous.

Usually No. 5 reinforcing bar is placed in the walls, within about 2 to 3 inches of the three corners. Reinforcing wire mesh (also called *remesh*), which is typically 6-×-6-inch welded wire, is laid out over the entire slab area. The mesh should be bent flat and supported about $1^1/2$ to 2 inches off the surface with wire chairs, small rocks, or bits of broken brick or concrete block. After a final check to make sure that everything is in order—this is your last chance—the concrete is poured.

Three-part

With the three-part slab, there is more opportunity for the do-it-yourselfer to become involved. The first step is to lay out the foundation (see Chapter 8) and then form up and pour the footings (see Chapter 7), which are keyed for concrete stem walls or flat for block. A physically active owner-builder can do this, especially with one or two helpers.

The next step is to form and pour the concrete stem walls (see Chapter 11) or build up concrete block stem walls (see Chapter 12). Forming and pouring concrete stem walls can be done by a serious do-it-yourselfer. However, considering the degree of difficulty and the potential problems—not to mention the physical labor involved—a professional crew is recommended. This is especially true where tall walls are involved. Block laying is another matter, and the entire construction of the stem walls can be readily undertaken by an amateur builder, especially if a stack-block system is used.

Once the walls are up and have cured for a week, you can backfill them, working up equally on both sides of the walls. The subgrade should be well compacted on the inside of the walls, but take care not to disrupt the green concrete or mortar. Then lay a minimum 4 inches of cushion material (6 inches is better) and compact that. Lay out the vapor barrier, with 6-inch minimum overlaps and a flap at each end. Lay the insulation next, followed by reinforcing mesh. Finally, have the slab poured and finished.

PWF

The PWF foundation is the easiest for the average do-it-yourselfer to tackle. As with the other types, lay out the foundation and have the trenches dug that are twice as wide as the footing plate. Locate and install all the plumbing, wiring, heating ducts, and other in -or below-floor items. Fill the footing trenches with coarse fill such as crushed rock (pea gravel works well), then rake it smooth and level at the proper depth. Lay the footing plate in place. Build up the wall sections and set them successively on the plate, check for plumb and level, and nail each to the previous one. Install rigid insulation panels as you go along.

As the final connections are made, level and plumb and align the walls again and tie them in place with temporary braces staked to the ground. Backfill the trenches on the inside with more gravel, and at the same time fill against the outside with spoil dirt. Continue spreading the gravel for the cushion, up to the subgrade level. Compact the cushion, then spread a vapor barrier, followed by rigid insulation if necessary. Roll out reinforcing mesh and set it. Drive the 16d keying nails down through the lower top plate, and add the upper top plate, noting the offset. Then have the slab poured.

Pouring the slab itself is not a job that an amateur builder should attempt, unless he also happens to be a concrete worker. A crew of several fairly rugged folks is needed, along with some specialized equipment, in order to do a good job.

The fresh concrete can be moved from a ready-mix truck drum by chute, a wheelbarrow and walkway, or a concrete pumper in a continuous operation. The entire area must be covered as rapidly as possible. Simultaneously, level the "mud" and check the position of the reinforcing mesh. Then re-do the surface screed and darby section by section. The depth should be minimum 4 inches, 6 inches is common. All utility elements in the floor must be covered by at least 1 inch of concrete. In some cases, strips of perimeter insulation or expansion joint material are inserted in the fresh concrete, against the interior faces of the stem walls.

After the concrete has started to cure and the water sheen is disappearing, trowel the surface. The texture of the surface can be controlled, from grainy and rough to super slick, by the amount of troweling done and the surface density achieved. Though troweling is still done by hand at times, especially on small floors like a one-car garage, in many cases large rotary power trowels are employed. They allow a better and much faster finish.

The last step is an important one, but even so it is often slighted. Here the owner-builder can take a hand. The slab should be damp cured for at least 5 days; 7 is better. No part of the surface should be allowed to dry off. Usual practice is to cover the slab with polyethylene film, 4- or 6-mil thickness, white or clear. A curing compound might or might not be sprayed on the surface first. Check the plastic often to make sure that wind has not lifted part of it and that there is still plenty of moisture beneath it. Watch out for tears in the plastic that will allow rapid evaporation and drying. More water can be flooded on with a hose as necessary, and planks or other weights placed on the plastic. Foot traffic is allowable within a day, but no heavy traffic, material storage, or construction should be allowed on the slab during the curing period. After the curing time the plastic and forms can be stripped and the building begun.

Chapter **10**

Pier foundation

Foundation piers are commonly used with continuous-wall crawl space foundations as a means of supporting girders. They are also used alone or topped with a wood or steel column to support decks, porches, and sometimes small additions. When correctly sized, piers do an equally good job of supporting an entire structure.

A pier foundation is easy to build, especially suitable for do-it-yourself construction, and is usually the least expensive kind of foundation. The system has other compelling attributes: It is readily adjustable to varying topography; minimal site preparation is required; there is minimal site disturbance; neither the foundation nor the house is susceptible to ground moisture or flooding damage; and the buildup of methane, radon, or other gasses is not possible. Note, that pier foundations higher than 4 or 5 feet above grade, depending upon topography, should be engineered for the specific task. Check local building codes for details and allowability.

There are three main types of pier foundations: poured concrete, concrete block, and wood post.

POURED CONCRETE PIERS

Calculate the number of piers required to support the weight and spans of the house, along with the footing size. The piers can be round, poured into cylindrical cardboard forms (FIG. 10-1). Or they can be square, poured into forms either scratch-built or assembled from stock form sections at the site.

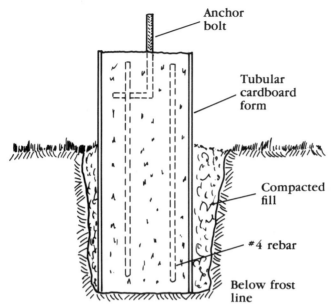

Anchor bolt

Tubular cardboard form

Compacted fill

#4 rebar

Below frost line

10-1   A typical arrangement for a poured concrete pier in a round fiberboard form.

Lay out the foundation lines and spot the places where the pier holes must be dug. Set the pier centers so that the outer edge of the first-floor sill will be approximately even with the outermost edges of the perimeter piers. Center interior piers under appropriate support points along girders or other structural elements.

Digging the holes

Double check the layout, then dig the pier holes. Digging by hand causes little disruption but a lot of blisters. A backhoe might be required for square piers, because the holes must be big enough to allow working room to set and brace the forms. Holes for round piers can often be drilled with a post hole auger mounted on a tractor. If no footing is needed, slip the forms into holes, then sift fill into the holes and tamp to keep the forms plumb and snug during pouring.

Often footings can be dispensed with if the piers are made a bit fatter. In any event, the holes should extend below average frost line depth—a minimum of about 24 to 32 inches, depending upon the nature of the soil—to allow decent stability. When the holes are set, pour the footings as required.

Pouring the footings

The next step is to place the forms. Cardboard tubing, because it is so easy to use, relatively inexpensive, and need not be stripped later, is most frequently employed for pouring piers. Set a series of taut lines over the pier locations to indicate the required pier top height. Cut the form tubes to length and set them in place; hold or brace them plumb and slowly and evenly backfill up around them. Tamp the backfill regularly, adding water periodically from a hose to help settle and compact the soil. Check for plumb and alignment frequently, because if a tube becomes misaligned you'll have to start again. Alternatively, build or erect wood or steel forms and brace them ruggedly in position.

When the forms are set, you can call in the ready-mix truck and fill them all in short order. If some or all of the piers are not readily reachable and you would have to use wheelbarrows and shovels to place the mix, consider hiring a pumper truck. If you are doing your own mixing and pouring, you can set forms and pour concrete piecemeal, as time and energy permit. After the forms have 2 feet or so of fresh mix in them, churn the concrete around with a stick or broomhandle to work out any air bubbles and consolidate the mix. Then stick in two or three or four precut lengths of No. 4 or No. 5 reinforcing bar, depending upon pier size.

Top up the forms and screed off any excess. Then insert anchor bolts or pins—or in some cases steel post or column bases—into the fresh concrete. Make sure the placement of such hardware is exactly right, because it can't be moved later. Slip a plastic garbage bag over each pier and secure with string or mechanic's black iron wire. This will keep the moisture in and aid in proper curing. Allow at least a week before loading the piers. Two weeks is even better, because the concrete will have almost reached its full strength by then. Wood or metal forms can be stripped after three days if necessary, but are better left for a week. Loose backfill can be shoveled in after three or four days, but leave any compacting until at least a week has passed. Cardboard forms can be left to rot away below ground, and the above-grade part stripped whenever you are able.

CONCRETE BLOCK PIERS

Concrete blocks make excellent piers, and are a good alternative where ready-mix concrete is not available. Blocks have ample strength to support nearly any kind of residential structure, they are easy to handle and work with, are readily available and relatively inexpensive. They are heavy, though, and costly to transport, so a nearby source is important.

Standard pier blocks, 8×8×16 inches and square-ended, are typically used for piers (FIG. 10-2). Common stretcher blocks will work just as well. For small piers you can use standard 8-×-8-×-8 half blocks, for heavy piers use standard 12-inch blocks. You can fill the hollow cores of the blocks with mortar or concrete for extra strength, and gain considerably more strength by inserting a No. 4 reinforcing rod in one or more of the filled cores. In the 16-×-16-inch type of pier pictured, filling and reinforcing two diagonally opposite cores, top to bottom, makes a rugged construction.

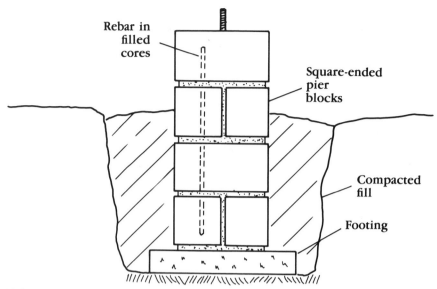

10-2 Piers can be built up quickly and easily using concrete pier blocks mortared together, grouted, and reinforced.

Digging and pouring the footings

Calculate the pier size, quantity, and footing size (necessary for block piers). Lay out the foundation lines and spot the pier locations. Dig pier holes. In firm soil you can hand-dig square-sided holes the same size as the footings, if they need not be more than about 32 to 40 inches deep. Then you can pour the footings directly on the bottoms of the holes without forming. Dampen the earth first. Otherwise, dig the holes with a backhoe, form up the footings, and pour them. Often as not they are small enough that you can hand-mix the concrete from a bagged dry mix, or mix bulk ingredients in a small electric batch mixer. Don't forget the reinforcing bar.

Remember that the depth of the pier hole, the thickness of the footing, the thickness of the blocks, and the thickness of the mortar joints between them, all interact with reference to the required overall height of the piers. This must be calculated well and checked as construction goes along.

Building the piers

Let the footings cure for five days or more before starting to build the piers. Lay the first block, or pair, in a full bed of mortar on the footing, about 1/2 inch thick. Fill the core that contains the anchor pin with mortar, and plumb and level the block(s). Then start building upward, spreading a shell bed of mortar for a 3/8-inch joint between blocks. This thickness can be adjusted slightly if you need to gain or lose a bit of pier height. Level and plumb the blocks as you build. Scrape off any excess mortar that squeezes out of the joints and tool the joints smooth and dense as the mortar starts to cure. Stop after laying the fifth course and allow the mortar joints to cure overnight. Then keep building upward.

After all the blocks are laid, allow the joints to cure for several days. Pour concrete, mortar, or grout into the cores and add reinforcing steel as desired. Set anchor bolts two courses deep into filled cores. If there will be no filled cores, insert a strip of hardware cloth or screen across the block cores, between the second and third course down from the top. Wad a piece of newspaper for a stopper and shove it down tight against the screen, then fill the core and insert the anchor.

Backfilling

Allow the mortar joints to cure for five to seven days before you backfill or load the piers. To backfill, use clean fill and shovel in about 18 inches or so all around, tamp it down with a post hole bar or heavy tamper, then soak the fill thoroughly. After the water drains down, shovel in another 12 to 18 inches, tamp, soak again, and so on. Carry the fill slightly up above finished grade line. This process will give you a dense, solid fill that approaches the native soil in degree of compaction, and locks the piers in tightly.

WOOD PIERS

Wood posts or poles are not as widely used as they might be. With today's excellent preservatives, wood posts provide an inexpensive, long-lived foundation system (FIG. 10-3). Wood piers are particularly suited to out-

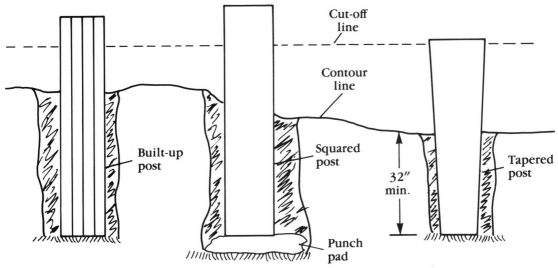

10-3 Wood piers can be made of built-up dimension stock, lengths of solid wood timber, or tapered poles.

buildings of all kinds, camps and vacation homes, and small residences, although many large homes have been so based.

This is probably the easiest of all foundations for the do-it-yourselfer to build. The job requires only minimal skill and experience and just a few ordinary tools. The system also has great flexibility: Hardly any site preparation is needed, site disturbance is practically nonexistent, and the piers don't take much time to set. Once they are set, the foundation is done and construction can start immediately.

Posts or poles can support an enormous amount of weight. If properly set they are unlikely to settle; they are held in place by soil friction along their sides as well as by the expanse of their ends. For added weight distribution they can be set on punch pads, either large flat stones or concrete footing-like pads. This extra step, however, makes the installation more difficult. It is usually better to simply use a thicker post or pole.

The material to use is wood that has been commercially treated for in-ground or direct burial purposes. The minimum size, except for a very small shed or similar outbuilding, is 8×8 inches or about the same diameter. Fully dimensioned timber is best from a strength standpoint, but you can make up posts by bolting together lengths of 2× PWF planking. These will be almost as strong and are less likely to twist.

New railroad ties, though a bit smaller than the timber, are usable. Never use second-hand ties; their useful life is over when they are removed from the railbed. Old telephone poles are equally useless. Don't use the so-called "landscaping timbers" or "garden timbers" either, because the preservative treatment is insufficient for this application. And, don't attempt to treat your own raw timbers or logs. An adequate job simply can't be done without the right industrial equipment, even if you could get the right chemicals—which you can't.

Digging the pier holes

As with the other kinds of pier foundations, calculate the size and number of piers needed, lay out the foundation outline, spot the pier locations, and run taut lines for height and alignment guides. Then dig the pier holes. You can do this by hand with a post hole bar and shovel, with a one- or two-man portable power auger, or with a power auger mounted on a tractor or truck. If possible, the holes should be just big enough around to accept the posts, which means that the holes themselves must be accurately located and dug vertically, not cockeyed. As a last resort, you can have the holes scooped out by a backhoe, although this is much less satisfactory. Depending upon local codes and conditions, the post bottoms might have to extend down below average frost level. In any event they should be at least $2^{1}/_{2}$ to 3 feet deep.

Backfilling

Set each post in place (tip downward for tapered poles) and shovel a foot or so of clean fill dirt around it. Check the plumb and alignment and tamp the dirt thoroughly. Wet the dirt to puddle stage, wait a few moments, and shovel in another foot of dirt. Repeat the process. Check the plumb and alignment often. If the soil is rocky and/or you had to dig a hole much larger than the post, you might have to brace the post in place while you work. Use some of the potato-sized rocks, driven in tight, as props around the post for the first 12 to 18 inches. Exchange rocky soil for some that will pack well. Carry the backfill up to somewhat above grade level.

Cutting the posts

There are two options for cutting the posts to the correct length. One is to cut each post ahead of time and set their tops exactly to a level taut line representing the proper sill height. This requires adjusting the level of the soil in the bottom of each hole, which can be tricky. The second method is to first cut each post long and set them all. Then cut them in place after achieving level by using a taut line or a sighting level. This is more difficult, because making a sideways cut in a heavy timber and keeping it square is not the easiest thing to do. There is, however, less chance for error.

Chapter **11**

Poured concrete foundation

One of the two most commonly used materials for continuous-wall residence foundations, either crawl space or full basement, is poured concrete. It makes a stable, solid, relatively inexpensive foundation that is adaptable to nearly all site conditions and structure design requirements. That is, provided ready-mix concrete is available and the site can be accessed by the heavy concrete mixer trucks, or reached by a pumper hose.

There are some drawbacks. The construction is physically demanding and requires expertise and equipment in most cases. The availability of ready-mixed concrete at reasonable cost is an absolute must. Unstable soils or special site conditions might require engineering and special construction methods, leading to increased costs. Also, for decent results the walls have to be correctly formed and poured, preferably during good weather.

The greater the mass of concrete, complexity of design, and extent of forming, the more difficult and complex the construction of poured concrete walls becomes. Small and simple installations can be handled by a do-it-yourselfer, with some help. Big jobs should be left to the professionals. Just where the dividing line comes is difficult to say. However, low, continuous stem walls, perhaps up to 3 feet high or so and 8 to 12 inches thick, pose few problems. An owner-builder and two or three helpers can handle both forming and pouring, if properly prepared. At that, some experience in handling concrete, even if only as a helper on a foundation job or two, is recommended.

Tall crawl space walls, buttressed or pilastered walls, full-height basement walls, stepped walls, and complex constructions with multiple openings, should be professionally designed, engineered, and built by a competent concrete contractor. If you hire a contractor, he'll read the plans and take it from there, and the chances are excellent that he will not want you to take any part in the work. If you want to build your own, or just want to know what the contractor is up to, here's how the job progresses.

FOOTINGS

The first consideration is to build suitable footings for the walls (see Chapter 7). There is an exception: Sometimes walls and footings are poured together using specially made forms. The wall flares outward on both sides near the bottom, and looks a lot like the precast concrete sections often used as highway lane dividers. Most often, though, the footing is the conventional type, rectangular in cross section and reinforced, with a keyway cast in the top surface.

FORMS

Next, forms must be built for the walls, to contain the fresh concrete mix. There are two possibilities. The first, and one that professionals employ, is reusable form sections. These may be shop-built from special plywood manufactured for the purpose, braced with wood dimension stock, or special interlocking steel panels of numerous types that allow forming practically any design. If you have experience in concrete work and know how to use this equipment, you might be able to borrow or rent a set; this does make the job easier. The second possibility involves building one-time forms on site. If possible, plan ahead so that the materials you put into the forms can be reused in the house later on. Remember, however, that you won't be able to get the surfaces entirely clean again.

Walls less than 4 feet

For walls less than 4 feet high, a typical construction (FIG. 11-1) employs exterior plywood $5/8$ or $3/4$ inch thick, braced with construction-grade 2×4s. You can also use nominal $3/4$-inch-thick boards. These should be tongue-and-groove, and even so are less satisfactory than plywood. If the footing is wide enough and you can build the forms immediately after stripping the footings, you can nail the bottom 2-×-4 plates right to the green footing concrete. Space the 2-×-4 studs about 24 inches apart for walls in the range of 2 feet high and 8 to 10 inches thick, assuming heavy plywood form board is employed.

Decrease the spacing for combinations of taller and/or thicker walls and/or thinner plywood form walls. Set the studs in opposing pairs, and

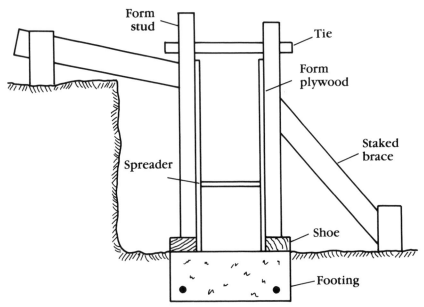

Form
stud

Tie

Form
plywood

Staked
brace

Spreader

Shoe

Footing

11-1   Typical form construction atop a concrete footing, for a poured concrete stem wall.

nail 1-×-4 ties to them across the form top. Install solid bracing at each stud, setting diagonals at about 30 degrees when possible. Drive anchor stakes well into the ground with a sledge. As the overall form construction proceeds, check the alignment often and make sure the walls remain exactly plumb and the horizontal alignment is as perfect as you can make it. Remember, your house is going to perch on top of these walls.

The form walls must be tied so they won't spread apart, but must also be stabilized at the outset with spreaders so the proper distance between them is maintained. The traditional method is to install wood spreaders and tie wires (FIG. 11-2). The spreaders are lengths of 1×2 or something similar, cut to the thickness dimension of the wall.

Set the spreaders about 2 feet apart both vertically and horizontally in a 3- to 4-foot wall; shorter walls need only one row about one-third height above the footing. These sticks must be removed as the concrete is poured. You can pick the upper ones out by hand just before they are buried. To retrieve lower ones, wrap a snatch wire solidly around each and leave the free end hooked down over the form side (FIG. 11-3). Pull the wire just before the upper spreader gets buried. Near each spreader, thread a tie wire of black iron mechanic's wire through small holes drilled in the form. Tie the loop off, insert a nail in the center, and twist the wire up tight.

Combination tie/spreaders (FIG. 11-4) are more commonly used today, and are readily available in several styles. They stabilize the form walls in both directions at once. This does away with having to cut, install, and later dig out wood spreaders. Threading in tie wire is also obviated.

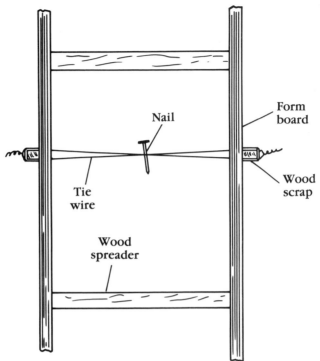

11-2 The traditional method of keeping form walls aligned is with wire ties twisted tight and wood stick spreaders.

11-3 For removing wood spreaders as the concrete is poured around them, attach snatch wires to them.

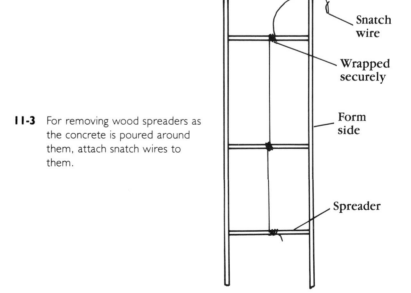

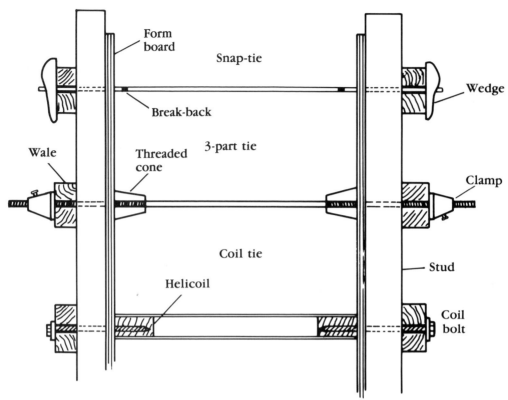

11-4   Combination tie-spreaders, quick and easy to install, are most often used in concrete wall construction today.

Snap ties consist of rods clamped in place through the forms, later to be broken off at designed weak points. Three-section ties use an inner rod connected by cone nuts to a pair of outer rods, which in turn are clamped against the form. Coil ties use a tubular inner spreader with helicoils in each end, into which bolts extending through the form walls are threaded.

Spacing for all of these ties is the same as for wood spreaders. Install them according to the manufacturer's instructions. They are made in different strength ratings, up to 50,000 pounds per square foot working load. At the 2-foot maximum spacing a rating of 3,000 pounds per square foot is sufficient for residential construction.

As you can see from TABLE 11-1, freshly poured concrete exerts an enormous amount of pressure on the form walls, depending upon the rate of pour and the ambient temperature. The rate of pour, in turn, depends in part upon the size of the foundation and how quickly the available workers can place the concrete. The greatest pressure is exerted along the bottom of the form walls, and especially at the form corners.

**Table 11-1   Relationship of Concrete
Temperature, Pouring Rate and Pressure**

Concrete Placement Rate, Feet/Hour	Approx. Concrete Pressure in Lb./Square Foot at Concrete Temperature of:			
	40°	*50°*	*60°*	*70°*
1	490	440	390	350
2	700	600	520	460
3	900	760	660	590
4	1100	920	800	700
5	1300	1080	930	820
6	1510	1240	1060	930
7	1700	1400	1200	1050
8	1790	1450	1250	1190

This is an inherent weak spot, so form corners must be carefully built and braced extra solidly. A broken form midway through emplacement is a major disaster. A lesser problem is gaps or splits in the form where cement paste can drool out. Avoid this, because it might cause dried-out and weak spots that will have to be filled later.

Walls higher than 4 feet

The construction of forms for walls more than 4 feet high is more complex and requires a lot more material. A typical construction is shown in FIG. 11-5. The studs must be supported by horizontal members called *wales*, and all bracing is larger and more rugged. The size and spacing of the materials is a variable combination of form wall thickness, stud size and spacing, wale size and spacing, and projected concrete pressures, all of which must be calculated carefully.

FOUNDATION WALL OPENINGS

Foundation walls always have some openings in them. Sleeves, such as might be needed to accommodate a sewer pipe, water line, electrical supply, or telephone wire, can be easily made by inserting lengths of pipe of a suitable diameter between the form walls, just like a wood spreader. If necessary, they can be locked in place with a tie wire or through-bolt. Ventilator or window openings are commonly positioned so that the house sill plate will serve as the top of the buck. To frame the opening, build a three-sided buck with key strips on the sides. Secure it between the form walls, flush with the top edges (FIG. 11-6). Cover the opening with a scrap board so the cavity won't accidentally get filled.

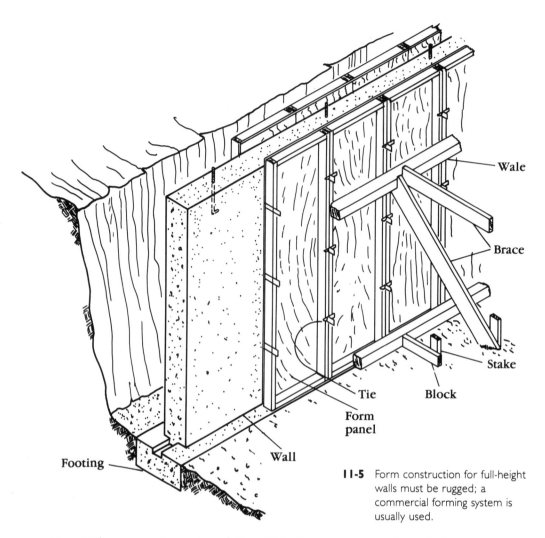

11-5 Form construction for full-height walls must be rugged; a commercial forming system is usually used.

For window or vent openings fully within the concrete, make a similar four-sided buck and position it accurately in the form. About 3 to 4 inches above the top of the buck, wire a pair of No. 4 reinforcing rods in place, equidistant from front and back, that extend at least 1 foot to either side of the buck (FIG. 11-7). If the opening is wider than about 4 feet, have this reinforcement scheme engineered for you. In small size, make the bucks of nominal 2-inch-thick stock. If wider or taller than about 2 feet, install removable bracing within the buck so that it will not distort under the weight of the fresh concrete.

To make a ledge near the outside top of the wall for a brick or stone veneer, you'll need a setback in the form (FIG. 11-8). Concrete pressure will not be great here, but this is inherently a weak point and must be reinforced. Make the top of the outside form wall 1½ inches higher than the

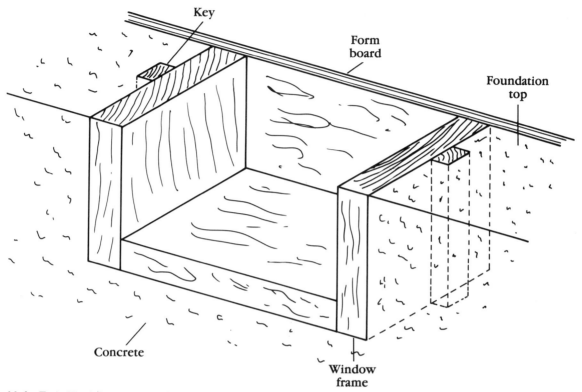

11-6 Typical buck/form construction for a window or vent located at the foundation wall top. The buck remains when the forms are stripped off, to hold the window or vent unit.

ledge point. Attach a horizontal 2× of appropriate width edgewise to the form, flush with the top edge. Attach the upper, outer form wall piece and its supporting studs solidly to this member, and brace everything well.

To make pockets in the foundation wall tops, in which girder ends will rest so that the girder top lies flush with the sill top, you need some specific dimensions to work with. These are: the width of the finished girder, plus 1 inch; the length of girder end that will rest within the wall pocket, plus 1/2 inch; the thickness of a redwood or treated wood pad upon which the girder will rest (typically 1 1/2 inches); the height of the girder; and the distance the girder end must extend above the foundation wall top to be flush with the sill top (also typically 1 1/2 inches). Putting these all together will give you the dimensions of the pocket. Make up chunks of wood or cut pieces of rigid insulation, and secure them in the appropriate spots to the interior face of the inside form walls.

POURING THE CONCRETE

When everything has been assembled, the next step is to double check the entire construction. When the pour starts, there's no turning back.

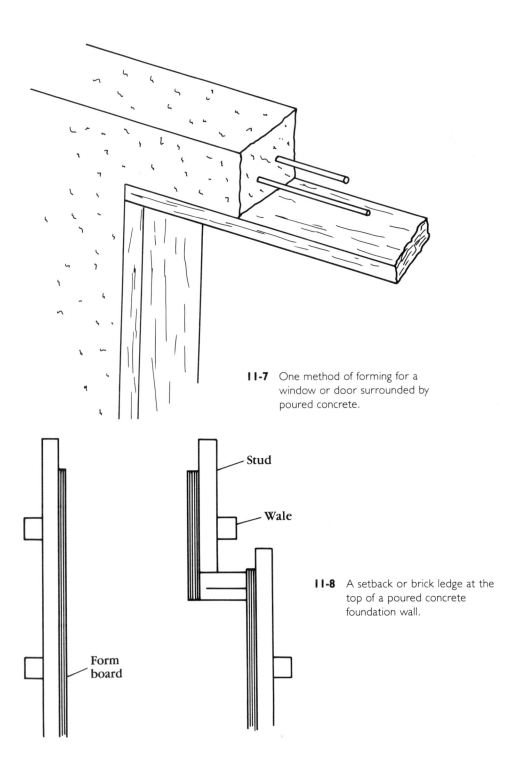

11-7 One method of forming for a window or door surrounded by poured concrete.

Stud

Wale

Form board

11-8 A setback or brick ledge at the top of a poured concrete foundation wall.

Make sure everything is well secured and braced, and aligned properly—especially at corners. Check that marker nails or string guidelines for pour levels are in place. All of the form work interior surfaces should be treated with a release agent. You can use old motor oil sprayed, brushed, or wiped on, but a commercial form oil is cleaner and works better.

Often pouring the concrete is the easiest part of the job. If possible, schedule your pouring for a time when the temperature will be between 50 and 80 degrees Farenheit; this makes the work much easier and will result in a better job. Above and below those numbers, you'll need to make special preparations and take special precautions in order to avoid improper curing.

Mixing the concrete

Typical mixes for foundation walls are one sack of portland cement to 3 cubic yards of sand to 4 cubic yards of gravel, or a similar 1:2^1/$_2$:5 mix. However, be guided by the recommendations of local builders or the ready-mix concrete company. Tell them what you're doing and they'll tell you what you need.

Preparations

Set up a pouring schedule with the ready-mix concrete company. Be ready for them when they arrive, and be prepared to get the job done expeditiously and in one pour. Have at least a couple of sturdy helpers on hand, along with shovels, rakes, hoes, and several wheelbarrows if the concrete has to be transported. Have truck access clear, plank walkways readied, and select a starting point and logical progression of work. Or, clear a spot for a pumper truck and concrete truck—if possible, one from which the entire foundation can be reached by the pumper boom and hose without shifting the trucks to another location.

Procedure

Place the concrete in layers about 1 foot deep or less, going around and around the foundation. If the temperature is over 75 degrees Fahrenheit, don't pour any more than 6 feet (height) in an hour. Below that temperature, keep the rate to less than 4 feet per hour. If you use a mechanical vibrator in the fresh mix to settle it, cut those rates in half, respectively. Use vibrators for no more than a normally paced count of 20 in any one area, and remember that the process puts a great deal of added strain and pressure on the forms. Vibrating is usually not necessary anyway in these comparatively low-volume pours, only convenient. You can "rod" the fresh concrete by pumping a length of 2×2 or 2×4 straight up and down in the mix every 2 feet or so, which will settle the mix nicely.

Spade the concrete along the wall faces as it is placed, by running a square-edge flat shovel or a big flat-bladed ice chopper up and down against the interior faces of the form walls. This will eliminate air pockets and honeycombs, and make for a smooth, dense concrete surface. Beneath the frames of openings like vent bucks, thump the forms solidly a few times with a hammer to accomplish the same purpose.

Pouring conditions

If you must pour in extreme temperatures or in foul weather, ask a specialist for advice on how to proceed. Consider the concrete mix, conditions likely at pouring time, and local weather forecast. In hot weather you might have to mix the concrete with cold water, chill it with ice, erect sun shades or windbreaks, and keep the forms cooled by watering them. In cold weather, you might have to use calcium chloride in the concrete, mix it with heated water, provide shelters over the forms, and heat the forms or even the entire area.

Screeding and curing

As the forms are topped up, screed the concrete by running a chunk of 2×4 along the top edges with a back-and-forth, sawing motion. Scrape off the excess concrete and even up the surface. Set whatever anchor bolts are required by shoving them down into the mix to the proper level and packing concrete back in around them; make sure they are plumb. Finally, cover the top of the foundation with polyethylene sheeting (construction plastic) and allow the concrete to cure.

Under good conditions, Type I concrete will attain two-thirds or more of its ultimate compressive strength within about three days, though it will still be green (not fully cured). Other Types might take more or less time, as will mixes containing additives. Usually three days is the minimum time and five or six the maximum for leaving the forms in place. After that you can strip them off, but be careful of corners and edges. Bucks and bushings stay in place, ties are broken or cut off, beam pockets are emptied, and framing other than bucks is removed at the same time. Allow at least a week, preferably more, before loading the foundation in any way—including placing backfill.

Chapter **12**

Concrete block foundation

*C*oncrete block ranks as one of the two most commonly used foundation wall materials—the other being poured concrete. Block is doubtless the most popular do-it-yourself material. It has the advantages of being relatively easy to handle, suitable for a person working alone, and fairly inexpensive. Working with concrete block requires little or no experience and a low-to-modest skill level to produce a creditable job, depending upon the system used. Also, the work can be done piecemeal over a period of time. A plain block wall is not as strong as a poured concrete wall, but it is ample for residential purposes, and any block wall can be beefed up substantially by design or with steel and grout reinforcing.

There are some drawbacks. One is the relative weakness just mentioned, especially against lateral forces. The blocks must be locally available, otherwise the shipping costs would be prohibitive. Blocks are more porous than poured concrete, so waterproofing in damp/wet conditions can cause problems. More time might be required to build a comparable block foundation than a poured concrete one.

BLOCK TYPES AND SIZES

Concrete blocks are modular and come in standard sizes and shapes; there might be small local variations. Standard or common block is the most widely available and frequently used, and is made in the greatest variety of shapes for specific purposes. Heavyweight blocks, usually employed in house foundations, are made of cement and an aggregate such as crushed rock or gravel, shale, or slag. Lightweight blocks are made from cement and cinders, pumice, vermiculite, or a similar light material. Select the type that is locally available and suitable for foundation purposes.

Concrete blocks are made most often in nominal 8-×-8-×-16-inch and 12-×-12-×-16-inch sizes. A 10-inch thickness is available in some areas, and 4-inch-thick blocks are used for partitions. The 8-inch size is sufficient for most residence foundations, including full-height basement walls. The 12-inch size might be necessary for an exceptionally large or heavy house, taller-than-normal walls, or unusual lateral force conditions. Actual sizes are typically $3/8$ inch less than nominal in height and length, so that when built up with a $3/8$-inch mortar joint, the dimensions will come out in even inches.

Because the blocks are modular, foundation walls (or any other constructions) should be designed on the basis of, preferably, 16-inch horizontal and 8-inch vertical increments. Failing that, use an odd number of 8-inch horizontal and/or 4-inch vertical increments. This obviates any necessity for cutting blocks to special sizes, plugging with bricks, or filling small spaces with mortar or concrete. Note that standard concrete block must always be fully dry when laid up, unlike brick, and should be free of dust and dirt. Keep the blocks well protected when they are stored prior to use at your building site.

There are block shapes made for numerous purposes (FIG. 12-1). The bulk of the blocks in a wall are stretcher blocks, with flanges at each end; these can be 2- or 3-cored. Corner blocks have one smooth, squared end. Pier blocks sometimes have two squared ends, as do half-blocks (8×8×8 inches). Cap blocks, used to top a wall, are solid and usually available in both full and half height. Jamb blocks are smoothly indented at one corner to accept steel or wood window or door side jambs, and header blocks are cut to accept door or window headers. Lintel blocks are oversize cast channels to be set over door or window openings and filled with reinforcing rod and mortar or concrete. There are many other shapes as well, and it's a good idea to check with local suppliers before you buy, to see what forms might be advantageous for you.

CONSTRUCTION SYSTEMS

There are three construction systems that can be used for concrete blocks. Various blocks can be intermingled, although it's best to stick with one. The traditional system is mortar joint construction, using conventional blocks, as just described, typically stacked in a running bond and joined with mortar. The surface bonded system also uses conventional blocks, but they are stacked dry (no mortar) and set as close together as possible. Note that this changes length/height wall dimensions. Then both inside and outside surfaces of the completed walls are plastered with a bonding material formulated for the purpose. The stack-block system uses specially made blocks that have tongues and grooves along the edges. They lock together when stacked, and some of the cores,

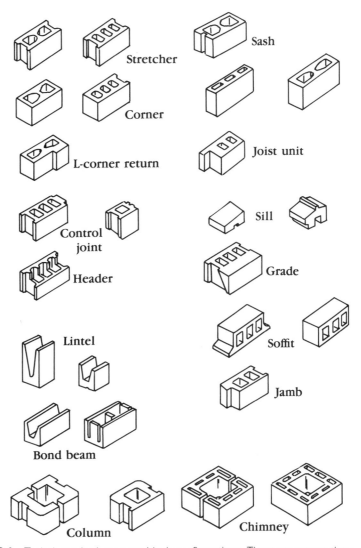

12-1 Typical standard concrete block configurations. There are many others.

following a prescribed pattern, are reinforced with steel rod and filled with mortar or grout as the construction proceeds.

POURED CONCRETE FOOTINGS

The starting point for any of these systems is with a suitable poured concrete footing. Typically no keyway is used and the footing top is smooth. However, a key does no harm. Some builders even install anchors consisting of right-angled lengths of reinforcing bar, bedded in the footings and protruding so as to extend up into block cores in the bottom course or two. Note that whenever mortar or grout is being used the weather conditions should be benign, the same as for poured concrete. Follow the same recommendations and take special precautions in poor conditions.

MORTAR JOINT CONSTRUCTION

To build a mortar joint block foundation, start by laying out guidelines, after the footings have had at least three days curing time. At one footing corner, spot a block corner location. From this point, snap a chalkline all the way around the footings to show the exact position of the blocks. They should be centered on the footings, so your chalkline should be either a half-block thickness to the inside or the outside of the footing centerline. Double check for accuracy when you're done. Measure the wall lengths and the distances between parallel walls, making sure that the wall tops will ultimately mate up properly at all points with the house sill. All corners should be exactly square (or at other planned angles). If the footings turn out to be a bit off-angle, adjust the block guidelines accordingly.

Placing the blocks

Lay out a full line of blocks on the footing, using no mortar. Approximate the 3/8-inch mortar joint between them, and see how they will fit up. Sometimes joints have to be thinned or fattened just a bit. Set the blocks off the footing in a row, and mix up a batch of mortar. Usual practice is to mix from bulk supplies.

Mortar mix

A good mix for general block laying is 1 part of masonry sand to $2^{1}/4 - 3$ parts of damp, loose sand, along with just enough water to make a plastic, workable mix. If the mortar feels too grainy and sandy and doesn't want to stick well, reduce the sand. If it's too goopy and seems not to have solid enough body, increase the sand. With a little playing around you'll soon find a mix that suits both you and the conditions. A good mix is a lot like a good peanut butter: It should stick together and to the block, but spread easily and smoothly. Mix only enough to see you through about $1^{1}/2$ hours of work (less in hot, dry, or windy weather), but keep track of your proportions and maintain them from batch to batch.

An alternative to scratch mixing is to use bagged dry mortar mix. This is more expensive, but also more convenient. Many of these mixes tend to be sandy; you can make a "fatter" mortar by adding about $1/2$ cubic foot of portland cement to each bag and mixing it thoroughly into the dry materials before adding water. You can mix either kind in a wheelbarrow or a mortar tub, or a power mixer. The latter obviously is easier and will produce a more uniform, smoother mix, but many a block has been well joined with barrow-mixed mortar. Hand mix each batch for at least 5 minutes, or power mix for about 3 minutes. And if you're working in strong, hot sun, be sure to cover the batch with a scrap of plywood.

Laying the mortar

Pick a handy corner and lay a bed of mortar on the footing that is a little more than four blocks long. Plop it down in full trowel loads, then furrow it down the middle with the trowel tip and spread it out a bit less than a block wide. Watch your guideline (FIG. 12-2). Set the corner block in place by lowering it straight down into the mortar bed. Push it down evenly until the excess mortar squishes out and the joint is about 3/8 inch thick (FIG. 12-3). Don't joggle or rock the block, or move it enough to break the mortar free. Check with a spirit level to make sure the block is both plumb and level. Stand the next few blocks on end and butter the flanges

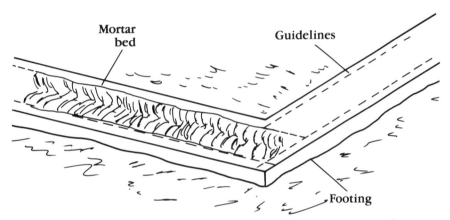

12-2 To start a block wall, lay a full bed of mortar for three or four blocks, furrowed down the middle, on the footing top.

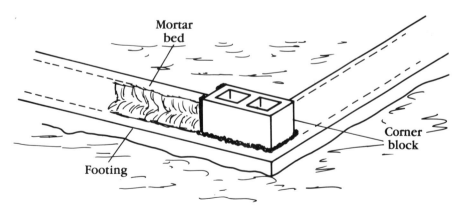

12-3 Set the first corner block in the mortar bed with an even, 3/8-inch bed joint and align it precisely.

of each. Set them successively, mortared end to dry end, by lowering them in a combined downward and forward motion. This should result in a ³/₈-inch bed joint at the bottom and a ³/₈-inch head joint between the flanges.

Check for plumb and level of each block, and make sure the alignment is correct by placing a long mason's level or a straightedge against the block faces. To make small adjustments, tap the blocks gently with the end of your trowel handle. If you break a block free of the mortar, remove the block and the mortar and start over with fresh mortar. When all the blocks are properly set, scrape the excess mortar away from the joints (FIG. 12-4). If it is still plastic and shows no drying, you can flip it back into the tub and mix it in for reuse, although many masons don't bother.

Now perform the same operation from the same corner but along the other wall. When that's done, start on the second course, same corner. Lay a face shell mortar bed (along the outer edges of the laid blocks but not across the webs), and butter the flange edges of the loose blocks as before. Set the corner block first, at right angles to the one below (FIG. 12-5). Follow up in the half-overlap pattern with the other blocks. Level,

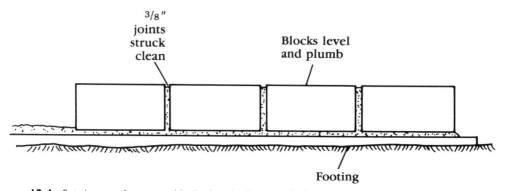

12-4 Set three or four more blocks. Level, plumb, and align them, and strike the joints clean.

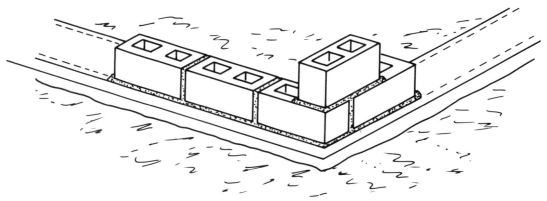

12-5 Start the second course with a half-overlap corner block at right angles to the first and precisely aligned.

plumb, and align as you go; this is crucial, and should soon become automatic. This course will be a half block short of the ends of the first course. Continue until you complete the corner pyramid. Then move to the next corner and build that one.

Walls that are too short for this procedure are built in the same way—doing the corners first and filling the middle space afterward. However, employ fewer blocks and work in a continuous operation—up to a height of four or five courses—before allowing a curing period.

To fill in between corners, follow the same procedure and lay more stretcher blocks with a 3/8-inch joint. Stretch a mason's line taut from corner to corner, aligned with a top edge of the course you're laying, to act as an alignment and height guide. Buy the bright yellow line; it's much more visible than plain white string.

Trim off excess mortar that curls out of the joints with your trowel as you go along. You can just leave the joints as is, flush with the block surface. This is common practice, especially on the outside, below-grade surfaces. Elsewhere, you might prefer to tool the joints before the mortar cures by going over all of them with a special tool made for the purpose. Use plenty of pressure to create a dense, solidly packed surface layer in whatever shape you've chosen.

Closer blocks

In each course you will eventually come to the point where you will need one full or half block to fill the gap and complete the course. This is called the *closer* block, and is placed a bit differently than the others. Butter the exposed outer edges of the lower course blocks with mortar, and do the same to the flanges of the adjacent same-course blocks. Then butter the full-block flanges or half-block corners as well. Hold the closer block directly over the opening, take good aim, and gently, slowly, slide it straight down without dislodging the mortar. It should just squish out a bit and join together (FIG. 12-6).

For a low wall, four or five courses or less, the block laying is complete. For more than five courses, wait a day for the mortar to cure. If you load them too much early on, the joints can break apart or squeeze down too thin. Then go ahead and build up the corners again, and afterward fill in the empty stretches between them.

Top course treatment

The top courses need extra attention regardless of wall height. They have to be sealed off. One method is to use solid blocks for the whole top course. Another is to lay a continuous strip of screening or hardware cloth along the top of the next to last course, bedded in the mortar joint. Then lay the top course and fill all the cores and between-flange spaces with mortar and strike the top surface smooth.

Anchor bolts must be installed to secure the house sill plate to the

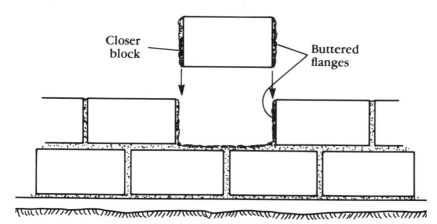

12-6 The closer block in every course is carefully slipped into place from directly above with fully buttered flanges.

foundation. Place a bolt about 1 foot from each corner and every 4 to 6 feet in between—or closer. Insert the bolts at least fully into the first course, or better yet, into the second. Follow local code requirements. Block off a core opening with a wad of newspaper or fiberglass insulation or a piece of screen, insert the bolt, and pack mortar around it. In a solid-block top course, use cored or partial blocks at the points where anchors must be installed.

Window and door openings

Window and door openings are built in as the job progresses. Calculate the sizes and positions of the openings to coincide with the block modules to save special cutting. You can build bucks or other opening frames from wood dimension stock. Or, use commercial steel frames, set them in place, and lay the block to them. You can also create the required openings unframed as you lay the block, employing the special shapes (jamb, lintel, header, etc.) as you build, then install frames and/or units later on. To form vent openings in crawl space walls, you can lay stretcher blocks on their sides with the cores open through. Setting the blocks back 3/4 inch or more allows a secondary opening into which you can fit a wood-framed summer screen and a wood winter door.

Reinforcing

There are several ways to reinforce a block wall. If the height is four courses or less, it is not usually necessary. If higher, reinforcement does no harm and might indeed be necessary or required. A good practice in any case is to place a length of reinforcing rod in the outermost core at each corner and pack the core full of mortar. Another good practice is to do the same at a logical point for every 10 linear feet or so of wall between corners. There are also various designs of wire reinforcement sections that can be bedded in the horizontal mortar joint about every four or five courses, or sometimes every other course, to combat unusual lateral forces and add overall strength.

SURFACE BONDED CONSTRUCTION

The surface bonded system has become popular with do-it-yourselfers because of its simplicity. However, it must be done correctly, under decent conditions, and exactly to the bonding material manufacturer's instructions if the job is to be successful. Although the standard concrete block products are readily available in most locales, the bonding material might not be; you will have to find a source. Typically this material is a special paste-like blend of glass fibers, cement, and various additives, that is designed to be applied like a plaster in a single coating about 1/2 inch thick.

Start the job just as for a conventional mortar-joint system. During early house planning stages, take into account the different dimensions involved. Stack the blocks carefully, and make sure they are plumb, level, and correctly aligned. Key points might have to be anchored, reinforced, or filled—or all three—depending upon the bonding material and the foundation design. Trowel on the bonding material in the prescribed manner, on both faces of the walls. The blocks must be dry and dirt-free. The top course should be filled or solid, and anchor bolts must be set as required.

STACK-BLOCK CONSTRUCTION

The stack-block system is equally easy but does require a considerable amount of mortar or grout, especially for full basement walls. This type of block is not universally available and it is more expensive than standard block.

To build stack-block foundation walls, follow the manufacturer's instructions explicitly; products and procedures differ somewhat. Stack the interlocking blocks with care and check for level, plumb, and alignment frequently. Insert reinforcing bar, cold-bent as necessary, in the corners and at other points as instructed. Then fill cores with mortar or grout as required. Skipping any part of the tying and reinforcing procedure might result in a weakened foundation that could cause trouble later on.

Chapter **13**

Grade beam foundation

*T*he grade beam foundation is one that is seldom employed in residential construction. Depending upon the overall house design, however, it is certainly worthy of consideration. This is an economical foundation that is especially advantageous where the soil is weak or unstable. It is sometimes a better choice than conventional construction where a full first-level concrete slab is planned. It is a combination of cast-in-place concrete piers, beams, and slab, where the piers support the bulk of the house load and the grade beams serve as sills and containment for the slab (FIG. 13-1).

The starting point for a grade beam foundation is a flat earth pad cut onto the building site, several feet larger all around than the structure will be. The pad surface should be undisturbed native subsoil. Lay out the foundation perimeter guidelines.

PIERS

Spot the locations for the piers, just as if building an ordinary pier foundation. The size of the piers, their number and placement, and their depth, must all be predetermined in accordance with the house weight and design, as well as the soil conditions at the site. Typically the piers range from 8 to 12 inches in diameter and are spaced 6 to 8 feet apart around the perimeter. Simple footings are used in normal fashion at points within the building envelope and beneath the slab where specific loads must be supported, such as load-bearing columns or walls.

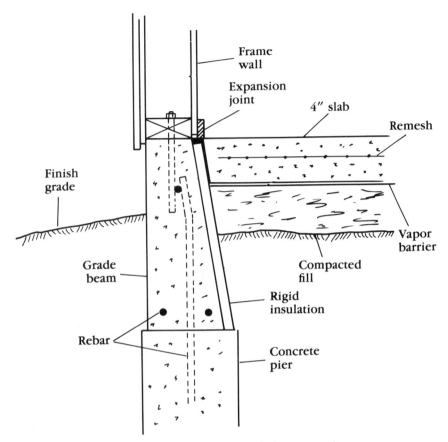

13-1 A typical grade beam foundation construction.

Digging pier holes

Dig the holes for the piers, preferably by drilling them. Dig holes as small as possible; the object is to cause minimum site disturbance. The piers can be poured in tubular cardboard pier forms, or you can construct square wood forms. Precast piers can also be used; these are sometimes made with a taper so that the bottoms are 2 or 3 inches wider than the tops. In any case, make sure they are accurately positioned and aligned with the house perimeter line.

Backfill around tubular cardboard forms right away to hold them in place. Wood forms have to be ruggedly braced in place with stakes and 2×4s; backfilling can't be done until a few days after the forms are stripped from the concrete. Precast piers can be set, aligned, and backfilled around immediately, and should be thoroughly compacted in place. While this is going on, electrical and telephone lines, water and sewer pipes, or any other items that must come in under the foundation and/or be buried in the slab floor can be installed.

Pouring the pier forms

Pour the pier forms full with concrete in a mix suitable for this purpose, such as 1 sack of portland cement to 3 cubic feet of sand to 5 cubic feet of coarse aggregate. Be guided by local practice or follow the recommendations of a ready-mix company. The pier tops typically lie a few inches below the working grade.

Each pier should contain one reinforcing rod centered in it, usually a No. 4 or No. 5 size. Have the rod extend downward to within about 3 or 4 inches of the bottom of the pier, and upward out of the pier top to within approximately 2 inches of the top of the grade beam. This temporarily protruding free length is variable, because the height of the grade beam will vary with different foundation designs.

Once the pier concrete has cured for about three days, the forms can be stripped. Remove wood forms entirely and peel cardboard forms back to grade level. Place whatever backfill is needed.

GRADE BEAMS

Next, set up the forms for the grade beams. They are continuous across the pier tops, and construction is much the same as for building footing forms. The beams have a flat, vertical outside face. The inner face is slanted back toward the exterior, with the taper figured so that the top surface of the beams is equal to the width of the sole plate of the first-floor walls. This is usually $3^1/2$ or $5^1/2$ inches in frame construction. The elevation and height of the grade beam should be calculated so that the top lies at least 8 inches above the planned finish grade. In some areas, local codes might require this distance to be a minimum of 12 inches. The beams are poured directly on undisturbed native soil, except for immediately around the piers; this backfill soil should be thoroughly compacted. Make sure that the forms are ruggedly braced, especially at the bottom of the slanted side, and put plenty of ties across the tops to keep the sides aligned.

Ballast beam foundation

Note that where the grade beams cannot be poured on undisturbed subsoil, or where the subsoil is loose or unstable, a variation called a *ballast beam* foundation can be used. This involves digging out the loose soil around the foundation perimeter between the piers, and creating a trench whose width and depth depends upon the specific soil conditions. (Soil conditions can vary from place to place, even within the same foundation.) The trench is filled with crushed rock or gravel, compacted to form a firm base, and built up to working grade level. The grade beams are poured on this surface (FIG. 13-2).

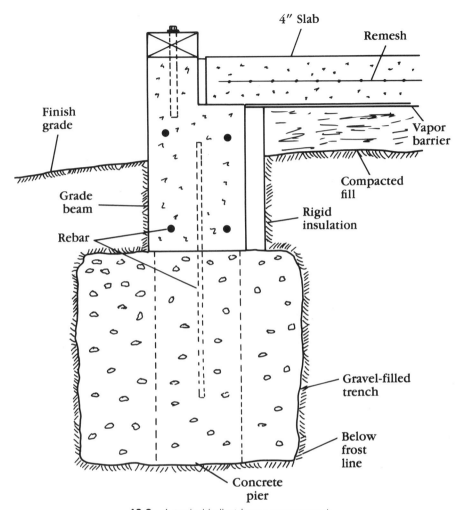

13-2 A typical ballast beam arrangement.

The ballast beam is a good system to use, too, when periodic or continuous ground moisture is expectable in the immediate vicinity. It provides excellent drainage and prevents moisture buildup under, and incursion into, the slab. In fact, ballasted trenches can be used in lieu of native subsoil under practically any site conditions.

Reinforcing rods

Once the forms are built, aligned, and supported, you can add the steel reinforcing rods, typically No. 4 or No. 5. Set a pair of rods lengthwise and spaced apart near the bottom of the beams, so that they will be covered in all directions by at least 2 inches of concrete. Set them on wire chairs to keep them in place. Slightly cold-bend the vertical rods protruding from the piers to better conform to the backslant of the inner grade beam faces. Run a single rod lengthwise about 2 to 3 inches down from the top of the beam and secure it to the vertical pier rods with a wrap of soft iron mechanic's wire. You can support it at midspan with a length of wire wrapped around a nail, which is driven in each top edge of the form sides and drooped down into the form to make a cradle (FIG. 13-3).

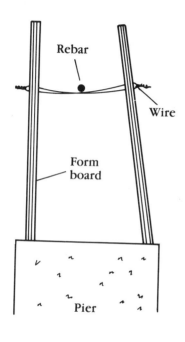

13-3   A cradle of soft iron wire will support the rebar temporarily in the grade beam form, and the tag ends are cut away after the concrete cures.

Pouring the grade beam forms

Pour the forms full of a suitable concrete. The same mix as was used for the piers can be used again, as can any appropriate foundation mix. Again, best results for the least effort and cost are obtained when the weather is good and the temperature is between 50 and 80 degrees Fahrenheit. In adverse conditions special procedures should be followed, as noted in Chapter 11.

Screed the top of the grade beam, then install anchor bolts or straps as required; usually this is the same arrangement as for poured concrete walls. Allow three to five days to pass before stripping the forms. Backfilling can be done any time after the forms are stripped, but be careful of the grade beams when moving equipment and materials in and out of the area. Until the backfill has set and the slab has been poured, which locks the beam in place, it can be easily damaged.

LEVELING THE GRADE

The next requirement is to bring the interior working grade up to finish level for the slab. All under-floor piping and ducting should be checked now for accurate positioning. Interior concrete footings, if required, should have been poured at the same time as the piers or grade beam. There should be a cushion about 6 inches thick directly beneath the concrete floor slab; in some cases a layer of rigid insulation is also installed. If this total depth is insufficient to bring the grade up to level, lay more fill in. The cushion layer typically is sand or 3/4-inch gravel, and this same material can be used to fill any extra space. Alternatively, crushed bank run or road base can be laid in and compacted first, followed by the cushion layer. All such materials are best spread in layers about 2 to 3 inches thick, then compacted.

Spread a vapor barrier of 6-mil or heavier polyethylene sheet over the cushion, lapped at least 12 inches at the seams. Place rigid insulation against the slanted face of the grade beam, extending from top to bottom. There are two exceptions. In locales with very benign year-round climates the insulation is left out entirely. In termite-infested areas a gap about 3/8 to 1/2 inch deep is left, to be filled later with caulk or tar.

POURING THE CONCRETE SLAB

The last step is to pour the concrete slab, which is done in the same manner as for a conventional slab-on-grade foundation. It is typically 4 or 5 inches thick. Place welded wire mesh or other reinforcement as required. Use a thin strip of wood around the perimeter, which is pulled out later, to form a gap for the anti-termite tar, if necessary. Cure the slab for several days.

Chapter **14**

Permanent wood foundation

*T*he PWF or permanent wood foundation system is a recently renamed version of the all weather wood foundation (AWWF), which has been around for a number of years. In the past decade or so the PWF system has been getting an increasing amount of favorable attention. Developed and thoroughly tested under the auspices of the American Plywood Association and others, it makes an efficient, effective, practical, and relatively inexpensive foundation. The materials are available almost anywhere, although you probably will have to order them from your local lumberyard unless you live in or close to a metropolitan area. The PWF system has been approved by the model building codes, as well as fire insurance, lending, and home warranty institutions, and federal agencies. The key to the system is that all the plywood and dimension stock lumber is pressure treated with special chemical preservatives, making the assembly extremely durable and long-lived even under severe conditions.

ADVANTAGES AND DISADVANTAGES

The PWF has some definite advantages. It is an excellent system for a do-it-yourselfer, because the entire foundation is put together in just the same way as any ordinary wood-framed, plywood-sheathed stud wall. No special equipment or expertise is needed, and the job is not physically demanding. All of the materials can be easily transported to any building site, including those that would be inaccessible for large, heavy trucks. For this reason it is an ideal foundation system for remote locations. The foundation can be put together as panels in a workshop, then transported to the building site and rapidly erected, a big plus in inclement weather. When built on-site, the whole job can be done rapidly. No concrete or mortar is needed at all.

Although full-basement PWF constructions usually feature a poured concrete floor, you can install a complete wood floor instead, using the same kind of materials. And, there are other technical advantages as well that make this system a better performer than other types of foundations in many circumstances.

This all sounds too good to be true: Are there any disadvantages? Only a few minor ones, depending upon circumstances. The system is not recommended for installation in Group IV soils (peat, organic clay and/or silt). When installed in Group III soils (inorganic silts, clays), it must be accompanied with an extensive foundation drainage system. Where termite infestation is moderate to severe, installation might not be recommended: Check with local authorities. Accuracy in construction is crucial. The foundation must be built to system specifications, using all the proper materials with no unapproved substitutions. The preservative chemicals are toxic, so care must be taken to wear gloves and masks when cutting and working with the materials, and scraps must be properly disposed of. Also, the overall techniques and procedures, as well as many of the construction details, are a bit unusual, so most carpenters or builders are unfamiliar with the routine. That situation is easy to overcome, because you can obtain a construction guide and technical information and help. Contact the American Plywood Association, P.O. Box 11700, Tacoma, WA 98411.

CONSTRUCTION VARIATIONS

There are several construction variations in the PWF system, depending upon the type of foundation or its purpose. In a typical full basement arrangement the walls are made up as panels, employing 2-×-6 or sometimes 2-×-8 studs set on 12- or 16-inch centers. These are attached to a top and a sole plate, sheathed on the outside with plywood (FIG. 14-1). The stud and plate size and the spacing on centers can be varied according to the amount of strength and rigidity required to adequately support the structure. This engineering information is available in the construction guide, to suit numerous conditions and designs.

The thickness of the plywood sheathing depends upon the stud spacing and the expectable lateral pressures against the foundation walls. Once the panels are erected and connected, the exterior of the sheathing is covered with a spot-bonded layer of polyethylene sheeting, secured with a recommended adhesive. The panels are set upon a wide footing plate, typically a nominal 12-inch treated plank, which in turn rests upon a wide, deep bed of gravel that has been compacted and leveled.

All fastening is done with stainless steel or galvanized nails or staples, depending upon just what is being fastened and its position in the foundation. All below-grade components, as well as those partly above and

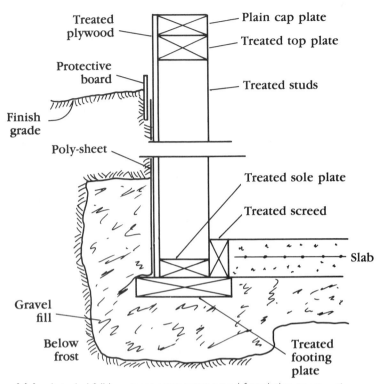

14-1 A typical full-basement permanent wood foundation construction.

partly below, are pressure-treated with preservatives. Some components that are wholly above grade, like an upper top plate, can in some circumstances be ordinary untreated construction lumber. The entire foundation must be put together, the first floor frame and subflooring laid, and the basement floor poured or constructed of wood, before the foundation walls can be backfilled. This chore must be handled with care, using only clean fill—preferably containing no rocks larger than first size.

The PWF system is also an excellent one for crawl space designs (FIG. 14-2), and construction is a bit simpler. Stud size is typically 2×4 or 2×6, and the panels are smaller and lighter. The foundation design can be either high-profile, low-profile, or above-grade (where there are serious drainage problems)—all of which differ slightly in construction. A stem wall arrangement can be employed where the first floor is a poured concrete slab on grade (FIG. 14-3).

Yet another design is used for a detached garage and is perhaps the simplest of all. And, there are certain ways to build for brick veneer, stepped foundation walls, bearing partitions, daylight basement walls, and other constructions. Because there are so many design variables, the detail of which should be faithfully followed, it's important to have a complete PWF construction guide on hand.

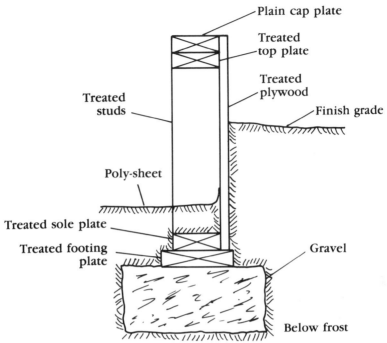

14-2 This permanent wood foundation arrangement is designed for crawl space application.

FULL BASEMENT CONSTRUCTION

For a general idea of what is involved, the construction sequence for a full basement proceeds as follows, depending upon house design and site conditions.

Digging the pad and footings

First, a flat pad is cut into undisturbed native subsoil. All utilities are trenched in as required, and backfilled. Preliminary work for the all-important foundation drainage system is undertaken now. The details of this system depend upon the groundwater situation—whether constant or periodic. A sump might be needed in the basement, connected to a drain line to a storm sewer, drywell, or daylight—but never to a septic tank. An alternative to the sump is a contour for footing drainage or a perimeter drain system.

The footing trenches, if required, are dug next. When a wall is almost entirely below grade no trench is needed, but those that are only partially backfilled might need an added footing depth. Usually these trenches are gravel filled in a PWF system. The trench width and depth is depends upon the size and weight of the structure, drainage considerations, the

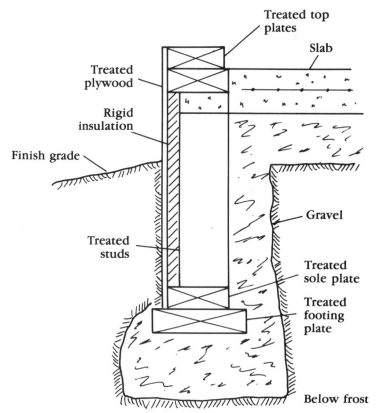

14-3   Another permanent wood foundation construction serves for a slab-on-grade design.

backfill height and finished grade, and the frost line depth. However, a PWF foundation can also be built upon a conventional, flat-topped, poured concrete footing with anchor bolts set in it, which requires a different sort of trench.

For a fully backfilled ordinary foundation, the next step is to place a cushion over the entire pad, extending about 12 to 16 inches beyond the outer edge of the footing plate. This cushion should be 4 to 6 inches thick, and may consist of crushed rock, gravel graded about 3/4 inch, medium-coarse roadbase, coarse sand, or a similar material. The material must be racked out smooth and level. Grade stakes spotted around the area help, and you can screed from stake set to stake set. At the same time, any required gravel for drainage purposes can be placed. Then the foundation perimeter must be staked out again, working from batter boards or other control points.

Building wall panels

Next come the wall panels, which can be shop-built or site-built. The wide footing plates can be attached as the panels are built, with joints calculated to lie beneath a panel and not at a panel joint. Alternatively, plates can be separately laid and the wall panels set upon them and then attached. The panels should have only a single top plate at this point. As many panels as possible should be made up in 8-×-8-foot size, with the plywood face grain at right angles to the studs. However, you can make the panels smaller—some of them will probably have to be anyway—and the plywood can be oriented either way on these.

Set up a panel at one corner first. Align it roughly and get it about level, then brace it solidly. Install the panel that forms the other leg of the corner and brace it; the two panels will also help support one another. Caulk the joint between meeting panel edges with an approved elastomeric caulk. Plumb and level both corner panels, then go ahead with placing successive panels. Keep checking plumb, level, and alignment, and caulk all joints as you go along. Drive small stakes or steel pins as necessary to keep panels from sliding out of place as you add new ones.

Once all the sections are in place, attached, and caulked, go around the entire structure once again and check for squareness and alignment, as well as plumb and level. Put the upper top (cap) plate on, with the joints staggered over the wall panel joints so that none coincide. Crosslap the corner joints, as in conventional wall construction. Drive a series of stakes or steel pins (short lengths of reinforcing bar work well) here and there along the edges of the footing plate, as necessary to keep the walls from shifting out of alignment. This is usually only a problem on long walls.

Pouring the basement floor and installing framing

The next two steps can be taken in whatever order is most convenient. Prepare the interior grade and pour the concrete basement floor in the usual manner, after completing construction of any required sumps or other drainage elements. Install the first floor framing as called for in the house plans, tying it to the top of the foundation walls as required under PWF specifications. Girders, posts, interior partition walls, and similar elements should also be installed now. Install the first-floor sheathing (subfloor) using the conventional method for the material involved.

Only after this is done can the foundation be backfilled. First, spot-bond sheets of 6-mil polyethylene to the outside of the foundation walls, at the finish grade line. Seal the vertical edge seams with adhesive in a 6-inch overlap. Spread the sheeting smoothly down the walls, hanging free, and let it lap outward a few inches over the footing plate. Install a grade board, made from a 12-inch-wide strip of treated plywood, over the top edge of the sheeting, caulked and nailed in place.

Backfilling

Now backfill, placing the material in 6-inch layers and tamping each one, up to about an inch or so below the top of the grade board. Take care not to damage the polyethylene, and keep heavy equipment well back from the walls to avoid excessive vibration and lateral pressures. Follow recommended backfill material and procedural requirements, depending upon the soil type and drainage considerations.

CRAWL SPACE CONSTRUCTION

A crawl space foundation is easy to build in the PWF system. Once the flat construction pad has been cut out, a perimeter trench can be dug. Typically this is twice the width of the required footing plate and deep enough to get down to average frost line and/or at least 6 inches below the interior grade. This, in turn, must be at least 18 inches below the foundation top. Fill the bottom of the trench with crushed rock or gravel and level. Set the wall sections and footing plates, make sure they are plumb and level, then attach them to one another. The joint caulking, polyethylene sheeting, and a grade board are not needed here.

Once all the wall panels are properly aligned and squared, attach the cap plate of ordinary untreated construction lumber in the usual fashion. Then the backfill can be placed, using the same material in layers on both sides of the walls. A depth relationship must be maintained between the interior and exterior backfill, and the exterior finish grade should slope away from the foundation at a rate of $1/2$ inch per foot for at least 6 feet outward.

DETACHED GARAGE CONSTRUCTION

The foundation for a detached garage (refer to FIG. 9-8) or similar outbuilding is done a bit differently, and is even simpler to construct. Cut a flat pad into undisturbed native subsoil, then dig a trench around the building perimeter. Typically the width is that of a backhoe bucket—12 to 24 inches. The depth is average frost line or a minimum of about 20 inches. The foundation walls should have about 12 inches minimum of gravel beneath them. They should extend a minimum of 9 inches below finish grade and a minimum of 8 inches above; some local building codes will demand 12 inches above. Thus, an easy total wall depth to work with is 24 inches, which is half a sheet of plywood cut lengthwise.

Fill the trench to within 12 inches of the finish exterior grade with crushed rock or gravel (pea gravel works well) and level it. Set the wall sections in place, fasten them together, level and plumb them. Make sure the corners are square; it's a good idea to attach long diagonal braces across them at this stage to keep them that way. Make sure the wall lines are square, too. At the overhead door openings you can continue the foot-

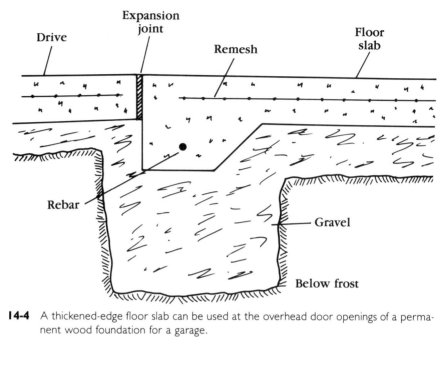

14-4 A thickened-edge floor slab can be used at the overhead door openings of a permanent wood foundation for a garage.

14-5 The garage wall sole plate is offset outward past the PWF top plate so the exterior siding will cover the joint.

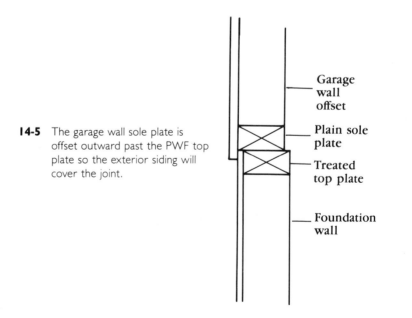

ing plate across to help keep everything lined up, and build in a thickened edge of the floor slab (FIG. 14-4). Or, you can build a shallow wall section that will be completely buried, with the slab edge poured over the top of it.

When everything is in order, start the backfill. Work from both sides in layers. Fill the inner side of the trench with gravel, the outer with soil backfill. Then continue with the gravel in the interior to build up a cushion about 4 inches deep for the concrete floor slab to rest upon. Drive a 16d galvanized common or box nail into each face of each stud at a point that coincides with the midlevel of the concrete slab. The nails will key the concrete to the walls.

The slab can be poured as soon as these chores are completed; this will completely lock the foundation walls in place. In some cases, though—as in inclement weather—it might be best to finish the building first in order to help protect the fresh concrete and allow better working conditions. Note that when the structure walls are built, the wall bottom plate is offset outward from the foundation wall top plate so that the exterior sheathing can lap down over the joint (FIG. 14-5).

Chapter **15**

Stone foundation

Stone foundations were traditional in certain parts of the country, and are in keeping with several styles of houses, such as the Cape Cod, saltbox, or log cabin. They were often built of natural fieldstone, laid up either dry or with mortar. They were also made of cut slabs of granite and other kinds of stone, sometimes topped with brick, in both random and ashlar patterns. Stone was used with full basement or crawl space foundations, and many were partial basements with crawl areas.

Stone foundations are not used often today because of high labor costs, a shortage of expertise, lack of materials, and the fact that local building codes often do not permit them. But stone makes an excellent foundation, and many houses a century or more old still stand four-square, without benefit of anchors or concrete or mortar, on such foundations. If you have a good supply of suitable stone, don't mind some hard work, have more time than cash available, and there are no code constraints, you might find the idea of a stone foundation compelling.

You can build full-height stone foundation walls, in the sense that it's possible if you know how and are an experienced stoneworker. But these days it's just not practical because there are other ways that are better and faster. This kind of stonework is a big job, especially for a sizable house, and one that has to be done just right to be effective and safe. Also, the entrance of ground moisture through a dry-laid wall can be a serious problem, and nearly as bad through a mortared wall. A crawl space arrangement, however, is a whole different matter.

CRAWL SPACE FOUNDATION

Stone walls laid up dry are likely to be more durable over the long haul than walls with mortared joints. This applies even in cold country, where every couple of years or so some of the top course stones might have to be readjusted or realigned a bit. Dry-laid stone works nicely in a crawl space arrangement (FIG. 15-1), where the total height of the walls is about 4 feet or less. The outside exposure should be 12 to 16 inches above finish grade—no more but not much less either—and about 2½ to 3 feet on the inside from crawl space floor to the bottom edges of the first-floor joists.

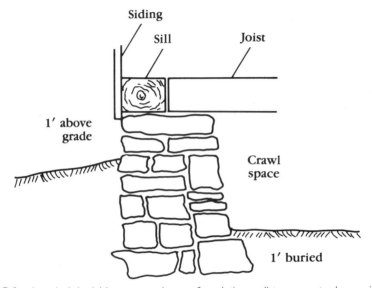

15-1 A typical dry-laid stone crawl space foundation wall to support a beam sill.

This means that about 1 to 1½ feet of stonework is buried in the ground as a locked-in base. Some additional crawl space headroom can be gained by mounting the first-floor joists on top of full sill beams, rather than setting them on a thin sill plate. This is a better arrangement atop a stone foundation, too. The thickness of the walls should be about 2 feet at the bottom; it can be considerably more if you wish but should not be less. The thickness at the top should be about 14 to 18 inches. The exterior face of the walls should be approximately plumb, and the interior face must therefore have a fairly substantial batter, slanting back from bottom to top.

PRELIMINARIES

Even a low stone foundation must be correctly and sturdily built if it is to stand up to the unremitting weight of a house and the ravages of time and weather. But it certainly can be done, and often has been. If you want to build such a foundation yourself, some preliminary study about stone masonry is recommended. Then start by building a stone retaining or garden wall or some such as a practice run. Stone laying is as much an art as a craft, and you need to get the feel of it by doing. A written explanation falls well short of conveying a picture of how stones should be set and fitted and nested, and how you'll eventually be able to spot the correct sizes of rock lying in a pile.

First, lay out the foundation perimeter on a suitable flat construction pad. Trench in utilities as required, and backfill. Compact the soil thoroughly wherever the stonework will cross a trench. Then cut a trench for the foundation about 12 inches deep into undisturbed native subsoil.

NON-MORTARED FOUNDATION

Bed the first course of stone into the trench, nesting the stones together and packing soil tightly around them (moistening helps) so that they are immovable. This course is often two stones wide with an occasional cross-lock stone. However, it might be one or three wide in places or entirely, depending upon the kind and size of stone available.

Build up the subsequent courses. This often is done by working to the top for a short section, then moving along to the next short section, and so on. Or, you can do one layer at a time all the way around. Much depends upon the bond you prefer and the kind of stone available. Common arrangements are random rubblestone or fieldstone, random ashlar, regular coursed ashlar, random coursed rubble, and cobble (FIG. 15-2).

The courses or layers must be laid up with care by fitting the stones together, with a little trimming and shaping, if necessary, to achieve the best fit. Set tie stones crosswise in each course about every 3 or 4 feet to help lock the rows together. Vertical tie stones that connect upper and lower courses are a good idea wherever they can be readily fitted in. All stones must lean in or sideways against one another, never outward, and they should be solidly set. The more regular, smooth, and brick-shaped, the easier the stones will lay up.

The laying up is a continuous process of fitting and adjusting. The trick is to fit them tightly, and follow the general principle of "one on two, two on one." This means that one stone should lie approximately centered over the joint between two stones below, and between two above as well (FIG. 15-3). You can't always do this, of course, but it is a goal to shoot for because the interlocking makes a strong construction.

As much as possible, use only sizable stones with fairly regular, preferably angular shape, in order to keep chinking to a minimum. You can chink with small flat or wedge-shaped stones as necessary. Arrange them so that they force the principal stones to wedge against one another and in toward the centerline of the wall, never toward the outsides of the wall. The chinking stones themselves must also be set so that they can't slip free, which usually means they have to be angled downward and inward.

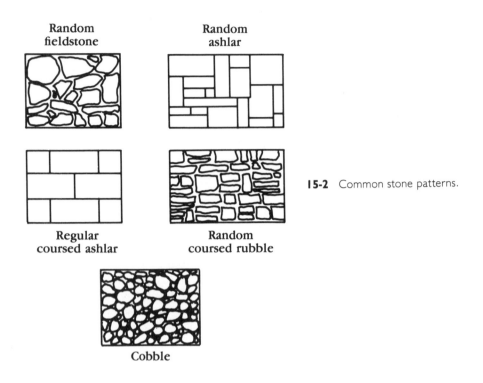

Random
fieldstone

Random
ashlar

Regular
coursed ashlar

Random
coursed rubble

Cobble

15-2 Common stone patterns.

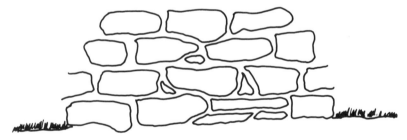

15-3 Dry-laid stone is fitted and laid one on two, two on one, so that joints do not align vertically.

It's also a good idea to not place small stones in the outside face of the wall above grade, because they tend to detract from the overall appearance of the foundation. This is where you want your coursing and the fitted joints to look best.

Pack soil into the outer and middle joints as you go along, until you reach the exterior finish grade line. This will help lock the stones together. Save the best stones for the top or cap course. Those have to be laid flat and level, and as many of them as possible should be wide enough to cover the entire wall top, front to back. It's a good idea to stretch out a taut line along the top of each wall section to act as a guide for both height and linear alignment. Cap rocks must be solidly set and well nested into the course below.

No anchor bolts are used in this kind of foundation, and the weight of the structure is relied upon to keep everything locked in place. No vent ports or other outside openings are needed, because the open joints will allow adequate cross ventilation of the crawl space in all directions. This assures that any buildup of moisture or gasses in the crawl space is unlikely. Access into the crawl area is best made from within the house: a trapdoor in a closet floor, for example.

MORTARED FOUNDATION

You can build stone foundation walls using mortar in the joints. There are a couple of advantages to this method. You can build a weather-, insect-, and rodent-tight foundation, and you can install sill plate anchor bolts if required by the local building code. With this arrangement you will have to build in vent ports, and access can be gained through an outside hatchway or from the inside.

A disadvantage, or at least an additional construction step, is that concrete footings must be poured, and usually has to reach below frost line. This, in turn, can mean more stone, depending upon the frost line depth, and can make stonework impractical entirely. Otherwise the results can be excellent, provided you don't fall into this common trap: Do not rely upon the mortar to provide the strength of the wall and to take up the slack between poorly fitted stones. If you do, the walls will be surprisingly weak.

Start by pouring a conventional footing, but instead of indenting a keyway or screeding the top flat, dish it so the top is slightly concave in an arc or a vee (FIG. 15-4). Then the bottom double row of stones will be canted toward one another. Build up the stonework just as for a dry-laid wall, fitting the stones together carefully. In this case, though, you fill the joints with mortar instead of soil, packed in well so there are no air spaces.

Make sure that all of the stones are clean of loose dirt. Keep the joints as small as you can, and use small chinking stones as described earlier. Use them sparingly but wherever necessary, mortared in place after being fitted. As the mortar begins to cure, scrape off any excess and tool all of the face joints, interior and exterior, by running the tip of a small trowel or a jointing tool over them. This packs the mortar to a greater surface density and improves its water resistance and toughens the joints, and at the same time improves the appearance.

When the visible above-grade exterior joints have cured just to the point where you can't make an impression with your thumb, carefully wash mortar residue off the stones with a scrub brush. Allow several days for curing before backfilling against the stonework.

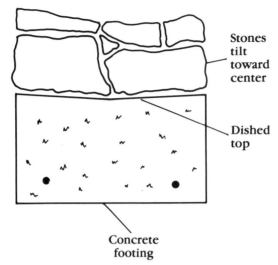

15-4 A dished footing top helps to tilt the stones inward to rest against one another.

PIER FOUNDATION

Stonework also makes an excellent filling between piers in that kind of foundation (FIG. 15-5). No weight is imposed on the stonework, so close, interlocking fitting is less crucial and the walls need not be as thick. If the walls will be low, less than about 2½ to 3 feet, you can dry lay or mortar. However, dry laying is much easier to adjust or repair, if necessary, and you won't have to fuss about cracked or crumbling mortar.

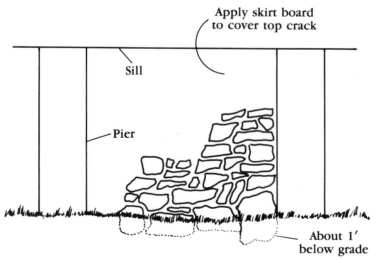

15-5 Stonework, dry or mortared, makes an excellent fill between foundation piers.

The easiest and quickest method is to cut a shallow trench in the ground at exterior grade level and between the piers, deep enough for all or most of the first course. Pack the rocks in place, well fitted, and build up the courses between the piers. Fit a skirt board to the bottom of the house that will overhang the top of the stonework by several inches and close off the small gap between the rocks and the sill.

If walls on the order of 3 feet high or more are needed to reach from grade level to the house sills, or if you want to cover the piers with stone to give the appearance of a full stone foundation, you are likely to be better off building mortared walls, unless you are fortunate enough to have stable, flat stones that you can dry-stack like bricks. Calculations have to be made ahead of time so that the piers can be set back or their faces indented enough to allow a thin facing layer of stone to be laid up over them, while remaining in alignment with the exterior wall face above. Plan on several vent openings to provide cross ventilation beneath the house, to avoid moisture buildup. Access to the crawl space can be gained through one of these vents, rather than down through the house floor.

Build the wall on a reinforced concrete footing poured between the piers. Lay up the stonework one or two rows thick. Where the wall crosses in front of the piers, change to thin, plate-like stones, preferably of sizable face area, as opposed to small shards and chunks. If the piers were built up from concrete block, masonry tie strip could have been set in the joints to tie the stone veneer to them in conventional fashion. However, the stone work can be tied, literally, to any kind of pier. Wrap a long length of heavy iron mechanic's wire around the pier, through the mortar joints, and twist the ends together right over the outer faces of a few of the stones. This will secure the stones tightly to the piers. When the mortar has cured, cut the knotted wire away on the outside, but leave the remainder in place. At least some of these veneer stones should lock back into the pattern of thicker stones to both sides of the piers.

POURED CONCRETE FOUNDATION

There is yet another way to build a foundation that appears to be solid stone with thick mortar joint lines. The method is suitable for either full basement or crawl space walls, and is based upon a poured concrete construction (FIG. 15-6).

Pour a footing and prepare for poured concrete walls as usual. Determine the height of the walls that will be visible above grade and add about 6 inches to that. Lay out a like amount of stone alongside the wall forms, set in approximately the pattern you want in the wall. You can usually get best results if the stones are no more than half the thickness of the walls and are relatively flat-faced; all of them should be clean. Run a taut line along the outside of the forms at a point that will be about 6 inches below finish grade.

Pour the concrete into the forms until you get to the level marked by the taut line; use a fairly stiff mix. Then nest the stones in a row with their

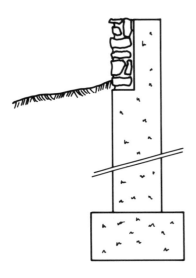

15-6 A poured concrete foundation wall can be veneered with stone over the above-grade portion to simulate a solid stone foundation.

faces set tight against the inside of the outside form panels. Back the stones with a layer of concrete of about the same depth, and start the next row, and so on. The less concrete squeezes through the back joints and out onto the stone faces, the better. Continue the process until the forms are topped up, making sure that no stones protrude above the foundation top. This will have to be screeded off flat.

Install anchor bolts as required, in the usual fashion. Strip the forms off as early as is practicable. Scrape off any globs of concrete on the stone faces, and with a small trowel finish filling the mortar joints to your satisfaction. When the mortar is just thumbprint hard, tool the joints smooth with the trowel point or a jointing tool. You can clean concrete or mortar residue off the stonework with muriatic acid after the joints have cured completely.

Chapter **16**

Veneered foundation

Most people aren't impressed by the appearance of a concrete or concrete block foundation; neither of these materials are very elegant. However, you can make such a foundation look like something it isn't without much difficulty, by giving it a nicer appearance and a finish that fits the character of the house. A concrete block, poured concrete, or wood foundation (which has the color of pea soup that eventually fades to a mottled brownish-greenish murk) can be made to look as though it is made of brick or stone. Or, the foundation can be given a unique appearance by facing it with ceramic tile. These treatments all involve applying an appropriate veneer to the original foundation walls, and constructing the walls in a certain way to accept the veneer.

PRELIMINARIES

The starting point for applying a stone or brick veneer is a concrete block or poured concrete continuous-wall foundation. The PWF system doesn't lend itself readily to this treatment. You will make the upper portion of the foundation walls—from slightly below finished grade level to the top—with a setback shelf that is typically the depth of a single course of brick, or about 4 inches. The shelf should not be taken back more than half the thickness of the wall; usually this is also about 4 inches.

In the case of poured concrete, the setback is made simply by forming it in place (FIG. 16-1). In standard concrete block construction, use half blocks set to the interior as a top course (FIG. 16-2). Reinforce the construction by adding reinforcing bars and grout or mortar to some of the hollow cores, tying the half blocks solidly to the full blocks. You can also

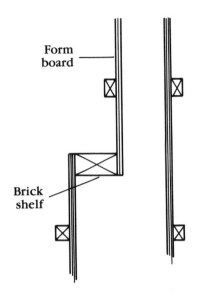

16-1 A setback shelf for masonry veneer is easy to form into a poured concrete wall.

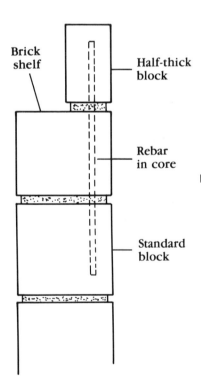

16-2 A setback shelf for masonry veneer can be made in a concrete block foundation wall by building the top courses with half-thick blocks and reinforcing the construction.

use solid cap blocks stood on edge, but the construction is not as strong. If you build using the surface-bonded system, either partition or cap blocks will work, but partition blocks are preferable, with reinforcement. If you use a stack-block system, half-thickness blocks might not be available. In that case, use standard cap or partition blocks mortared in place, with reinforcement.

The sill anchoring system has to be modified from standard. Spacing should remain the same (see Chapter 12), but you will have to make up anchor bolts. You can do this in any of three ways. Bend right-angle hooks at the head ends of sufficiently long 1/2-inch diameter bolts. Or, bend lengths of threaded rod in the same fashion. Or, bend lengths of plain steel rod in the same way and thread the upper ends for about 1 1/2 inches. Set these anchors at least 8 inches deep into the thick portion of the foundation walls and extend them up alongside the thin portion, protruding above the foundation top about 1 to 1 1/2 inches more than the thickness of the sill plate material.

Put in masonry ties as the foundation is built, too. There are a couple of approaches for poured concrete. One is to drill holes through the form material that retains the face of the setback. Space the holes about 32 inches apart in horizontal rows about 16 inches apart, with the rows staggered vertically. Insert lengths of iron wire (12 to 14 gauge) through the holes, looped between holes on the inside with free ends several inches long on the outside. The concrete will trap the loops (FIG. 16-3). An alternative is to nail standard metal masonry tie straps to the green concrete face at appropriate points immediately after the forms are stripped, using masonry nails angled downward. In concrete block construction, just bed wire or metal strip ties into the mortar joints. Or, bend and lock them into the cores in a mortarless system, at appropriate points as you lay up the blocks.

BRICK AND STONE VENEERS

For a brick veneer, use face brick or any other type you like. The bricks must be able to survive the elements. Any kind of stone will work except soft sandstones and shales, which tend to come apart as they weather. Decorative cast concrete masonry units are another possibility.

Applying the veneer is simple enough, and can be done piecemeal as time and energy permits. When you work with uniform, similar pieces such as brick, just mortar them in place successively. Spread on a full mortar bed with a medium-sized trowel, lay the unit in place, and tap it plumb and level.

For nonuniform, random-sized and shaped units like fieldstone or river rock, first make sure the surface is clean. Throw a substantial glob of mortar into the designated spot and settle the unit into position, then pack more mortar around it; often a small pointing trowel is useful during

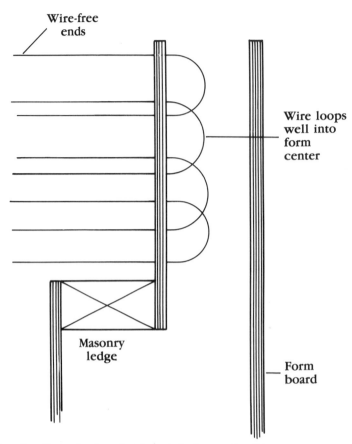

Wire-free ends

Wire loops well into form center

Masonry ledge

Form board

16-3 Lengths of iron wire threaded through the form walls will be trapped by the concrete and the ends serve as ties for the masonry units as they are being laid up.

this process. Bed the wire or metal strip ties into the mortar as you go. The wire ends can be wrapped across irregular stones and the ends twisted together for temporary support, and the exposed portion clipped away later.

Bagged dry mortar mix is fine for the purpose, and you can fatten it a little with a cup or two of portland cement per bag if you wish. Mix thoroughly with clean water. Establish mortar joints about 3/8 inch thick for uniform units. Fit nonuniform units closely together to keep the total amount of mortar used as low as you can. Minimum joint thickness should be about 3/8 inch. There is no maximum, but excessive mortar detracts from the appearance and may make for a weak veneer. In either case, scrape the joints back with the tip of your trowel as you go along.

Later, as the moisture sheen leaves the mortar surface and it starts to cure, go back over all the joints and tool them. Pack the joint surfaces down hard and smooth them with a tool made for the purpose, a bent chunk of reinforcing rod or whatever else is handy. This greatly increases the surface density and thus the weatherproofing of the joints. For random unit shapes and joints just indent to a reasonable distance. For uniform shapes and joints there are several joint patterns you can choose from (FIG. 16-4). After the joints have cured for several days, you can go back over all the surfaces and clean off mortar residue with muriatic acid. This is available at any good paint or hardware store; carefully follow the directions for use on the container.

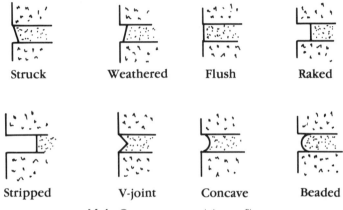

Struck   **Weathered**   **Flush**   **Raked**

Stripped   **V-joint**   **Concave**   **Beaded**

16-4 Common mortar joint profiles.

CERAMIC TILE VENEER

Applying a ceramic tile veneer to the above-grade portion of a foundation is easier. You can make the application on a poured concrete, concrete block, or PWF foundation with no modification to the foundation. You simply build it in the usual fashion. The only change in construction occurs in the structure above. The sill plate must extend outward past the outer surface of the foundation walls for a distance equal to the thickness of the tile to be used and the adhesive bed that will secure it. Then the exterior siding will overlap the foundation face in the usual fashion (FIG. 16-5). This usually means that the overall framing dimensions of the structure should remain strictly modular so as not to introduce extra cutting and material waste, while the overall foundation dimensions should be shrunk a bit to accommodate the added tile thickness.

Select the tile type and adhesive during the early planning. Both must be suitable for exterior service, and there is a tremendous range of tile choices: from 1/4-inch squares to 16-inch squares, numerous fancy patterns, loads of colors, and different degrees of sheen from flat to high-gloss. The adhesive and grout typically used are epoxy-based thinset. Application procedures for the tile are no different than for any exterior wall—a swimming pool, for example. The surface should be thoroughly

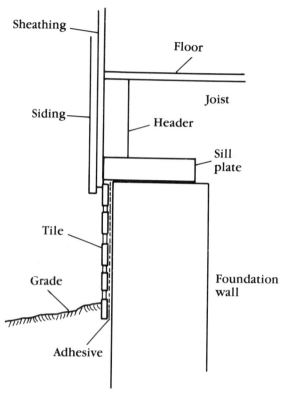

16-5 Where a tile or other facing is applied to a foundation wall, the sill plate should be set outward an equal amount so that the exterior sheathing/siding will lap over the top joint.

clean and dry; concrete should be well cured and block joints should be left flush with the surface. PWF joints should be filled with a suitable caulk.

Chapter **17**

Foundation drainage

One of the keys to a long-lasting, stable foundation is proper drainage of groundwater away from the building. This is especially true where the below-grade portion of the structure contains finished living quarters, although it is important for the well-being of any foundation arrangement. Any foundation material that you use—concrete, concrete block, wood, or any other—should be protected. Damp-proofing or waterproofing treatments help, but do not provide the sole solution. Nor are they necessarily fully effective, especially over a long period of time and against substantial quantities and pressures of moisture. The one exception might be a foundation made up of poured concrete piers, but even those should be protected from the ravages that moisture can cause over time.

The problem is not just dampness, or even soaking, although those can be deleterious enough. Even worse are the freeze-thaw cycles, swelling and shrinking of expansive soils, subsidence, shifting, and general degradation that can cause the foundations to crack, misalign, tilt, rise or sink, or disintegrate—with disastrous consequences to the structure above. If a building is to realize its full potential of a long life and remain in good condition, the foundation must retain its complete integrity. This means protecting it from moisture incursion as much as possible. This does not mean that if a foundation gets damp it will dissolve. Virtually all foundations will nearly always be surrounded by at least a slight degree of moisture. The trick is to reduce that moisture to a minimum and keep what little remains from migrating into the foundation material and the structure. Even houses built in arid locales can benefit from protective measures.

PRELIMINARY PROTECTIVE MEASURES

Protecting foundations from moisture initially involves dampproofing or waterproofing the foundation. This will be covered in the next chapter. Another concern is the large quantities of moisture that are introduced around the foundation when the house is built, and this is roof runoff. Methods of properly channeling this runoff are covered in Chapter 48.

What we will discuss here are ways of minimizing the presence of free moisture in the vicinity of the foundation, occurring either as ground water or surface water, that can affect the foundation. Drainage systems are built to handle such problems, but before planning these, consider ways that moisture can be avoided in the first place, or diverted. Ground and surface moisture is handled in three ways: avoidance, diversion, and foundation drainage.

Avoidance

The best defense against free ground or surface water is to avoid it altogether. Boggy, marshy ground, whether the condition is seasonal or perpetual, is unsuitable for building. Some areas might have a dry surface layer but a high water table, suitable only for a shallow-depth stem wall foundation or a floating slab. A site next to a stream probably will not be a good one for a full-depth basement. Obviously a dry wash is not a safe site and flood plains should be well defined, but there are other watercourses much less obvious that occasionally flood and cause problems. Even a nearby street or highway might periodically become a canal and overflow onto the building site, for example. All such possibilities should be thoroughly checked early on, and the building site changed if necessary.

Diversion

Diversion can only be practically accomplished with surface water, and should be given consideration on any building site. One essential that should always be followed is sloping the finished grade down and away from the structure on all sides at a pitch of at least $1/4$ inch per running foot, for a distance of at least 10 feet. *Never* should there be a slope toward the foundation.

On any site there will be a pattern of surface drainage. In any situation where drainage might approach the structure, a diversion should be created to lead moisture away. For example, if a nearby hill or even a rise in the ground drains moisture toward the building site, the ground should be recontoured to channel the moisture harmlessly away. In most cases this can be done without a major upheaval. Sometimes just a couple of retaining walls or a shallow, broad dip or ditch will do the job, and they can be made part of the overall landscaping effort (FIG. 17-1). Whatever the situation, you must take care that any moisture thereby drained from your

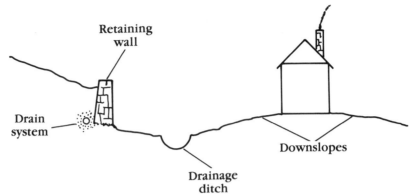

17-1 Retaining walls, drainpipe systems, drainage and diversion ditches, and downslopes all can play a part in keeping moisture away from house foundations.

building site doesn't inundate your neighbor. Moisture diversion is sometimes a neighborhood, or even municipal, effort.

FOUNDATION DRAINAGE SYSTEMS

Foundation drainage systems are straightforward and usually easy to install. As the old saying goes, no home should be without one.

PWF foundations

If the foundation is a PWF system, drainage is a crucial matter and is an integral part of the design: The deep gravel base under the footing is the key element. In a crawl space foundation built in soil that drains moderately to very well, continue that gravel base in one or more trenches leading away from the foundation and sloping downward. Cover the top of the trench, which should be about 1 foot wide and 1 foot deep, with 6-mil or heavier plastic sheeting, and continue the trench to daylight (FIG. 17-2).

An alternative is to install 4-inch-diameter or larger perforated plastic pipe in the gravel around the foundation. Orient the perforations downward, and set the pipe about 1 foot outside the foundation line and a few inches below the bottom of the footing plate. Connect this loop to one or more runs of solid-wall pipe leading away to daylight or a storm sewer system. Also, tee a vertical riser into the loop at each corner, fitted with a cleanout plug (FIG. 17-3). Do not run the line to a dry well, and never to a septic system.

If the soil drainage is modest to sluggish, install one or more gravel-filled trenches leading from the footings to a sump filled with gravel. If drainage is poor, install a 4-inch-diameter perforated drainpipe in the sump. Connect that to a solid-wall line running to daylight or to a storm sewer system (FIG. 17-4).

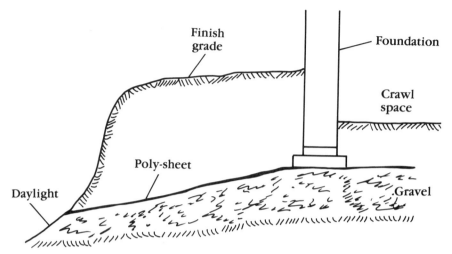

17-2   This drainage arrangement is common to PWF foundation systems, but the basics can be installed for any foundation.

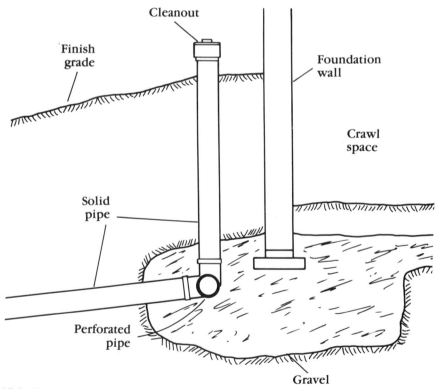

17-3   This footing drainpipe system uses vertical cleanout risers at the corners, along with runoff pipes to daylight.

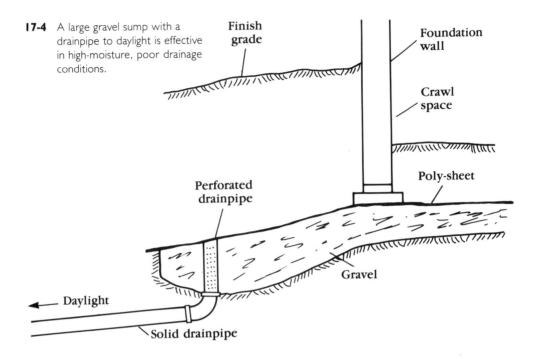

17-4 A large gravel sump with a drainpipe to daylight is effective in high-moisture, poor drainage conditions.

Full basement foundations

The treatment is a bit different for full basement foundations. If the soil is well drained (Group I, better than 4 inches per hour perc), the perimeter drainpipe arrangement just described (run to daylight or a storm sewer) should be adequate. For Group I soils that don't drain as well and Group II soils, a sump pit must be dug beneath the basement floor and filled with gravel (FIG. 17-5). The vertical perforated drainpipe should be connected to a solid line running to daylight or a storm sewer. Fit the drainpipe with a removable cover for cleanout purposes.

In Group III soils, a lined sump pit with removable cover must be provided in the basement floor (FIG. 17-6). A section of concrete pipe can be used for this, in 2-foot or greater diameter, surrounded by and set upon at least 2 inches of gravel. A drain line of solid-wall pipe runs to daylight or a storm sewer. In some locales it is permissible to run internal sump lines to a municipal sewer system. In this case, a trap must be connected in the line to prevent the backup of sewer gasses into the house.

Note that in all of these arrangements the solid-wall drain line that carries moisture away from the foundation must be pitched uniformly downward at a rate of at least 1/4 inch per running foot.

Poured concrete and concrete block foundations

The footing drainage system used with poured concrete or concrete block foundations, either crawl space or full basement, is inexpensive,

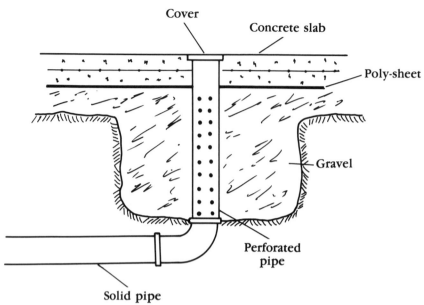

17-5   A typical sump pit arrangement beneath a full-basement floor, for use in soils of medi-ocre drainage capability.

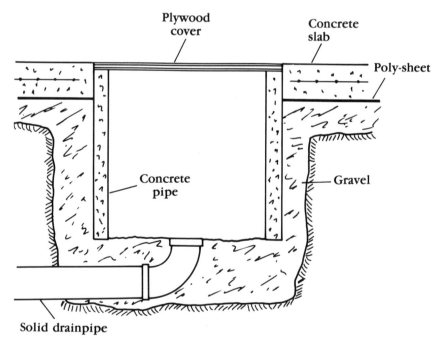

17-6   Where drainage conditions are poor, a large lined sump like this might be required in the basement floor.

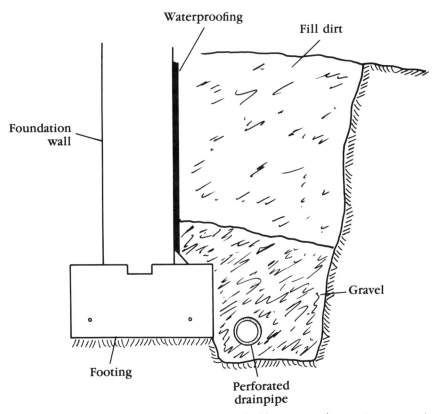

17-7 A typical drainage system that can be used with any poured concrete or concrete block foundation in virtually any soil conditions.

easy to install, and effective (FIG. 17-7). It is useful in any kind of soil, and essential in Group III soils. The first step is to spread a bed of gravel, about ³/4-inch size, alongside the footing and extending outward about 12 to 18 inches minimum. The poorer the soil drainage characteristics, the wider this bed should be. Lay a line of 4-inch-diameter (or larger) perforated plastic drainpipe on the gravel, coupled together, holes downward, about 2 inches or so from the footing as a moisture collection loop. (You can dispense with the couplings and cover the joints with a strip of tar paper, but the couplings help keep the pipe lengths aligned). If possible, arrange the pipeline so that it pitches slightly downward to one or more runoff lines.

Attach those solid-wall pipe lengths, coupled together, to the drainage loop with tees at the most convenient points. The runoff lines should be trenched to daylight or to a storm sewer system. In some cases a sump or drywell may be employed. Risers are not typically installed, but could be if you wish. Run them up from corners of the collection loop. You can cap them with solid cleanout plugs, or slip on elbows and leave them open

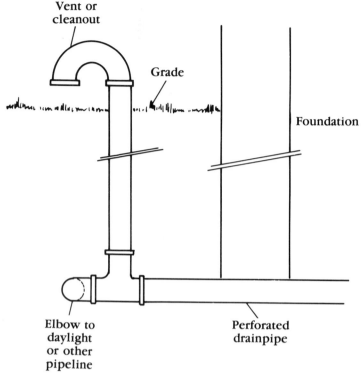

Vent or cleanout

Grade

Foundation

Elbow to daylight or other pipeline

Perforated drainpipe

17-8   Foundation drainpipes can be equipped with riser pipes capped with vents/cleanouts.

for venting (FIG. 17-8). Backfill the runoff lines with spoil dirt. Cover the collection loop with more 3/4-inch gravel to a depth at least 2 inches over the top of the footing. Then cover the gravel surface with a strip of 6-mil or heavier plastic sheet or a layer of roofing felt or tar paper. Backfill the foundation in the usual way.

There are two more points to consider about all of these drainage systems. First, the outlet end of all runoff drainpipes to daylight should be set in a concrete collar or a jumble of earth-bedded rocks to hold them steady and prevent erosion around them. And they should be terminated in a screen cap to prevent small creatures from nesting in the system. Second, downspouts or leaders from roof guttering systems should never be plugged into the foundation drainage piping at any point, including a sump or drywell.

Chapter **18**

Foundation dampproofing/ waterproofing

*D*espite the installation of surface water diversions and foundation drainage systems, foundation walls can become periodically and sometimes even continually damp, or they can leak free moisture into the interior. Poured concrete and concrete block walls are hygroscopic by nature: They have the ability to pick up and to retain moisture, and to transfer it from one surface to the other, even from low-moisture sources. Capillary action, the "wicking" effect, can occur in both materials. In addition, because concrete block is porous, and hollow cored, it is a sieve to free moisture. With both types of foundations there is always the possibility of shifting or settling and the development of cracks, leaving wide-open paths for the entrance of moisture.

Moisture incursion through foundation walls can range from annoying to disastrous, depending upon the circumstances, and should be avoided. This means that preventive steps in the way of dampproofing or waterproofing should be undertaken as the structure is built. Remedial steps attempted later are always less than fully successful, and always expensive. If done at the outset, effective sealing is cheap and easy—so omitting those steps shouldn't even be considered.

Dampproofing/waterproofing is part of PWF foundations and is undertaken during construction. The details depend upon the foundation design and the site soil conditions, as well as the latest recommendations from the American Plywood Association.

For poured concrete or concrete block walls, there are several standard procedures. Except in perpetually arid locales, crawl-space stem walls should get a light-duty dampproofing. Only in unusual or extreme circumstances is waterproofing required. The object here is to keep crawl space moisture at the lowest practical level, making ventilation more effective and minimizing the possibilities of rot, termite invasion, or other difficulties.

In semiarid locales and those in the moderate rainfall category—30 inches or so per year—all full-basement walls should have the heavy-duty dampproofing treatment, whether the area enclosed is initially intended to serve as finished living quarters or not. Where the climate can be classed as very damp to wet and annual rainfall is high, foundation waterproofing is in order. There are many possible procedures for this, some quite sophisticated and complex, suitable for earth-sheltered houses.

LIGHT-DUTY DAMPPROOFING

Light-duty dampproofing is a simple procedure and a common practice. The first step is to apply a broad fillet of mortar along the exterior joint between the bottom of the foundation wall and the top of the footing (FIG. 18-1). Then apply a coating of foundation waterproofing, usually a bituminous liquid, to the entire below-grade portion of the foundation.

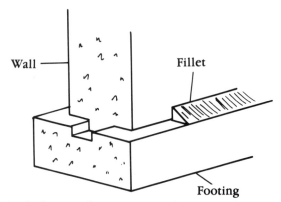

Wall

Fillet

Footing

18-1 The first step in dampproofing or waterproofing a foundation is to place a mortar fillet along the entire exterior wall/footing joint.

Depending upon the kind of material selected, it may be brushed or rolled on cold, or mopped or sprayed on hot. A single coat (in the absence of manufacturer's instructions to the contrary) is sufficient on poured concrete, but two might be in order on concrete block to completely seal the pores. For greater moisture control, a layer about 1/4 inch thick of special heavy asphaltic mastic can be troweled on. Another alternative is to apply a liquid coating, and immediately drape a sheet of 4- or 6-mil plastic onto the sticky surface and roll it flat. Laps can be sealed with more liquid brushed on.

Another effective method, especially useful on concrete block walls,

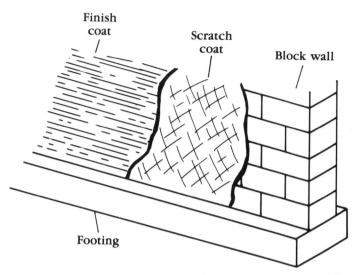

18-2   Parging, a method of applying a thick scratch coat of cement mortar followed by a second, densely packed finish coat, is one method of dampproofing a foundation wall.

is called *parging* (FIG. 18-2). There are several approaches. If soil drainage is reasonably good, lightly dampen the walls and then trowel a single coating of Type M mortar 1/4 inch thick over the entire exterior wall surface. Pack the surface hard, and extend the coating up about 6 inches above grade level. Feather it off to nothing there, and lay a fillet or cove along the bottom footing/wall joint. Damp-cure this coating for 48 hours; it should not be allowed to dry out at any point.

Effectiveness can be increased by applying one or two coats of portland cement-based paint, damp-curing each for 24 hours minimum. If still greater moisture control is required, apply a first coating and immediately scratch the surface with a broom to roughen it up a bit. Cure the coating for 48 hours, then apply a second layer of mortar, also 1/4 inch thick, and cure that for 48 hours. If necessary, one or two coats of a bituminous or similar foundation sealer can be applied over the parging after it has completely cured and there is no appreciable moisture remaining.

Some of the methods just discussed actually go beyond mere dampproofing. Just where the line between dampproofing and waterproofing should be drawn is not clear. There are situations where extra precautions are indicated in order to preserve the integrity of below-grade constructions and prevent any moisture incursion whatsoever, even though soil moisture conditions might be difficult and variable. When such situations arise, the builder should always seek out the latest information on foundation waterproofing, because techniques and materials are continually being developed and upgraded. At present, there are several systems that are useful; there are none that are absolutely foolproof.

FULL WATERPROOFING

Full waterproofing involves installing a sealed-seam membrane over the entire below-grade expanse of foundation wall and sealing it to the footing. The old tried and true method, which still works, is to apply multiple layers of roofing felt—or for better results—fabric. The felt is typically 15- or 30-pound weight. The best fabric used to be an open-weave cotton, but a glass fabric has supplanted it. Each layer is glued up and sealed with hot coal-tar pitch or a similar substance. Ten such layers will withstand hydrostatic pressure equivalent to a head of water of about 30 feet. A lack of elasticity and self-healing properties and a susceptibility to mechanical damage are drawbacks to this system.

A similar arrangement employing polyethylene sheeting in various thicknesses along with assorted different kinds of mastics has been found to work well. This is the basis for PWF waterproofing systems, in fact. Experimentation with the application of unbroken flexible membranes also shows promise, because of good bridging capability and flexibility. Neoprene, butyl rubber, and similar products are being used.

In conditions that are both fairly severe and constant, application of a natural clay soil called *bentonite* has been found to be effective. In one method, the material is applied as sheets that look much like ordinary plasterboard. Another uses a sprayed-on mix of bentonite and mastic, laid about $1/2$ inch thick. In either case, the bentonite swells up so much when it becomes damp that further moisture cannot penetrate it, and it forms an impervious seal.

Chapter **19**

Concrete basement and garage floors

*T*he material of choice for basement and garage floors, and those in many kinds of outbuildings as well, is concrete. Because this is also a primary ingredient of most foundations, installation of these floor slabs is often considered a part of the foundation construction and may be poured and finished by the same crew. The job can be done in the early stages, even immediately after the foundation is finished, or it can take place weeks and even months later. Because installation can be done almost anytime and usually has no direct interconnection with the rest of the building program, it is often a task that an active owner-builder can accomplish along with a couple of helpers. This is especially true of the relatively small and noncritical slabs, such as for a small detached garage or shop.

CONSTRUCTION

Though demanding physically, concrete floor construction is not complex. Figure 19-1 shows typical slab construction. The general routine is as follows:

Laying insulation and fill

The first step is to clean up all debris from the grade. If there are areas of loose fill, either compact the areas, or shovel the loose material down to undisturbed native soil and take it away. If required (as for a three-part slab-on-grade arrangement), place sheets of rigid thermal insulation against the inner faces of the foundation stem walls and shovel fill in

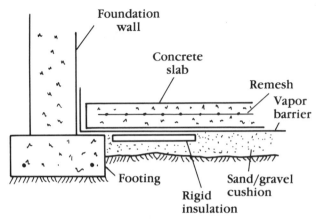

19-1   A typical concrete slab construction for a basement floor.

against them. Compact the fill as much as possible without harming the insulation. Next, have enough cushion material hauled in to cover the whole area at least 2 inches deep; 4 inches is better. Crushed bank run, road base, sand, pea or 1/2- to 3/4-inch gravel all will work, and the smaller materials will spread easier and level better. Emplace the material in whatever way is easiest—chutes, wheelbarrow, direct dumping—and rake it out smooth and level. Road base or damp sand might require compacting.

Vapor barrier

Lay out a vapor barrier of 6-mil polyethylene sheeting atop the cushion, and overlap the seams by about a foot. Leave enough extra material at the ends and sides to lap up the wall about 8 inches. Top this with sheets of rigid thermal insulation if required. This might only be needed around the edges of the foundation, but sometimes covers the entire floor area. If a fibrous or flexible expansion joint material is needed around the perimeter of the slab against the walls, set this in place now.

Reinforcing wire mesh

Roll out reinforcing wire mesh. Typically the 6-×-6-inch size in 10-gauge welded wire is used. Sometimes it's easier to roll it out, flatten it, and cut off suitable lengths out in the open where you have room to navigate, then take the cut lengths inside and flop them down.

While mesh is adequate for most installations, you might prefer to install reinforcing bars in a garage or workshop floor, for greater strength and resistance to cracking. A grid of No. 4 or No. 5 rods on 2-foot centers, wired together at the intersections, is ample. In either case, support the reinforcing material on wire chairs or small rocks or chunks of brick so that it will lie just about at the center of the slab.

Pouring the concrete mix

The concrete slab should be at least 4 inches thick. Many builders prefer a 5- to 6-inch thickness, perhaps because forming with standard 2-×-6 planks results in a 5½-inch-thick slab. Calculate the required volume of mix needed in cubic yards and add 10 percent for waste. When the truck arrives, be ready to emplace the mix with shovels, hoes, rakes, wheelbarrows, and arm power, as required. Usually the truck chute or a concrete pumper can place most or all of the mix in good position for leveling. Rough-level the mix as it is placed, then go back and screed it off flat with a long straightedge. Keep checking the remesh or rebar to make sure it stays midway in the slab. Watch out for dips and humps in the surface too; the slab thickness should be as uniform as you can make it.

Once you have a level surface, use a darby to further smooth the surface (FIG. 19-2). Do this as soon as possible after leveling, a section at a time. Float the darby gently over the concrete surface, embedding pebbles and knocking down small bumps of mix and smoothing off the ripples left by the screed. You shouldn't be scraping off much, if any, excess concrete. This process brings up concrete paste and a thin layer of moisture.

Floating

After an hour or so the water sheen will begin to disappear from the concrete surface, indicating that it is starting to cure. Now the surface should be floated. For this process you can use a wood float, moving from section to section as the concrete appears to be ready. Work from kneeling boards placed on the concrete to keep your knees and toes from digging in; 2-foot squares of plywood work fine. Sweep the float back and forth over the surface with the blade tilted slightly upward into the direction of

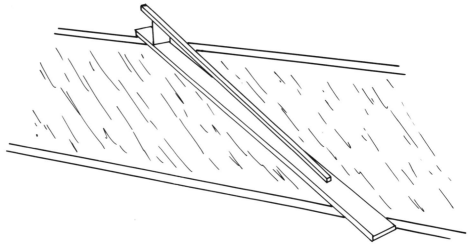

19-2 After the fresh concrete has been leveled by screeding, it is further smoothed with a darby.

travel (FIG. 19-3). Use light pressure, smooth out any bumps, and erase any marks or ripples. Try not to repeatedly go back over the same area; you do not want to raise another visible surface sheen of moisture. If that does happen, move on immediately.

19-3   The next step in finishing a concrete slab is to float the surface as it starts to cure, to further smooth and pack the surface.

FINISHING THE SURFACE

If you want a fairly coarse, sandpapery surface texture, floating one time with a wood float is all you have to do. If you want the surface somewhat smoother, go over it all again with a steel float. Again, do not use much pressure, but let the sweeping action and the weight of the tool and your arm do the work. You can use a small hand float and work from kneeling boards, or a large tool called a bull float (rentable). This long-handled float allows you to work a large area in a short time from a standing position, and produces a relatively smooth surface.

If an even smoother surface is desired, wait for just a few moments for the surface to firm up and all traces of free moisture to disappear. Then go over the whole area with a steel trowel; a 10- to 12-inch tool will probably work best for you. The action is similar to hand floating, but there are differences. You have to tilt the trowel in the direction of travel, but just slightly—the blade must be kept as flat as possible to the surface to prevent ripples from forming, yet you can't let the edges dig into the surface. Keep the strokes even, side to side or out and back. Exert steady, even, moderate pressure on the blade, packing the concrete and increasing the density of the surface layer. Make a couple of passes over each swath, but rework as little as possible. One complete pass will result in a smooth, nongrainy surface. You can go around again if you wish, or even twice, using a smaller trowel and more pressure each time. Eventually you can achieve a glass-smooth surface that is slick and even a bit shiny—and also dangerously slippery if it becomes wet.

Cutting control joints

There is one more procedure that is sometimes employed on garage or outbuilding floors, but not on basement floors. In cold-winter country where there is substantial precipitation, and especially where soil drainage is moderate to poor, frost heaving and subsequent cracking of a concrete slab is likely. This is particularly true of an unheated or periodically heated garage or outbuilding.

Using a grooving tool, you can cut control joints (FIG. 19-4) in the slab at intervals of approximately 8 to10 feet in both directions. This should be done after the surface has been floated and is fairly firm, but before the concrete sets up so much that running the tool is difficult. The cuts introduce planned weak spots in the slab, and most if not all of the cracking and shifting that occurs will follow the cuts without much disturbing the integrity of the slab. Subsequent expansion and contraction will also be mostly absorbed by the cuts.

19-4 A special tool is used to cut control joints into large concrete slabs, to minimize cracking elsewhere.

CURING

The final step is an important one: curing. The slab surface should be kept damp or even wet for at least 3 days, and preferably for 5 days. The easiest way to do this is to mist the entire slab surface gently with water. Do this after all the finishing work has been completed, but before any part of the surface has a chance to dry out instead of curing—this can lead to powdering and spalling. Any time you see a patch starting to turn lighter gray, get some water on it quickly. After misting, spread a layer of plastic sheeting over the surface, well overlapped at all seams. Pull it out flat, and if necessary set planks or other weights on it to keep wind from displacing it. Cover over any holes or tears in the plastic. Inspect it periodically to make sure it remains damp; it should hold for several days. Rewater if necessary.

Keep all but light foot traffic off the slab for the first 3 days, heavy loading for at least a week. Take the plastic up at the end of the curing period and allow the slab to dry naturally, preferably without benefit of sun, wind, or artificial heat. Note that large quantities of water vapor will be released into the air for some time, so be careful what you store in the area for the first several weeks.

Chapter **20**

Foundation wall and concrete slab insulation

If you live in an area where the annual cost of cooling a house exceeds that of heating, the foundation of your house does not need to be fitted with thermal insulation. If heating and cooling costs are approximately equal, then you should consider thermal insulation. Over time, it will be worthwhile. If you will have substantial heating costs and do little or no cooling, it is absolutely necessary to thoroughly insulate your foundations as you build. The payback period could be less than a year, and the livability (and salability) of the house is markedly increased.

A concrete or block foundation, despite its mass and thickness, has about the same insulating value as a pane of glass: practically none. The portion of the foundation that is above grade and exposed to the elements will radiate heat at a high rate. The earth that lies against the below-grade part of the foundation will act only as a partial insulator and only part of the time, so a lot of heat will be lost via that path as well. Except for the uppermost shallow layer of soil, the below-grade temperatures year-round will be lower than the ambient air temperature inside the house—below freezing in frost-filled ground, and seldom above 55 degrees or so down around 3 meters' depth and below. Thus, the soil around your house will wick heat away constantly from an uninsulated foundation.

For these reasons, any full basement, crawl space, or slab foundation should be insulated against this heat pilferage. This is best done on the exterior, mainly because it is both more effective and more efficient than interior insulation by as much as 10 to 20 percent. The effectiveness of both interior and exterior insulation is measured in terms of ''R-values.''

The higher the R-value, the greater the material's resistance to the passage of heating (or cooling).

The insulation must be a rigid type, and there are only a few that will adequately do this job. For houses, the insulant of choice is extruded polystyrene in the tongue-and-groove pattern. Another possibility is expanded polystyrene or "bead board," and a third is a urethane foam board. Neither of these do the job as well as extruded polystyrene.

FULL-DEPTH BASEMENT FOUNDATION

There are three general methods of insulating a full-depth basement foundation. The most important method is to cover the above-grade area, because that's where most of the heat loss takes place—both directly and from heat migrating upward through the foundation walls from the below-grade portion. Cover this surface to a distance of about 12 inches below the finished grade (FIG. 20-1). Apply the sheets of insulation to the foundation faces with an approved adhesive that will not "melt" the insulation, or attach it with masonry nails and washers. If there is enough thickness involved, apply the insulation in two layers with staggered joints, even if the panels join with tongues and grooves. This increases thermal effectiveness.

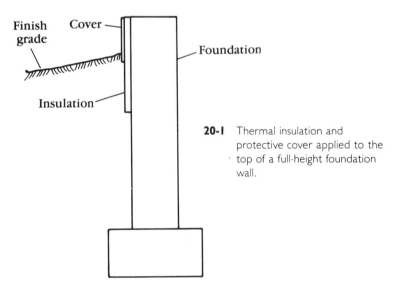

20-1 Thermal insulation and protective cover applied to the top of a full-height foundation wall.

Cover the joints with a seam tape made for the purpose. Exception: For every 150 square feet of above-grade material, leave a joint about 1/4 inch wide for expansion and contraction. Fill this joint with a good elastomeric caulk; silicone works well.

Cover the entire surface of the insulation with a sunlight protectant. This may be a solid sheeting such as fiberglass panel, or a plaster-like material that is troweled or brushed on. The top edge of the insulation should be protected from moisture with a strip of Z flashing.

The second method of installing the insulation copies the first and adds a skirt of rigid board all the way around the foundation (FIG. 20-2). This increases efficiency and reduces heat loss further.

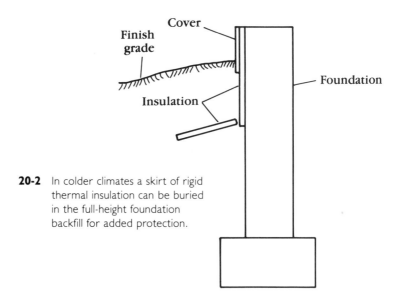

20-2 In colder climates a skirt of rigid thermal insulation can be buried in the full-height foundation backfill for added protection.

The third method (FIG. 20-3) is the most complete, and carries the insulation all the way to the bottom of the wall. Installation procedures are identical to the first method. The added cost lengthens the payback period, but also affords the best thermal protection and the highest interior comfort level. Higher inside wall-surface temperatures are maintained, so this is the first choice for below-grade living quarters.

Crawl-space walls

Crawl-space walls, when insulated at all, are often covered on the inside with fiberglass or mineral wool blanket. However, insulating the exterior is likely to prove more satisfactory. The job is easier, cleaner, and more effective. Also, the thermal mass of the foundation walls helps to store interior heat, and the overall cost is likely to be lower. Proceed just as for a full basement; the most advantageous arrangement is to carry the sheets of insulation all the way down to the footing top.

Slab-on-grade and grade-beam foundations

Slab-on-grade and grade-beam foundations also should be insulated, and just how this is done depends upon the foundation design. A three-part

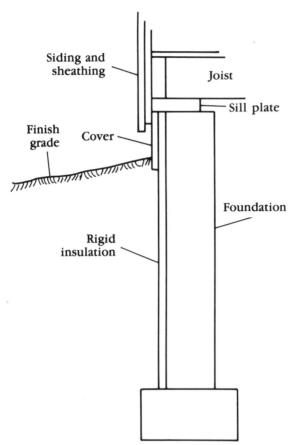

20-3 For maximum protection in cold climates, apply rigid insulation top to bottom of full-height foundation walls.

arrangement is often insulated as shown in FIG. 20-4, with the insulation board extending down at least 2 feet below the finished exterior grade and around the perimeter in a band about 2 feet wide. The narrow perimeter strip between the slab edge and the stem walls serves as an important thermal break, and also doubles as an expansion joint. In colder climes, add the optional exterior insulation, installed just as for a crawl space.

The situation is much the same for a monolithic slab-on-grade. Typically the rigid insulation board is installed on the exterior wall faces to full depth, but only along the slanted portion of the inside faces. A perimeter band about 2 feet wide should be laid flat on the sand or gravel cushion (FIG. 20-5). Insulation is often installed only on the slanted inner face of the beam in a grade-beam foundation, usually to the full width. However, this leaves ample area for heat to be dissipated. In cold country, the exterior faces should be insulated as for a crawl space. In addition, an exterior

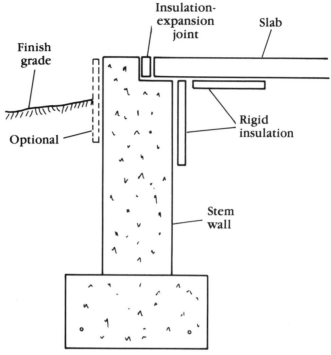

20-4 A typical arrangement for placing rigid thermal insulation in a three-part slab-on-grade foundation.

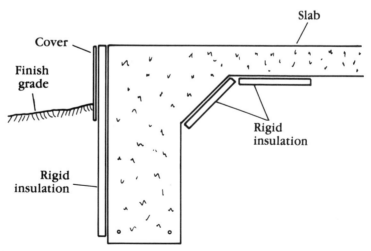

20-5 This insulating arrangement allows maximum protection for a monolithic slab-on-grade foundation.

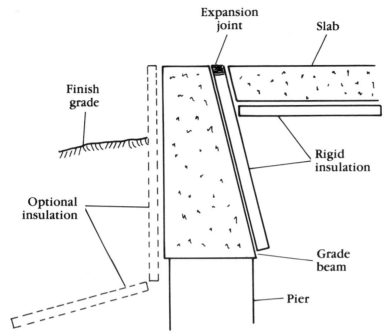

Finish grade

Expansion joint

Slab

Rigid insulation

Optional insulation

Grade beam

Pier

20-6   Thermal insulation arrangements for a grade beam foundation, using rigid panels.

band about 2 feet wide and extending outward and slightly downward from the bottom edge of the grade beam (FIG. 20-6) (as is done with full basement foundations) will increase effectiveness.

CONCRETE SLABS

Concrete slabs, whether part of an on-grade foundation or a basement or garage floor, are frequently ignored when it comes to insulation. And in fact, energy analysis to determine optimum insulating values in such locations is extremely difficult and seldom fully accurate. But, leaving these slabs uninsulated is not a smart move, especially since the initial cost is low and there is no way at all to make an equally inexpensive and effective retrofit. The soil beneath the slab, whether at finished grade or basement subgrade, is always at a substantially lower temperature than the house interior. Therefore, it will always bleed heat away from an uninsulated slab. If heating costs tend to be equal to or greater than cooling costs in your locale, consider installing full slab insulation. In heating-only areas, this should be considered a necessity.

The procedure is not difficult, but does require some extra time and care. There are two possibilities for insulants. The most common, least expensive, and most readily available is the same extruded polystyrene discussed earlier. It is relatively tough and crush-proof. An alternative is cellular glass foam in sheets, which is impervious to ground moisture and chemicals, and has very high compressive strength: about 10 times that of polystyrene. Its main drawback is that a thickness twice that of polystyrene is needed for the same approximate R-value.

To make the installation, lay the sheets out on a layer of 6-mil polyethylene sheet, atop a level—and compacted if necessary—sand or gravel cushion. Lay out the reinforcing mesh or rod on top of the insulation. Here is where glass foam works well: You can (carefully) walk around and work on it without causing damage. If you use polystyrene, opt for the 2-inch thickness for extra strength. Then pour the concrete in the usual fashion.

An alternative method if several workers are available is to spread the entire vapor barrier atop the cushion, and make ready all the rest of the materials. Then, as you pour the concrete in successive segments, lay out the insulation and remesh in sections at the same time, working backward away from the pour. This will minimize the damage potential and result in a better job.

Chapter **21**

Termite control

*E*xcept for the most arid parts of the United States, and at elevations from about 8000 feet up, there is no area that is completely safe from termites. Their concentration is greatest in the damp and humid southern states, but their range covers the entire United States. In many locales the danger of extensive damage caused by termite infestation is more than enough to warrant special preventive measures as a house is built. Those measures are simple and reasonably effective, if they are coupled with regular inspection and maintenance, and the cost is low.

TYPES OF TERMITES

There are three generally recognized kinds of termites: subterranean, damp wood, and dry wood. The subterranean are the most common by far in terms of numbers, the most destructive, and the hardest to spot. Fortunately they are also the easiest to control. Damp-wood termites are also very destructive and hard to spot, but less prevalent. Dry-wood termites are the easiest to find and to track, as well as the least prevalent. They cause comparatively minor damage, but are difficult to control. A fourth type, the Formosan termite, is extremely destructive and will seemingly gnaw through anything short of armor plate. Fortunately, this type is not widespread and is found only in parts of the Deep South.

Subterranean termites live almost entirely underground and particularly like warm and moist soil. They must have moisture to survive, and their diet is cellulose. They tunnel vigorously and build earthen tubes above ground to reach food supplies. The damp-wood termites are similar, except they live entirely in damp wood. Dry-wood termites do not need moisture to survive, and they live partly above ground, flying to wood and boring into it. All three types appear in the spring, equipped with wings, for their annual breeding and migration rituals.

METHODS OF TERMITE CONTROL

The first control measures against these miserable critters can be formulated during the house planning stages and carried out during construction. For example, an open pier foundation affords the least opportunity for entry into a structure, and a continuous-wall poured concrete foundation, properly built, is next best. Block foundations must be solidly capped with either a poured concrete top layer about 4 inches thick (FIG. 21-1) or a cap course of solid concrete block (the former is preferable). Slab foundations inevitably crack after a time and afford easy entrance for termites, especially since most of the cracks are hidden and measures are seldom taken to make repairs or stop the invasion. Wood foundations of any sort are not recommended in locales where termite infestation is common and severe.

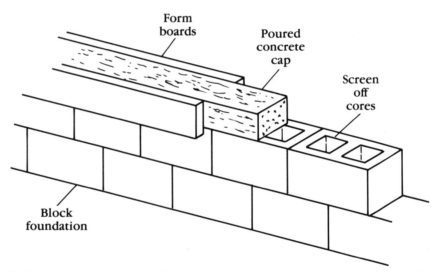

21-1 A poured concrete cap should be installed on a concrete block foundation wall in locales where termite infestation is a problem.

Adequate moisture control

Foundation moisture diversion and drainage systems are particularly important. They should be extensive, efficient, and well constructed in termite country. The drier the ground, the fewer the termites. Surface water and roof run-off in particular should be routed as far away from the structure as possible. In many locales, thermal insulation is best installed on the inside of the foundation walls (despite the contrary recommendation in Chapter 20). Termites will not eat exterior polystyrene or foamed glass insulation, but they can and will burrow between the insulation and the foundation surface. This gives them a warm and cozy place to colonize, a situation no homeowner needs. Interior insulation means the soils outside the foundation remains cold and relatively uninhabitable for them.

Removing debris

As you prepare the building site, be sure to remove all wood left from tree and brush clearing. During construction, make sure that the site is regularly policed and cleaned up. Don't leave any scraps of wood, paper, or cardboard around that might nourish the start of a colony. Never follow the age-old lazy builder's custom of burying all the trash and scraps in utility trenches and along the foundations when the backfilling is done. That's an invitation for the termites to come feast on your domicile. If it contains cellulose, they'll find it.

Preservative-treated wood

Pressure preservative-treated wood that does not come in contact with the ground is effective against termites. All exterior wood surfaces that are near the ground should be treated initially, then re-treated every few years with the most effective preservative available. Sill plates and any other wood components close to the ground should be commercially pressure-treated stock where the termite hazard is high. Elsewhere, you could make them of redwood, cypress, or cedar heartwood.

Polyethylene sheet

Cover all crawl space floors with a double layer of 6-mil or heavier polyethylene sheet. Overlap seams 12 inches or so. Allow ample ventilation to keep moisture at the lowest possible level. All wood surfaces inside a crawl space, such as first-floor joists and the underside of the subfloor, should be treated with preservatives. Sleeves or holes where pipes or wires go through the foundation must be completely sealed from both sides with roofing compound or an elastomeric caulk.

Chemicals

For decades the time-tested termite control method consisted of liberally dosing the soil surrounding a building with chemicals of one sort or another. The old chemicals were not only extremely toxic to termites, but to everything else as well. Environmental enlightenment has led to disuse and outright bans on most of those chemicals, as well as a reduction in the amount of soil poisoning that is done. The few chemicals that are currently being employed are less toxic but also less effective. Research continues, and procedures and chemicals are in a state of constant flux. There are still occasions when chemical control or preventive measures are called for, but any such work must now be done by trained and licensed personnel. Obtain details from a local exterminating or pest control company. Under no circumstances should you try do-it-yourself chemical eradication.

Termite shields

Another time-honored method of termite control is the installation of metal termite shields between the foundation top and the sill plate of the structure, as well as on any other convenient pathways from soil to building. This system has fallen somewhat into disfavor for two reasons. First, unless the system is complete and installed properly, it is ineffective. Likewise, if it is damaged or broken during construction, or any time later on, or if general deterioration sets in, it becomes ineffective. Termites will soon find any breach in the defenses. And second, building owners and tenants are left with a false sense of security and feel they do not have to worry about any further protective measures

If there is damage or deterioration to the metal shield, repairs must be immediately made. Also, a shield system does not prevent the entrance of termites, it merely forces them to tube out and around the barrier, where presumably they can be more readily seen. Sometimes in the real world, however, homeowners simply do not follow through with regular inspections, immediate repairs, and correct initial installations. Coupled with the false security, enormous damage can result.

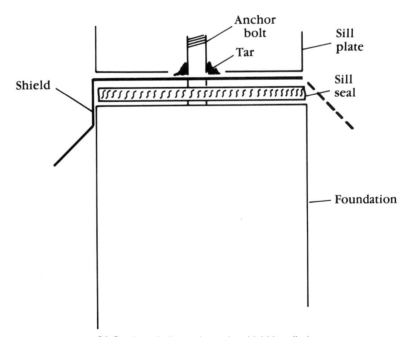

21-2   A typical metal termite shield installation.

This is not to say that a termite shield system should not be used as another line of defense against this determined bug. It can be worth the effort and cost. Shields made of 24-gauge or thicker copper will last longest and the material is easy to work. Aluminum, sheet zinc, and galvanized iron are also used; they are less expensive but also shorter lived and less satisfactory. All seams are best soldered, but may be overlapped by several inches and sealed with elastomeric caulk or roofing compound, and the sections riveted together.

On a continuous-wall foundation, place the shield directly on top of the wall with the sill seal and sill plate on top of that (FIG. 21-2). The whole foundation top should be covered, with the metal extending straight outward for about 2 inches and then slanted downward at about a 45-degree angle for another 2 inches. Make this extension to the outside on full basements and slab-on-grade foundations, and to both outside and inside in crawl space construction. The shields should extend out and down all the way around piers. Seal all holes in the shield, such as for sill anchor bolts, with caulk or compound.

Chapter 22

Sill installation

*I*n the Dark Ages of house construction, the starting point for the structure was a continuous horizontal perimeter made up of several timbers placed end to end. This was collectively called a *sill*. Typically the timbers were 8 by 8 inches or larger, of whatever wood species was handy: oak, chestnut, pine, and fir were all common. The *long sills* were located under the longest walls, usually front and back, and the *cross sills* tied them together. Sometimes the timbers were placed right on the ground, hence the term *mud sill*. More often the sill was placed on a stone foundation, and in timber framing construction the sill remains the starting point for the structure.

In the modern stick framing systems the massive sill has become a pale reflection of its former self. Now it is called a *sill plate* or a *foundation plate*, with no differentiation between long or cross, and is made up of nominal 2× dimension stock laid flat on the top of the foundation. The floor joists need only bear upon the sill plate for a distance of $1^1/2$ inches at each end, so 2×4s are sometimes used for the purpose. Most builders prefer to lay out 2-×-6 stock, however, and 2×8s are also used. The latter will cap almost the entire width of the foundation, or they can be set out to overhang the foundation face slightly to protect exterior foundation insulation.

Model building codes specify that all sill plates resting upon concrete or masonry foundations of whatever sort be pressure preservative-treated wood or redwood heartwood graded for foundation purposes. Where the termite and moisture hazards are moderate, a lesser grade of redwood or a top-grade cedar heartwood may be used. Where termite hazards are low, other species of wood may be acceptable to local inspecting authorities.

However, in view of the relatively minor added cost and the importance of the continuing structural integrity of the sill plate, it makes sense to install either preservative-treated or heartwood redwood stock, regardless of local conditions.

CONTINUOUS-WALL FOUNDATION

Installing the sill plate on a continuous-wall foundation is probably the easiest job you will encounter in the entire construction process. Even so, it should be done carefully and correctly; alignment is important for easy subsequent construction.

Leveling the area

First, check the foundation top all the way around for damage, low spots, protruding chunks of mortar or concrete, or anything else that might prevent the sill plate from lying flat and level. Repair any such problem spots; humps and dips can cause difficulties. Check the sill plate with a straight-edge. When the top is ready, sweep off any debris.

Fitting the sill plate members

Now you can get the sill plate members ready. Set them in place on the foundation, cutting lengths of dimension stock to fit as necessary. The longer the unbroken runs of plate, the better. Many framers join the members with flat butt joints and consider that adequate. Perhaps it's a small point, but good workmanship suggests that joints along the walls should be flat scarf or double rabbet joints, and the corners flat rabbets (FIG. 22-1). This affords a better fit and decreases the degree of air infiltration potential. Set the lengths of plate on the foundation top and mark the points where holes will have to be drilled to pass the anchor bolts. Position these marks accurately, so you won't have to oversize or elongate the holes to get the plates to align properly. Drill the holes about 1/4 inch larger than the anchor bolt diameter.

Applying sill seal

Next, apply the sill seal. One widely used material is thin, narrow fiberglass blanket that is made for the purpose and comes in rolls. A better material where air infiltration is a concern is a gasketing substance made of polyethylene foam. This is typically available in rolls, usually 1/4 inch thick and either 3 1/2 or 5 1/2 inches wide. Both materials compress and conform to the foundation surface, filling any gaps. Although foam does a better job; both can be used in double layers, if necessary. If the weather is good and the air calm, you can roll the material right out on the foundation. Or, you can staple it to the bottom of the sill plate members as you install them.

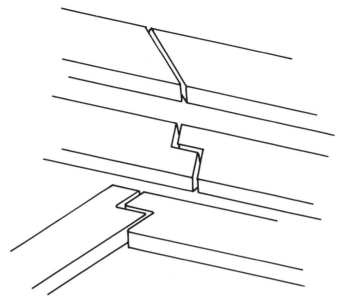

22-1 These joint patterns for sill plates are better than plain flat butts.

Positioning the sill plate

Set the sill plate pieces in position on the foundation top, with the sill seal sandwiched between. Place washers and nuts on all the anchor bolts and draw the nuts down snug. Then check the alignment and dimensions, to make sure that the overall size matches what is called for in the plans. Corners should be square or properly angled, and all the plate pieces set properly. Make any necessary adjustments. Take the anchor nuts down another turn or so until the washer bites into the wood. Depending upon the position and kind of splices, you might want to tie them together with a 10d toenail or two. That completes the job.

PWF FOUNDATION

The procedure for a PWF foundation is different, in that there is no discrete sill plate. The foundation walls are built like any ordinary stud wall, and in most designs the top plate of the wall is doubled. That top plate actually serves as a sill, in the sense that the first-floor joists, or in some cases another wall, will rest directly upon it (FIG. 22-2). Most often the lower plate is PWF treated lumber, while the upper plate of the pair can be ordinary construction grade material. There are no anchor bolts either; the upper assembly is nailed or sometimes through-bolted to the foundation top plate.

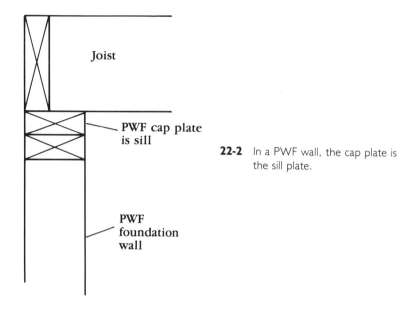

22-2 In a PWF wall, the cap plate is the sill plate.

PIER FOUNDATION

The procedures are also different for a pier foundation. There are three principal choices for sill material. Heavy beams like those used in timber framing can be installed, but they are expensive, hard to work with, and prone to twisting. Another possibility is laminated beams, often called "glue lams," made to order for the job. These are more effective than solid timbers, but also relatively expensive. An alternative is to make up beams from construction grade dimension stock, in the same way girders are conventionally built up.

Sizing sill beams

There is no handy rule of thumb to use for sizing the sill beams, because the cross-sectional dimensions required depend upon the spans between piers and/or supporting girders, the kind and grade of wood selected, the total weight that will be imposed on them, and the distribution of that weight. Thus, the sill details have to be engineered on an individual basis. However, a sill beam is essentially a girder. If the imposed loads will be evenly distributed, and if you can determine those loads with accuracy, you can use the girder sizing information in the following chapter, along with TABLE 23-1.

Placing the beams

Once past the design hurdle, installation is simple enough. No sill seal is required, of course, but if the sills are not made up of redwood or treated lumber (which is likely) they should rest upon heartwood redwood pads

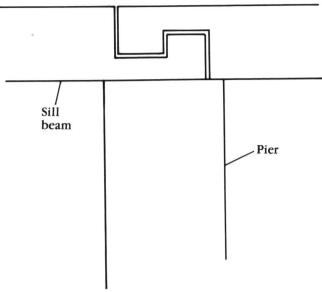

22-3 Splices in sill beams should be made only over a pier. This is a squared splice.

set atop the piers. Place the beams accurately, aligned and squared, and secure them to the piers with anchor bolts, straps, or other hardware.

Adjusting the sill

If the foundation layout is slightly off-line, now is the time to make corrections by adjusting the sill position. Avoid splices if possible in solid sill beams. When they must be made, they should occur only centered over a pier (FIG. 22-3). Splices in continuous built-up beams should also occur over a pier. Place them no less than 4 feet apart and always stagger them when the beam is composed of short rather than full-length pieces.

Chapter **23**

Girder installation

*I*t is possible in some designs to install floor joists over spans as great as 20 feet, but usually not advisable. When joist spans become too great, the floor assembly is weak and begins to take on the characteristics of a trampoline. Again, depending upon the framing design, once the floor joist spans go much beyond the 10- to 12-foot range, consideration is given to supporting the joists from below. The support is typically introduced at midspan in average-sized residence structures, but can also be placed at two or more equidistant points in spans of any length.

There is a complex interdependence of factors at work here, all of which must be addressed to determine just what approach will result in the most advantageous and economical construction. These factors include the total imposed loads; load distribution; joist span lengths; joist size; joist spacing on centers; the size, type, and material (and the species if wood) of the supporting member; and spans between supports.

The means of support for first-floor joists in a full-basement design, especially when finished as living quarters, may be a series of load-bearing stud frame walls built in the usual fashion. However, in many full-basement designs and also in crawl space designs, the means of support consists of one or more girders. The girders in turn are generally supported by posts or columns placed at predetermined intervals (FIG. 23-1). Girders are also sometimes employed as support for second-floor framing, with the support posts disguised or concealed in some fashion.

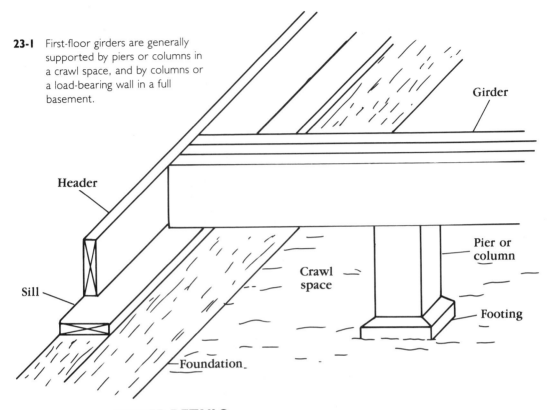

23-1 First-floor girders are generally supported by piers or columns in a crawl space, and by columns or a load-bearing wall in a full basement.

GIRDER DETAILS

Girders can be solid wood timbers, or commercially made up of laminated lumber (glue lams). They may be steel beams, although these are not often used in residential construction, especially in smaller houses. The most common practice in residential construction is to build up girders from nominal 2× dimension stock right on the job site. Because these are load-bearing members and the health of the structure is dependent upon their being correctly sized for the loads imposed, the details should be engineered to suit each individual case.

There are exceptions. Often a builder can use the empirical approach because he knows from experience what will work and what will not. Girders can also be obviously overbuilt and oversupported for the job at hand with successful results, but only on a basis of past specific experience. For the amateur owner-builder, girder details are best called out on the house plans or in an engineering report.

You can, however, get a safe approximation by first calculating the total load—live and dead—imposed on the girder. First get the per-square-foot load on the floor area supported by the girder. In a typical center girder design with nonload-bearing endwalls (a Cape Cod, for instance), this is the area equal to the girder support to girder support distance, mul-

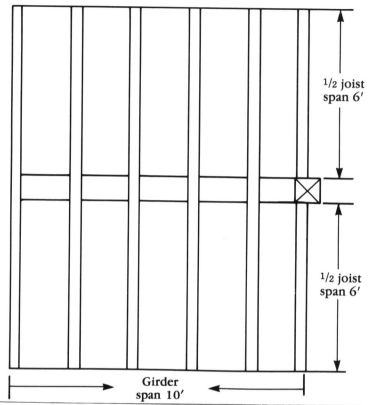

23-2   The load imposed on a girder equals that imposed over the total area covered by the girder span, multiplied by half the joist span to each side combined.

tiplied by half the joist span from girder to wall on each side in the other direction. If the girder span is 10 foot and half the joist span to either side of the girder is 6 feet, 10×(6 + 6) = 120 square feet (FIG. 23-2). If the total load imposed is 50 pounds per square foot, that amounts to 6000 pounds. Consult TABLE 23-1 to see what size built-up construction-grade lumber girder will support that total load over the 10-foot span. In the example given a 6×10 would do the job.

Girder length should be equal to the distance between the two foundation walls which will support the girder ends, plus a minimum of 3 inches at each end. Four inches is better, and recommended if the foundation walls are concrete block. The foundation pockets (FIG. 23-3) in which the ends will lie must be at least 1 inch wider than the girder, and allow a gap of at least 1/2 inch at the girder end. The depth of the pocket must be such that the girder top lies flush with the top of the sill plate. An alternative to the pocket system, especially useful when more headroom below the girder is desired, is to set the girder atop the sill plate.

The girder ends should never be set directly on concrete or masonry.

Table 23-1 Safe Loads for Girders, Equally Distributed in Lbs.

Size	\multicolumn{5}{c}{Span}
	6′	7′	8′	9′	10′
6×8	7000	6000	5500	5000	4000
6×10	10,000	9500	8500	7500	7000
6×12	13,000	12,500	12,000	11,000	10,000
8×8	9500	8000	7000	6500	5000
8×10	13,000	12,500	11,500	10,500	9500
8×12	18,000	17,500	16,500	15,000	13,500

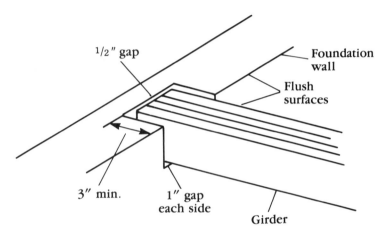

23-3 Girders frequently are set in foundation wall pockets.

The girder ends should never be set directly on concrete or masonry. Instead, set them on steel bearing plates in the pockets, and adjust the height of the girder with steel shims slipped between the plate and the girder bottom. For foundation top placement, if shimming is needed, use only steel shims at least 1 inch wider than the girder, placed between the sill plate and the girder. The girder should also be secured to the foundation with strap anchors.

BUILDING THE GIRDERS

Girders should be built up of kiln-dried lumber to minimize shrinking and warping. The members can be nailed or bolted together, or both. Bolts should be at least 5/8-inch diameter and spaced in a staggered upper-lower pattern every 20 inches. Use hex head bolts with flat steel washers or plates beneath both heads and nuts. Build up a two-piece girder by nailing the planks together from one side with 10d nails in a staggered pattern, spaced about 16 inches apart. For a three-part girder, use 20d nails in a staggered pattern, driven from each side and about 30 inches apart. Build up a four-part girder by nailing another layer to the three-part with 20d nails staggered every 30 inches. All joints must be staggered and separated by 4 feet minimum; no two should be opposite one another. Also, joints should be calculated to fall directly over support columns or posts.

Intermediate supports (FIG. 23-4) for a girder are usually spaced 8 feet apart; 6 feet can be considered the narrowest spacing and 10 feet the practical maximum. The supports can be wood posts, which should be of the same width as the girder. A 6-inch nominal girder requires a 6-×-6 nominal post. However, steel columns are the more common choice. They may be fixed-length with a flange welded on each end, and sometimes concrete filled, or they may feature adjustable screw tops. A common alternative in crawl space foundations is a series of piers, either poured concrete or built up of concrete block. Whatever is used, the support must be solidly anchored at both ends.

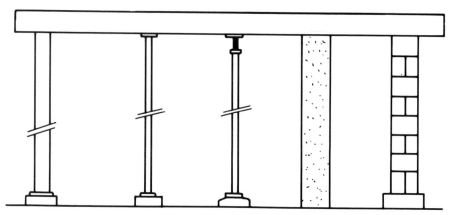

23-4 Girder intermediate supports can be (left to right) a wood post, fixed steel column, adjustable steel column, poured concrete pier, concrete block pier, or (not shown) a frame wall.

FOOTING SUPPORTS FOR GIRDERS

The supports must also have supports; you cannot just plunk them on the earth or a concrete slab. The traditional method is to pour a suitable reinforced concrete footing at each support column location, with the top level with the grade.

Following the previous example, if the plan is ground loading is at 1000 pounds per square foot, a footing area of 6 square feet each would be needed. A precast concrete pier is mortared to the footing. If the column is wood, a redwood or treated wood pad is inset into the pier top. If it is steel, suitable anchor bolts are used. The arrangement remains as is in a crawl space; in a basement the slab floor is simply poured over the footings and around the piers. Steel columns are sometimes anchored directly to the footing top. Wood posts should never rest less than 6 inches from a slab or earth grade, unless they are preservative treated.

Chapter 24

First-floor framing

A floor frame consists primarily of a series of joists, along with a few other auxiliary members. Its purpose is to support the weight of the flooring, partitions, and variable portions of the other live and dead loads of the structure, and transmit them to the girders and/ or foundations. The floor frame design is dependent upon several interrelated factors, all of which must at some point be considered. These include: the total live and dead loads that will be imposed, joist span between supports, joist size, joist spacing on centers, joist wood species and grade or construction (for trusses), the specific modulus of elasticity (E), the extreme fiber stress in bending (Fb), and the kind of subflooring that will be installed.

If you change the value of one of these factors, others might have to be changed as well. For example, by shortening a given joist span you might be able to use narrower joists, impose a greater load, increase the spacing between them, or install a thinner subfloor material. If you increase a given load, you might have to set the joists closer together, use wider stock, increase the subfloor thickness, or shorten the joist span, or maybe all of the above.

A floor frame design can be determined for any application through appropriate engineering and calculations, and there is a wide range of design possibilities. Much sophisticated data has been developed and tabulated for this purpose. However, in conventional residential frame construction there are some convenient starting points, and some generalities that can be put to work, all of which has come about through many years of building experience and thousands of successful houses.

A floor frame must be strong, more than enough to support the imposed loads over an indefinite period without sagging or deforming, and it must be stiff. There are few things more annoying and disconcerting than a floor that shudders and joggles when your 50-pound hound lopes across it. Making a stiff and strong floor is not at all difficult. If your house design is unusual and has some peculiarities, an engineered design by a competent architect might be for you. For conventional designs, use the following information.

CONVENTIONAL FLOOR FRAMING

Traditional residential joist spacing is 16 inches on centers (from the lengthwise centerline of one joist to the next). This is in accord with the 4- and 8-inch and 4- and 8-foot modular building system. Sometimes, when imposed loads are high or there is a need for a particularly strong or stiff floor, 12-inch centering is selected. In the past, 24-inch centering has been shunned in most constructions, but in fact it works nicely if you use the proper joist and subflooring materials. Currently 24-inch spacing is often recommended in houses whose walls are framed with 2×6s instead of 2×4s. Stud spacing in this system is 24 inches o.c. (on centers), so the floor joists, studs, and roof rafters can be similarly spaced and aligned with one another, affording greater structural strength and integrity than would otherwise be achieved. In certain flooring systems, it is also possible to use 36- or 48-inch o.c. spacing. Although this is an excellent system, it is rarely used.

Floor loading capabilities

Once you have selected the joist centering dimension, you need to calculate the floor loading capabilities in terms of pounds per square feet of floor area. The rule-of-thumb figure for dead load, including stud partitions (and in the absence of special engineering data or local code requirements to the contrary), is 10 pounds per square foot. The live load now almost universally required by codes is 40 pounds per square foot minimum. If there are no special weights involved, like an 1800-pound pool table or a 1000-gallon hot tub, and if local codes do not require a heavier load factor to be used, these are adequate figures.

Choosing the materials

The stock conventionally used for joists is 2×6, 2×8, 2×10, and 2×12. The next step is to find out specifically what kind of lumber is available to you at your local lumberyard for joists. You need to know the wood species and the grade being offered. Because grades vary and the designations might be confusing, it's better if you can find out the modulus of elasticity (E) value and the extreme fiber stress in bending (Fb) factor for that particular material. Or simply ask what all the local builders are using these days for floor joists, and do the same. Either way, you can then go to a table of allowable spans for floor joists with a 40-pound-per-square-foot live load. Select your spacing and *E*, and look for a joist size and suitable *Fb* that will cover your intended span.

An alternative, if you don't want to bother with all this and don't care if your floor frame might be somewhat overbuilt (which isn't a bad idea) is to assume a low *E* and a low *Fb* and select the span accordingly. TABLE 24-1 lists safe spans for floor joists with a total 50-pound load factor, rounded back to the nearest half foot. If your requirement is for a length between a half foot and the next highest full foot, don't go up to that foot, go back to the half foot; for 9-9, go to 9-6 instead of 10-0.

Table 24-1 Safe Spans
(50 Lbs./Sq. Ft. Load)

	Spacing	
Size	*16"*	*24"*
2×6	8–0	7–0
2×8	10–6	9–0
2×10	13–6	11–6
2×12	16–0	14–0

Note that these are minimums, as are almost all such tables. Often the numbers are predicated on allowing a commercial builder to get the job done in the most economical but still adequate fashion. The finished product will be solid enough but not necessarily superior. If you want an even stiffer, stronger floor frame, you can reduce the span by one-fourth, decrease the joist centering by one step, or go the next larger joist size (2×8 instead of 2×6). Substantial stiffening and strengthening can also be accomplished in the subfloor construction, which is covered in the following chapter.

Building the floor frame

To build a floor frame, start with the header joists, which rest upon the long sill plates at right angles to the common joists. Toenail these members to the sill plate with 10d nails driven from the outside every 16 inches. Then set the end joists on the short sills and secure them the same way. Also, nail the end/header corners together with three 16d nails each (FIG. 24-1). Next, lay out the locations of the common joists on each header joist.

Note that if the common joists run straight through over girders, the pattern will be the same on opposite headers. If they overlap, as is often the case, one pattern will be a joist thickness out of step with the other. Usual practice is to mark both sides of each location with plumb lines,

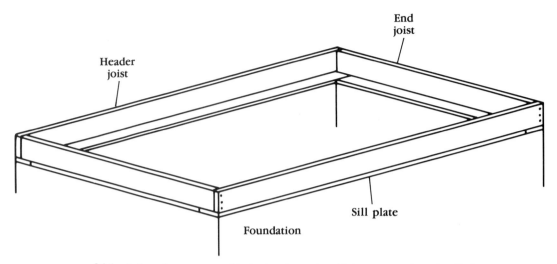

24-1   A floor frame starts with the header and end joists mounted on the sill plate.

using a try square (FIG. 24-2). This avoids confusion and improper placement. Center-to-center spacings should all be identical except where
additional joists are installed. These spacings should always be less than
the norm, not greater.

Next, install the common joists (sometimes called *stringers*). The way
they are nailed is important and should never be skimped; check local
codes for specifics, too. Set the joists in place, making sure that the
crown, if any, is upward on each (FIG. 24-3). Face nail one end of each to
the header joist with three 16d nails, and toenail into the sill plate with
one 10d nail on each side. There are several ways to secure the opposite
ends. If the joist butts against another header, follow that same procedure. If the joist ends butt the faces of a girder and rest in steel hangers,

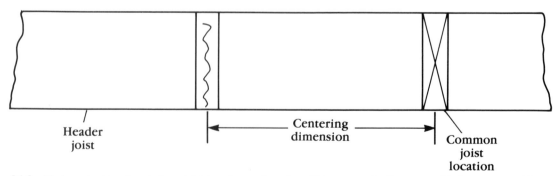

24-2   Mark each side of each floor joist location and mark an X between the lines to avoid placement problems.

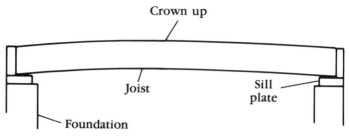

24-3 When installing joists, always place the crown upward.

use the hardware manufacturer's recommendations for nailing; you can also anchor to headers that way. If the joists ends lie on top of a girder, they should overlap each other by a minimum of 4 inches. Toenail each end to the girder top with one 10d nail on each side. Also, face nail the ends of each overlapping pair to one another with at least four 10d nails.

FLOOR FRAMING FOR HEAVY LOADS

At any point where there will be unusual and concentrated weight resting upon the floor, and the subfloor will be nominal 1-inch boards or $1/2$-inch or thinner plywood, it is wise to double the nearest joist or two. Such loads include parallel partitions (especially if load-bearing), cast-iron bathtubs or large-capacity tubs of any sort, or extra-heavy appliances or equipment—especially heavy machinery that might vibrate when operating. You can nail the joists together with 10d nails staggered up and down about 16 inches apart. In the case of a parallel partition, where there might be a need to get pipes or wires up into the wall above, you can space the joists apart with 2-×-4 blocks secured on end between the joists. Use two 10d nails on each side (FIG. 24-4).

Framing an opening

Framing an opening in a floor frame requires some special components and a particular sequence of steps. Face nail all butt joints with three 16d nails, and all side-by-side doublings with 10d nails staggered on 16-inch spacings. If the opening is no wider than the space between two joists, just fit a pair of short headers between them to form the required opening length (FIG. 24-5). For a larger opening, first install a common joist at the nearest prescribed joist location beyond the opening, on each side. Fit a primary header joist between the two common joists, $1^{1}/2$ inches shy of the specified opening length, on each side. Then fit however many tail joists are needed between those headers and the sills or girders, placed in the prescribed locations on centers.

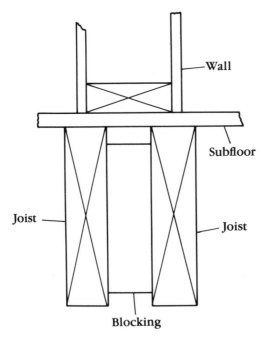

24-4   One method of installing doubled joists beneath a parallel wall.

24-5   Two headers between adjacent joists are sufficient to frame a small opening; add a trimmer as needed.

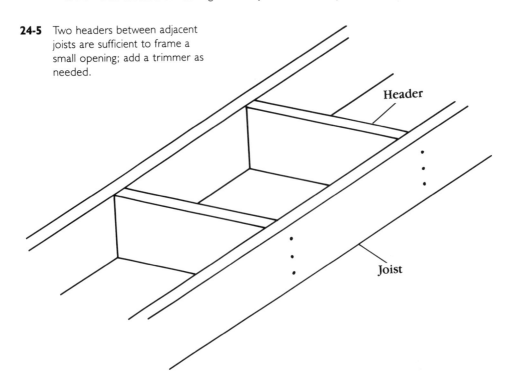

Now nail a secondary header to each primary header, and face nail them through the common joists as well. Toenail a pair of trimmer joists in place to finish out the opening to the required size, if necessary. Reverse toenail into the top and bottom at each end with 16d nails, and through the sides as well with two or three more. Finally, double each of the bordering common joists on the outside. Figure 24-6 shows the arrangement and the sequence. Note that the common joists can be set in some cases to provide the sides of the opening, eliminating the short trimmers and themselves becoming trimmer joists. Note too that much of the assembly can be put together with joist hangers instead of direct nailing, which can make construction both easier and stronger.

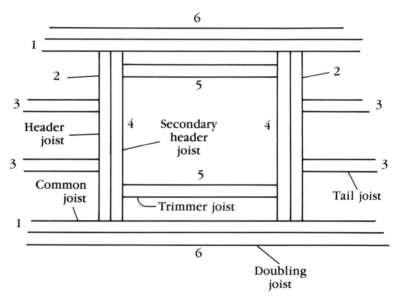

24-6   Large rough openings in a floor frame require more complex construction; follow the sequence shown.

Installing bridging

There is some argument about whether or not bridging should be installed. The purpose of bridging is to keep the joists aligned and to prevent them from warping, going out of plumb, and spreading laterally under concentrated weight from above. The argument against bridging is that it adds nothing structurally, increases time and cost, and is not necessary because modern kiln-dried joists don't warp. Also, some builders believe bridging members often are responsible for squeaks and creaks in the floor. In fact, kiln-dried joists do warp, sometimes badly in arid and semiarid areas, and they can spread apart. The added cost and time is not a big factor, especially in an owner-built house, and many building codes require bridging.

There are two alternatives in cross bridging. The conventional method employs lengths of 1×4 cut to fit diagonally between joists in cross pairs (FIG. 24-7). Place a single row positioned at right angles to the joists halfway between supports, or on maximum 8-foot centers. Spans over 16 feet require two equidistant rows. Toenail the top end of each piece with a pair of 8d nails. Leave the bottom ends loose until the sub-flooring is installed, then secure them with another pair of 8d nails each.

The other method is more satisfactory and requires less work. It consists of preformed steel struts that may be secured with integral teeth or with whatever nails are recommended by the manufacturer.

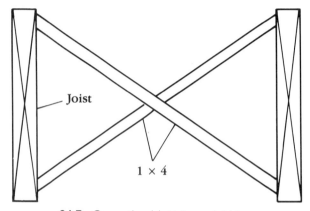

24-7   Conventional 1-×-4 cross bridging.

Installing solid blocking

Solid blocking should be installed between joists where they overlap atop a girder. Toenail at the top ends and/or face nail whenever possible with 16d nails as the joists are set, with the blocks in a straight line along the centerline of the girder (FIG. 24-8). Also, toenail 10d nails into the girder from both sides of each block. Solid blocking can also be effectively used in place of cross bridging, and helps distribute floor loads and stabilize joists. You can install the blocks in staggered lines in the pattern shown in FIG. 24-9, face nailing through the joists into the block ends with three 16d nails each. Or, you can run the blocks in straight lines for a slightly more stable construction, nailing as shown in FIG. 24-9. Face nail straight on from the open end, and face nail at an angle at the other.

Cantilevered floor joists

Floor joists can be cantilevered outward beyond the sill plate a certain distance in some constructions. You can safely install unsupported extensions in frame constructions without recourse to special materials and engineering, as long as you keep the projection to 4 feet or less. Make sure that the interior length of the joists is at least three times that of the exterior (4 feet

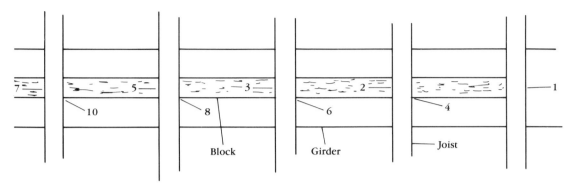

24-8 Straight-line solid blocking is easy to install in this pattern.

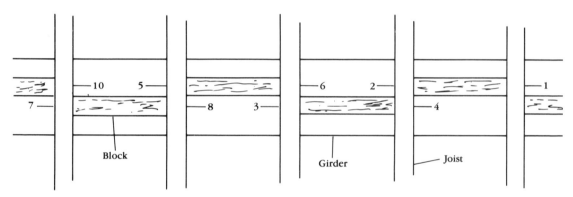

24-9 Staggered solid blocking is a bit less effective than straight-line, but easier to put in.

out, 12 feet in), and that the framing is properly done and the members solidly anchored. If the cantilevered joists run parallel with the common joists, just extend them outward. It is a good idea to double the outside joists and outer header. Install solid blocking across the bearing surface in continuation of the common header, and secure the inner ends of the joists with steel framing anchors (FIG. 24-10).

If the cantilevered section lies at right angles to the run of the common joists, double the interior anchor joist. Install the outermost of the cantilevered joists first, then put in all of the cripple joists that run parallel with the common joists. Install the remaining cantilevered joists (these are called *lookout* joists) and double the header and outside joists if required (FIG. 24-11). Anchor the inboard joist ends with steel joist hangers placed upside down, stirrups on top.

Extensions

You can also make first-floor extensions of any sort by securing joists to the outside faces of the header or to end joists with framing anchors. Or, run extra-long joists outward, and support them at the far end (or close to

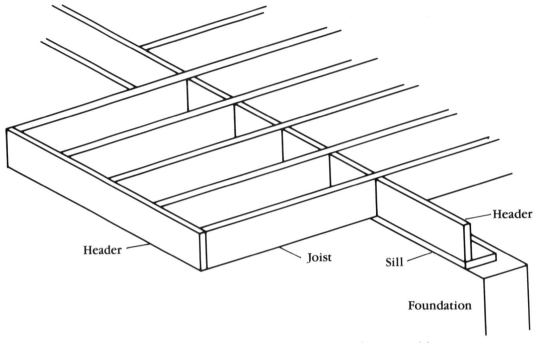

24-10 A cantilevered floor section parallel with the main common joists.

it) on a girder set on piers. No special construction techniques are needed.

OTHER FLOOR FRAMING POSSIBILITIES

Although conventional lumber joist floor framing remains the most economical and widely used system in residential construction, there are other possibilities that have their advantages. The cost of these is decreasing and they are becoming more available, and will be used much more in coming years. One is the closed or solid web floor truss, which consists essentially of a narrow plywood panel glued between solid wood top and bottom stringers (FIG. 24-12). There need be no waste with these joists. They can be made to whatever length you need, are very lightweight, and are easy to handle and to work with. In addition, they will support a greater load and/or span greater distances than solid wood joists, shrinkage and warping are negligible, and all the pieces are uniform.

Another possibility lies in the various kinds of open web joists, which may be all wood, wood and steel, or all steel. These will also cover greater spans than lumber joists and handle greater loads. They provide a broader floor support and nailing surface than either conventional or

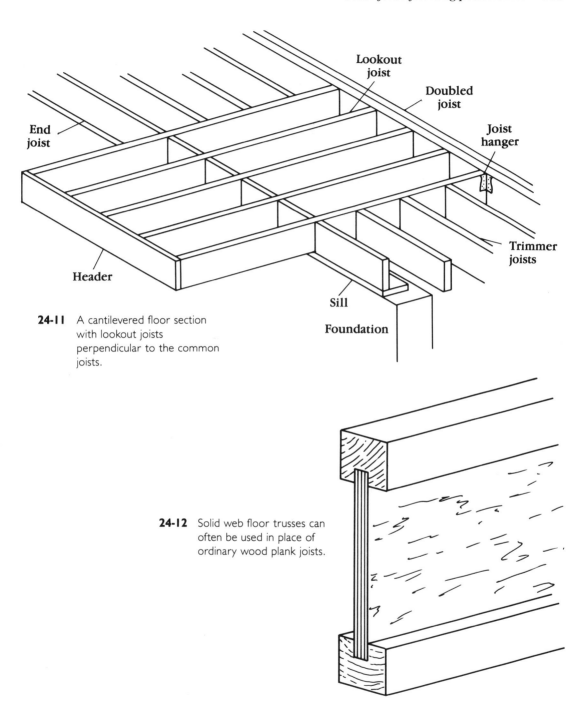

24-11 A cantilevered floor section with lookout joists perpendicular to the common joists.

24-12 Solid web floor trusses can often be used in place of ordinary wood plank joists.

closed web joists, and they are very stiff. These joists are fairly heavy, but easy to install. Running pipes, ducts, and wires through them is a simple task.

All of these specialized joists are proprietary products that vary in characteristics and properties. In order to use such a system, first determine which might work best for you. Then obtain the necessary technical data, application notes, and installation instructions from the manufacturer or dealer. In most cases, a company representative will work out exactly what materials you need for a given floor system.

Chapter **25**

First-floor sheathing

*T*he next step in frame construction—again, with the exception of slab-on-grade house designs—is to sheath the first-floor frame. This creates the platform that gives the platform framing technique its name. There are several ways to accomplish this; no one way is necessarily better than another, but each has its own advantages and disadvantages.

PRELIMINARIES: TRIMMING THE JOISTS

Before you start putting down a subfloor, however, there is one chore to take care of. All of the floor joists should have been installed with the crown upward. Check each joist with a taut line stretched from one end to the other along a side to see how much upward bow is present. On any joist where the crown exceeds about $1/16$ inch at any point, snap a chalkline along the joist side. Then trim each joist top off flat to the line with a power plane. Lay a long straightedge across the joists at right angles in various locations and check for high spots. Trim as required. This process will ensure that your finish floor lies reasonably flat, with a minimum of distracting dips and humps.

SUBFLOORING BASICS

The traditional method of laying a subfloor, which will be covered later with a finish flooring, consists of nailing down individual boards. This is an easy approach for the amateur builder, and is no less effective a system now than it was a century and more ago. Nominal 1-×-8, or preferably

1×-6—S4S (surfaced four sides) squared-edged boards can be used, but a tongue-and-groove pattern is better. You can lay the boards at right angles to the joists, but placing them on a diagonal will give you a stronger floor because of the bracing effect. If the boards are perpendicular to the joists, the finish flooring should be parallel with the joists. If the boards are run diagonally, the finish flooring can be oriented in any direction.

Use only kiln-dried lumber. When laying the boards at right angles to the joists, start flush with the outer edge of a header joist. If using tongue-and-groove lumber, the tongue can be oriented either inward or outward. Nail the boards to each joist with a pair of 8d nails, angling them slightly (FIG. 25-1). Keep a scrap of board handy to use as a block for driving the boards tightly together. When laying diagonally, choose one corner and first measure off 8 or 10 feet along the header joist, then along the end joist. Snap a diagonal chalkline between them across the joist tops. Start laying at the line, working away from the corner (FIG. 25-2). Use the shorter cut-off pieces that result from laying the major portion of the subfloor to fill in the corner areas. All joints must be located on the centerline of a joist, with the board ends securely toenailed. As soon as a section of subfloor is finished, it's a good idea to cover it with a sheet of polyethylene for moisture protection until the building is made weathertight.

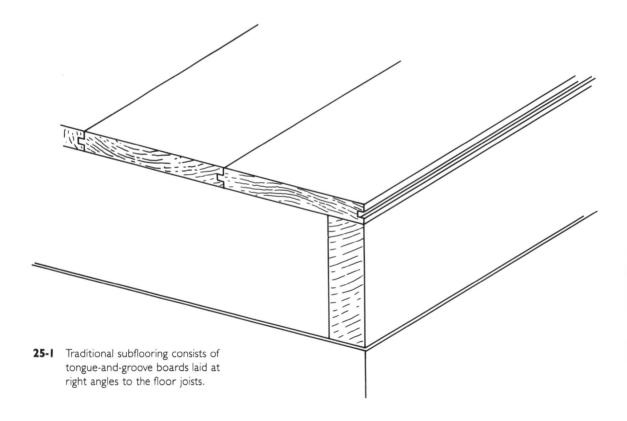

25-1 Traditional subflooring consists of tongue-and-groove boards laid at right angles to the floor joists.

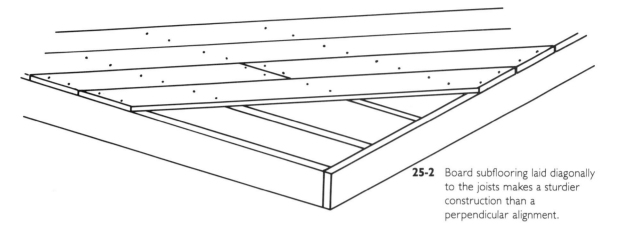

25-2 Board subflooring laid diagonally to the joists makes a sturdier construction than a perpendicular alignment.

PLYWOOD SUBFLOORING

The material of choice for subflooring today is plywood. It is strong, stiff, economical, and lays rapidly—at least 32 square feet at a clip for full sheets. Because several thicknesses are available, it can be tailored to fit a variety of joist span/spacing and loading or stiffness requirements. And, several kinds of finish flooring can be laid right over the smooth, flat, virtually unbroken surface plywood provides. About the only drawback for a lone do-it-yourselfer is that the sheets are heavy and awkward to handle, trim, and position.

For subflooring, APA (American Plywood Association) rated sheathing, Exposure 2 C-D plywood is a logical choice. It is best covered with poly-sheet for protection from the weather, as necessary. Exposure 1 C-D plywood at a slightly greater cost is also a good choice because weather has little effect on it and short-term protection isn't a concern. For normal residential purposes, over joists spaced 16 inches o.c., install the 5/8-inch thickness. For a 24-inch o.c. spacing, lay 3/4-inch plywood. For a stiffer flooring with either joist spacing, go up to 3/4 inch and 7/8 inch, respectively. In any case, a C-D grade of panel is the usual choice.

Laying plywood subflooring

To lay plywood subflooring, start at one corner of the floor frame and lay a full panel. Place the best face up, with the long length or face grain set at right angles to the joists. Lay the next panel with a 1/16-inch end gap, and continue. In the next and subsequent rows of panels, stagger the joints by a half panel, and leave a 1/8-inch gap between all the sides (FIG. 25-3). If dampness or very high humidity is a constant local condition, double those expansion gaps. Make sure that no cut piece bears on less than three joists. Fasten the panels with 8d common nails (recommended), or use box or ring-shank nails. Space them every 6 inches around the perimeter and 12 inches at intermediate points. Chalklines snapped on the panels

25-3 Plywood panels laid in this fashion comprise the most popular subflooring in modern house construction.

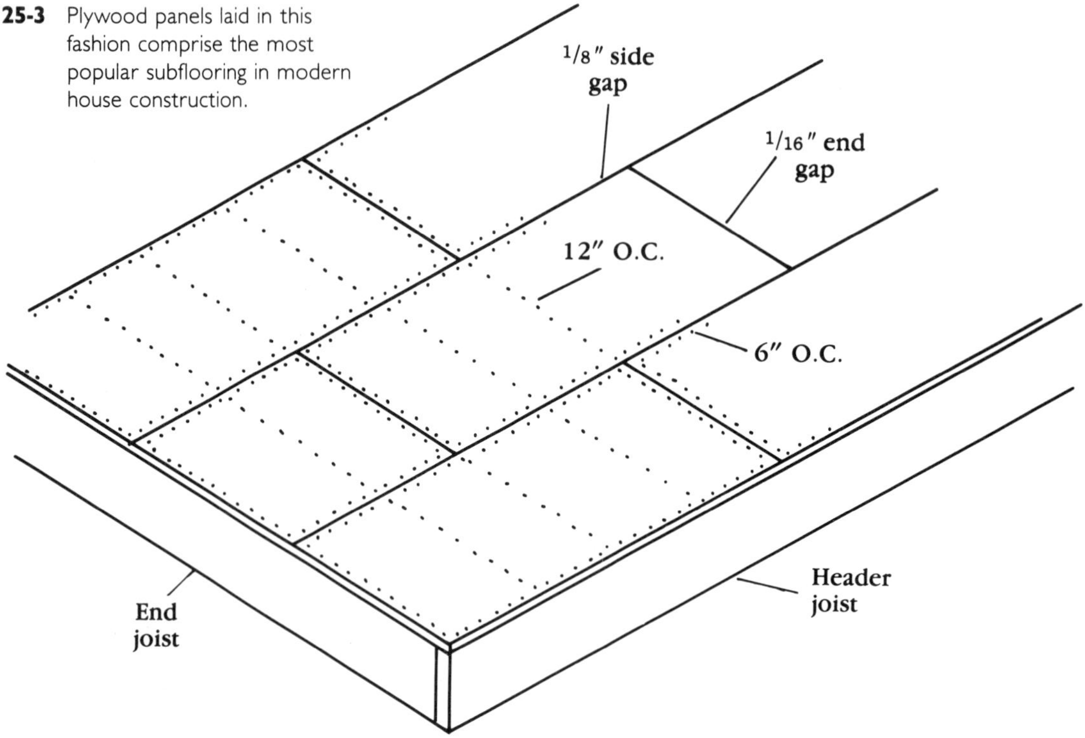

1/8" side gap

1/16" end gap

12" O.C.

6" O.C.

Header joist

End joist

over the joist centerlines will help you keep the intermediate nails properly positioned. A pneumatic nail gun (rentable, along with an air compressor) will speed the process; just make sure the plywood is lying flat and tight to the joist top surface as you nail.

GLUED SUBFLOORING

You can make a substantial improvement in conventional plywood sub-flooring construction by installing a glued subfloor. A bit more expense and time is involved, but the result is a stiffer, stronger floor (the joists become interconnected T beams) and a virtual elimination of squeaks and popped nails. You can use the same thickness of standard plywood panels as previously outlined. If the finish floor will be hardwood strip, you can downsize by 1/8 inch.

Laying the glued subflooring

To lay a glued plywood subfloor, set a panel in place at a corner and trim to fit as necessary. Mark its boundaries on the joist tops. Flip the panel back out of the way and make sure the joist tops are clean and dry. Apply an approved construction adhesive in a 1/4-inch continuous bead along the joist tops, stopping at the boundary marks. Reset the panel and align it carefully; it might move off-line on the glue. Nail the panel down using 6d ring-shank nails for 3/4-inch or thinner plywood, 8d nails for thicker material. Space the nails 12 inches apart at all bearing points. *Note*: Some building codes might require closer nail spacing and/or larger nails. Continue in the same way with subsequent panels, staggering all joints and leaving a 1/8-inch expansion gap at all joints.

SUSPENDED CONCRETE FLOOR

Plans might call for a ceramic tile, slate, paver, or similar finish floor in certain areas, typically the bath, entryway, or kitchen. A concrete substrate or other alternatives are often desirable for this kind of installation, which might require a modified subfloor. The joists must be sized/spaced to carry the added load. Then, fasten ledger plates to each side of each joist with 10d nails spaced 6 inches apart and staggered up and down. Chamfer each joist upper edge. Cut strips of plywood, minimum thickness 3/4 inch in a rated sheathing Exposure 1 C-D grade plywood, with the face grain oriented lengthwise. Nail the strips to the ledgers with 8d common nails spaced 6 inches apart (FIG. 25-4).

STURD-I-FLOOR®

APA rated Sturd-I-Floor® is a proprietary product that is very strong and stiff. It can be installed on joists spaced anywhere from 16 to 48 inches,

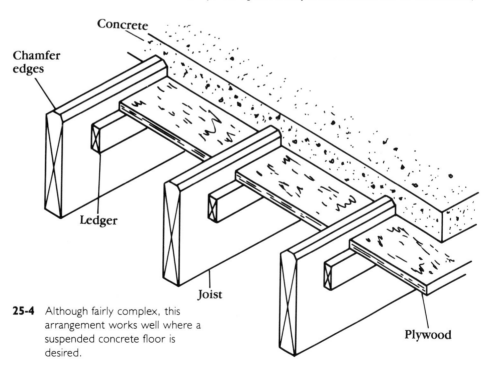

25-4 Although fairly complex, this arrangement works well where a suspended concrete floor is desired.

depending upon thickness and other details. The panels, obtainable in tongue-and-groove form, are combination subfloor-underlayment and can be laid in a single thickness for direct carpet and pad installation. The panels can be laid dry or be installed with adhesive. There are numerous variables, so the best bet is to tailor each Sturd-I-Floor® installation to suit. Additional information can be obtained from the APA.

FIVE-QUARTER PLANKING

Conventional plywood or board subfloors, as the name implies, start as a working platform and later are covered with a layer of finish flooring, or an intermediate layer of underlayment and then a finish floor covering. But sometimes a single-layer flooring is desirable, which combines the subfloor function with the finish floor appearance. One such possibility is called five-quarter (5/4) planking. These boards typically are 6 to as much as 12 or 14 inches wide, and an actual $1^{1}/_4$ inches thick. They may be S4S or tongue-and-groove, end-matched or not. Many different wood species can be used, such as maple, birch, yellow pine, pecan, butternut, or oak, though the softest woods generally are not used. The planks are laid by blind-nailing through the edges, securing them with screws capped with plugs, or face-nailing with decorative-head nails.

DECKING

Another popular single-layer flooring is called *decking*. Readily available through most lumberyards, this is usually nominal 2-×-4 or larger stock with either a single or a double tongue-and-groove. It has great strength and allows for a firm, tight, stiff floor.

Decking is usually laid at right angles to the joists (or often wide-spaced beams), starting flush with the outside edge of a header joist. The grooves face outward and tongues to the interior. Toenail through the inner edge of the tongues with 16d nails, one into each joist face. Butt joints must be made over joist centerlines, and the planks should be driven as tightly together as possible. Decking can be protected during construction, then sanded and given an applied-coating finish afterward, or it can be covered with an underlayment and/or finish flooring. Also, the underside of the material can be given an attractive applied finish for an "open" ceiling below, as in a basement rec room.

Chapter **26**

Wall framing

*P*robably the easiest phase of the entire residence construction project is framing the walls. There are only three basic components in a plain, unbroken wall, whether it is exterior or interior: common studs, sole plate, and top plate. The design is simple and you can readily assemble the parts with all the members set flat on the first-floor platform, then tilt the frame up into position afterward.

CHOOSING THE MATERIAL

The material used in the majority of houses is construction or stud grade 2× dimension stock, available at any lumberyard. Wood species vary in different locales. Most houses continue to be built with 2-×-4 studs set on 16-inch centers, with plates of the same size. This construction is amply strong and adequately stiff and vibration-free. Stretching the centers out to 24 inches has been done, but can't be recommended as a good construction practice even for interior partitions. Though the support afforded is strong enough, the walls are a bit too limber. Also, most building codes don't allow any spacing greater than 16 inches in walls that support an upper floor; 24 inches is a maximum in any case. Interior nonload-bearing walls can be framed with 2×3s set no more than 16 inches on centers, but this too results in flimsy walls.

In recent years the exterior walls of many houses built in colder climes have been framed with 2×6s. These are nearly always set on 24-inch centers, which affords excellent strength and stiffness. The purpose is to allow extra in-wall space for thermal insulation, making a more energy-efficient structure. Many local building codes in such locales now require the thermal insulating value of walls to be greater that can be readily accomplished with the conventional 2-×-4 stud and fiberglass batting type of construction.

The material used for the plate components of the wall frame must be the same size as the studs, except for a few special applications, and is usually the same or similar grade when the frames are to be set on a wood subfloor. In the case of a slab-on-grade or a grade-beam foundation, the sole plate lies directly upon concrete. This member should be either heartwood redwood or preservative pressure-treated stock. In all cases the plate material should be clean, straight, dry stock, preferably in long lengths to reduce or eliminate the need for splices.

Both exterior and interior stud walls are typically framed as 8-foot-high sections. Many lumberyards stock precut studs sized so that when sandwiched between a sole and a top plate, the overall height will come out just right. Some designs, though, call for taller walls. Usually 14 feet is considered a maximum height for 2×4s and 20 feet for 2×6s, in the absence of lateral support framing. If ceilings lower than 8 feet are desired, this is often accomplished by leaving the wall height at 8 feet and simply lowering the ceiling on a subframe. However, walls can be framed lower than 8 feet. Most codes set 7 feet 6 inches as a minimum, with only a few exceptions.

One further point with regard to the material: It pays in the long run to install studs of good quality that are straight and clean with a minimum of knots, and kiln dried to 15-percent moisture content. Even if you have to go to a better grade than your local supplier offers for the purpose, the extra cost might be worthwhile. The reason is that between the time the wall frames are erected and the exterior sheathing and interior covering is applied, low-quality and/or moisture-laden studs are likely to twist, bow, and warp. This will give you fits when you try to finish the walls and make them look decent.

CONSTRUCTING A SIMPLE STUD WALL FRAME

To make a simple stud wall, start by selecting straight pieces of stock for the sole and top plates. Lay them out flat on the floor, edge to edge, with the ends aligned. Tack them to the floor with a few 8d nails. The plates are best made up of one single length each, but if this is not possible, arrange the butt joints to fall about midway between two fully spaced joists.

Measuring and marking

Next, measure out the stud spacing, marking both plates at the same time. Start at a corner of the sole plate, measure in 1¹/₂ inches, and strike a squared line. Mark an X in this slot; this is the first corner stud. Measure along the plate 15¹/₄ inches and strike another squared line; move along 1¹/₂ inches and strike another. Make an X between the lines to show the location of that stud. Now measure along the plate in 16-inch increments, from stud centers or stud faces to either side (FIG. 26-1). Mark out each slot, so there will be no possibility of fastening a stud on the wrong side of a single mark. The spacing between the last and next-to-last stud can (and probably will) be less than your selected spacing (16 or 24 inches), but should never be more. Add extra studs whenever necessary. If the wall is to be set on concrete or concrete block, lay out the anchor bolt locations and drill holes for them that are about 1/4 inch greater in diameter than the bolts.

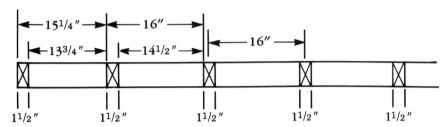

26-1   The starting layout for the studs on the plates of a wall frame.

The method you use to make the stud/bolt layout doesn't matter. Carpenter's tape measures have 16-inch center markings on them, and are easy to use. Some professionals use a premarked pattern board made of a straight piece of 1×2 or something similar that can be set next to a pair of plates. Precise spacing measurements can then be transferred with a square to a pair of plates in just a few seconds. You could even use a good yardstick; the key is accuracy.

Cutting the stock

Next select a straight, flat piece of stud stock and trim it to length as necessary. Use this piece as a pattern to cut all the remaining studs. When not in use, store it out of the sun and moisture. Do not use each cut stud as a cutting pattern for the next one, because you'll eventually discover (usually after you nail them up) that each one is a tad longer than the last.

Nailing

Turn the plates up on edge and separate them, and set the corner studs between them. Face nail through the plates into the stud ends with a pair of 16d nails each. Set all the remaining studs and nail them up in the same way (FIG. 26-2). If two sections of plate must be spliced, cut a length of 2× to fit over the joint and between two studs. Nail this piece to the plate with several 10d nails (FIG. 26-3), and through the studs into the ends of the splice plate with a pair of 16d nails. The finished frame is the simplest form of stud wall frame, typical of a blank interior partition wall that fits between two others.

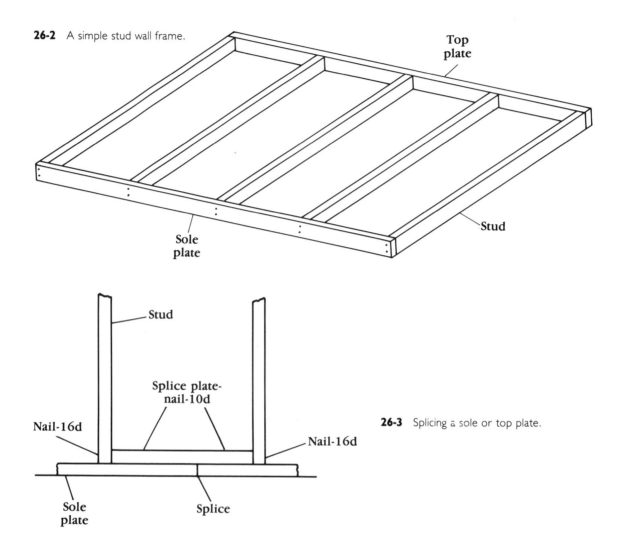

26-2 A simple stud wall frame.

Top plate

Stud

Sole plate

Stud

Splice plate-nail-10d

Nail-16d

Nail-16d

26-3 Splicing a sole or top plate.

Sole plate

Splice

FRAMING CORNERS AND INTERSECTIONS

All walls, whether interior or exterior, end at a corner. The simplest is an open end that forms a corner of the wall itself. Just double the end stud (FIG. 26-4), securing one to the other with a series of 10d nails staggered about every 10 inches. When you set exterior walls, the short walls always go between the long ones. The short walls end in single studs, as in the simple frame just discussed. The long walls, however, end in double studs that can be set in various ways; the purpose is to provide bearing and nailing surfaces for the later application of both inner and outer sheathings.

The most common and easiest arrangement is to place a stud 1½ inches inboard from the long-wall corner stud, leaving a 1-inch bearing surface on the inside corner. Some builders leave the space between the

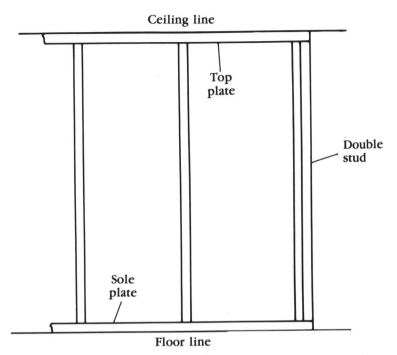

Ceiling line

Top plate

Double stud

Sole plate

Floor line

26-4   When a full-height wall frame terminates in the open and connects with no other framing, double the free-end stud.

studs open, others install two studs to make a solid three-stud corner post. The first method doesn't make a rigid enough mounting surface, the second is wasteful. The best bet is to nail scrap 2-×-4 cut-off ends, three or four of them, between the two studs (FIG. 26-5). Nail each block to a stud with three or four 10d nails, then nail the second stud to the blocks. Or, slip the blocks between two already nailed-up studs and nail them in place.

Other corner combinations, less popular but used by some builders, are shown in FIG. 26-6. These methods can be used for either inside or outside corners.

In conventional framing, extra studs must also be set wherever a partition wall intersects with either an interior or exterior wall (FIG. 26-7). There are two common practices. One is to space a pair of studs 1½ inches apart with scrap 2-×-4 blocks nailed between them, as in a corner post. The post must be set so that its vertical centerline coincides with that of the intersecting wall. This arrangement allows ½ inch of bearing surface at each inside corner, which is rather scant and must be carefully controlled. The second method takes more material but allows a full 1½ inches of bearing surface at the inner corners. Space a pair of studs 3½ inches apart by nailing a third stud edgewise between them and flush with the inside face of the wall frame. Fasten with 10d nails about 12

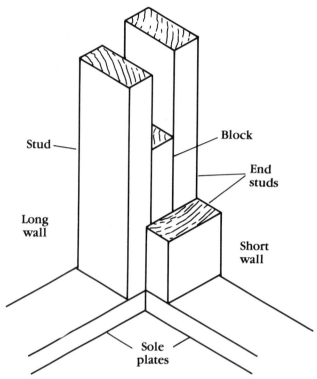

Stud

Block

End studs

Long wall

Short wall

Sole plates

26-5 One of the easiest and most common arrangements for constructing stud wall outside corners.

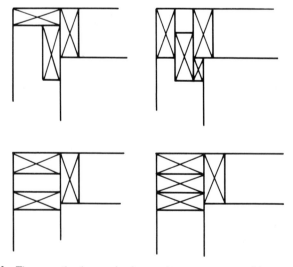

26-6 These methods can also be used to construct outside corners.

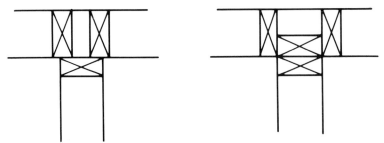

26-7   Two common methods of arranging wall intersections.

inches apart, through the side studs and into the edges of the center stud. Align the vertical centerlines of the post and intersecting wall.

There is another method of joining wall frames that requires fewer studs. The system, although not yet widely used, is less wasteful than the other methods, but equally effective and simple to use. It incorporates floating joints at the inside corners that minimize cracking and allow installation of more thermal insulation. This method is based on the installation of drywall or backup clips, small metal devices that clip to the drywall edges and are in turn nailed to an adjacent corner or end stud (FIG. 26-8). Intersection posts are eliminated completely, and corner posts

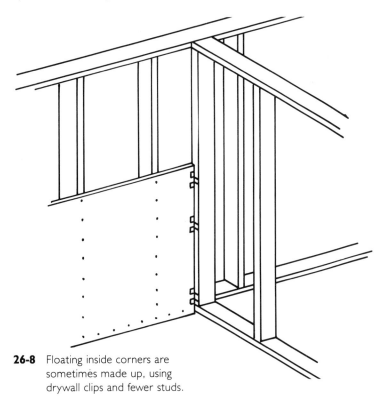

26-8   Floating inside corners are sometimes made up, using drywall clips and fewer studs.

are made up of only two studs with no spacers. Follow the manufacturer's instructions for installation. This method is approved by model building codes and recommended by the National Association of Home Builders.

ERECTING THE WALL FRAME

Erecting a completed stud wall frame is simple enough. Some builders prefer to put on the exterior sheathing first, others do not. Handling and alignment is generally easier with the frame alone, though. Either way, choose a time when the wind isn't blowing heavily. On a wood platform floor, in the case of an exterior wall, you can nail some scrap pieces to the outside of the sill to protrude above the floor level and act as stops. Anchor bolts serve the same purpose on concrete slab floors. Scoot the frame into position and line it up with corners, edges, anchor bolts, intersection posts, etc. Have some long braces right handy for first or other temporarily freestanding walls. Tilt the frame up, being careful not to overbalance and lose it in the opposite direction, and thump it into approximate position.

Nail up the braces (FIG. 26-9) and fasten the sole plate using either 16d nails spaced every 16 inches, or anchor nuts. At corners or intersections,

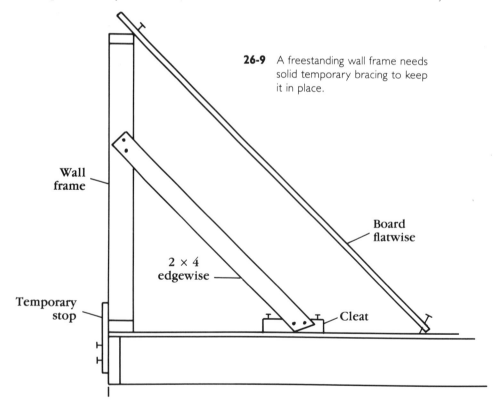

26-9 A freestanding wall frame needs solid temporary bracing to keep it in place.

Wall frame

Board flatwise

2 × 4 edgewise

Temporary stop

Cleat

carefully plumb and square adjoining frames as required. Nail the studs and posts together. Use 10d nails for 3-inch thicknesses, 16d for greater thickness. Make sure all free ends and long expanses of framework are well braced before leaving them.

Normal practice is to construct all the wall frames on a given floor level and secure them in place. The tops should all be level and matching; each section should be plumb and squared up; each length of wall must be straight, with no bows in or out; all intersections and corners should be firmly tied together; and all corners should be at right or other planned angles. Then the upper member of the top plate, the cap plate, can be installed.

INSTALLING CAP PLATES

When installing the cap plates, use straight pieces, preferably the full length of each wall section or distance from corner to intersection. Start with partition walls, and set the cap plate in a cross lap over the adjacent lower top plate member (interior or exterior), with the end flush with its outer edge (FIG. 26-10). Lap all the corner joints in similar fashion. Fasten the cap to the top plate with 16d nails spaced 16 inches apart.

There is a variation on this arrangement that can be safely employed in partition wall frames that are nonload-bearing only. You can dispense with the doubled top plate. Instead, cut the single top plate so that the

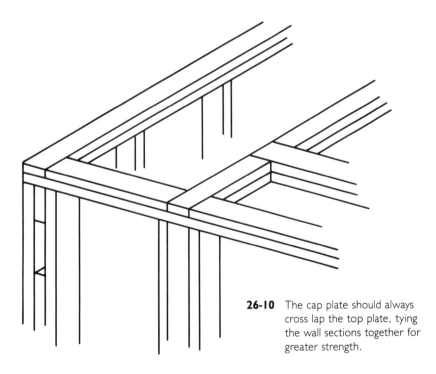

26-10 The cap plate should always cross lap the top plate, tying the wall sections together for greater strength.

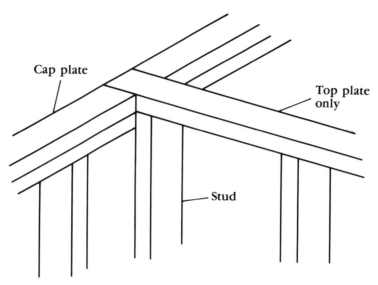

26-11   A nonload-bearing partition top plate can be cross lapped with the cap plate of other walls, and its cap plate dispensed with.

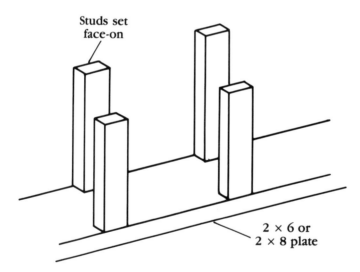

26-12   A common method of building an extra-thick partition to accommodate pipes or ductwork.

ends overhang the endmost studs by 3 1/2 inches, and trim all the wall studs 1 1/2 inches longer. Thus, these top plate ends will lie on top of the top plate on the mating load-bearing walls (FIG. 26-11) instead of flush with them. Double the rest of the top plate with a cap in the usual way.

CONSTRUCTING EXTRA-THICK PARTITION WALLS

Occasionally extra-thick walls are needed, usually in interior partition walls, to accommodate a soil stack or ductwork. Sometimes a standard 2-×-6 frame will do the trick. If more space is needed, another possibility is to set a double run of 2-×-4 frames back to back, or separate them to whatever extent is necessary. Yet another construction, which requires less material, consists of setting a 2-×-8 or wider sole and top plate and installing 2-×-4 studs, usually on 24-inch centers (FIG. 26-12). Because of their bulk and awkwardness, these walls are generally built upright and in place, piece by piece.

Chapter **27**

Window and door framing

Only a few walls in any given house design are blank, with no openings at all. That means the simple stud wall frame described in the previous chapter must be modified. Most exterior wall frames require framed openings for doors and windows, and many interior walls include doorways. Other openings might be needed, too, for pass-throughs, vent fans, fireplaces, or ventilation louvers. Creating openings in a wall frame means losing some structural strength and rigidity by virtue of deleting part of the studding. To replace that, and to provide support for whatever is to be set into the opening, some auxiliary members must be added to the wall frame. Some are structural, some serve as nailers. There are several variations, depending upon job details.

PLANNING THE OPENINGS

In all cases, you can realize savings in time and materials by planning for as many openings as possible to be bounded on at least one side by a common stud. Each opening, called a *rough opening* or *r.o.*, should have specific dimensions that are slightly greater than the size of whatever unit will be placed in the opening. For windows and some units like vent louver sets, exhaust fans, patio door units, or mechanical equipment, the rough opening sizes for best results and easiest installation should be the ones specified by the manufacturer. Rough opening sizes might also be specified for doors by their manufacturers, but stock doors (unlike windows) tend to be more generic and mostly of standard dimensions. A useful rule of thumb for a door r.o. is the door width plus 2½ inches and the height plus 3 inches. However, this depends partly upon the dimensions of the stock used to make the door or window frames and other parts.

DOOR FRAMING

In traditional door framing (FIG. 27-1) a rough opening is bounded by a trimmer stud on each side, attached to a common stud on each side, with a header above. One or more cripple studs are set between the top of the header and the bottom of the top plate. A window opening has much the same layout, with trimmers and common studs at each side and a header and cripples above. To square out the opening, a rough sill runs across the bottom of the opening, supported by one or more cripple studs.

To frame a door opening, start with a common stud at one side or the other. This can be one on the regular centering module, or you might have to insert one. Install another common stud with its face the r.o. width plus 3 inches (trimmer stud thicknesses) from the first. Cut a pair of trimmer studs to length, equal to the r.o. height minus 1$\frac{1}{2}$ inches (sole plate thickness) and fasten them to the inner faces of the full studs. Use 16d nails staggered on 24-inch centers, clinched over on the backside.

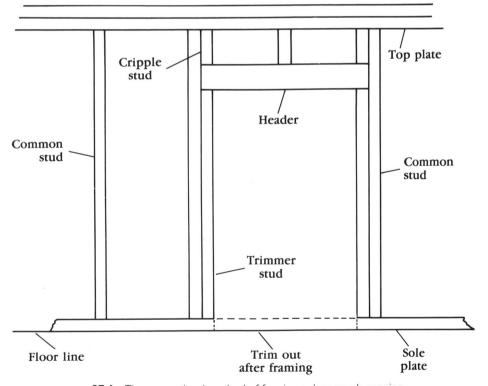

27-1 The conventional method of framing a door rough opening.

Note: Many carpenters prefer to stagger 10d nails about 12 to 16 inches apart.

Make up a header by cutting a pair of 2×4s to r.o. width and inserting shims between them to gain the full wall thickness (FIG. 27-2). Set the header atop the trimmers, and fasten it with four 16d nails through each side stud into the header ends. Cut a cripple to fit between the header and the top plate, center it, and toenail it with four 8d nails at each end. Two cripples are often used above openings greater than 2 feet 6 inches. Cripples may also be on the regular stud spacing pattern.

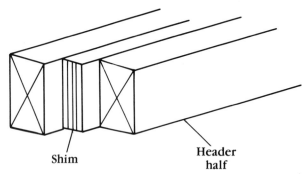

Shim   Header
                                            half

27-2 A header consisting of two 2 × 4s on edge with a shim between them to match the width of the wall frame.

WINDOW FRAMING

To frame a window opening in the conventional way (FIG. 27-3), follow the same pattern. Set the common studs first, then attach the trimmers to them. If the window is no wider than 3 feet 6 inches in a single-story house, or 3 feet if there is a second story above, you can build in the same kind of header as for a door. For widths greater than this, refer to TABLE 27-1.

The makeup of the header is the same for all sizes. With the header set, fasten the rough sill in position 1¹/₂ inches below the bottom of the

Table 27-1   Dimensions for Residential Construction

Max. Span (Feet)	Header Size (Inches)
3.0	Two 2×4
4.0	Two 2×6
6.0	Two 2×8
7.5	Two 2×10
9.0	Two 2×12

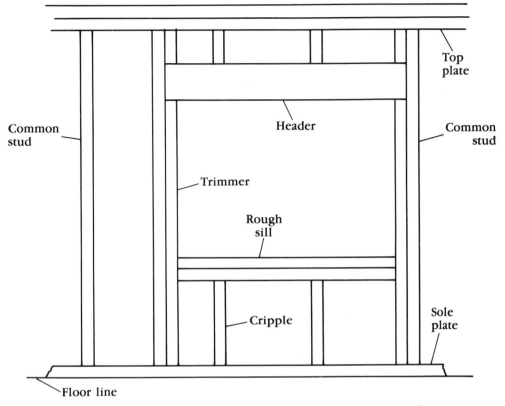

27-3 The conventional arrangement for framing a window rough opening.

r.o. Reverse toenail back through each side of each trimmer into the sill end using 16d nails. Fit cripple studs above the header and below the sill, set on the regular center spacing. Facenail the lower cripples through the sill and sole with a pair of 16d nails at each point. Toenail the upper cripples with four 8d nails at each end. Last, install the rough sill cap on top of the sill. Nail through the ends with 16d nails and face nail down into the sill with 10d nails.

VARIATIONS

The short cripple studs above windows in particular are difficult and time consuming to install. Wherever the spacing between the top of the r.o. and the bottom of the top plate works out (and you can usually plan it that way), you can install a solid header (FIG. 27-4). This can be made up in a number of ways, and is designed to fill the entire space between the window or door framing and the top plate, eliminating the cripples.

Another variation makes the sill easier to install (FIG. 27-5). Cut the trimmer studs to reach only to the bottom of the rough sill. Place the

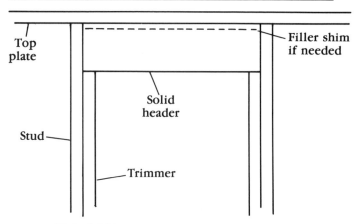

27-4 Solid header installation above a door opening.

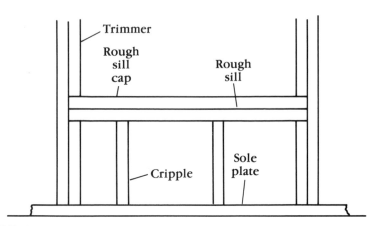

27-5 In this construction the rough sill and cap are installed before the trimmers.

rough sill on top and secure it to the trimmer ends with a pair of 16d nails each. Put in the lower cripples the same way. Install the rough sill cap, then fill the area between it and the headers with continuations of the trimmers.

Conventional framing practices have in the past made little distinction between load-bearing and nonload-bearing walls as far as rough openings are concerned. However, new methods do recognize the difference, and there are some relatively recent procedures that you can safely follow, provided local codes permit.

In a load-bearing wall, there is no structural load on a window rough sill, so this can be a single member instead of doubled (FIG. 27-6). Nor need any of the lower cripples be doubled, as they sometimes are. In a nonload-bearing wall the trimmers can be eliminated, as can the rough sill

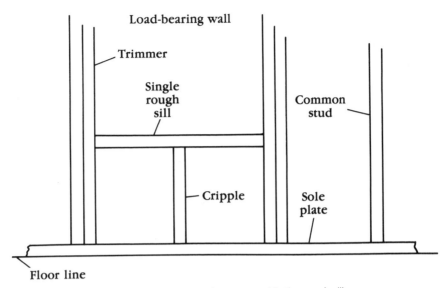

27-6 This variation does away with the rough sill cap.

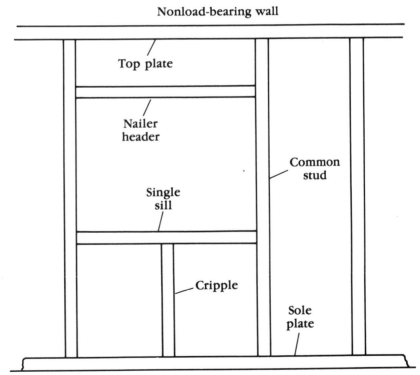

27-7 This method of framing a window rough opening is considered adequate in a non-load-bearing wall.

cap, and the header can be a single member laid flat. Both the header and the rough sill are attached directly to the side studs (FIG. 27-7).

There is also another, easier method of installing headers, either door or window. In a load-bearing wall, size headers as usual, but install them tight to the bottom of the top plate, with the trimmer studs directly supporting them. Then attach a single subheader across the top of the r.o. (FIG. 27-8). This merely serves as a nailer for the window or door trim and the wall sheathing.

Load-bearing wall

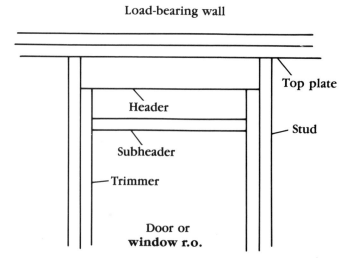

27-8 In a load-bearing wall the header for either a door or window opening can be moved up against the top plate, supported by the trimmers, with a subheader installed for nailing.

There are two problems with long headers. The first involves adequately supporting the load above. That and the required size of a solid header leads to the second problem: A large header means lots of shrinkage and the potential for warping or twisting, which cracks open drywall or plaster, causing problems with the fit and operation of windows and doors. One solution is to install conventional trussed headers built along the lines of those shown in FIG. 27-9, made up of 2×4s and 1×4s or 1×6s. They are a lot of work, but they do the job.

Stressed skin or box headers are a bit easier to make and will carry even greater loads. They also do not shrink, twist, or bow much, if at all. These can be made up as individual units or beams and sized to whatever width, height, and length is required. Use single 2×4s for shorter headers, doubled for longer ones, and space them apart with short sections of the same. Cover both sides with 1/2-inch-thick plywood, the face grain set lengthwise (FIG. 27-10). Glue the panels with construction adhesive and fasten with 6d ringshank or 8d box nails every 6 inches to each member.

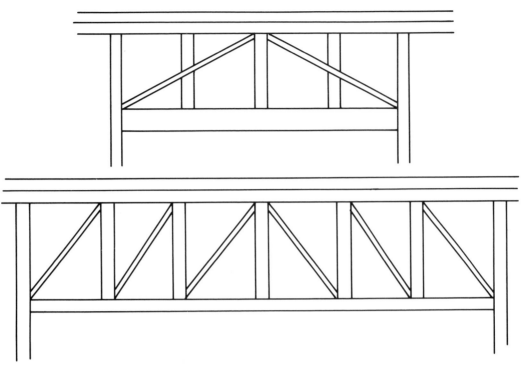

27-9 Truss headers can be installed over wide load-bearing window or door openings.

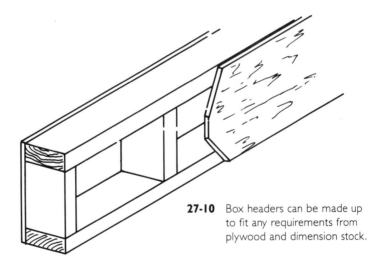

27-10 Box headers can be made up
to fit any requirements from
plywood and dimension stock.

An alternative method is a built-in variety using a single header atop the r.o. with cripples between it and the bottom of the top plate, spaced at 24 inches on centers. The plywood skin is glued and nailed to the header and both the top and cap plates, as well as the cripples, taking the place of

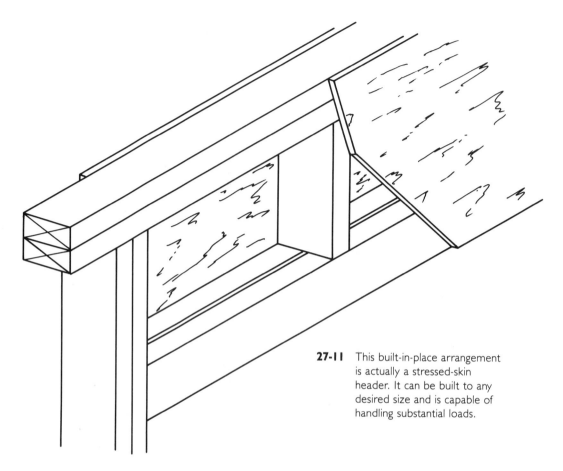

27-11 This built-in-place arrangement is actually a stressed-skin header. It can be built to any desired size and is capable of handling substantial loads.

¹/₂-inch drywall (FIG. 27-11). Nailing space must be left on the side studs for the drywall material to be applied later, or a separate nailer can be installed.

Openings for other items can be similarly framed. The sides of the openings in load-bearing walls should consist of studs with trimmers, headers above, and support cripples. Single members are sufficient for any small openings, as between two standard-spaced studs in any kind of wall, and for larger openings as well in nonload-bearing partitions.

There is another point to keep in mind with regard to all wall openings. Even though a particular framing method is sturdy enough to do its required job in complete safety, that does not necessarily mean the finished wall will be stiff and vibration-free. If you want walls that will never resound and windows that will never shiver when you slam a door, as well as totally trouble-free operation of both doors and windows, you'll have to have heavy, braced framing—as well as solid construction and quality materials elsewhere.

Chapter **28**

Wall blocking, bracing, nailers, and ties

Several minor components common to frame wall constructions are: blocking, braces, nailing strips or nailers, and ties. They are variably necessary, depending upon structure design details, and some are required by code in some instances and in some locales. Many of these items are frequently deleted in cheap construction, and sometimes they are ignored or sometimes forgotten in the rush of construction, only to be incorporated later at extra cost and effort. Good building practice suggests that each be given due consideration.

BLOCKING

At one time blocking was regularly installed in good construction. These days continuous wall blocking has been largely discontinued as a cost-saving measure. However, installing a line of blocking at the midpoint of all walls, both interior and exterior, will help to stiffen the walls and minimize twisting and bowing of the studs before the sheathings are applied.

The process consists of installing lengths of 2×4 (or 2×6 in that type of construction) between the studs about 4 feet above the floor. They can be staggered, which makes for easier nailing, or straight-line, which is a bit more effective. Fasten staggered blocks by face nailing through the studs and into the block ends, using two 16d nails at each point. For straight-line blocking, nail in the manner shown in FIG. 28-1.

There are other reasons to install this kind of blocking. Building and/ or fire codes in some locales require similar installations in certain parts of the structure. They serve as firestops in areas such as ceilings where the wall studs continue upward (FIG. 28-2). Where vertical planking is to be

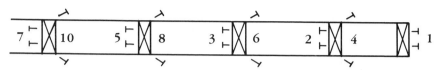

28-I Straight-line blocking can be installed between the wall studs most easily using this sequential method.

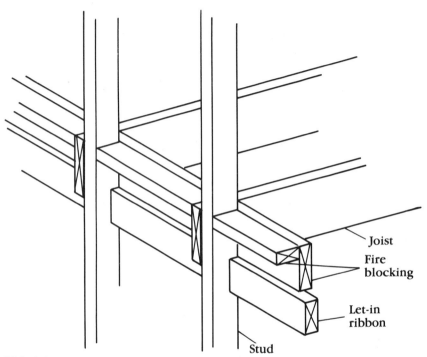

28-2 With balloon framing, and sometimes with platform framing, fire blocking is required to close off long airways.

installed, either as interior wall covering or exterior siding (board-and-batten, for example), install wall blocking. The blocks should be straight-line so that the nailing can also be done in straight lines. Install two rows in the frames of those walls, separating them roughly in thirds (FIG. 28-3).

Other uses for blocking occur at isolated points where backing or support will be needed for appliances or fixtures. Support for the back rim of a built-in bathtub is a typical example, as are wall-hung toilets or toilet tanks, shower fittings, anchoring points for grab rails in bathrooms or stairs and any other item whose exact position can be anticipated before the wall sheathing is put on. Where the loading factors are light, the blocking may consist of 1×4 or 1×6 nailed to cleats, which are in turn nailed to the stud faces (FIG. 28-4), all with 8d box or ring-shank nails. You

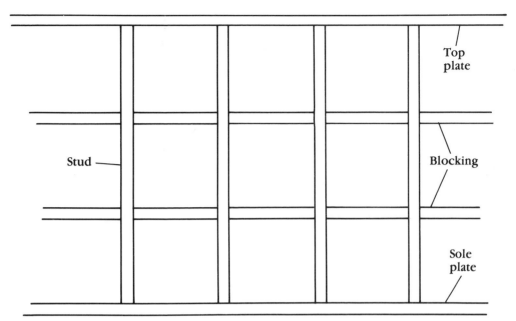

28-3 Two or three rows of straight-line blocking can be installed for nailing up vertical interior or exterior board finish.

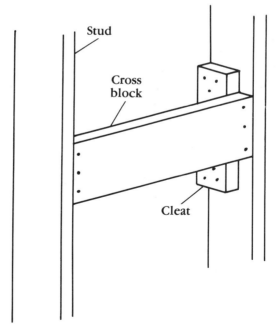

28-4 A cross block can be attached to cleats on the wall studs to provide a solid anchoring point for some article to be later installed, such as a bathroom grab rail.

can also block out useful storage areas in inside walls by positioning pairs of cross blocks between studs at appropriate locations (FIG. 28-5). These are great for medicine cabinets, canned goods, and such.

BRACING

Proper bracing of the exterior wall frames is crucial to the integrity of the structure and is required by all building codes. There are several ways to go about it. The first step in all cases is to make sure that the frame is perfectly in square. Depending on the method used, bracing may be accomplished with the frame still flat on the floor, or upright and nailed in its final location.

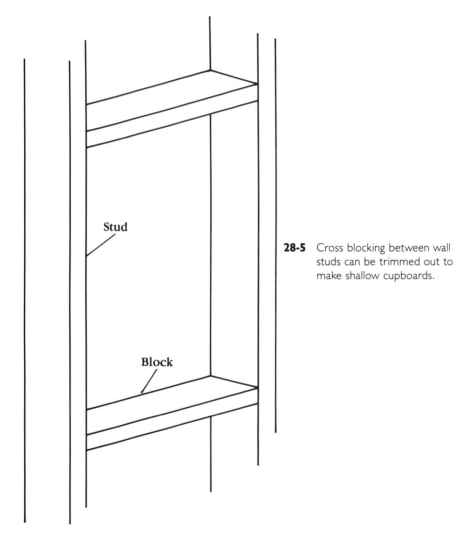

Stud

Block

28-5   Cross blocking between wall studs can be trimmed out to make shallow cupboards.

The traditional method, now largely abandoned because it takes a bit of time, is called *let-in* bracing (FIG. 28-6). Place a length of 1×4 at each corner, angled from the sole plate upward across at least three studs to the top of the top plate. This angle is not critical, and can be varied if necessary to clear window or door openings. Note, however, that where required by code, the angle typically must be between 45 and 60 degrees off horizontal. Tack the piece in place temporarily and mark each point of passing on the studs and plates. Remove the piece, set the shoe of your circular saw to a 3/4-inch cut depth, and cut the studs and plates at each mark. Knock the waste pieces out with a wood chisel and smooth the bottoms of the notches as necessary. Set the brace into the notches and fasten it with a pair of 8d nails at each bearing point.

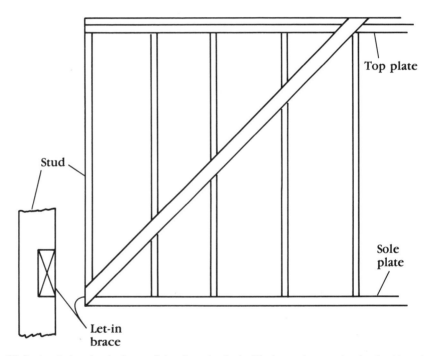

28-6   Let-in bracing is the traditional method of stiffening and strengthening load-bearing stud wall frames.

There are other bracing methods. An old favorite when board sheathing was popular was to apply the sheathing diagonally. This system still works. The boards can be square edged or tongue-and-groove, and must be at least 5/8 inch thick (actual). Or, you can apply sheets of plywood at the corners, 4 feet wide, with the face grain vertical. The minimum thickness for 16-inch stud spacing is 5/16 inch, 3/8 inch for 24-inch spacing.

Another possibility involves certain kinds of fiberboard sheathing. Apply a full 4-×-8-foot sheet vertically at each corner and nail with 11/2-

inch, 11-gauge roofing nails. Space these 3 inches apart around the perimeter and 6 inches at intermediate points. Certain types of rigid foam thermal insulation panels can be applied in a similar fashion; check current specifications and code requirements. Or, you might use 1/2-inch-thick gypsum sheathing or gypsum wallboard panels in 4-×-8-foot sheets. Again, check local codes.

NAILERS

Nailers are nothing more than strips of wood, usually 1×2 or 1×4, but occasionally heavier. They are fastened to the wall framework to provide a solid surface on which items may be attached after the wall sheathing/covering has been applied. To install nailers, a continuous horizontal ribbon might be let into the studs, much like let-in bracing, about 3 feet above the floor so that the top ends of wainscot planks can be easily nailed in place. Another example is a let-in ribbon of 1×4 to which wall-hung cabinets, towel or clothes racks, shower fittings, or similar items are attached (FIG. 28-7).

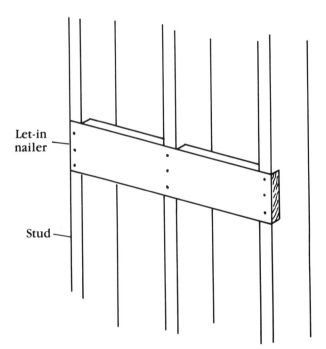

28-7 Let-in nailers can be installed across wall studs to support heavy articles like laundry tubs or toilet tanks.

One kind of nailer of particular importance is the one attached to the cap or top plate of a nonload-bearing wall that runs parallel with and in between a pair of joists. Of similar nature are the short nailers that must

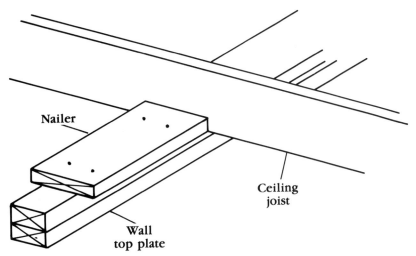

28-8 Wide nailers are often required atop wall top plates as ceiling attachment points.

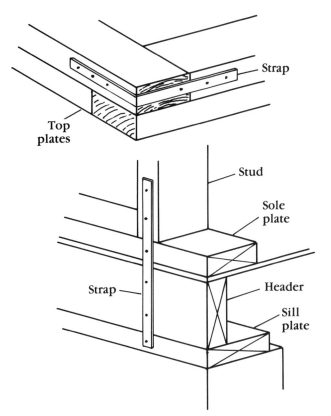

28-9 Steel strap and other types of ties and anchors can be used in a variety of ways to help strengthen a structure: at a cap plate (above), and from stud to sill (below).

be fastened to the top or cap plate of any wall, at right angles to the ceiling joists. Without these nailers (FIG. 28-8) there is no surface to which the ceiling edges can be attached. They should be attached solidly using canted 10d common or box nails or 8d ring-shank nails closely spaced on 1-×-6 stock. Use 16d nails for 2-×-6 stock (this is a sturdier arrangement).

TIES

Ties (FIG. 28-9) are a relatively recent innovation, and are being increasingly employed in a number of ways, particularly in regions where seismic shocks and/or high winds are common or periodically expectable. They may take the form of steel straps of various sizes, or steel framing anchors of different configurations. One technique is to bind all the top cap plate corners together with thin straight straps. Those same straps can be employed to lock the bottoms of studs across the sole plate and to the end or header joists on outside walls. Or they can run from outside stud edges up and over the plate and down onto the opposite stud edges in a secured loop. Framing anchors and hangers can be used in numerous ways, as in solidly connecting stud bottom ends to the sole plate.

Chapter **29**

Ceiling joist installation

*I*n a single-story house that features flat ceilings with an uninhabitable attic area above, and where roof trusses are not used, the next phase of construction involves installing ceiling joists. The purpose of these joists is to support the ceiling material, but they also tie opposite walls together, anchor intermediate partition walls, and help oppose roof rafter thrust.

JOIST SIZING AND SPACING

In this situation, ceiling joist size is often different than the first-floor floor joist size. Whenever possible the spacing on centers should not only be the same as the wall stud spacing, but the joists should actually be set directly over the studs. Nominal 2-inch-thick dimension stock is always used, typically construction grade. Joist width is determined by the span, the spacing between them, the wood species and specific grade, and the loads imposed, as well as by any local building code mandates. Selection can be made via the engineering route and appropriate span tables, as is done with floor joists (see Chapter 24).

You can also use a similar alternative method to the one described in that chapter: you can overbuild somewhat. Assume a low E and a low Fb and choose joist widths to suit the required spans. Commonly used loading factors for joists to which a drywall ceiling will be applied and for a roof slope that is 3 inches in 12 or less are 5 pounds dead and 10 pounds live weight. Where there might be some attic storage and the roof slope is greater than 3 inches in 12, and the ceiling drywall or plaster, those factors change to 10 pounds dead and 20 live. You will find both categories

Table 29-1   Safe Spans in Feet for Ceiling Joists*

Size	Low Slope Spacing		High Slope Spacing	
	16"	*24"*	*16"*	*24"*
2×4	9−0	7−6	7−0	6−0
2×6	14−0	12−0	11−0	9−6
2×8	18−0	16−0	14−6	12−6
2×10	23−6	20−6	18−6	16−6

*Low slope not exceeding 3-in-12: live load of 10 lbs./sq. ft. plus dead load of 5 lbs./sq. ft. High slope over 3-in-12: live load of 20 lbs./sq. ft. plus dead load of 10 lbs./sq. ft.

in TABLE 29-1, listing maximum safe ceiling joist spans. When making your selection, always size up a notch or drop back to the nearest half-foot, rather than the reverse. Also, make sure you meet local code requirements, if any. For odd designs, extra-heavy loading factors, or other peculiarities, consult an architect or builder.

SETTING THE JOISTS

Ceiling joists are usually set across the narrow dimension of the house or section. Even when they cross a supporting partition it's best if they are in one piece. This is a stronger arrangement and also does away with having to handle two or more pieces per total joist run and having to make splices. As with floor joists, they should always be set with the crown upward. Also, in nearly all designs the ceiling joists must have their outer, upper corners clipped off (FIG. 29-1), because they protrude upward above the rafter line. A good procedure to follow is to cut one joist to length for each particular configuration needed, determine the lie of the crown, and trim the one upper corner to align with the roof rafter angle. Use this piece as a pattern to cut all the remaining joists for that section, or for the entire structure if they are all the same, ascertaining the lie of the crown each time. Then when the joists are put in, they will automatically be correctly set.

Splicing

Although one-piece ceiling joists are best, in fact they frequently must be spliced because of the long lengths involved. You can do this in either of two ways. One is to overlap them at the bearing point (FIG. 29-2). Fasten each joist to the cap plate at each end using three 8d common nails. Secure the overlap with four 16d nails driven at an angle, with the protruding ends clinched over.

This method can throw one end of each lap-spliced joist out of line with the wall studs, which may be undesirable. Also, in some constructions, such as a gable roof design, each end of each joist should lie up against the side of a roof rafter, and this doesn't work out with lap-joined

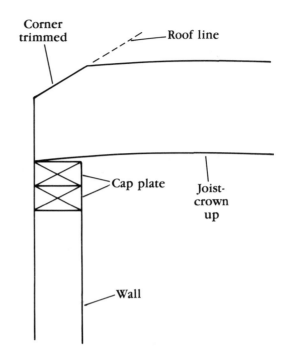

29-1 Often the upper corners of ceiling joists have to be clipped off to match and fit under the roof rafter line.

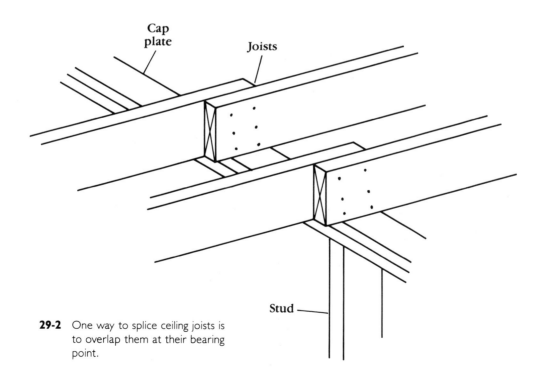

29-2 One way to splice ceiling joists is to overlap them at their bearing point.

joist sections. To get around the latter problem, fasten a nominal 2-inch-thick spacer block between the joist sections. Make the spacer about 12 inches long, and secure it to each joist member (or vice versa) with four 16d nails each, clinched over. Set the spacer block on the joist spacing centers, which will allow the joist ends to straddle the rafter position (FIG. 29-3). Again, there will doubtless be a misalignment with the wall studs, and it is more advantageous in many designs for the roof rafters to be aligned with the studs than with the ceiling joists.

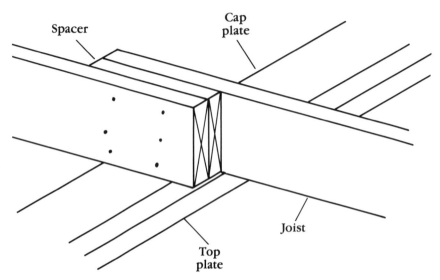

29-3   This method of splicing ceiling joists allows them to straddle and be secured to the rafters.

The straight-line method allows you to align joists with rafters and place each set centered over a wall stud. You must plan ahead a bit. Abut the joist ends over the partition centerline and toenail each to the cap plate with a pair of 8d nails. Then attach splice plates 2 feet long of similar stock to the joists, using four 16d nails angled and clinched at each end. Toenail these to the plate with a pair of 8d nails (FIG. 29-4).

Running joists in two directions

There are occasions when the best arrangement is to run the ceiling joists in two directions in order to take advantage of the narrowest dimensions and shortest spans. This means setting a joist parallel with and secured to a partition wall cap plate. Its inner face should lie flush with the inner edge of the plate; fasten it with 10d nails toenailed about every 16 inches. Then set the other joists at right angles (FIG. 29-5), fastening them to the end joist with three 16d nails each.

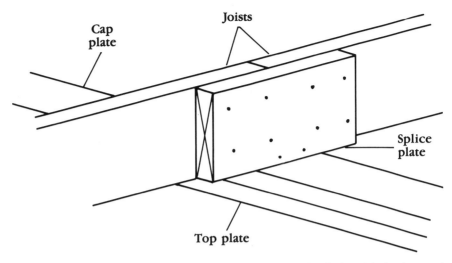

29-4 Ceiling joists can be spliced together at their bearing points by butt jointing them and attaching a plate to one or both sides, as well as to the bearing member.

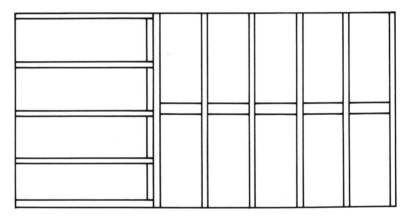

29-5 Ceiling joists can be set in two different directions in order to take advantage of shorter spans.

INTERMEDIATE SUPPORTS IN LARGE ROOMS

Sometimes the span from wall to wall is too long for individual joists, such as in a large living room or the increasingly popular "great" room. Intermediate support must then be provided by a flush beam.

Flush beams

Flush beams are typically built up in the same fashion as a floor-support girder: of two, three, or even four lengths of 2× material spliced and nailed together with 20d nails staggered on 32-inch centers. An alternative is a commercial glue-laminated beam. Either should be engineered for the job at hand.

The beam is set atop the wall cap plate at the required intermediate point, supported by a similar set of wall studs and fastened with four 16d toenails at each end. Sometimes the joists are set on ledger strips attached to each face of the beam. Fasten the ledger to the beam with 10d nails staggered on 12-inch centers, and toenail the joists to the beam with five 8d nails. A better arrangement is to use metal joist hangers fastened according to the manufacturer's recommendations, with a steel strap placed across the top of the beam to bind the joist ends firmly (FIG. 29-6).

Another method consists of setting one or more exposed beams with the joists resting upon them and secured in the usual way. Instead of resting atop the wall cap plate, the beam ends are supported within the walls with their tops flush with the cap plate surface (FIG. 29-7). Often more and/ or larger beams than required by the loading factors or spans are installed, for the decorative impact. The beams may be built up from ordinary dimension stock and then cased and trimmed with finish material. They

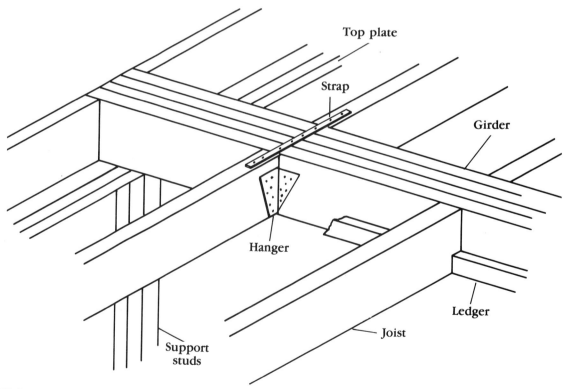

29-6   The strap and hanger arrangement is a good method of joining joists to a girder in a flush fit. Toenailing over a ledger plate is a second choice.

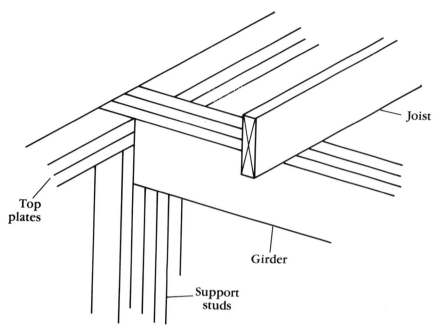

29-7 This method mounts the girders in wall pockets, and the joists rest atop the girder.

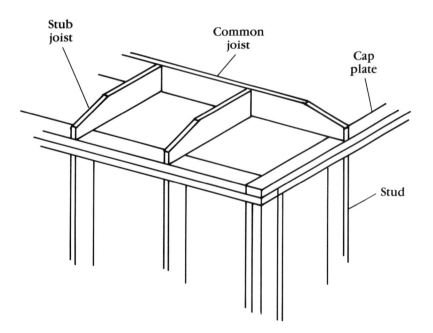

29-8 Sometimes stub joists must be installed like this under a low-slope roof, to provide adequate bearing for the ceiling close to the wall.

may also be finished glue-laminated beams or built-up plywood and block spacer constructions suitable for finishing. The ceiling material is applied to the joists between the beams, often with the help of nailers.

STUB JOISTS

In low-slope roof designs there might be no room for a ceiling joist running close to and parallel with the roof edge, leaving a too-wide gap between the wall and the last joist in the row. In this case, stub joists must be installed to provide sufficient attachment points for the ceiling (FIG. 29-8). Place them on 16-inch centers, running at right angles from the last full joist to the cap plate. Secure them with three 16d nails into the tee ends, and toenail with three 8d nails at the cap plate end.

Openings are usually not required in ceiling frames of this sort. Small ones, such as to admit passage of a metal appliance chimney, need only be blocked between a pair of joists with short members of the same material. Similarly, small hatchway openings to permit access to an attic crawl space, often located in a closet or hallway, don't require doubled headers. Larger openings such as might be needed for a sizable masonry chimney or a disappearing stairway should be framed in the same way as in a floor frame: with doubled joists and headers.

Chapter **30**

Second floor/attic considerations

*I*f a partial or full-height second story is part of the plan, or whenever an attic space will be inhabited or used for storage, the construction details for installing ceiling joists are different than in a single-story, no-attic design. One major difference is in the joist selection, because the loading factors are different. The two-story frame must act as a combination floor and ceiling joist system.

As with a first-story frame or a ceiling joist system, the joist size, spans, wood species, and spacing all can be determined through the engineering process. This can also be done empirically, on the basis of prior actual experience. For the owner-builder, the easiest way is to refer to TABLE 30-1.

The spans listed allow a substantial margin of safety because they are predicated upon stock with low *E* and *Fb* ratings (see Chapter 24). The spans will be governed by the relative locations of the outside walls and the partitions, and the spacing should be the one you have already selected for other building sections. The wood species will be whatever is locally supplied for joist purposes. Select appropriate joist widths for the spans involved, and if you want extra-solid, extra-stiff flooring go up one size. Use 30-pound live and 10-pound dead loads for a floored attic, or for rooms (or areas) that will be exclusively sleeping quarters. Use 40-pound live and 10-pound dead loads for joists beneath all rooms or areas that will be used for other purposes, such as a second-floor sitting room. And in any event, be guided by local building codes, which might require framing for heavier loads.

Table 30-1   Safe Spans in Feet for Floor/Ceiling Joists*

Size	Active Areas Spacing		Inactive Areas Spacing	
	16"	*24"*	*16"*	*24"*
2×6	8−6	7−6	7−6	6−6
2×8	11−0	9−6	10−0	8−6
2×10	14−0	12−6	13−0	11−0
2×12	17−0	15−0	15−6	13−6

*Loading for inactive areas is 30 pounds live and 10 pounds dead per square foot. Loading for active areas is 40 pounds live plus 10 pounds dead per square foot.

JOIST INSTALLATION

Unlike a simple ceiling joist system, this framework is installed with header and end joists, as in a first-floor frame. These perimeter members are called *bands* or *band joists*. Stand them on edge with their outer faces flush with the outside edges of the first-floor wall top plate and toenail them using 16d nails on 16-inch centers, alternate sides. Then set the common joists in the same way as for joists in a first floor or simple ceiling frame (FIG. 30-1). Fasten them by toenailing into the cap plate with

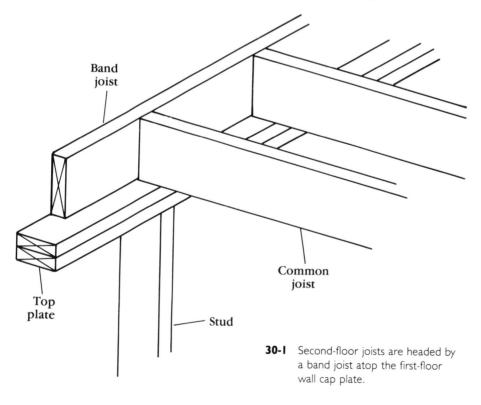

Band joist

Common joist

Top plate

Stud

30-1   Second-floor joists are headed by a band joist atop the first-floor wall cap plate.

three 8d nails and face nailing through the band into the joist ends with three 16d nails.

As with the simple ceiling frame, combination ceiling/floor joists are usually set across the long walls and parallel with the short ones. When common sense dictates that some of the joists be run at right angles to others in order to take advantage of a short span, they are installed just as for a simple ceiling. The last joist in a row is secured to a partition top plate and acts as a header for another series of perpendicular joists.

Sometimes a partition runs parallel with the joists and lies between them. In that case, nail cross blocks between the two joists—2×4s are fine—flush with the bottom edges and set every 16 inches (FIG. 30-2). Face nail through the joist into the block ends with a pair of 16d nails at each point. Then, after making sure that the partition is plumb and straight, face nail down through the blocks and into the cap plate of the partition. Use a pair of 16d nails at each bearing.

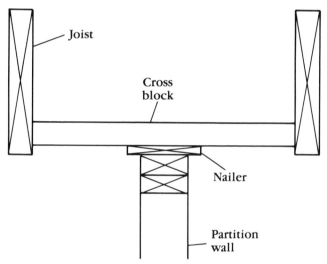

30-2 A first-floor wall frame running parallel with and in between second-floor joists is secured to cross blocks installed every 16 inches between the joists.

SECOND-FLOOR OVERHANG

Some house designs call for a shallow second floor overhang; the garrison style is one example, bay windows constitute another. Without special engineering and construction, such an overhang can extend as much as 4 feet as a practical maximum, but most second-floor projections are considerably less than that: typically 18 to 24 inches at most. The interior unsupported length of the joists should be about three times that of the exterior: 2 feet outside, 6 feet inside. When the joists lie at right angles to the exterior wall, run them across the cap plate directly above first-floor studs (FIG. 30-3). Strap-anchor or otherwise solidly secure the interior ends, and toenail to the cap plate with three 8d nails at each bearing point.

When the joists run parallel with the exterior wall, double the interior attachment joist and install lookout joists set over the first-floor wall studs (FIG. 30-4). Fasten the inboard ends with steel framing anchors, preferably the stirrup type mounted upside down to counteract the cantilever thrust. Fasten a band joist to the outer ends in either case by face nailing with three 16d nails into each cantilevered joist end.

FRAMING OPENINGS

As with the frame for the first floor, all small openings (between two joists) can be framed by blocking with single headers of the same size as the joists. All larger openings should have doubled headers and trimmers. Often the same kind of subflooring is installed as well, but just as often there is reason to select a different material or method, depending upon what is to be installed in the way of finish flooring. For example, 1/2-inch-thick plywood is satisfactory under a 3/4-inch-thick oak strip finish flooring, but not under sheet vinyl. Boards or cut-off scraps of plywood could be used in a low storage attic. In half-stories or any other area where the

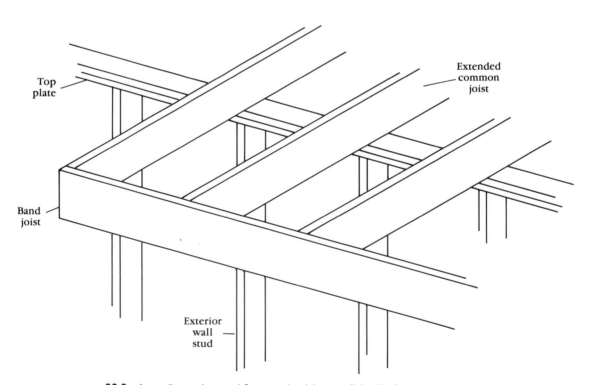

30-3 A cantilevered second-floor section lying parallel with the common joists.

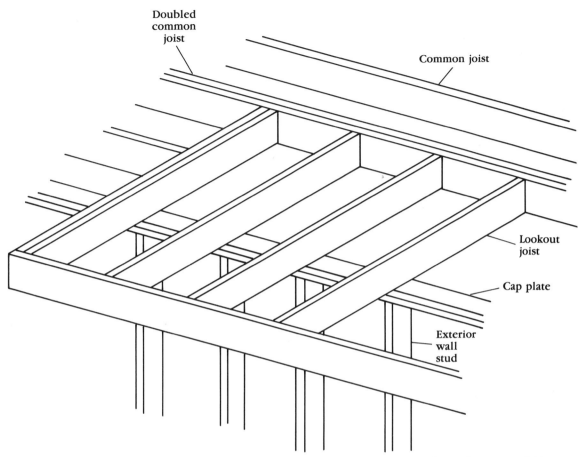

30-4 A cantilevered second-floor section with lookout joists running at right angles to the common joists.

flooring extends only to kneewalls or low roof points, blocking should be installed between the joists to support the subflooring edges. Otherwise, installation procedures are the same as for a first-floor platform.

Chapter **31**

Upper-level wall framing

*T*he details of framing walls for the second or any other upper level of a house don't vary much from those for the first-floor walls. The materials and procedures are the same, although the shapes and sizes might be a bit different. There are four kinds of frames to consider: full-height walls, stem walls, endwalls, and kneewalls.

These frames are secured by nailing them directly to ceiling or ceiling/floor joists and/or blocking, either directly or through a subflooring material. When an upper-level partition frame lies parallel to and between joists, it needs more support than just a subflooring beneath it. If the partition is load-bearing, an auxiliary joist—doubled if the loading warrants it—should be introduced beneath the partition as a bearing surface. If the partition is nonload-bearing, the same arrangement can be used, but a series of nailing blocks fastened between joists every 16 inches should suffice.

FULL-HEIGHT WALLS

Full-height walls enclose and partition upper-level living quarters where all the ceilings are at least 7 feet 6 inches high. This area might consist of a complete second or higher story, or might lie over only a portion of the first-level structure. Either way, the walls are framed in the same pattern as first-floor walls, including window and door framing, blocking, bracing, and other details.

Often as not, these walls are framed on the floor platform, then tilted into place as usual. If so, it's a good idea to nail temporary restraints—scrap ends of 2×4s work fine—to the outside of the band joist. This keeps the bottom end of exterior frames from scooting over the edge (FIG. 31-1). Also, most builders take care to nail props to the frames before tilting them all the way up. Then, with the anchoring spots made ready ahead of time, outside wall sections can be quickly tied off. Another safety measure is to wrap a rope or two around the top plate and secure or simply hold the opposite ends so that the frame can't go beyond the upright position. Once an upper-level wall goes over the edge, it's gone!

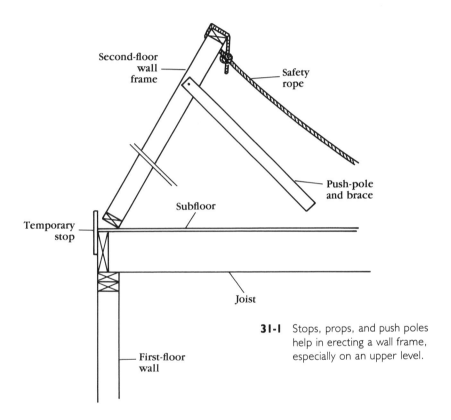

31-1 Stops, props, and push poles help in erecting a wall frame, especially on an upper level.

An alternative method of constructing the frames of exterior walls is to first lay out the sole plate, all marked for stud locations, and face nail it in place with one 16d nail every 16 inches. Then build up the corner posts and toenail them to the sole as usual, and install temporary props to keep them upright. Next, attach a top plate between the corners. Finally, start filling in with studs and rough opening frames. All these members are put together in the usual way, except that the bottom ends of the studs are toenailed to the sole plate with four 8d nails each. This method eliminates the danger of losing a whole frame over the side. However, it also requires working right next to the edge of the upper-level floor platform, which can be even more dangerous.

Partition wall frames are typically built after the exterior wall frames are in place, but this depends upon how much open floor space is available to use for assembling frames. One method that is sometimes advantageous is to make up all or most of the frames—this can even be done on the ground—and stockpile them, then move them all into position in one effort.

STEM WALLS

Stem or stub walls are simply abbreviated full walls. They may be short, individual frames—or if exterior walls, they may be extensions of the framework below. For example, a design might include a stem wall only 3 feet high at the rear of a two-plane roof in a modified saltbox arrangement (FIG. 31-2). Assuming a first-floor wall height of 8 feet, that frame could be built to a height of about 12 feet (exact dimensions would vary), with the

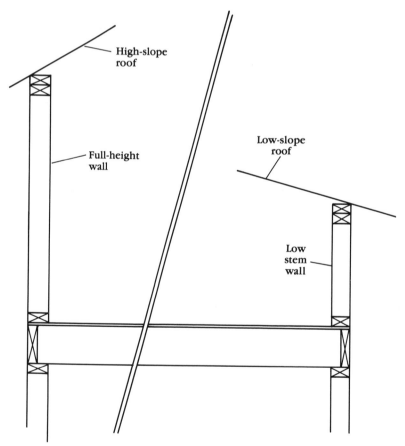

31-2   In this arrangement the rear stem wall has been built by the conventional platform framing method. It could also be framed straight through from the lower floor.

ceiling/floor frame attached at the 8-foot level. Or, the first-floor frames could be built in the usual way. Then a stem-wall frame 3 feet high would be attached to the upper-level band joist directly above it.

Partition walls can also be stem or partial walls, and the framing is done in the same way as for full walls. An example would be a wall frame running parallel with the rafters in an upper half-story, perhaps to close off a bedroom, bathroom, or closet (FIG. 31-3).

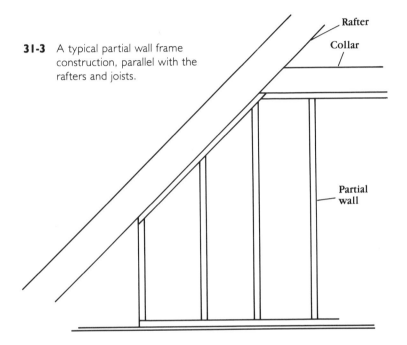

31-3   A typical partial wall frame construction, parallel with the rafters and joists.

KNEEWALLS

Kneewalls are stem walls of a particular sort. Typically they are found in story-and-a-half designs like Cape Cod houses, running at right angles to the rafters and floor joists and closing off the under-eaves area. There are several ways to construct them, and they may be simple nonload-bearing divider partitions or help to support some of the roof load. In some cases they serve as rafter supports where a two-plane roof section changes slope. The height of a kneewall for general use is considered to be 5 feet minimum. However, where headroom is not required a kneewall can be lower, and they are sometimes built as low as 3 feet.

One of the simplest constructions is to run 2-×-4 studs from the top edges of the joists to the side of each accompanying rafter. Toenail into the joist tops with four 8d nails each. Face nail into the rafters with four 10d nails each, or with three 16d nails clinched over. Then install 2-×-4 nailer blocks between stud and rafter pairs as in FIG. 31-4, as attachment

31-4 A simple kneewall construction method.

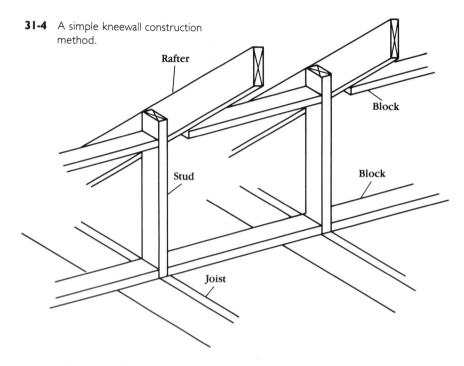

Rafter

Block

Stud

Block

Joist

points for drywall panels. Also, install edge blocking between joists along the kneewall edges as support and nailing points for the subflooring, as required. (This is not necessarily needed for heavy decking, thick plywood, and some other constructions.)

Another method is to lay a sole plate first, secured directly to the joists or through a subflooring material, using two 16d nails each. Then toenail the joists to the sole plate with four 8d nails each, and anchor the top ends to the rafter faces as just described (FIG. 31-5).

A simple nonload-bearing arrangement involves installing a sole plate and an angled top plate with a beveled edge rip-cut from 2-×-6 stock (FIG. 31-6). Alignment with joists and rafters is unnecessary, and this system obviates the need for nailing blocks in the kneewall, and possibly in the rafters as well, because the kneewall can be installed after the drywall is applied. Then the ends of the drywall can be fastened to the kneewall top plate from behind. This assembly can be put together on the floor and slid into place. Use a pair of 16d nails at each end to secure the plates to the studs, and a pair of 16d nails through the plates into each joist and rafter.

If the kneewall is to support roof rafters, it is built like any wall frame, with a sole plate and a doubled top plate (FIG. 31-7). In this case it is set in place before the roof is put on. The rafters for a single-plane roof must be notched to fit over the kneewall cap plate, and each is fastened to the plate by toenailing with three 8d nails. If the roof breaks to two planes, two sets of rafters are involved. A porch roof might break to a shallower slope, a

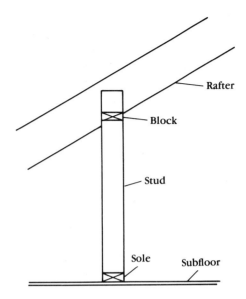

31-5 This kneewall construction starts at a sole plate rather than the joists.

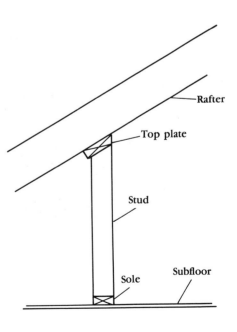

31-6 Simple kneewall construction using a single angled top plate.

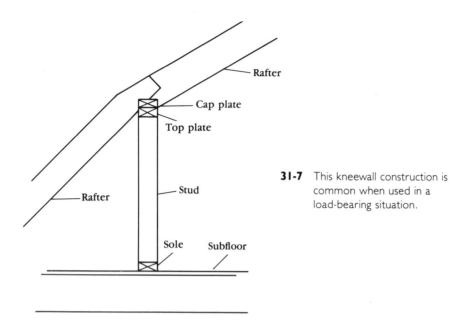

31-7 This kneewall construction is common when used in a load-bearing situation.

gambrel to a steeper one. The rafters must be trimmed to suit each plane, with one end of each attached to the kneewall top plate.

ENDWALLS

Houses with uniform, single-style roof patterns like the flat, mansard, pyramid, tent, or hip require no special endwall framing. The exterior walls are of the same construction no matter what their position in the structure. With styles such as the shed, saltbox or gable, bow, or gambrel, as well as combinations of these with others, upper-level endwalls are required to close off the under-roof space. Their construction varies depending upon whether or not there is to be a roof overhang. And for either case, the actual outline of the endwall doesn't much matter. The construction techniques are the same, just the sizes and placement of the pieces change.

If there is no overhang at the roof rake and only a slight extension of trimwork to finish out the joint between the exterior wall and the roof, the endwall is often framed in place after the roof rafters have been set. However, it is also possible to build up the endwall framing flat on the floor platform and then tilt it into position before the rafters are set. There are two methods for that procedure: One requires that the pattern rafter be made up beforehand, the other does not.

Framing in place

To frame an endwall in place, start after the end rafters have been set. If a subfloor material has been installed, lay a sole plate down and secure it through the subfloor to the wall cap plate below. Use 16d nails on 16-inch centers. If there is no subflooring, you can work directly on the cap plate of the wall below. Lay out the stud placement markings as you would on any sole plate, using 16-inch centering. Trim each stud to fit its individual slot, cutting the top end to an angle that matches the roof line. Cut a notch out of each to accommodate the roof rafter; the outside edges of the sole and cap plates, studs, and the rafter faces must all be flush. Each stud should be about 1/4-inch shy of being flush with the top edge of the rafters, to allow for shrinkage (FIG. 31-8). Toenail each stud to the sole or cap plate. Use four 8d nails at the bottom and a pair of 10d nails through the edge of the upper end and into the rafter face.

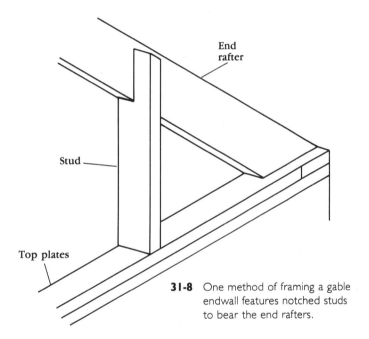

31-8 One method of framing a gable endwall features notched studs to bear the end rafters.

Building a tilt-up endwall

To build a tilt-up endwall complete with the end rafters in place, first use the pattern rafter to cut the required number of end rafters. Note that if a ridgeboard will be used, each of these rafters must be longer than the other common rafters by half the thickness of the ridgeboard. Make up a sole plate that extends full width of the endwall and mark the stud locations. Lay it on edge and align the rafters with it. Trim and fit all the studs, notch them, and fasten them to the sole and rafters. Use two 16d nails up through the sole into the bottom ends, and two 10d nails edge nailed at the top. Tilt the whole works into place and secure it with 16d nails on 16-inch centers through the sole plate. Anchor the wall with temporary props.

The alternate method (FIG. 31-9) does not require having the rafters on hand, because they can be installed at any time, along with the other common rafters. However, you do have to know the exact set of the rafters because the end ones will lie directly on top of the endwall and must fit up perfectly. To build an endwall in this fashion, lay out a sole plate and top plate to the endwall outline. Mark out the stud locations and assemble the wall in the same way as any stud wall. Tilt it into place, fasten it, and brace it. When the time comes, the end rafters should fit atop the top plate. They can snug up to one another at the peak, or to a ridgeboard.

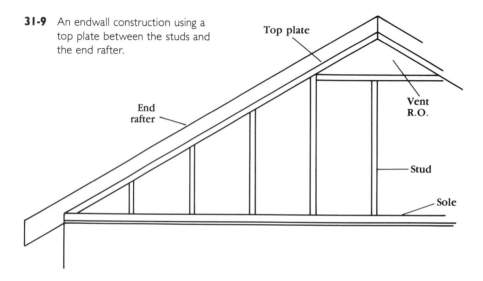

31-9 An endwall construction using a top plate between the studs and the end rafter.

Lookout ladder

If there is to be an overhang at the roof rake, the roof framing must include a construction called a *lookout ladder* (FIG. 31-10). Construct the endwall as just described, but add a cap plate to the top plate. The upper surface of the cap plate should be at the same level as the bottom edges of the roof rafters if the roof overhang is more than about 18 inches. This will allow the use of dimension stock the same size as the roof rafters in making the ladder.

For short overhangs the ladder stock is often 2×6 or even 2×4, so the height of the endwall cap plate has to be adjusted accordingly to make up the difference. The endwall frame can be built up in place or done tilt-up fashion, but usually is in place before the rafters go up (or at least, the last inboard rafter). Rafters can be set either with or without a ridgeboard. A ridgeboard can be braced to the endwall peaks before setting the rafters, making that operation a bit easier.

Gable endwalls have been shown here because that is probably the most common framed shape. Changing the shape of the endwall, however, doesn't change the framing procedures. A saltbox endwall is a gable

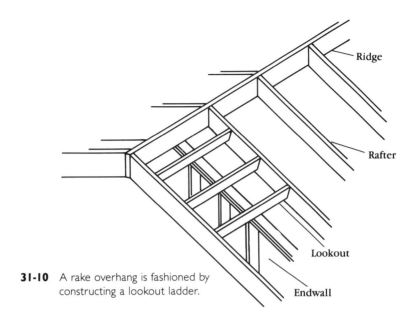

31-10 A rake overhang is fashioned by constructing a lookout ladder.

with two different halves, a gambrel endwall just has a humped-gable outline, the endwall under a shed roof is half a gable, and so on. All you have to do is add or subtract members as common sense suggests. Note also that endwalls frequently contain openings for doors, windows, and especially louver vents. Frame them just as you would any opening at any other wall location.

Chapter 32

Roof types and components

*I*n many cases the roof is the most complicated construction of a frame house and the most difficult of all the selections to put together. If premanufactured roof trusses are installed, as they are on many small houses and particularly "tract" houses, the roof construction is relatively easy. But trusses have their drawbacks and are not suitable for many house designs, especially if the roof patterns are complex. That means the roof will have to be built from scratch. In order to do a creditable job of constructing a roof frame, the builder has to have a good working knowledge of roof configurations, frame components, and terminology.

STYLES

There are several main styles of roof (FIG. 32-1), and a few lesser ones as well. There are variations and embellishments on some of these styles, and frequently two or more styles are employed on the same structure. While the frames for all of these roof styles feature the same kinds of components, each is built according to its own plan. When two or more are used on the same structure, they are sometimes grafted to one another, sometimes integrated. These main styles are as follows:

A *flat* roof is not often used as a main residential roof, although it is common to commercial buildings. It is sometimes used over small sections of a house. A flat roof is seldom really flat; usually there is a slight pitch to aid moisture runoff. In commercial buildings this pitch is sometimes to the center of the building, where interior drainpipes carry runoff away. On houses the pitch is typically to the outside. Because a flat roof

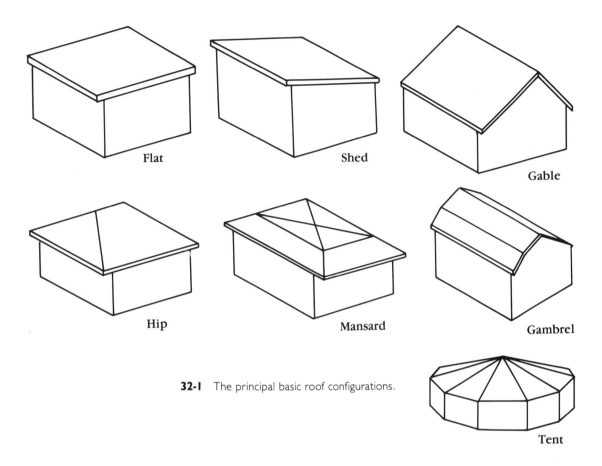

32-1 The principal basic roof configurations.

can sometimes carry huge loads, it must be heavily framed and solidly built.

The *shed* roof, a familiar style, is used on many houses. It is a flat expanse built in one plane and may be pitched to nearly any angle. It may be freestanding and cover an entire structure, or it may extend from another part of the building. Two or more shed roofs are frequently used on residences, and a shed roof is often used along with another style.

The *gable* roof is essentially a pair of shed roofs opposing one another and meeting at a peak; a triangle is thereby formed at each end, and these are the actual gables. Sometimes the pitch is equal on both sides, sometimes it is not, and there may be several such roof assemblies on one structure. A variation is the *bow* roof, where the gables instead of being flat are bowed outward. Another variation is the *A-frame*, which combines the roof and the sidewalls of the principal structure.

The *hip* roof, instead of having two sloping sides like a gable roof, has four: The end sections also slope to the ridge. If the house is square and all the roof panels are the same, the result is the *pyramid* roof.

A *mansard* roof looks a bit like a hip roof with the top lopped off. The lower portion of the roof is a hip style. The upper portion may be flat, but usually is pitched at least slightly in four directions. Sometimes, too, the lower 2 or 3 feet of the roof are kicked outward at a shallower angle.

The *gambrel* style is a familiar one often seen on barns. This is essentially a gable roof with two-plane sections on each side, and the endwalls thus formed are also called gables. A variation, sometimes called the *Dutch barn*, has a three-plane roof on each side, with the bottom few feet (sometimes only a few inches) extending at a shallower pitch than the center section.

A *tent* roof is composed of several triangular panels set against one another and rising to a central peak like the roof of a circus tent. This complex structure is used atop hexagonal, octagonal, and similar geometric house plans.

PARTS AND TERMS

A complete roof structure only has a few main parts (FIG. 32-2). The basis for the roof is the frame, which itself has numerous components that will be considered separately a bit later. In some constructions the roof frame may support a ceiling, or actually be a visible part of the ceiling. Roof insulation may be below, in, or above the frame, or all three. The topside of the frame is covered with a sheathing, or in some cases, a decking. In many cases another layer is applied to the sheathing, the underlayment.

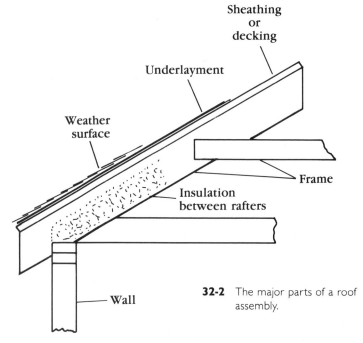

32-2   The major parts of a roof assembly.

Finally, the whole assembly is topped off with what is variously called the weather surface, the finish covering, or just "roofing." Exactly what materials are used, and just how, in all of these parts depends upon the overall roof design.

The terms used in roof frame layout can be confusing, but a working knowledge of them is essential. As FIG. 32-3 shows, the *span* is the distance between the two opposite walls that support the roof, as measured from outside to outside. The *run* is the distance from the outside of one supporting wall to the centerline of the *ridge*, which is the line of intersection of two opposing roof sections. In an equal-sided gable, the run equals half the span. However, in an off-centered ridge design the runs will be different for each roof section. In a flat or shed roof where there is no intersecting line, the span and the run are the same.

The *rise* of a roof is the total distance that the rafter is above the plate, at the uppermost point of its longitudinal centerline. The *unit rise* is the amount of rise expressed in inches for every foot of run. The *unit run* is always expressed as 12, meaning inches. *Rafter length* is the distance between the outside edge of the supporting wall plate and the centerline

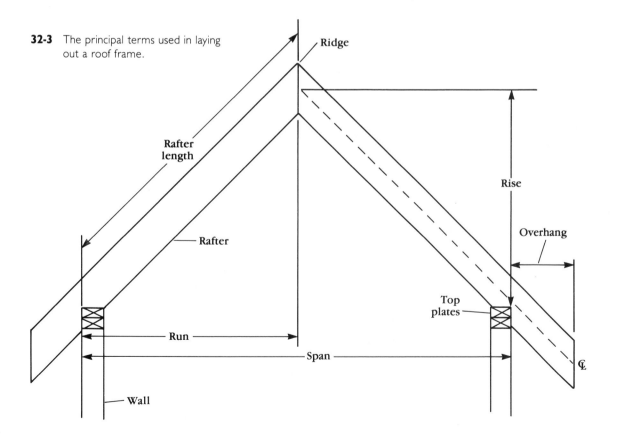

32-3 The principal terms used in laying out a roof frame.

of the ridge. The *true* or *linear rafter length* is the same as the rafter length when there is no ridgeboard, or the rafter length minus one-half the thickness of the ridgeboard when it is present.

The relationships of span, run, and rise determine two more crucial factors, roof *pitch* and roof *slope*, both of which signify the degree of roof incline. The terminology often gets mixed up. Pitch is the ratio of the rise to the span, expressed as a fraction and calculated in terms of the total length in feet of each (FIG. 32-4). Thus, if a roof has a span of 20 feet and a rise of 5 feet, the ratio is 5:20, or $^5/_{20}$, or $^1/_4$-pitch. If the span is 30 feet and the rise is 3 feet, that's a ratio of 3:30 or $^1/_{10}$-pitch. Slope, on the other hand, is the ratio of rise to run rather than span, and is calculated in terms of inches of rise per foot of run (FIG. 32-5). Thus, if a roof has a rise of 6 inches per foot it is called a 6-in-12 slope. If the rise is 48 inches over a 24-foot run, that is 2 inches per foot or a 2-in-12 slope.

Note that slope and pitch are only sometimes the same: when the run is half the span. A 6-in-12 slope is the same as a $^1/_4$-pitch when the span is double the run. But when the run is the same as the span, for example (as in a shed roof), a 6-in-12 slope, or 1 foot in every 2, is a $^1/_2$-pitch (FIG. 32-6). To put it another way, consider a gable roof with equal runs, a 20-foot span and a 5-foot rise. That's a $^1/_4$-pitch roof with a slope of 6-in-12. A shed roof with a 20-foot span also has a 20-foot run and is a $^1/_4$-pitch with a 5-foot rise, but it's a 3-in-12 slope. And if the same 20-foot span with a 5-foot rise is broken in one 15-foot and one 5-foot run, there is one 4-in-12 roof panel and one 12-in-12. They all have the same pitch but four different slopes. For obvious reasons, these are called *unequal-pitch* roofs.

To add to the confusion, the words slope and pitch are often used interchangeably, and loosely, with specific meaning only to the user of the word. A $^1/_4$-pitch might be termed a 4-pitch, and a 4-in-12 slope might be called a 4-in-1 slope or a 4-in-1 pitch, or a $^4/_{12}$, or also just a 4-pitch.

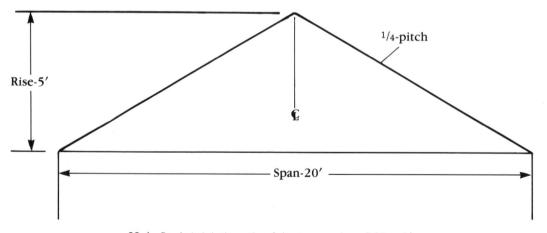

32-4   Roof pitch is the ratio of rise to span, here 5:20 or $^1/_4$.

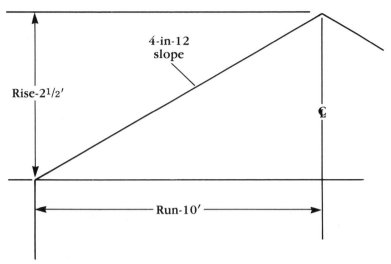

32-5 Roof slope is the ratio of rise to run expressed in inches of rise per foot of run, here 4-in-12.

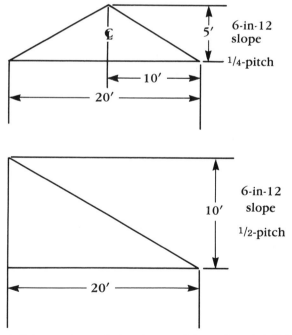

32-6 Slope and pitch are only equal when the run of the roof equals half the span. Otherwise, they are unlike.

The best bet is to think consistently in terms of inches of rise per foot of run and call the foot 12 inches; 5 inches of rise in every 12 over a run of 14 feet, for example. Then the relative roof inclines will be the same no matter the roof shape or style, as long as you follow the proper definition of roof run.

ROOF FRAME COMPONENTS

A roof frame has a number of component parts (FIG. 32-7). Many frames have one or more *ridges*, along which runs a horizontal member called a *ridgeboard* or *ridgepole*. It is not present in some roof styles, like a flat or tent roof, nor need it be present in others even though there is a ridge. In simplest form a roof frame is composed of *common rafters*, individual members that run from the plate to the ridge. The plate can be the cap plate of the supporting wall, or a separate plate installed atop an upper-level floor platform. *Hip rafters* always extend downward at an angle to the common rafters, from the ridge to the plate to form an outside corner (which need not necessarily be a right-angle corner). *Valley rafters* are their inside-corner counterparts, also extending downward at an angle to the common rafters from the ridge to the plate.

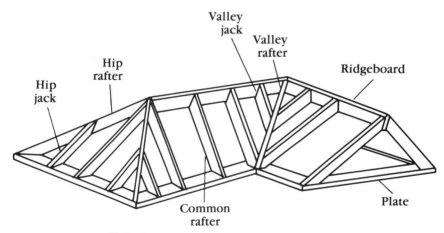

32-7   The principal components of a roof frame.

Jack rafters are shortened members that come in three flavors. A *hip jack* is trimmed at the upper end and runs up from the plate to the side of a hip rafter. A *valley jack* is trimmed at the bottom and extends down from the ridgeboard to the side of a valley rafter. *Cripple jacks* are trimmed at both ends and run between hip and valley rafters. *Lookout rafters* form the rungs of *lookout ladders* used to frame a roof overhang on both flat and pitched roofs. A *king rafter* is sometimes installed at the corner of a double overhang, especially in a flat or low-pitched construction, for extra strength. A *collar beam* or *collar tie* is an auxiliary member often installed between opposing rafters to stiffen and strengthen the frame.

A rafter only extends from the ridge to the outside of the plate FIG. 32-8). It may be trimmed off there, but more often it continues. The portion that extends beyond the wall is the *rafter tail*, and the distance between the wall and the outermost part of the rafter tail is the *overhang* or *projection*.

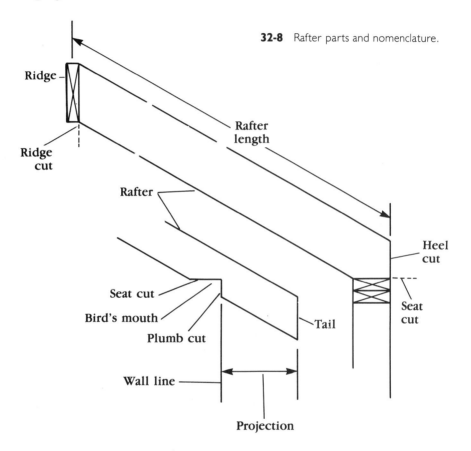

32-8 Rafter parts and nomenclature.

If the rafter is cut off flush at the wall line, that is the *heel cut*, and the cut made to rest the rafter heel on the plate is the seat cut. But if the rafter is notched to seat on the plate, the notch is a *bird's mouth*. The horizontal cut is the *seat cut*, and the vertical one is the *plumb cut*. Out at the end of the tail, where the rafter is trimmed is called the *tail cut* (FIG. 32-9). The tail cut can be a *square cut* (at right angles to the piece), a *plumb cut* (vertical), a *level cut* (horizontal), or a combination of plumb and level. Occasionally *scroll cuts* or *taper cuts* are made in exposed rafter tails for decorative purposes. The rafter can be cut off flush at the heel and a separate decorative extension piece added to it; this is a *false rafter* or a *separate tail*, and

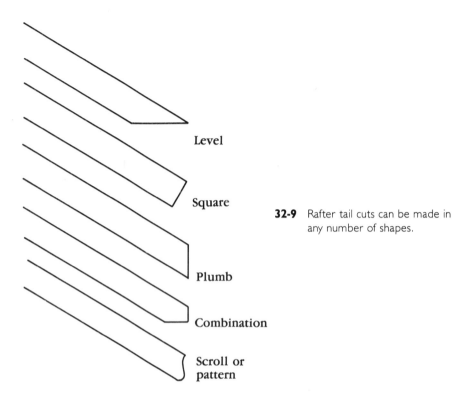

Level

Square

Plumb

Combination

Scroll or
pattern

32-9 Rafter tail cuts can be made in any number of shapes.

can be reduced, curved, or straight. At the opposite end of the rafter, the cut made to set the rafter against the ridgeboard, ledger plate, or another rafter is the *ridge cut* or *upper plumb cut*. The angled cuts made on hip, valley, and jack rafters are *cheek cuts* or *side cuts*.

RAFTER SIZE

Rafter size usually refers to the thickness and width of the stock, rather than the length. In platform framing when trusses are not installed, standard 2-inch (nominal) dimension stock is almost always used. Most of the time the widths will be 8, 10, or 12 inches. As with floor and ceiling joists, the rafter width, span, and spacing are interdependent and must be determined in conjunction with other facts as well. The slope of the roof plays a part, and so do wind and snow loading factors, and the weight of the finish roofing to be installed. Because the roof is the ultimate protective cover over the structure and because it takes a terrible beating year in and year out, selecting the right stock to make a sturdy frame is extremely important.

As with floor and ceiling joists, you can make that selection in several ways. If you are using published stock plans or an architect's custom plans, those details have already been determined. Otherwise, you can hire an engineer or an architect to verify your design, or to draw up a complete roof framing plan. You might consult with a local builder or two, and/or copy what has been successfully done in other houses of a similar design in your area. If you have made up a plan, your local building department will tell you whether or not it is satisfactory (but don't expect them to design a roof for you). And finally, you can work out the engineering details yourself with a bit of study and perhaps the aid of a calculator. Once you know the local wind and snow load requirements, you can turn to either the formulae for determining rafter spans for given rafter dimensions, spacing, wood species, and grades, or consult any of the many published tables used for the same purpose.

Chapter **33**

Using the framing square

*E*xpertise with a *framing square*—also called a *carpenter's* or *rafter square*—is not essential for building a good roof. If you fuss long enough with angle finders and tape measures and your pocket calculator, you can get the job done well enough in due course. However, the particular purpose of this tool is to avoid a lot of that bother and enable you to lay out any kind of pitched-roof rafters with greater ease, accuracy, speed, and with considerably less chance for error than would otherwise be the case. Familiarity with the use of a framing square is a decided advantage in constructing a roof structure, especially if complex. You can also use it to solve all manner of other difficult carpentry problems, such as finding brace lengths, laying out stairs, determining board measure, and converting hundredths to sixteenths.

The two parts of a framing square are set exactly at right angles to one another, so you can use it for all squaring-up jobs. The wide leg of the square is the body, the narrow one is the tongue. The outside edge of the body is 24 inches long, handy for 24-inch centering; the outside edge of the tongue is 16 inches, handy for 16-inch layouts. Graduations are in sixteenths, twelfths, tenths, and eighths (and of course quarters and halves) of an inch. The outside corner of the square is the heel.

LAYING OUT AN OCTAGON

On the front of the tongue, centered lengthwise, is the octagon or eight scale, which is used for laying out eight-sided figures. To lay out a large octagon, make up a smaller one with the square to scale for the larger one. As an example, for a 20-inch octagon, first lay out a 20-inch square. Divide

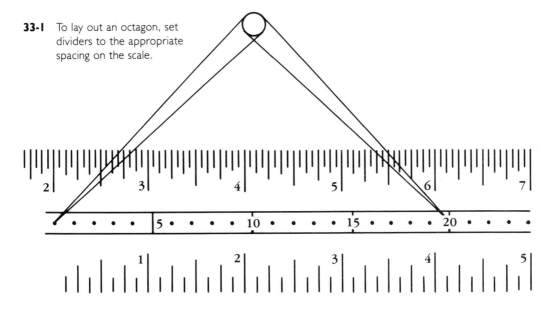

33-1 To lay out an octagon, set dividers to the appropriate spacing on the scale.

the square exactly into quarters. Set a pair of dividers to 20 dots on the eight scale (FIG. 33-1), and step off that dimension from each quadrant line to the perimeter line on each side. Connect the marks to form the octagon (FIG. 33-2).

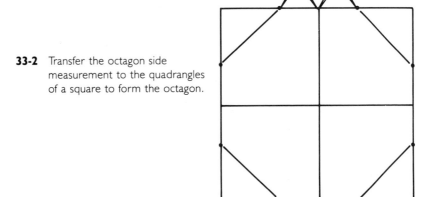

33-2 Transfer the octagon side measurement to the quadrangles of a square to form the octagon.

CALCULATING BOARD FEET

On the back face of the framing square in the corner is a line 1 inch long, divided into hundredths at the top and sixteenths at the bottom. You might need a magnifying glass to see it. This line is for quickly converting decimal measurements to practical sixteenths. The back of the blade features a handy board measure table, based on nominal 1-inch board thickness. This table allows you to determine the number of board feet (12 × 12 × 1 inches nominal) of lumber in any given piece. You can also work it backwards to determine how many pieces of material of a given size you need to cover a particular area. Here's how it works.

Below the 12-inch mark on the outer edge of the blade is a column starting with 8. These are the piece lengths in feet, and this is where calculations begin. For this process, the inch marks along the top edge of the blade represent the widths of the pieces. The numbers in the other columns of the table are the board feet. Where there are two digits, the left one is a whole foot, the right is a fraction of a foot in terms of the number of twelfths of a foot: 9 2 means 9 and $^2/_{12}$ board feet. So, if you have a 1 × 10 that is 14 feet long, find 14 in the length column under the 12-inch mark. Go left along that line to the column under the 10-inch-wide mark to find 11 8, or 11 and $^8/_{12}$ board feet, which would be denoted 11$^2/_3$ (FIG. 33-3). For a 2 × 8 that is 16 feet long, which is off the scale, calculate an 8-foot 1 × 8 and multiply by 4.

DIAGONAL BRACE

On the back face of the tongue there is an arcane string of figures along the center; these are common brace lengths. This is most useful in post-and-beam or braced-frame construction, but is sometimes handy for other jobs as well. The purpose is to easily determine the overall length of a diagonal brace running from a vertical to a horizontal member, which is simply the hypotenuse of the triangle formed by the three pieces. So, taking the first set of numbers as an example, a brace running across a 24-inch rise and a 24-inch run will be 33.94 inches long (FIG. 33-4). Checking the hundredths scale, that's about 33$^{15}/_{16}$ inches, or near enough.

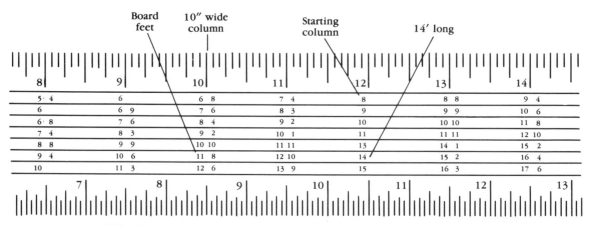

8	9	10	11	12	13	14
5·4	6	6 8	7 4	8	8 8	9 4
6	6 9	7 6	8 3	9	9 9	10 6
6·8	7 6	8 4	9 2	10	10 10	11 8
7 4	8 3	9 2	10 1	11	11 11	12 10
8 8	9 9	10 10	11 11	13	14 1	15 2
9 4	10 6	11 8	12 10	14	15 2	16 4
10	11 3	12 6	13 9	15	16 3	17 6

33-3 This table on the framing square is used to determine board foot measure.

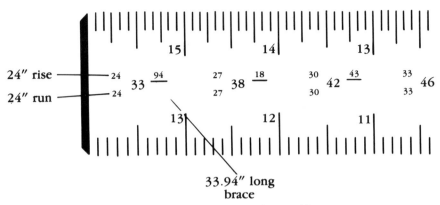

24" rise —— 24
24" run —— 24

33 $\frac{94}{}$ 27 $\frac{18}{27}$ 38   30 $\frac{43}{30}$ 42   33 $\frac{43}{33}$ 46

33.94" long
brace

33-4 The framing square brace table.

RAFTER LENGTH

Now, back to the rafter table. The first line gives the length of common rafters in terms of inches of length per foot of roof run for various rises. Suppose, for example, the rise of a roof section is 4 inches in every foot of a 14-foot run. Find the 4-inch mark at the top of the blade; directly below are the numbers 12 65 (FIG. 33-5). That means 12.65 inches of length per foot of run, so multiply by 14. The answer is 177.1 inches, or 14.758 feet,

Length in inches
per foot of run

Rise in inches
per foot of run

6		5		4		3		2		1
3	42	13	00	12	65	12	37	12	16	
8	00	17	69	17	44	17	23	17	09	
7	875	17	33	16	87	16	49	16	22	
6	83	26		25	30	24	74	24	33	
0	¾	11	¹⁄₁₆	11	⅜	11	⅝	11	¹³⁄₁₆	
1	⁵⁄₁₆	11	½	11	¹¹⁄₁₆	11	¹³⁄₁₆	11	¹⁵⁄₁₆	

33-5 The first line on the front face of the framing square blade is used to determine rafter length.

which would be rounded to 14 feet 9¹/8 inches. This length is along the measure line. If the rafters are installed in butting pairs with no ridge-board, that is the true length as well. If there is a ridgeboard, half its thickness must be subtracted to get the true rafter length (FIG. 33-6).

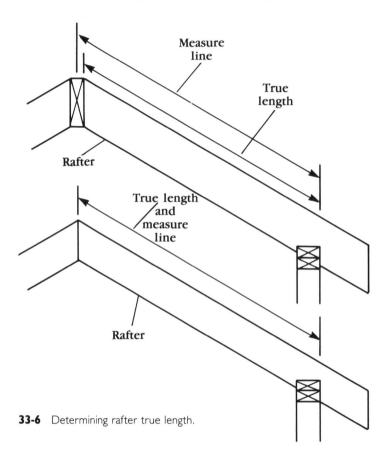

33-6   Determining rafter true length.

HIP AND VALLEY RAFTER LENGTHS

The second line of the table gives the length of valley or hip rafters in inches per foot of roof run under the common rafters. Using the same example as above, under the 4-inch mark for rise are the figures 17 44 (FIG. 33-7), meaning 17.44 inches of length per foot of run. That times 14 equals 244.16 inches or 20.35 feet, or about 20 feet 4³/16 inches. Again, this is the length along the measure line. That measurement is taken along the top edge centerline of the hip from the plate end to the centerpoint of the ridge or ridgeboard. The hip must be trimmed to fit into the intersection of the ridgeboard and the common rafters, so the first step is to deduct one-half of the diagonal thickness of the common rafter from the measure line length to get the true hip rafter length (FIG. 33-8).

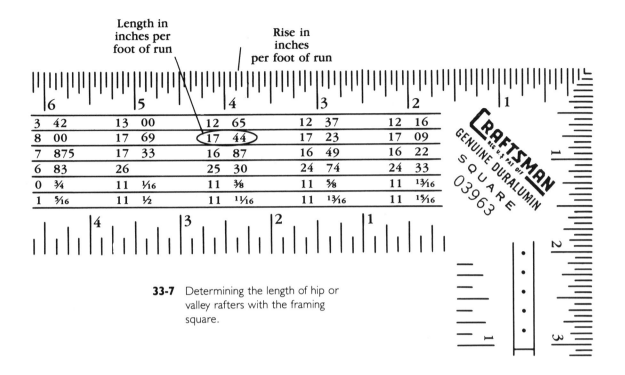

Length in inches per foot of run		Rise in inches per foot of run			
6	5	4	3	2	1
3 42	13 00	12 65	12 37	12 16	
8 00	17 69	(17 44)	17 23	17 09	
7 875	17 33	16 87	16 49	16 22	
6 83	26	25 30	24 74	24 33	
0 ¾	11 ¹⁄₁₆	11 ⅜	11 ⅝	11 ¹³⁄₁₆	
1 ⁵⁄₁₆	11 ½	11 ¹¹⁄₁₆	11 ¹³⁄₁₆	11 ¹⁵⁄₁₆	

33-7 Determining the length of hip or valley rafters with the framing square.

SIDE CUTS IN HIP AND VALLEY RAFTERS

In order to make the fit, you have to make the side cuts, shaping the end like an arrowhead. The rafter tail is also an arrowhead for a hip, but like an arrow tail for a valley. These are compound-angle cuts (FIG. 33-9). That brings us to the bottom line of the table. Following the example again, look at the bottom figure in the column under 4, for a 4-inch rise, 11¹¹⁄₁₆ (FIG. 33-10). Place the square on the front (top) of the hip or valley rafter, heel down, tongue to the left with the rafter top end also to the left. Set the 12-inch tongue mark and the 11¹¹⁄₁₆-inch blade mark on the near rafter edge, with the tongue edge intersecting the lengthwise centerline of the rafter and the plumb cut line. Draw a line against the tongue from the rafter centerline back to the near edge. Flip the square over and repeat, with the marks aligned on the far edge of the rafter. This will give you the correct side cut angles for making the plumb cut (FIG. 33-11).

JACK RAFTER DIMENSIONS

Now we come to lines three and four of the rafter table, indicating the common difference between jack rafters set 16 o.c. and 24 o.c. (on centers). Valley, hip, and cripple jacks all lie in the same plane as the common rafters. When they have equal spacing, they have a common difference in length; the second is double the first, the third three times the first, the

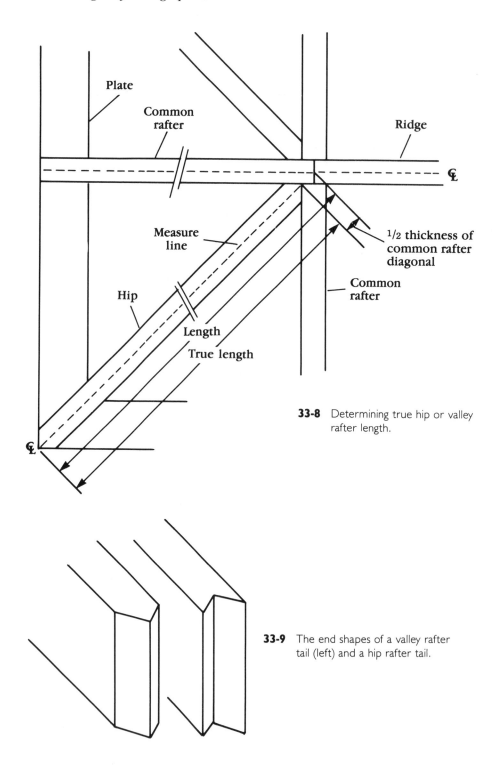

Plate

Common
rafter

Ridge

Measure
line

½ thickness of
common rafter
diagonal

Common
rafter

Hip

Length

True length

33-8   Determining true hip or valley
rafter length.

33-9   The end shapes of a valley rafter
tail (left) and a hip rafter tail.

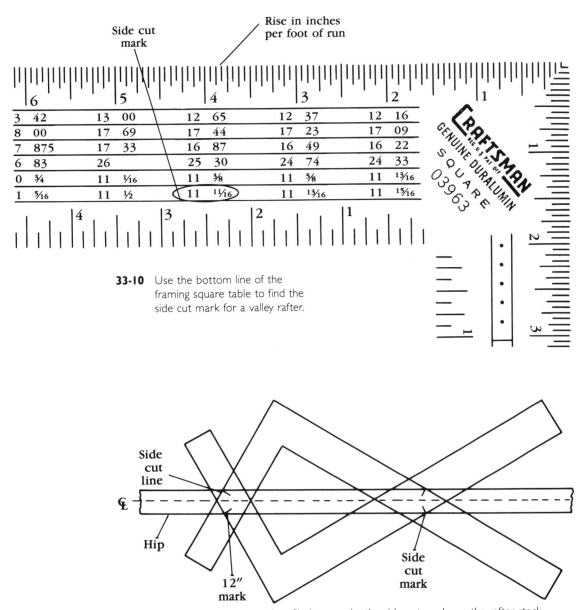

33-10 Use the bottom line of the framing square table to find the side cut mark for a valley rafter.

33-11 Set the square, then flip it, to make the side cut marks on the rafter stock.

fourth four times the first. Again following the example as above, under the 4-inch mark the figures in that column for 16-inch centering are 16 87, or 16.87 inches, or close enough to 16⅞ inches (FIG. 33-12). So, the first jack will measure 16⅞ inches, the second one 33¾ inches, and so on. Once again this is along a measure line, and the jacks must be short-

Common difference
in inches

Rise in inches
per foot of run

6	5	4	3	2	1
3 42	13 00	12 65	12 37	12 16	
8 00	17 69	17 44	17 23	17 09	
7 875	17 33	16 87	16 49	16 22	
6 83	26	25 30	24 74	24 33	
0 ¾	11 ¹⁄₁₆	11 ⅜	11 ⅝	11 ¹³⁄₁₆	
1 ⁵⁄₁₆	11 ½	11 ¹¹⁄₁₆	11 ¹³⁄₁₆	11 ¹⁵⁄₁₆	

33-12   This line of the framing square table gives the common difference dimensions for jack rafters set to various equal-pitch roof slopes.

ened by one-half the diagonal thickness of the rafters to which they will mate.

JACK RAFTER SIDE CUTS

Also, at this end of the rafters side cuts must be made. That brings us to the remaining line of the table, line 5. In the example, the figure under the 4-inch mark in that line is 11³⁄₈ (FIG. 33-13). Draw the arrowhead on the top edge of the jack by setting the square on that number and 12, in the same manner as making the side cut layout for a hip or valley rafter. The cuts at the opposite ends from the side cuts are the same as those used at the rafter ends, either plumb or seat.

RIDGE AND SEAT CUTS

Common practice in roof construction is to select the best piece of rafter stock available—straight, uncrowned, with no bow or crook—and make a master pattern rafter from it. Then use it to lay out all the remaining common rafters. Make as many pattern rafters as are necessary for different rafter sets.

Staying with the example, the rafter needed for a 14-foot run and 4-inch unit rise is 14 feet 9¹⁄₈ inches. Assume no ridgeboard is installed, and assume no rafter tail. Also assume that the seat cut will go all the way across the end of the rafter. Set the unit run mark—12 inches—on the

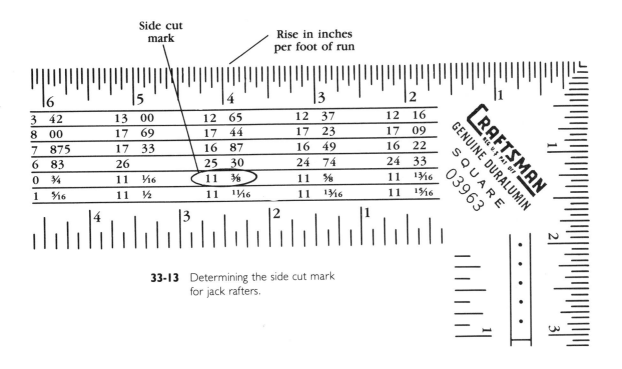

33-13 Determining the side cut mark for jack rafters.

blade edge of the square and the unit rise mark—4 inches—on the tongue edge, aligned on the edge of the rafter stock. The level line you draw against the blade is the seat cut, and the plumb line against the tongue is the ridge cut (FIG. 33-14). The two will always be in the correct relationship.

To get the proper distance between the two cuts, measure along the rafter side from the toe or point of the seat cut 14 feet 9¹⁄₈ inches. Reset the square in the same position as for the seat cut and mark the plumb cut. If there were a ridgeboard involved, you would subtract one-half its thickness from the measurement and strike the plumb line at that point.

BIRD'S-MOUTH NOTCHES

A rafter, however, seldom features a full seat cut. It usually fits down over a plate in a notch. What then? Then you cut the bird's-mouth notch or a simple seat and heel first, and establish a measure line from that. Assume no rafter tail, and that the rafter will sit atop a 2-×-4 plate on a 3¹⁄₂-inch seat. Strike the seat line, measure in along it from the back (underside edge) of the rafter 3¹⁄₂ inches, and strike a plumb line. This is the heel cut. From the heal/seat corner, run a line parallel with the rafter edge. This is the measure line. At a point 14 feet 9¹⁄₈ inches from the heel/seat corner, reset the square on the unit rise-unit run marks and strike a ridge cut line (FIG. 33-15).

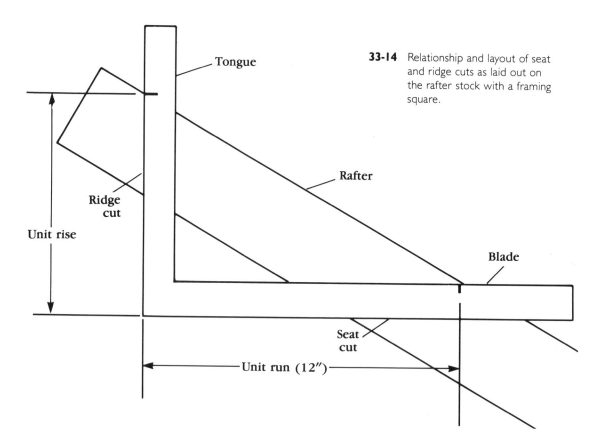

Tongue

33-14 Relationship and layout of seat and ridge cuts as laid out on the rafter stock with a framing square.

Rafter

Ridge cut

Unit rise

Blade

Seat cut

Unit run (12″)

Now assume that there will be a tail on the rafter. That means no heel cut, but rather a bird's-mouth notch with a seat and a plumb cut. Strike the seat-cut line as usual, and measure in from the back edge of the rafter a distance equal to the seat length you want. This might be just enough to bear on a 2-x-4 or a 2-x-6 plate, for example. Then strike a plumb line at this point, and make the vertical cut to form the bird's mouth. From the notch corner, run a measure line back along the rafter parallel with its edge, measure off the rafter length, and strike the ridge-cut line. Note that you can make the seat as long as you wish and fashion the tail however you like by changing the position of the measure line, but the measure-line length stays constant (FIG. 33-16).

STEP-OFF LAYOUT

There is an alternative to using a measure line that some carpenters use. It is called the *step-off layout*. Set the square on the pattern rafter stock at the left end with the tongue to the left, on the 4 and 12 marks. This is setting the square to the cut of the roof, which is a 4-in-12 slope. Strike a plumb line against the tongue; this will be the ridge cut. Now move the

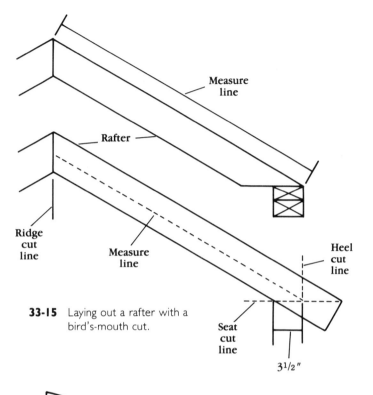

33-15 Laying out a rafter with a bird's-mouth cut.

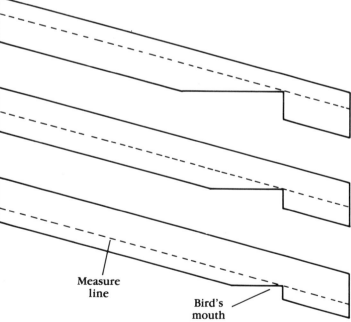

33-16 The seat cut can be made any length and the measure line moved, but the measure line length stays the same.

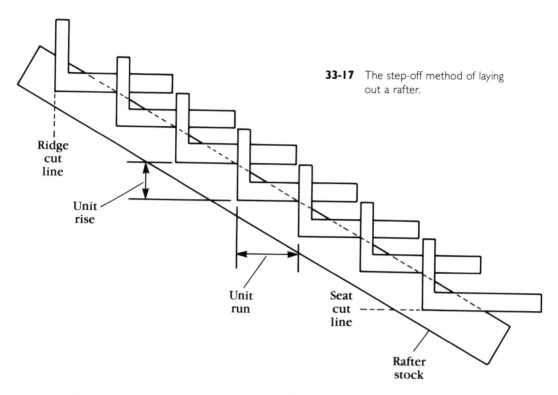

Ridge cut line

Unit rise

Unit run

Seat cut line

Rafter stock

33-17   The step-off method of laying out a rafter.

square, still set to the cut of the roof, along 9¹/8 inches from the plumb line. Mark the rafter edge at the 12-inch mark on the blade. Reset the square and repeat 13 times to get to the building line and bird's-mouth notch or heel (FIG. 33-17), then beyond for whatever distance is needed to reach the rafter tail cuts, if any.

Chapter **34**

Flat roof framing

*A*lthough flat roofs are not popular for covering an entire house, they are sometimes used in conjunction with other styles. In deep-winter country they have a reputation for being prone to leaks, but modern methods and materials have helped to cure that difficulty. If properly designed and constructed, they can be expected to serve well in any climate.

Flat roofs are less complex structurally and somewhat easier to build than other roof styles, but their construction is a bit different than either floors or other kinds of roofs. And even though they are called flat, in fact they should have a pitch of at least 1/4 inch per foot of run from the highest point to facilitate moisture runoff. In the building trades, any pitch less than about 2 inches per foot is commonly called flat. Only membrane and/or built-up weather surfaces can be installed on flat roofs; shingles, metal panels, roll roofing, and similar materials are not weathertight on shallow slopes.

Flat roof framing is similar to floor framing and the construction techniques are about the same. However, there are some important differences. A flat roof is itself heavy and periodically carries heavy live loads, and in some parts of the country that weight can be practically prohibitive for house construction. Wind load is less of a factor than with a pitched roof, but snow load can be very high, and water load can be substantial as well. In addition to these weights and its own weight, the roof frame must hold heavy sheathing; insulation; a ceiling; and numerous layers of membrane, tar, gravel, or other materials. Some flat roofs are also decked and may have special imposed loads. This all means that the framing must be stout, stiff, and well made.

Roof framing members are typically 2×10s or 2×12s, perhaps heavier, often doubled, and often supported on short spans by intermediate girders and/or bracing. (The principal members are called roof joists, rather than rafters.) The upshot is that unless there are some local examples to copy that have stood successfully for some time, a flat roof frame to cover an entire structure or a large area should be carefully engineered for the specific conditions.

ROOF CONSTRUCTION WITH NO OVERHANG

A flat roof can terminate flush with the building lines or faces of the exterior walls, or be contained within a continuous parapet, or overhang the walls. The latter arrangement is advantageous in that it keeps moisture runoff away from the structure walls, especially at the vulnerable upper joints, and also affords some helpful shade and weather protection. The first two constructions are put together like an upper-level floor frame. Install a band joist around the perimeter atop the wall top plate, set the joists on their predetermined spacings, and apply the sheathing (FIG. 34-1). The top of the structure can later be treated with rim trim or parapet walls, either of which can be designed to contain/restrain the roof weather surface, whatever that might be.

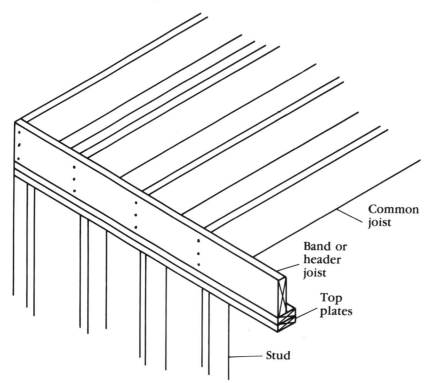

Common joist

Band or header joist

Top plates

Stud

34-1 Flat roof construction with no overhang.

OVERHANG CONSTRUCTION

Overhang construction is done a bit differently (FIG. 34-2). The intermediate joists are set in the usual fashion, typically on 12- or 16-inch centers. They must be set on a doubled wall top plate, and if the centering is 16 inches, the roof joists should lie directly over the wall studs. They project to the extent of the overhang.

Set the outboard joists parallel with the other walls approximately two or three times as far from those walls as the extent of the overhang. Install a series of lookout rafters at right angles to the outboard joists, keeping to the same centering and setting them above wall studs if possible. Nail the inboard ends of the lookouts with three or four 16d nails through the common joist face, and fasten the outer ends to the cap plate with four 8d toenails. Then install another joist alongside the one that anchors the lookouts. The roof corner should be further boxed out. Fit a short lookout anchored at right angles to the first in the row of full-length ones, then another one parallel to the row and anchored to the right-angled one. Then fit a very short lookout parallel with the first short lookout.

When the overhang gets out to more than 2¹/₂ feet, the construction at the roof corners should be modified for greater strength (FIG. 34-3).

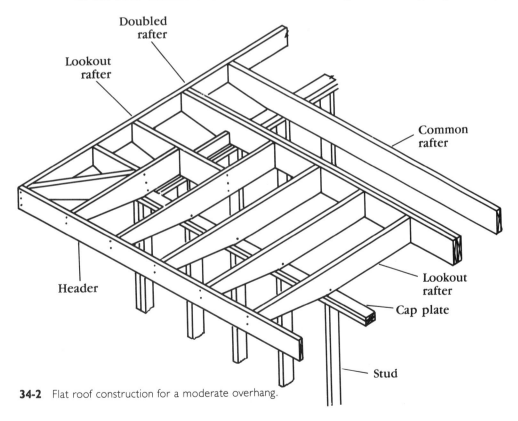

34-2 Flat roof construction for a moderate overhang.

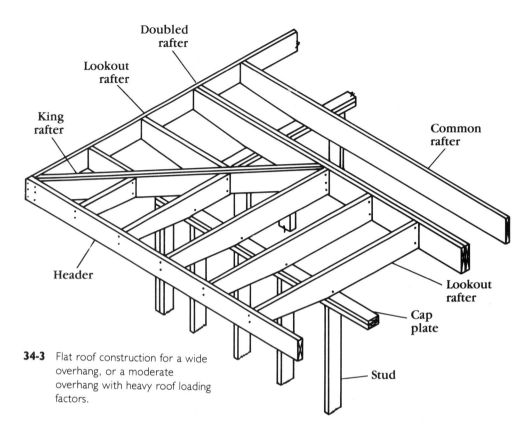

Doubled rafter

Lookout rafter

King rafter

Common rafter

Header

Lookout rafter

Cap plate

Stud

34-3 Flat roof construction for a wide overhang, or a moderate overhang with heavy roof loading factors.

First, the lookout joists should extend farther inside the structure. Make the inside length at least three times the outside, and a bit more when practical. Install the series of full-length lookouts. Fit a doubled king rafter diagonally across the corner. Then box in with short lookouts, maintaining appropriate spacing on centers.

Although not crucial, good building practice suggests that a nailing header be attached to the open ends of the joists. This will help keep the joists aligned and restrain them from twisting easily. It will also allow plenty of nailing area for a decorative fascia, soffit, and any other trim. Because roof joists are often so wide, the bottom edges sometimes are cut in a taper from the building line to the tail end (FIG. 34-4). This de-emphasizes the apparent bulk and create a lighter, more balanced appearance. Thus, the fascia trim might be a 1×6 instead of a 1×2 or wider.

VENTILATION

In all flat roof constructions it is important to allow for ventilation. There must be substantial space between the thermal insulation and the underside of the roof sheathing to permit ample free air movement. Air motion is provided by outside air movement, so the soffits must have screened

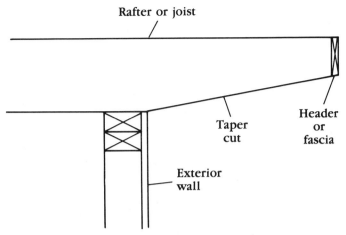

34-4   The joist or rafter tails of flat roof overhangs are sometimes cut to an upward taper for a less bulky appearance.

openings in them, evenly spaced, in the ratio of at least 1 square foot of net free ventilating area for every 250 square feet of roof area. These openings act as combined inlet and outlet vents. Do not install solid blocking in the roof frame if it will interfere with air circulation. Fit boxed-in areas at the roof corners with at least two small vent plugs each to reduce heat and condensation buildup.

METHODS OF ENCOURAGING MOISTURE RUNOFF

Gaining the necessary pitch for moisture runoff can be done in different ways. For example, at $1/2$ inch per foot of run, the center of a flat roof 30 feet wide and pitching to two sides would have to be $7 1/2$ inches higher than at the outboard building lines. This could be done by building the endwall frames to suit, supporting the roof center with a longitudinal load-bearing partition, and slanting the outboard wall top plates just a bit. Steeper slopes could be made in the same fashion as any other kind of pitched roof, although the framing square would be of no use.

Another possibility is to install cellular foamed glass or extruded polystyrene roof deck insulation panels atop completely flat roof sheathing. The material is available in tapered sheets for just this purpose, and the weather surface is applied directly over the insulation.

Chapter **35**

Shed roof framing

Single or multiple shed roofs, either alone or in combination with other roof styles, are extensively used in residential construction. They are also called *lean-to* roofs because they so often cap a structure or addition with that appearance. Shed roofs are the easiest to build of all the pitched-roof styles. They can be built at a low slope—3 inches or less—but typically have a slope of 4 to 6 inches per foot of run, sometimes more.

A shed roof can be freestanding, covering an entire structure, or it may be only a section attached to another roof or a wall. In the latter case the roof can attach at the ''front'' or highest point, or adjoin a structure at one end or side.

FREESTANDING SHED ROOF

A freestanding shed roof may be made with no overhang at the *rakes*, the edges along the endwalls that run parallel to the rafters. Lack of a front overhang on a freestanding or side-attached roof will do no real harm, but eliminating a rear overhang, even if only a short one, will eventually result in unnecessary damage to the rear wall.

As an example, consider a freestanding shed roof with a short rear overhang and none at the front or sides. The first step in building the frame, which is made up almost entirely of common rafters, is to lay out and cut a master pattern rafter. In this case the span and the run of the roof are the same, but note that one or the other (or both) are sometimes measured from the outside of the lower wall to the inside of the higher one (FIG. 35-1).

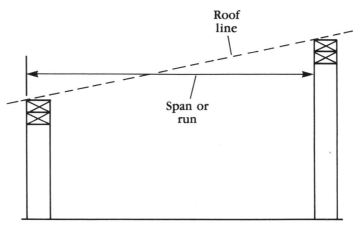

35-1 The span of a shed roof is sometimes measured from the outside of the lower wall to the inside of the higher one.

Start by setting your square to the cut of the roof and striking a plumb line at what will be the upper end of the rafter. Set the measure line or step off the rafter length, and strike the lines for the bird's-mouth cuts and the lower end, along with the tail cut.

Making seat and plumb cuts

Now, unlike common rafters in other roof designs, you must make seat and plumb cuts at the upper end that match those of the bird's-mouth cut. This will allow the rafter to sit flat on top of and against the ridge plate (FIG. 35-2). The notch is not deep in a low-slope roof, but the steeper the pitch the larger the notch becomes. For a full seat, a substantial amount of wood may be removed. This creates a problem, because

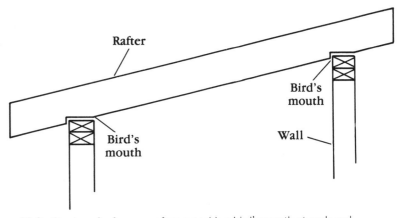

35-2 Shed roof rafters are often cut with a bird's-mouth at each end.

notching a rafter or joist end weakens it (FIG. 35-3). If you cut a 2-inch-deep notch from the bottom corner of a 2×8, you have the support capability of a 2×6.

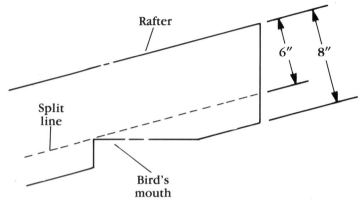

35-3 A bird's-mouth or any other notch in a rafter diminishes its effective strength.

Preventing rafter weakening

There are methods, other than keeping the notch as shallow as possible, to prevent weakening of the rafters. You can size the rafters up one step to compensate for the notch, or install a beveled ledger strip immediately beneath the rafters, or side-cleat each rafter just behind the notch. You can also provide extra support and strength by installing framing anchors; this is probably the easiest and least expensive, and the most advantageous to boot.

Setting the rafters

Set the pattern rafter in place to make sure that it fits up properly. Cut the common rafters, and lay out the rafter locations on the wall top plate. Then start at one end and set the rafters in place. The outer faces of the end or outboard rafters lie flush with the building line, as do the upper ends of all the rafters. Fasten each end by toenailing to the plate with four 8d nails.

Endwalls

There are several possible arrangements at the endwalls. The end rafters may lie directly atop the top plate of discrete endwall frames. Or, endwall frames may now have to be constructed to fill the open space between the plate and the end rafters. Or, the studs of the endwalls may be individually installed after the rafters are secured, with each stud notched and beveled to fit under and against the end rafters. (Refer to Chapter 31.)

RAKE OVERHANGS

If you want an overhang at the upper end of the roof, the only change is that bird's-mouth notches must be cut and the rafter heads extended, just as is done at the rafter tails for a rear overhang. Rake extensions are handled differently. The endwalls must be in place, with the height of the cap plate calculated to accept a lookout ladder set at the proper level (FIG. 35-4). If the overhang is less than 18 inches, 2-×-4 stock may be used for lookouts, extending inward about 3 feet. For greater overhangs, the lookouts are usually made of the same size stock as the rafters. Rake overhangs seldom exceed 3 feet; beyond that they are likely to be built as a roof extension supported by columns.

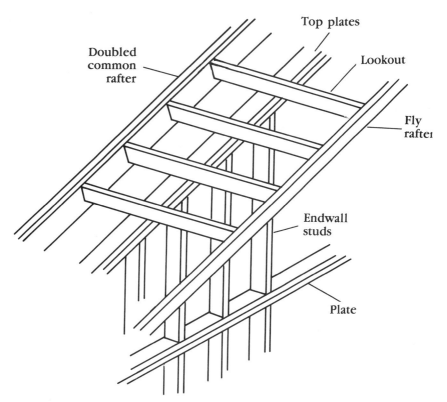

35-4 Shed roof rake extensions require a lookout ladder set upon an endwall frame, level with the rafter tops.

To build rake overhangs, install a series of lookouts set on a double plate and over the wall studs. Anchor the inboard ends to the header rafter, using two or three 16d nails driven through the header. Fasten the outboard ends to the cap plates with four 8d toenails. Secure a band or nailer across the open ends of the lookouts and across the rafter tails and heads. Box out the corners as necessary with short lookouts interconnected, and install a king rafter in long overhangs.

Securing wide overhangs

This arrangement is the same one that is used for the flat roof overhangs, as described in the previous chapter. Wide overhangs on shed roofs (and flat roofs) tend to be windcatchers. In locales where wind is apt to be a problem, securing the rafters to the plates with framing anchors or straps rather than just nailing them is a good idea, and might be required by local codes.

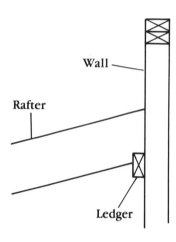

35-5 The upper ends of the rafters in an attached shed roof section that faces the main structure rest upon a ledger plate.

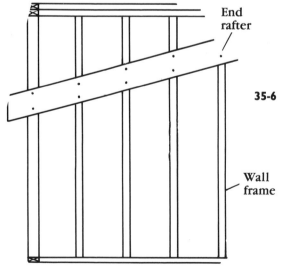

35-6 An end-attached shed roof has its inner end rafter fastened directly to the wall of the main structure.

ATTACHED SHED ROOF SECTIONS

The construction of attached shed roof sections differs only in the few details of their connection to the main structure. When set against a wall, for example, the higher end of the roof is supported by a ledger plate fastened flat to the wall (FIG. 35-5), rather than a wall top plate. In an end attachment, the end rafter may be secured directly to the adjoining wall studs (FIG. 35-6), and the endwall of the shed-roofed structure eliminated. In a dormer construction, although the roof may appear to be a flat shed type, it actually is little more than a jacked-up section of the larger roof to which it is attached.

Chapter **36**

Gable roof framing

*G*able roofs, so named because of the triangular endwall shape they form, are probably the most popular of all the roof styles. A simple gable roof consists basically of two shed roofs tilted against one another, although there is a bit more to it than that. One of the easiest gable roofs to build is the two-section, plain variety with a ridgeboard, no rake overhang, a short eave overhang, and equal slope on each side.

GABLE ROOF WITH RIDGEBOARD

The entire construction (except for the ridgeboard) is made up of common rafters. To begin, lay out a master pattern rafter, then use it to cut the required number of rafters. Select the ridgeboard stock. Nominal 1-inch board is satisfactory, although 2-inch stock is sometimes employed, especially on a long ridge. Either way, the width of the board should be no less than the length of the rafter ridge cut, so the rafter ends will bear fully on the ridgeboard. Nor does a little extra ridgeboard width do any harm.

Making ridgeboard supports

Next, make up two or three (or more) temporary ridgeboard supports (FIG. 36-1). A pair of short 2×4s for a base, a straight length of 1×4 or 2×4 for the upright, and a couple of small scraps of 1×2 are all you need for each support. The top end of the upright should lie exactly at the bottom edge position of the ridgeboard.

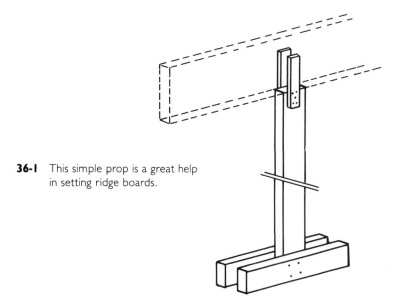

36-1 This simple prop is a great help in setting ridge boards.

Snap a chalkline on the floor platform that lines up with the length-wise centerline of the ridgeboard position. Mark the centerline of the ridgeboard props, position them centered on the chalkline and in between rafter locations, and tack-nail them in place. Then attach diagonal braces from near the top of the uprights to the floor. Lay out the rafter positions on one side of the ridgeboard with double lines and mark the space between them as you did for joist or stud layout. Likewise, lay out the seat locations on the plates. (If the rafter ends lie against appropriately positioned joists, this step isn't necessary.) Drop the ridgeboard into the slot atop the supports.

Setting the rafters

With a plumb bob or a straightedge and spirit level, align one end of the ridgeboard with the endwall building line. This should automatically align the other end if it was correctly precut. Boost a rafter into place, with the bird's-mouth cut resting flat on the plate and the ridge cut against the ridgeboard (FIG. 36-2). Secure the lower end by toenailing with three or four 8d nails, and the upper end by driving two 10d nails through a 1-inch ridgeboard. Use 16d nails for a 2-inch ridgeboard.

Set the mating rafter in place and align it with the first. Fasten it by toenailing two or three 10d nails at the upper end (FIG. 36-3), three or four 8d at the lower end. Skip three or four rafter locations and install another pair, and so on; this will quickly anchor the ridge and solidify its position. Then fill in the empty slots afterward. Where the lower ends of the rafters lie against joists, fasten them by face nailing to the joists with five 10d

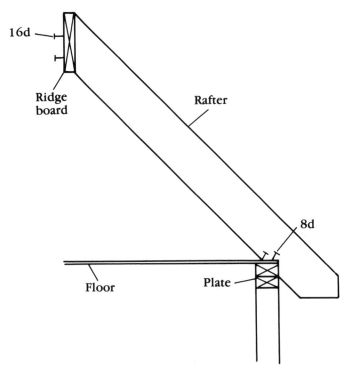

36-2 The first rafter of a set in position against the ridge board.

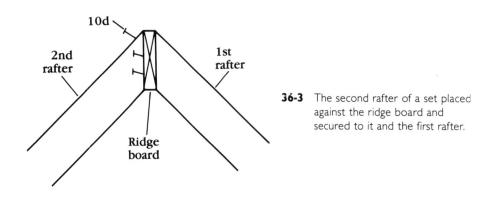

36-3 The second rafter of a set placed against the ridge board and secured to it and the first rafter.

nails, two from one side and three from the other. If there is a 1¹/2-inch gap between the rafter and the joist, nail in a spacer block.

INSTALLING COLLAR BEAMS

In a pitched-roof design, the tendency is for the rafters to sag downward and their ends to push outward, even though they support one another at the ridge. Collar beams or collar ties will counteract this downward and

36-4 A collar tie in place on a rafter set.

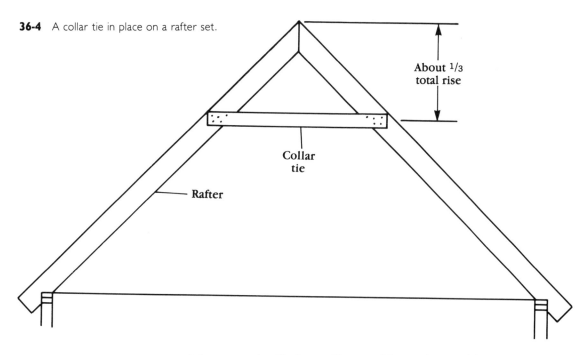

About 1/3
total rise

Collar
tie

Rafter

outward thrust, and will also stiffen a gable roof assembly against strong wind pressure. Often the beams, which are actually boards or planks, are placed only on every third or fourth rafter set, which is fine for them but does nothing for the rest. The stiffening and antisag effect does not transmit equally to other parts of the structure.

Place 1-×-6 stock about one-third of the way down from the ridge. Face nail it to one side of every rafter set with five 8d nails (FIG. 36-4). This must be done if the collar beams will be used as ceiling joists in a finished attic space. In that case, adjust the height of the beams to be at least 7 feet 8 inches above the subfloor. You might also prefer to install 2-×-4 or 2-×-6 beams, which afford more nailing surface for the drywall. Face nail them to the rafters with two 16d nails at each end, clinched over.

GABLE ROOF WITHOUT RIDGEBOARD

Often gable roofs, especially if small in overall expanse, are constructed without a ridgeboard. This involves making up the rafter sets ahead of time, then raising each set and bracing it in place. The rafter sets can be assembled on the floor platform, a set of sawhorses, or on a level patch of ground. Usual procedure is to align a pair of precut rafters tip to tip and fasten them together with a gusset plate of 1/2-inch plywood at the top and a 2-×-6 collar beam about a third of the way down. Use both construction adhesive and plenty of nails, and for best results stack the sets and allow the adhesive to fully cure before setting the rafters. Meanwhile, lay out the rafter positions on the plates.

Erecting rafter sets

To erect rafter sets from an upper-level floor platform, start with one inboard several feet from an end of the structure. Lay the set down flat with the ends approximately positioned on the plate and raise the tip until the assembly is vertical. Hold it in place with braces nailed to floor cleats. Position the next rafter set in line, swing it up, and brace it. Then tie the two together at a couple of places on each side with boards nailed across the upper edges. Continue until all the sets are in place; those toward the building ends will have to be boosted into place more or less upright. Finally, double check the alignments and plumb, make any needed adjustments, and rebrace if necessary.

A variation on this theme, handy in small buildings like garages where there are no ceiling/floor joists, is to hang a series of rafter sets upside down inside the building, wedged against the plates. Then they can be swung up into place and stabilized with pick-poles and ropes, and braced in position. Again, the last few have to be lifted straight up onto the plates.

ADD-ON GABLE ROOF

A gable roof grafted to another gable roof is a common arrangement. This can be a small roof extending out over a porch or a large roof covering a full-sized ell. Or, the roof can extend from a central part of the main roof or cover a full corner of the main structure. The gable roof may be situated in any number of different ways, but the construction basics remain the same. Valley and valley jack rafters are required. Note the position of the valley rafters in the frame; they support the ends of numerous valley jack rafters and thus an added load. Therefore these rafters are often a size larger than the common rafters: 2×8 common and 2×10 valley. This also affords a full bearing surface for the angled side cuts of the valley jacks.

Depending upon the design and positioning of the gable roof section to be added to or grafted onto another, you'll probably have to determine ahead of time just where the lengthwise centerline of the ridge of the add-on gable will lie, as well as the plate locations of the valley rafters. Get the main ridgeboard installed along with some of the main common rafters, so that part of the construction is stable. Leave a suitable gap for the add-on gable.

Installing ridgeboard

Assuming the add-on gable lies at the same height as the main roof (FIG. 36-5), locate the position of its secondary ridgeboard end on the main ridgeboard. Set it in place with temporary props and anchor one end to the main ridgeboard by face nailing. Use two or three 16d nails, 10d for a 1-inch ridgeboard. Then set most or all of the common rafters in the add-on section in the usual manner, to stabilize the whole frame. Lay out the valley rafters with the square and trim them to fit snugly into each side of

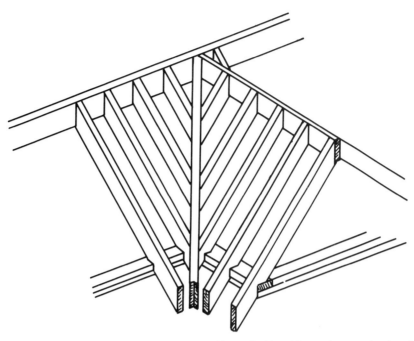

36-5 This is the arrangement for an add-on gable roof with a ridge at the same level as the main ridge.

the intersection of the two ridgeboards. If there is an overhang, the projection of the rafter tail will be greater that that of the common rafters. Lay out a right triangle with base and elevation equal to the amount of the common rafter projection. Measure the hypotenuse; which will be the length of the valley rafter tail.

Installing jacks

Finally, use the rafter square table to determine the lengths and cut details of the valley jack rafters. Working in pairs, cut and install the jacks. Lay out their positions on the ridgeboard and the valley rafter faces. Set the jacks flush with the ridgeboard top, but a little above the top of the valley rafters so the roof sheathing edges will abut smoothly. Fasten them in opposing pairs, using four 10d toenails at the valley joints and three or four at the ridge. Start about in the middle of each row, and make sure the valley rafters stay straight. The best method is to leave all nails short of fully driven until all the jacks are set, then go back and finish driving them tight.

Installing an add-on roof that is lower than main roof

If the ridge of the add-on roof is lower than the main roof (FIG. 36-6), the situation is a bit different. In the case of a fairly small add-on, install the

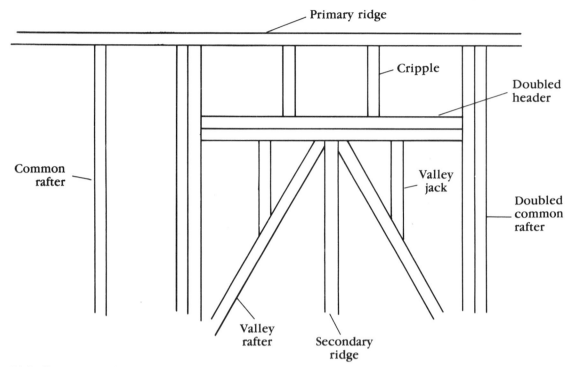

36-6 The component layout for an add-on gable roof with the ridge at a lower level than the main ridge, in plan view.

main common rafters as before, leaving the full opening for the add-on section. Install a single header between the two common rafters that bound the opening, positioned just above the point of the ridgeline of the add-on roof. From the header vertical centerline establish the ridgeboard and valley rafter locations, and install them in the usual manner. Double the header, then fit jack rafters between the doubled header and the ridgeboard. Secure all pieces with 16d nails, face nailed where possible. Otherwise, use 10d nails. Then fit the jack rafters as usual.

Installing supporting valley

Another method is more commonly employed when the area of the add-on roof is substantial (FIG. 36-7). Once the main roof frame has been erected, a single valley rafter—called a *supporting valley*—is installed from ridgeboard to plate. It can be set to either left or right. Then install a shortened valley rafter attached to the supporting valley. Trim the secondary ridgeboard to fit the intersection of the valley rafters and install it along with some common rafters (if possible) to secure its position. Finally, install all the jacks, making side cuts as necessary. One or two valley cripple jacks will have to be fitted between the shortened and the supporting valley rafters.

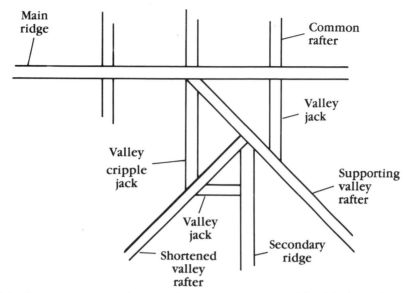

36-7 This arrangement is often used for a large gable add-on with a ridge lower than the main ridge.

OVERHANGS

Gable roofs almost always have overhangs at both eaves and rakes, and the details of the cornice construction required in this case are covered in a later chapter. In two instances, however, support members for the overhang and cornice have to be built into the roof frame. The simplest of these arrangements is for overhangs that extend anywhere from 8 to 18 inches from building line (FIG. 36-8).

The first step is to calculate the ridgeboard length to extend a certain distance beyond the last common rafter and the building line. The exact amount of extension depends upon the desired overhang width, including trim, drip edge, and the rake extension of the finish roofing. After installing the common rafters, fasten a nailing header across the rafter ends. Allow the ends to project an amount equal to the ridgeboard extension. Then nail a fly or outrigger rafter to the ridgeboard and soffit nailer ends. This rafter sometimes matches the others, but often is narrower to allow a stepped cornice return.

When the rake overhang exceeds 18 inches, construction follows the same pattern as for a flat or shed roof overhang (refer to these chapters). Build a lookout ladder supported by the endwall top plate (see FIG. 35-4). The lookouts can be the same width as the rafters, or narrower, depending upon the extent of the projection. Anchor the ends to a doubled inboard common rafter, and attach a fly rafter to the lookout ends. It is also a good idea to install nailing blocks between the lookouts, with their top flush with the rafter tops (FIG. 36-9). This provides a secure bearing surface for the roof sheathing.

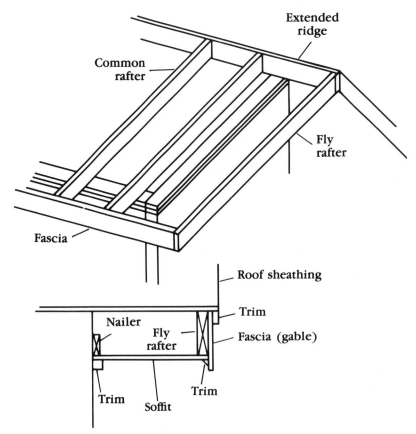

36-8 A simple arrangement for a rake extension of approximately 8 to 18 inches beyond the building line.

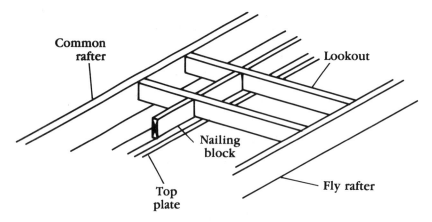

36-9 On a wide rake overhang, install nailing blocks between the lookouts to provide adequate bearing for the roof sheathing.

Chapter 37

Hip and pyramid roof framing

While not as popular as the gable roof style, hip roofs are often seen in residential applications. The principal frame members are the hip and hip jack rafters. The hip rafter is the opposite of the valley rafter; the valley descends and forms an inside corner, while the hip ascends and forms an outside corner. Layout, measuring, and trimming is handled in the same way as for valley rafters, and the same table lines on the rafter square are employed. And like valley rafters, hip rafters take a lot of load and strain, so are often one size larger than common rafters. In a simple hip roof all four sections can be set to the same slope, which makes for easier construction, but the end sections might differ from the other two. In fact, there could be four different slopes, but the appearance would seem awkward.

SETTING COMMON RAFTERS

To build a simple, symmetrical hip roof, first lay out the positions of the common rafters on the plate. Cut the ridgeboard to a length equal to the distance between the outer faces of the outside common rafters. This, in turn, is equal to the length of the building (or that part of it being covered by this roof), outside to outside, minus the span, plus the thickness of a rafter. Prop the ridgeboard in place just as for a gable roof and set the common rafters in the usual fashion. Then, drop a common rafter from each end of the ridgeboard and aligned lengthwise with it to the center of the endwall plates (FIG. 37-1). These two rafters match the other common rafters.

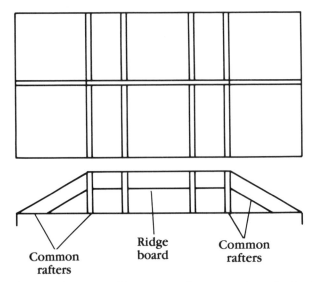

37-1   Hip roof construction starts with common rafters set to the ends of and aligned with the ridge board.

LAYING OUT AND CUTTING HIP RAFTERS

Next, lay out the hip rafters. The procedure is the same as for laying out common rafters, except that you use the 17-inch mark column to figure from rather than the 12-inch mark column. When an odd measurement for the hip rafter is involved, allow the extra inches left in the run of a common rafter to be the sides of a square. Lay out the square and measure the diagonal. (Or, find the length of the hypotenuse of the right triangle described.) The answer will be the actual odd-unit dimension for the hip rafter, which you measure out as usual (FIG. 37-2).

Note that if you cut a hip rafter tail to the same length as a common rafter for a matching projection at the building corner, you'll be disappointed—it will be too short. The end of the tail must be cut to a point. The distance from that point back to the corner of the plate is equal to the diagonal of a square whose sides are the same length as the projection of the common rafters (FIG. 37-3).

Once you have made a pattern hip rafter, try it for proper fit, adjust as necessary, and make up the remaining hips. If you were to install the rafters as they are, you would run into yet another problem. The top edge of the hip rafters will lie above the tops of the hip jacks a certain amount, depending upon the roof slope. There are two solutions. You can drop the hips by trimming the seats, or you can back (bevel) the edges (FIG. 37-4). You have to do one or the other, or the roof sheathing won't line up properly.

To determine the amount of drop needed, set the square on the rafter to the cut of the roof and draw a line in from the edge that is equal in length

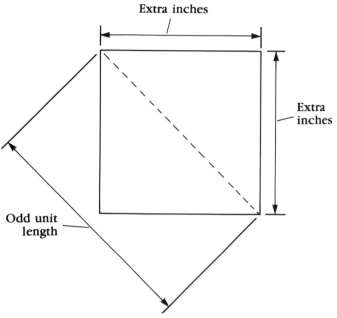

37-2 The diagonal of a square whose sides equal the odd inches of hip rafter length equals the odd-unit rafter length to be added to the even-unit measurement.

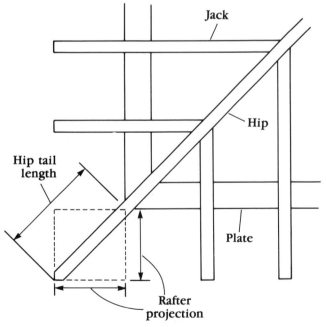

37-3 The length of a hip rafter tail is equal to the diagonal of a square whose sides equal the common rafter projection.

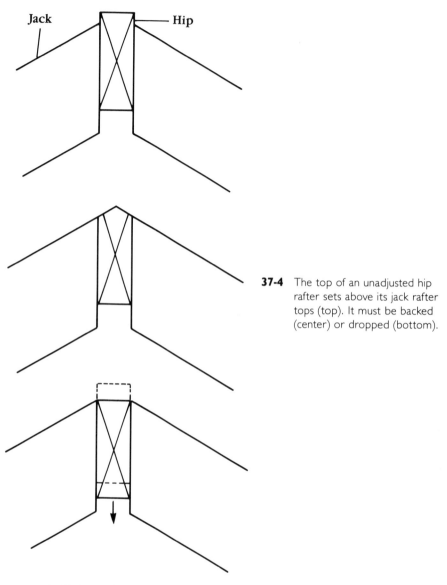

Jack — Hip

37-4 The top of an unadjusted hip rafter sets above its jack rafter tops (top). It must be backed (center) or dropped (bottom).

to one-half the rafter thickness (typically 3/4 inch). Measure the vertical distance from the inner end of this line to the upper edge of the rafter. Cut that amount from the rafter seat (FIG. 37-5). To line out backing cuts, set the square the same way and measure inward one-half the rafter thickness and mark a point. Draw a line through this point that is parallel with the rafter edges, full length, on both sides. Draw another line down the centerline of the top edge of the rafter, full length (FIG. 37-6). Trim to the lines with a power plane. Or, set a table or radial arm saw blade to the proper angle with the fence to the proper distance, and make a pair of rip cuts.

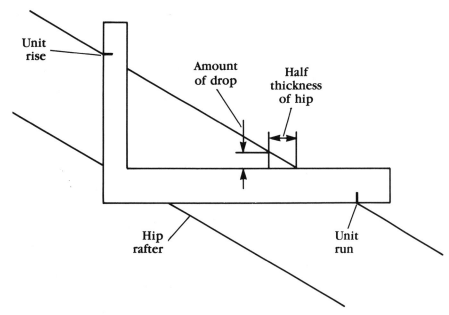

37-5 Use the framing square to determine the amount of drop needed in a hip rafter installation.

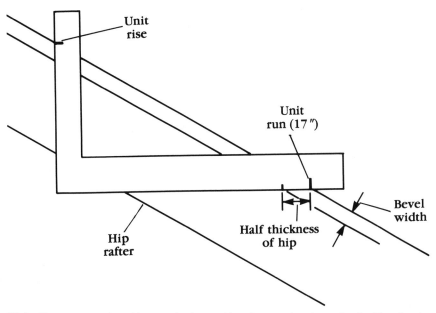

37-6 The amount of backing required on a hip rafter can be determined with a framing square.

LAYING OUT AND FASTENING HIP JACK RAFTERS

Once the hip rafters are made up and set, you can lay out the positions of the hip jack rafters. Trim them to size in pairs or fours, just as for valley jacks, and install them successively in the same fashion. Lay out their positions on the hip rafter faces and the plate, then start fastening them in pairs. Use four 10d toenails at the rafter joint and three or four 8d toenails at the plate, starting about at the middle of the row. Make sure the hips stay straight; brace them if you have to (FIG. 37-7). Leave the nails short of being fully seated until all the jacks are installed, then go back and drive them home.

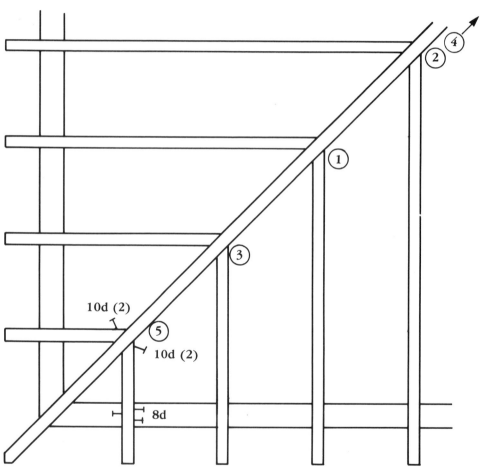

37-7   Fasten jack rafters to a hip rafter in opposing pairs, starting about at the midpoint of the hip and working back and forth.

TWO METHODS OF SETTING HIP RAFTERS

Instead of two short and two long hip sections, a pyramid roof has four equal triangular panels that meet in a point at the center. For this arrangement the building, or the area to be covered, must be square. There are two approaches to setting the hip rafters.

Method 1

The most craftsmanlike method is to cut the peak end of each to mating compound angles. Tie one opposing pair together with a collar beam, temporary or permanent, several feet below the peak. Stand the pair in place and brace it, and secure the bottom ends to the plate. Then set the remaining two, supported by the first at the peak and fastened at the bottom. Secure a collar beam to these two, and nail the four together with a few 16d nails at the peak (FIG. 37-8). If you want to be like a cabinetmaker about it, back the top edges of the hip rafters to correspond with the roof angle.

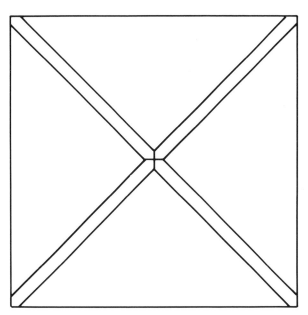

37-8 One method of fitting the four hip rafters together at the peak of a pyramid roof frame.

Method 2

The second method is cruder, but it works. Pair two of the hip rafters, butted end to end at the peak. Toenail at the top and set a collar tie further down. Erect the pair and brace them, and fasten them at the plate. Set the third rafter against the pair, centered on the joint between them, and toenail through the pair into the single with 16d nails. Set the fourth rafter the same way, and fasten it with 16d nails driven through from the opposite side of the first pair (FIG. 37-9).

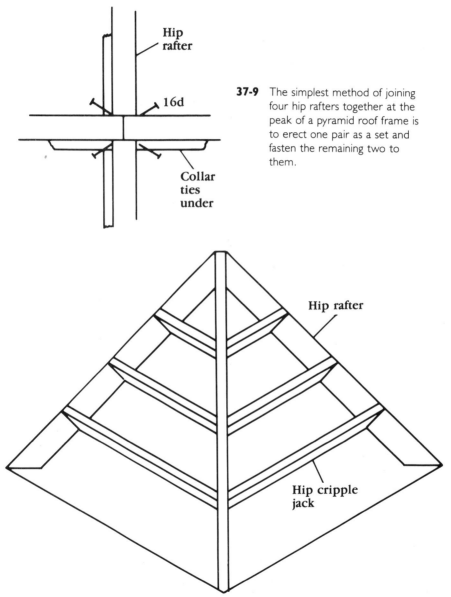

37-9 The simplest method of joining four hip rafters together at the peak of a pyramid roof frame is to erect one pair as a set and fasten the remaining two to them.

37-10 Instead of installing hip jack rafters, in some constructions you can use hip cripple jack rafters (purlins) instead.

INSTALLING HIP VALLEY CRIPPLE JACKS

In most roof frames of this sort the hip jack rafters are laid out and installed in the usual fashion, and the hips adjusted to suit their lie. But if the roof is small and relatively steep, and the snow/rain loading and wind factor is negligible, there is another way. You can dispense with the hip jacks, and instead install hip cripple jack rafters, (also called *purlins*). These members run horizontally between the hip rafters (FIG. 37-10). They are made of the same size stock, or sometimes one step narrower, with their ends trimmed to the required compound angle, opposing at opposite ends. Typically, 16-inch centering is used. Depending upon the required overhang, there may be an outrigger rafter or two beyond the building line.

Because the combination of a secondary gable and a hip close-coupled is common, this seems a good spot to introduce that construction,

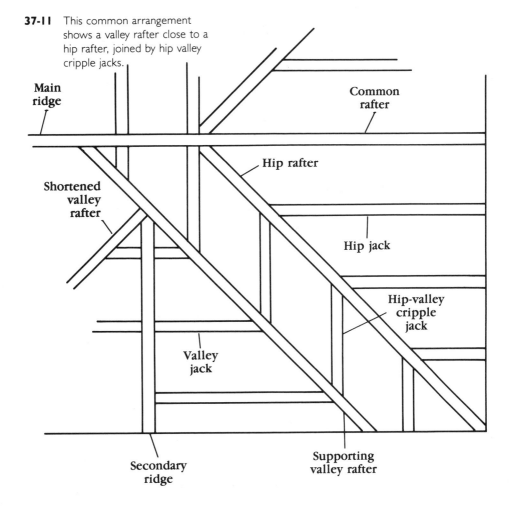

37-11 This common arrangement shows a valley rafter close to a hip rafter, joined by hip valley cripple jacks.

Main ridge

Common rafter

Hip rafter

Shortened valley rafter

Hip jack

Hip-valley cripple jack

Valley jack

Secondary ridge

Supporting valley rafter

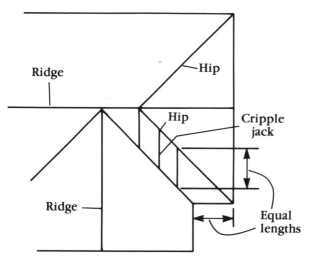

37-12 Where close-coupled hip and valley rafters are parallel, as is usual, the cripples will all be of the same length and have identical side cuts.

which requires installing special shortened members. Often the valley rafter of a gable roof sets an inside corner so close to an outside corner that is described by a hip rafter on a main roof that there is no space for a common rafter to drop to the plate from the main ridge. In this case the valley and hip rafters have to be bridged by hip valley cripple jacks (FIG. 37-11).

In most constructions the valley and hip rafters are parallel with one another. Thus, all the cripples will be the same length, with equal diagonal side cuts facing the same way. The rafter length is equal to the distance along the plate from the valley rafter centerline to the hip rafter centerline (FIG. 37-12). The side-cut figure is half the cripple thickness, typically 1¹/2 inches. Lay one out and check it for fit, adjust as needed, and use it as a pattern to cut all the rest.

To install the cripples, proceed as with any set of jacks. Work in pairs, starting from around the middle of the run. Tack them all in place, ensure the main rafter alignment, and finish securing them. Unequal slopes and nonparallel rafters mean that the cripples will all have to be individually measured and fitted.

Chapter **38**

Gambrel and mansard roof framing

*T*he gambrel style of roof is a standard for barns and smaller outbuildings as well, and it is also used on residences, especially in rural areas. In its most common and simplest form, a gambrel roof has four sections and two slopes. In the "Dutch barn" variation there are six sections and three slopes. Construction can be done in either of two ways, depending upon the desired end result. The mansard roof, an old French style, is actually a variation of the hip roof and is less commonly seen today than either the hip or the gambrel. Its construction can be tricky, but the design is relatively straightforward.

GAMBREL ROOF

The four-section gambrel has one ridge, two purlins or purlin plates, and two sets of common rafters. In the layout it is treated as two individual roofs (FIG. 38-1). The upper two sections comprise one roof, the lower two comprise the other. The common rafters do not butt at the purlin but they do align in a straight run from ridge to wall plate. The span of the lower roof is from outside to outside of the wall plate, and the rise is measured from the top of the wall plate to the top of the purlin or purlin plate. The run is measured from the outside of the wall plate to the outside of the purlin or purlin plate, same side, on a horizontal line. The span of the upper roof is from outside to outside of the purlins or purlin plates, and its rise is from the top of the purlins or purlin plates to the top of the ridge. The run is measured from the outside of the purlins or purlin plates to the center of the ridge. Figure 38-2 shows these relationships.

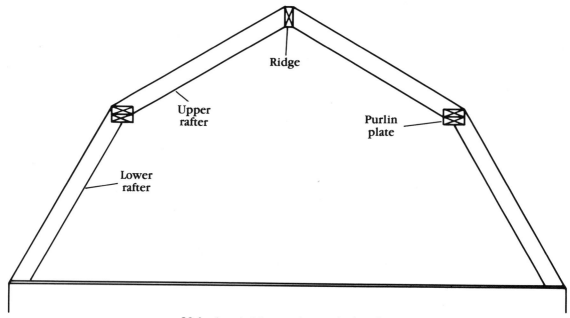

38-1 A typical four-section gambrel roof.

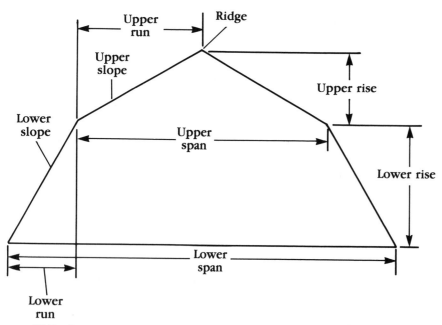

38-2 Gambrel roof layout separates the construction into two separate roofs.

Method 1

As mentioned, there are two construction methods that can be used for a gambrel roof. The first is a clear-span gambrel roof frame.

Make up pattern common rafters for the two roofs. Lay out the rafter positions on the wall plate and on the ridgeboard. Align and prop the ridgeboard in position, just as for a gable roof. You can also set the center studs of the endwalls at this point, as added (and permanent) support for the ridgeboard. And, you can build the endwalls and erect them before building the roof frame or not, as you wish (see Chapter 31).

Prop the purlins in place, after laying out the rafter locations on them. Working in double pairs, install opposing rafter sets at or close to the ends. Tack-nail them solidly, but don't drive the nails completely in. As soon as they are in place cut and fit a collar beam (2-x-6 stock is typically used for this) and install it from purlin top to purlin top (FIG. 38-3).

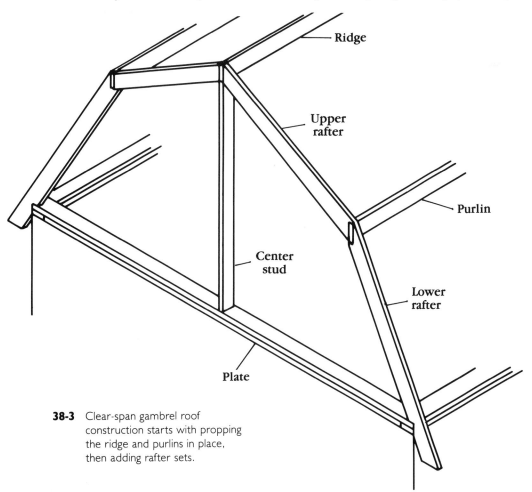

38-3 Clear-span gambrel roof construction starts with propping the ridge and purlins in place, then adding rafter sets.

Skip three or four rafter locations and install another set, and so on. Then check the purlins and ridge for straightness, and finish driving all the nails. Finally, go back and fill in the open positions with rafters sets and collar beams. Face nail collar beams with two 16d nails at each end, clinched over. Toenail rafter ends to the plate and purlins with three or four 8d nails at each bearing. Secure the first rafter of a pair to the ridgeboard by face nailing with three 10d nails into the rafter end (16d for a 2-inch ridgeboard). Secure the second rafter of the set to the ridgeboard by toenailing with four 8d nails. Fasten the lower common rafters to the joists with three 16d nails at each crossing, clinched over.

Method 2

The second method of construction is a bit easier, and works well in residential construction where the living area will be confined to the usable

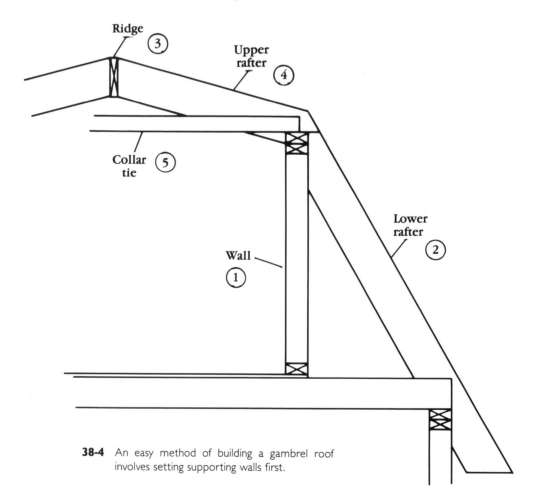

38-4 An easy method of building a gambrel roof involves setting supporting walls first.

full-headroom space beneath the upper roof. Instead of purlins to support the rafter ends, purlin plates—which are actually the top plates of partition walls—bear the load (FIG. 38-4).

These walls are built in the usual way and erected first. Then the rafters can be easily set, along the same lines as just described. Collar beams may be installed, but are sometimes left out for an open-ceiling effect, especially when the upper roof is small and/or loads are light. If there is a free choice, though, installing collar beams will give you a more stable roof.

Flared gambrel

There are several approaches to constructing the flared three-section type of gambrel roof. One easy one is to make the rafters of the lower roof without tails; just make a heel cut, flush with the building line. Install soffit lookouts for whatever eave projection is desired; 2 x 4s will do the job here, although 2 x 6s afford better bearing and nailing surfaces. Then run a set of false rafters from the common rafters to the lookouts (FIG. 38-5).

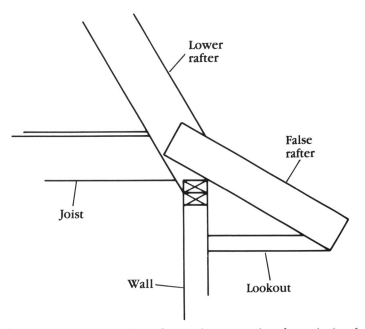

38-5 One method of adding a flare to the eave section of a gambrel roof.

The angle and projection can be set to whatever amount appeals but should be in proportion to the rest of the roof. Making a full-sized mock-up ahead of time is a good idea. You can trim the false rafters ends to a heel cut, or continue them in an exposed decorative tail beyond the main soffit. Either way, install blocking between rafters at the break point, which is located between the lower and the flared roof sections. These serve as nailers for the edges of the roof sheathing. In fact, a double set of blocks to handle both angles is a good idea and not much extra trouble.

MANSARD ROOF

A mansard roof is a steep hip roof with the top lopped off and replaced with a shallow hip roof. There are eight sections, four of a moderately to very steep slope and four that are gentle to nearly flat. The two sets of sections each have equal shapes and slopes so the roof is symmetrical; if it were not, construction would be difficult and the appearance would be strange. This roof almost always entirely covers a single or main structure, usually rectangular but sometimes square. Upper-level windows are often installed by means of dormers (usually gable) or by indents or setbacks. The roof overhang can be substantial, and in some cases the upper-level floor is cantilevered out over the lower on all sides. Either construction, together with a steep slope in the lower roof sections, can be designed to allow upper-level partition walls to align flush with the lower exterior walls, and their top plates to serve as the purlin plates for the upper roof sections (FIG. 38-6).

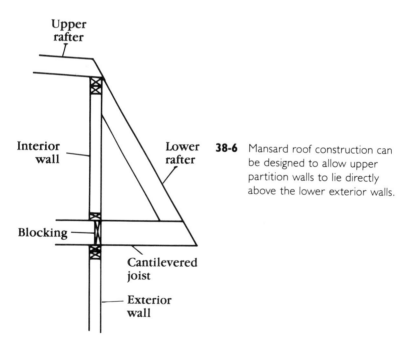

38-6 Mansard roof construction can be designed to allow upper partition walls to lie directly above the lower exterior walls.

The easiest way to build a mansard roof is to first install partition wall frames around the perimeter, along a precalculated line. Brace these walls solidly. Install any other interior partition walls, too. They will help brace the perimeter walls and, depending upon location, can be useful in sup-

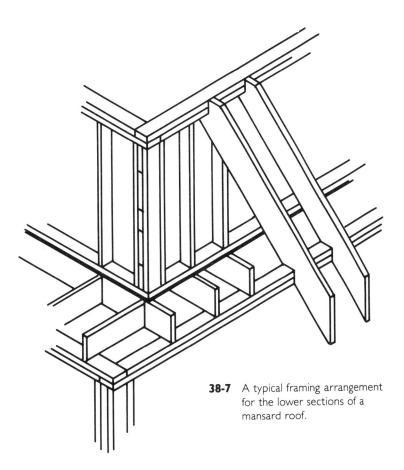

38-7 A typical framing arrangement for the lower sections of a mansard roof.

porting portions of the upper roof structure. Follow the methods for framing an ordinary hip roof. Install all the lower rafters—most of them are commons—in the usual fashion (FIG. 38-7). The upper ends of these rafters will have plumb and level cuts to bear upon the wall plates, much like those in a gambrel roof lower frame.

There are two possibilities for the upper roof sections, depending upon the slope desired. For a shallow slope, install a flat roof frame. After the frame is sheathed, or decked, lay thermal insulation in rigid panels that taper downward from the center to the outer edges. Cellular foamed glass and extruded polystyrene are available for this purpose. Arrange the taper to rise in four planes to a central peak. For a steeper slope, build up a frame in the same way a pyramid roof frame is constructed. Set opposing pairs of hip rafters based on the purlin plate corners. Then fill with hip jack rafters, or if the span is short, hip cripple jacks. If the slope is relatively steep and the span substantial enough to allow space for additional framing, install a series of collar beams from plate to plate.

Chapter **39**

Unequal-pitch and other roofs

Many modern and stylistic residence designs, not to mention the traditional saltbox, call for a two- or multiple-plane treatment, where the pitches of the roof sections are unlike. The rise per foot of run is different for the various sections, and in fact there might be several pitches. In such cases each discrete section is treated as an individual roof and constructed according to the normal procedures for that style. This creates no problems when the roof section is a simple extension, such as a shed-type porch roof, and few difficulties in many biplanar designs like the saltbox. Some arrangements, however, can be quite complex. Making a full-sized layout on the subfloor is an excellent idea. You can see exactly what needs to be done, how the cuts and joints are made, and what the mating angles are. You can also draw a layout to large scale, but that is not as satisfactory. Ridge and common rafter work is the same as for any other roof, but other aspects become more complicated. Following are the situations that can arise.

CONSTRUCTING AN UNEQUAL-PITCH ROOF

The unit run of a hip or valley rafter in an unequal-pitch roof is not 17 as in an equal-pitch roof. Instead, the unit run equals the diagonal of a rectangle, two of whose sides equal the unit run of the primary roof and the other two the unit run of the secondary roof (FIG. 39-1). So to get the total run of a valley or hip, lay out a rectangle in full size, using the actual measurements of the two roof sections (FIG. 39-2). The length of the diagonal is the length of the valley or hip run. Next, lay out a right triangle with the base equal to the total valley or hip run and the height equal to the total

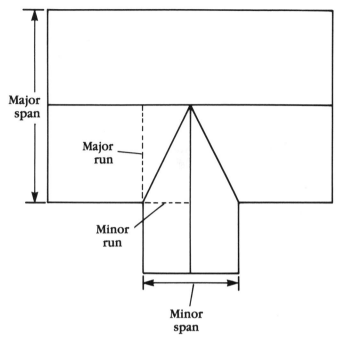

39-1 The unit run of a hip or valley rafter in an unequal-pitch roof equals the diagonal of a rectangle whose sides equal the unit runs of the major and minor roofs.

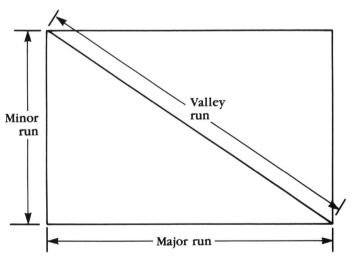

39-2 The total valley run in an unequal-pitch roof equals the diagonal of a rectangle whose sides equal the actual lengths of the major and minor roof runs.

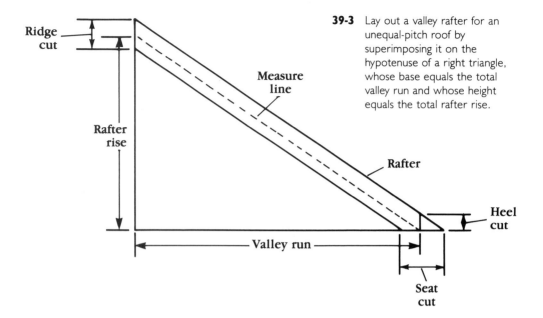

39-3 Lay out a valley rafter for an unequal-pitch roof by superimposing it on the hypotenuse of a right triangle, whose base equals the total valley run and whose height equals the total rafter rise.

rafter rise. The length of the hypotenuse is the line or unadjusted length of the valley or hip rafter (FIG. 39-3). Make the layout full size, and superimpose the outline of the rafter with its line length, now a measure line, on the hypotenuse line and coinciding with the heel point of the rafter. Use the outline to mark out the trim cuts. Ridge, side, and tail cuts will be different from side to side; take these also from a full-sized layout.

As usual, valley rafters do not need to be backed or dropped, because they are already lower than the jacks. And as usual, hips set too high. Where the degree of inequality between roof sections is not great, either backing or dropping can be carried out in the same way as was explained in an earlier chapter. Where the difference is great, you might have to do both. Make a drop first, as great as seems practical. If that is insufficient, back the high edge of the hip and leave the other; it won't interfere with anything.

The plumb cuts of jack rafters are the same as those of the common rafters of the respective roof sections. Lengths and side cuts, however, require some special attention. To get jack lengths, simply take the length of a common rafter for that roof section and divide it equally by the number of jacks needed (FIG. 39-4), according to the center-to-center rafter spacing being used. To get the other cuts, take them from a full-sized layout. An adjustable-angle square is helpful for marking locations and cut lines.

Lots of problems occur when two or more unequal-pitch roofs overhang the building line and must be fitted with a continuous cornice. Making cornice returns at rake overhangs can be a trial, too. Full-size layouts are a must here, so that you can visualize how to make the necessary

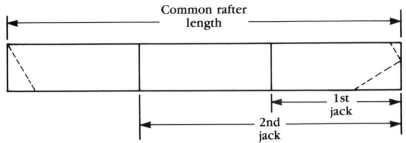

39-4 You can determine jack rafter lengths by dividing a common rafter equally by the number of jacks required.

adjustments. Heel cuts and level cuts, positions, extensions, all will be awry between differing roof sections. The rafter tails might have to be designed from the fascia/soffit back toward the building line, so there will be even, plumb, and level attachment points. Raising the wall height might also be necessary under the steep-pitched sections, and slight pitch alteration could be helpful.

OTHER ROOF STYLES

There are numerous house designs that call for roof styles not yet discussed, which might or might not have unequal-pitch sections. Although the framing patterns are different, construction proceeds according to the same principles and techniques already discussed. Here are the general patterns for a few of the more popular styles.

A-frame

The A-frame is a popular style, especially for vacation homes. In this arrangement, the roof doubles as the two sides for the structure (FIG. 39-5); the endwalls merely fill the gaps and are nonload-bearing. The pitch is typically very steep and the rafters made of wide stock, depending upon the specific span and pitch involved. The common rafters are best made full length, although they can be spliced at transverse load-bearing kneewalls. Floor/ceiling or loft joists act as collar beams and must be sized to serve both purposes. Construction is the same as for a conventional equal-pitch gable roof.

Butterfly

A butterfly roof is a gable roof turned inside out, or a pair of shed roofs back-to-back instead of face-to-face (FIG. 39-6). The higher ends are supported by load-bearing exterior walls, and the joined lower "ridge" is supported by a load-bearing interior wall. There must also be secondary pitch of both sections to allow moisture runoff down the valley they form. In a more fanciful version, the outer tips can be curved, and the two

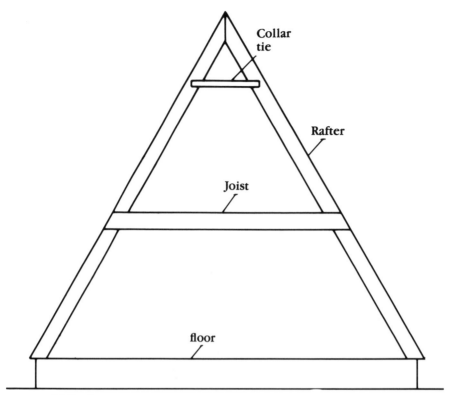

39-5 The A-frame is a popular roof style, especially for vacation homes.

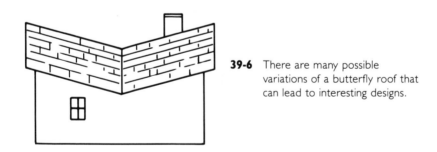

39-6 There are many possible variations of a butterfly roof that can lead to interesting designs.

sections can also be individually bowed or crowned. Construction is much like making a couple of shed roofs, except that the rafter seat cuts must be made to a side angle to match the equal tilt of the two sections.

Diagonal

A diagonal roof is just a freestanding shed roof twisted 90 degrees to the building walls (FIG. 39-7). Instead of the upper and lower eaves being paral-

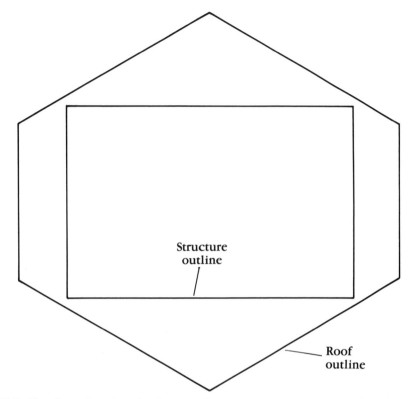

Structure
outline

Roof
outline

39-7 The diagonal roof can be altered to fit over almost any structure, and can be shed style or gabled.

lel with the front and back walls and the rakes parallel with the sides, the diagonals of the roof bisect them. The front and back exterior walls of the building must be constructed with canted top plates, and the side walls must set the roof pitch. Typically the slope is fairly steep and the overhangs substantial. Construction is much like a shed roof. This roof can be broken along a diagonal into a pair of gabled triangles that are either equal or unequal in size, pitch, or both.

Tent

A tent roof (FIG. 39-8) is commonly used on a round, hexagonal, octagonal, or other regular polysided structures. On an octagon, for example, there would be eight hip rafters running from a central point to each 45-degree corner. They could derive support from one another, or be aided by a center support column. There are several ways to make the joining plumb cuts. The most logical is to mate one rafter pair and erect it, then join an opposing pair as in a pyramid roof frame. Make side cuts on the remaining four and set them in the intersections of the first four. This

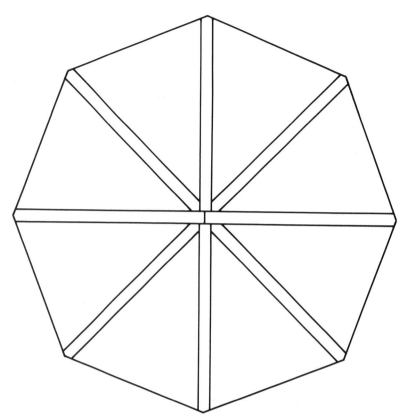

39-8   The tent-style roof is appropriate for round, hexagonal, octagonal, and other regular polysided structures.

makes a flat-topped peak, but the sheathing and finish roofing hide that. The seats at the plate are made in the usual way.

Then you can set hip jack rafters, working in pairs from both sides of each hip. This will mean that all the exterior walls will be load-bearing. Alternatively, you could install hip cripple jack rafters from each hip to the next. In that case, the hip rafters should be either extra-wide or doubled, because they will bear the entire roof load and transmit it to the corner posts of the walls. The corner posts thus become load-bearing columns requiring full support beneath them, and all the exterior walls are non-load-bearing or curtain walls.

Chapter **40**

Roof trusses

Roof trusses are the alternative to conventional rafter framing, and are being used more and more in residential applications. An individual truss is made up of several parts, which collectively take the place of rafters, floor-ceiling joists, wind braces, collar ties, and even stem walls in some instances. Most trusses are commercially manufactured and delivered preassembled. However, you can get trusses in knocked-down form, requiring some job-site assembly. It is also possible to construct trusses from scratch on the job site; special hardware is used for this purpose.

ADVANTAGES OF TRUSSES

There are good reasons for the increasing popularity of trusses; they have several advantages. Because most are factory-built, quality and precision assembly can be closely monitored and the units are uniform. They go into place rapidly and easily, so weathering is not a problem, and a structure can be roofed over and protected in short order. Trusses are engineered and designed for specific jobs (although there are numerous general-purpose designs as well), and so they usually require less material than a conventional frame. Because they are carefully engineered and built with prime material, they can be manufactured in clear spans of 30 feet and more. And finally, they are frequently more cost-effective than conventional roofing.

Trusses can be designed for almost any purpose. The ones often seen in residences are the standard gable trusses, typically with a span of about 26 feet and a 4-in-12 slope (FIG. 40-1). Usually they are seen marching in a

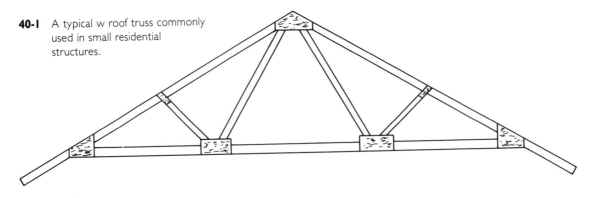

40-1 A typical w roof truss commonly used in small residential structures.

rank across a fairly small, single-roofed structure. In fact, trusses can be made to fit virtually all parts of a roof, so practically any roof design is possible. In addition, you can combine trusses with conventional framing. For example, you might frame all the center section of a hip roof with trusses where the common rafters would ordinarily be set, and then install hip rafters, end commons, and hip jacks in the old way.

TYPES OF TRUSSES

There appears to be a widespread misapprenhension that trusses are flat-bottomed, allowing only a conventional flat ceiling to be installed. Not so. Apart from trusses that can be specially engineered and shaped for extraordinary purposes, there are some standard designs of different configurations (FIG. 40-2). For example, either a scissors, vaulted scissors, or a cambered truss will allow a sloped ceiling under a gable roof. If you want a wide-open, cathedral effect, a three-hinged arch truss will do the job. To get away from the gable effect, use a mono-pitch or a stub, or a gambrel or a broken-pitch. A dual-pitch truss will give you the saltbox look, and if you want a conventional gable with attic, use a set of attic trusses. One way or another, you can do about anything you want to with roof trusses.

Build your own

If you decide to build your own trusses, be guided by a good set of plans of proven worth, or have the design made up for your particular purposes, engineered and approved. Use only top-grade stock in constructing them—the wood characteristics, species, and grade should be spelled out—and use the proper hardware and adhesive. Build the trusses carefully, keeping both the stock and the completed units protected from the weather.

Ready-made

If you buy ready-made trusses, there are some precautions to be heeded. Have them scheduled for delivery when you're ready for them, not any

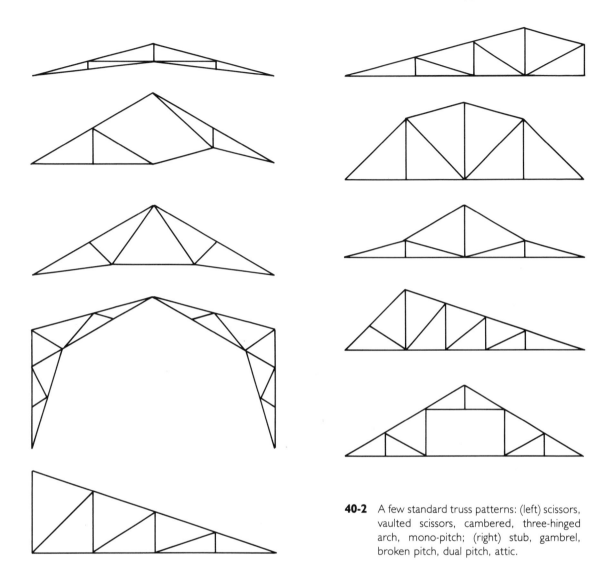

40-2 A few standard truss patterns: (left) scissors, vaulted scissors, cambered, three-hinged arch, mono-pitch; (right) stub, gambrel, broken pitch, dual pitch, attic.

old time beforehand. However, be prepared to warehouse them under cover if the scheduling doesn't work out; new trusses should never be left lying around in the weather. When you store them, even if only for a short while between taking them off the truck and putting them up on the plates, stand them up vertically, bottom chords down. That's the only direction in which they have any appreciable strength and rigidity. If you have to lay them flat, make sure they are truly flat, such as on a concrete pad, not propped up on a few 2×4s. When you handle or carry the trusses, keep them upright if possible so they won't distort or loosen from wracking. In some instances you can sling them upside down from the wall top plates and swing them up into position with ropes and pick poles, as is done with some ordinary rafter sets.

INSTALLATION

Trusses can also be installed in the same way as conventional rafters or rafter sets. Make the layout the same way, and boost or swing the trusses into place successively. Don't skip locations as with conventional rafters. Brace the first truss in place, then secure the second one to the first with a couple of boards tacked across the top edges. Keep going this way, adding braces and boards as necessary to keep the whole assembly solid. There is no ridgeboard; plumb and spacing have to be checked constantly. You can secure the ends at the plate by toenailing with three or four 8d nails. However, toenailing often is not the best method, especially if the chord stock is small or has a tendency to split, or if you have a nail through plywood gussets. Steel framing anchors are apt to be easier to use, and will give you a neater, stronger installation.

Chapter **41**

Roof openings and wind braces

Many roofs require at least one opening to be made in part of the framework, to admit passage of an appliance or masonry chimney, a skylight, or a roof window. Framing for dormer construction also requires a large opening in the main roof frame. In these cases, additional framing and anchoring is recommended, and often required by building codes, for locales where strong winds are a frequent occurrence. The same system, wind bracing, can also be employed in heavy-snow country.

FRAMING FOR SMALL ROOF OPENINGS

The smallest roof openings, such as for drainage system vent stacks or small roof air vents, require no additional framing. All that's needed is a suitable small hole in the roof sheathing. To frame a small opening between two adjacent rafters, such as might be needed for a metal chimney support basket, install a pair of single headers between them. If the opening needs to be narrowed, as when nailing support might be needed for the item to be installed in the opening, insert a trimmer between the headers (FIG. 41-1).

FRAMING FOR LARGE ROOF OPENINGS

Large openings in the roof frame need to be done a bit differently. If roof loading is light and the gap will span no more than two rafter spaces, the side rafters need not be doubled. Just install a single header above and below the opening to box it out. Then extend head rafters from the ridge-

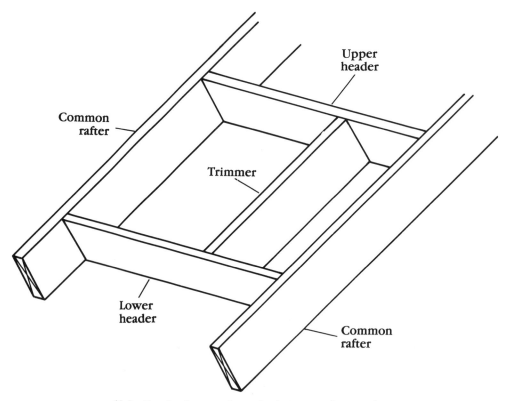

41-1   Framing for a small opening between adjacent rafters.

board to the upper header, and carry through with tail rafters from the lower header to the plate. Install one or two trimmers, as needed, to properly size the opening (FIG. 41-2).

If the roof load is moderate to heavy, and/or the gap spans more than two rafter spaces and necessitates removing part of two or more rafters, the side rafters should be bolstered from ridge to plate by doubling them. The headers should also be doubled. The sequence is as follows (refer to FIG. 41-3): 1) Install the side rafters. 2) Install upper and lower single headers face nailed with 16d nails through the side rafters. 3) Put in head and tail rafters face nailed through the headers with 16d nails. 4) Add upper and lower doubling headers face nailed through the side rafters with 16d nails and to the headers with 10d nails. 5) Add side doubling rafters face nailed to the side rafters with 10d nails in a staggered pattern every 16 inches or so.

Again, you can install single trimmers as necessary between the headers to reduce the opening size and provide attachment surfaces. This might be required for a skylight curb, for example. In all cases, the size of the dimension stock used should be the same as the common rafter stock.

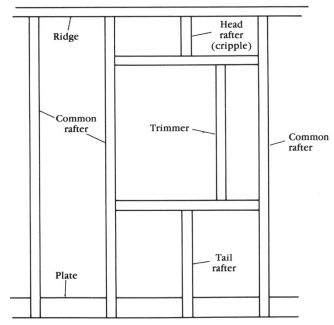

41-2 Framing for an opening spanning no more than two rafters, with light to moderate loading.

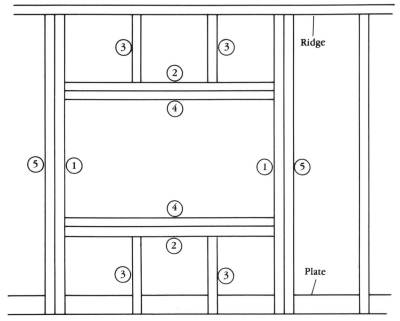

41-3 Framing for a large roof opening, any loading.

Plate and ridge ends of the rafters can be fastened with any of the appropriate usual procedures.

WIND BRACING

Wind bracing is not needed if the roof frame is made up of truss assemblies, because bracing is integral in truss design. In conventional rafter framing, however, such bracing might be advisable. In its mildest form, ordinary collar beams will serve a limited wind-bracing function in a gable roof, provided there is one attached to every rafter set. Otherwise, and also when the roof style is a modified gable or some other shape, different measures can be taken.

A typical arrangement is to add truss-type bracing to the rafters, which in a gable roof would normally be arranged as shown in Fig. 41-4. The 2-×-4 braces are angled to anchor at about the midpoint of the rafters with a pair of 16d nails clinched over, and attached to the upper edges of the ceiling joists with 8d toenails. Gusset plates of 1/2-inch plywood are face nailed with 8d nails to each side to further anchor the braces to the joists. This installation is best made on every rafter set, rather than only on every fourth or fifth, as is sometimes done. Positioning braces in roof frames of different configurations is a matter of common sense. Angle the braces to transmit as much load as possible from rafter midspans to load-bearing walls or columns and make truss-like patterns in the process.

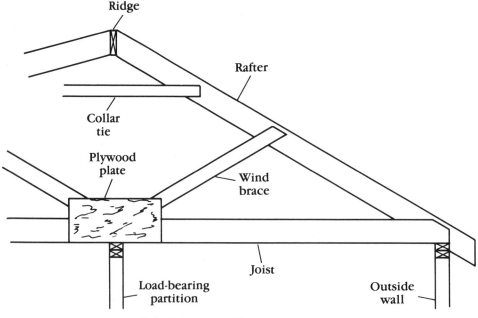

41-4 A typical wind bracing arrangement.

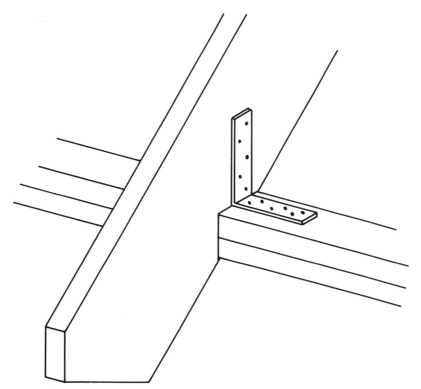

41-5 Either truss or rafter ends can be tied to the wall frames with steel hangers, brackets, or straps.

Under normal circumstances any of the ordinary nailing procedures are more than sufficient to anchor a roof assembly to the walls of a house for an endurance of many decades. However, high winds can loosen and destroy a roof. This can occur from constant battering and jolting, and the only preventive is top-quality materials and workmanship. Damage also occurs when wind pulls a roof section loose, and/or gets beneath portions of it and actually lifts it up. The greatest likelihood for failure occurs at the joint between the plate, rafters, and joists, especially if there is a substantial overhang at the eaves.

The preventive is simple. Install steel strapping or similar framing anchors that will solidly affix the rafters to the plates (FIG. 41-5). This can be done so as to fasten each rafter to the wall plate, or across the plate to a stud. When a rafter/stud connection cannot be made, it's a good idea to install steel straps or other anchors from plate to studs, then from rafters to plate. The joists can be similarly anchored, then nailed to the rafters in the usual way.

Chapter **42**

Dormer framing

*D*ormers can be used for architectural emphasis and to provide added light, ventilation, and living space in the upper story or half-story of a house. With few exceptions they are fitted with either a gable or a shed roof and can be attached to several different main roof styles, especially gable and hip. Dormers range in size from a width of only a couple of rafter spaces to nearly covering an entire main roof section. Regardless of size, however, the construction techniques remain the same. Dormer walls are built using the same materials and procedures as in the rest of the house, while the roof frames are designed and built for local conditions, as would be any roof of comparable size and shape.

FRAMING SMALL DORMERS

One of the most common dormer arrangements consists of one, two, or three small gable-roofed units that are attached to a main gable roof, often on both sides, with the dormer ridges lower than the main ridge.

Framing the opening

To construct a dormer of this sort that is only three or four rafter bays wide, begin by framing the opening in the main roof (FIG. 42-1). With the two side or trimmer rafters in place, install a single header set at right angles to them in both planes, and secure it by face nailing with 16d nails. Its location on the rafters must be calculated so that when it is doubled, the top edge of the dormer ridgeboard will lie flush with its lower top edge and at the proper height.

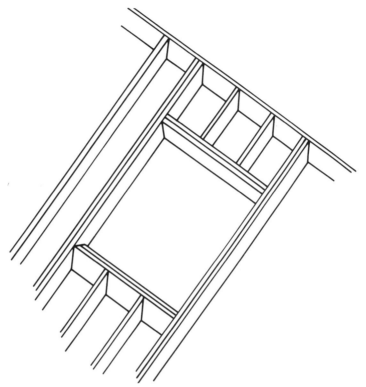

42-1   A framing arrangement for the rough opening under a small dormer.

Install the short head rafters next, between the header and the ridge-board, again face nailing with 16d nails. Double this header, nailing as for the first one, and also by face nailing to the first one with staggered 10d nails. Then install a single lower header, this time with the face plumb instead of perpendicular to the rafter edges. Put in the tail rafters, face nailing the upper ends to the header with 16d nails and the lower ends to the plate with three or four 8d nails, or other conventional methods. Double this header as you did the upper one. To complete the opening fram-ing, double the trimmer rafters and fasten them together with 10d nails staggered about every 16 inches.

Building the dormer frame

Start the dormer frame (FIG. 42-2) by erecting the two front corner posts of doubled 2×4s. Toenail each with six 8d nails, then fasten a top plate across them. Set the two top plates for the sidewalls, with the front ends on top of the front wall top plate and flush with the front wall face, extending back on a level line to the double trimmer rafters. The trim cut at the back ends of the plates must match the cut of the main roof. Face

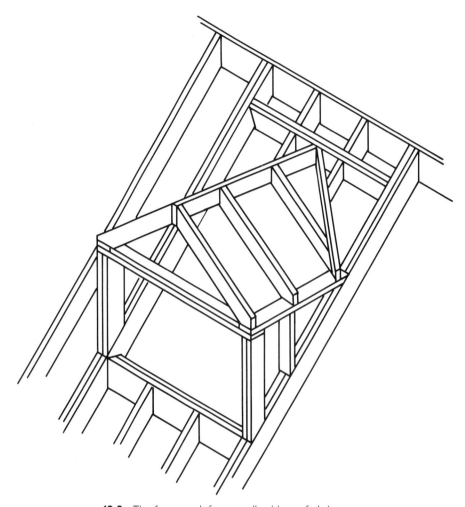

42-2 The framework for a small gable-roofed dormer.

nail at both ends with a pair of 16d nails at each bearing. Fill across the front between the sidewall plates with a front cap plate face that is nailed to the top plate with staggered 10d nails.

Now install the wall studs. Trim the bottom ends to the cut of the main roof and square the top ends. Set them with their inner edges flush with the inner faces of the double trimmers. Face nail at the top with a pair of 16d nails each, and toenail the bottoms with three or four 8d nails.

Locate the plumb centerline of the header. Attach the ridgeboard aligned on that centerline and propped at the front; a short length of scrap 1×4 tacked to the front wall top plate and the ridgeboard end will do the job. Toenail the ridgeboard to the header with 8d nails. Lay out the dormer valley rafters. Make the side cuts at one end of each to fit into the header/ridgeboard intersections. The opposite ends must be shaped with a side cut to lie against the trimmer face, a notch to fit over the sidewall top plate, and an angled heel cut to match the line of the sidewalls and common rafter ends. Toenail with 8d, 10d, and 16d nails as appropriate.

Working in pairs, cut and fit cripples between the valley rafters and the header, and valley jack rafters between the valley rafters and the dormer ridgeboard. Face nail with 16d nails at ends where possible, toenail with 8d and 10d nails elsewhere. Finally, lay out a pattern common rafter, check it for proper fit, and cut the remaining common rafters. Install them in the usual fashion.

The face of a small dormer is often dimensioned to exactly accept a single window, requiring no further framing. Otherwise, install whatever additional framing is required for a window rough opening. Also, attach nailers to the outside faces of the trimmer rafters along the length of the dormer sidewalls, to provide a bearing and attachment surface for the roof sheathing.

FRAMING LARGE DORMERS

Larger gable-roofed dormers can have a ridge at the same elevation as the main roof, and might be substantial enough to cover a larger portion of that roof. Construction details, however, remain essentially the same. The dormer ridgeboard is attached to the main roof ridgeboard as though another full gable roof were being built; there is no header between common joists. The valley rafters attach at that point also and usually extend further down-roof than they would for a small dormer. However, they eventually intersect with doubled trimmer rafters, which must be sized to carry the added load imposed by the dormer weight and its load. In some cases the dormer face is flush with the building line, but more often it is set back a few feet or more. This entails constructing a lower doubled header as for a small dormer, and installing tail rafters as usual. Other aspects of the framing remain the same as for a small dormer.

Shed roof

Dormers with shed-style roofs are commonly seen on residences, especially on modern ranch designs, and they are in fact a bit easier to construct than gable-roof dormers. These dormers often extend from the main roof ridge full-span to the building line, although they can also start at a point lower than the main ridge, stop well short of the building line, or both. In the latter two cases, install doubled headers—upper or lower, or both—to box out the opening, as is done with a gable-roofed dormer. Conversely, you can use the following details to frame the front wall of a gable-roofed dormer flush with the building line (FIG. 42-3).

To begin, set doubled trimmer rafters (sized for the substantial loads imposed by a shed-roofed dormer) at the outside edges of the main roof opening. Face nail these doubles together with staggered 10d nails about

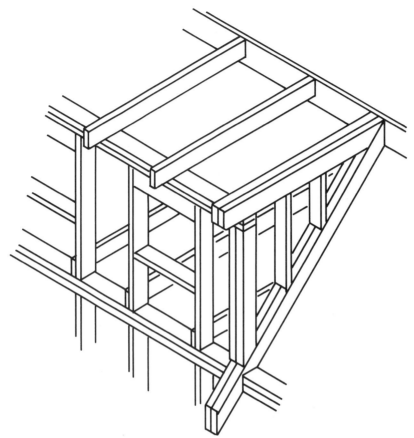

42-3   Framing for a large shed-roofed dormer starting at the ridge line, the face flush with the exterior building line.

16 inches apart. Erect the two doubled 2-×-4 front corner posts, squared at the top and trimmed to the cut of the main roof at the bottom. Nail the doubles together with 10d nails staggered; toenail them to the trimmers with six 8d nails. Fasten a front top plate to the corner posts by face nailing with a pair of 16d nails at each end. Brace both posts. Install the common studs, face nailing them to the ceiling/floor joists with four 10d nails each, and face nailing down through the top plate with a pair of 16d nails each. Frame in window openings as required. Then add a cap plate, face nailed to the top plate with 10d nails staggered.

Lay out a pattern common rafter, check it for proper fit, and cut all the remaining rafters. Trim the ridge end of two of these rafters to the cut of the roof, to serve as side rafters that will mate properly with the trimmers. Install these rafters first, secured with several 8d toenails at each end, then fill in with the remaining common rafters. Attach a collar tie from each dormer rafter to each main roof common rafter opposite; these will serve as ceiling joists and should align with those in other parts of the main roof. Install the sidewall studs; trim their bottom ends to the cut of the roof and notch the top ends to fit against the side rafters. The inside edges of the studs should be flush with the inside faces of the trimmers. Finally, install a nailing strip on the outer faces of the trimmers, flush with their upper edges, as a bearing and attachment surface for the roof sheathing.

Depending upon the way the main roof common rafter tails are fashioned and the kind of eaves overhang planned, you might have to add false rafter tails at the bottom end of each dormer front wall stud in order to carry the eaves design through.

Chapter **43**

Bump-outs,
bays, and bows

One of the more popular and interesting features found in contemporary house design goes by the unlovely name of a *bump-out*. This is a square-sided, right-angled projection that typically extends outward from an exterior wall anywhere from 18 inches to 3 feet or a bit more. Most project at floor level, though they can be built with their floor at any desired level above the main floor of the house. A bump-out may have its own individual roof, or the house roof may extend down over it. Occasionally they are built with solid sidewalls and windows only in the front, but usually tall narrow windows are fitted in the sidewalls as well. Bump-outs are seldom less than 2½ feet wide and seem most appropriate in the 4- to 8-foot range, but are sometimes wider and sometimes built in pairs with a 2- or 3-foot main wall separation between them.

BUMP-OUTS

Bump-out construction (FIG. 43-1) is straightforward and not difficult. The first step is to build a cantilevered floor frame section, as described in Chapter 24. Once that is covered with a subfloor, the bump-out walls can be built and anchored in place as part of the exterior wall construction. Frame a rough opening in the main wall as you would for a patio door assembly, for example, complete with a substantial header across the opening. Make the bump-out walls shorter than the main walls. If the house roof will continue down over the bump-out, configure the walls to the roof slope. The main roof rafters will extend to the bump-out top plate and be fastened there.

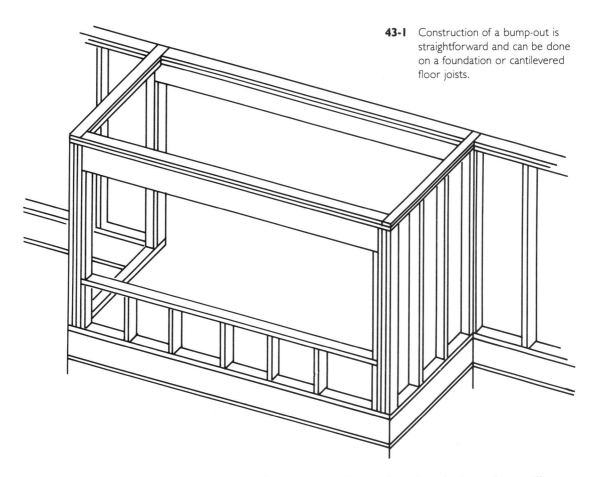

43-1 Construction of a bump-out is straightforward and can be done on a foundation or cantilevered floor joists.

Because most bump-out walls are largely window, they will most likely be topped with headers rather than a top plate. Run joists from the top of the headers back to the header in the main wall, for ceiling attachment. If the bump-out will have its own roof, set rafters from the headers back to the main structure. Their upper ends usually are secured to a ledger plate that serves as a ridgeboard, which in turn is fastened to the main framework.

You can also build a bump-out with its bottom well above the floor: About 20 inches, for example, would be a good window seat height. In this case, frame an opening as for a window that would sit 20 inches above the floor. Anchor a floor framework of 2×4s or 2×6s to the main wall and build abbreviated bump-out walls to suit. The roof construction is as previously described. Sheath the exterior bottom of the bump-out and then, if it projects more than about 18 inches and/or will be used for seating or other weighty purposes, install heavy-duty finish brackets underneath for added support, about 2 or 3 feet apart (FIG. 43-2).

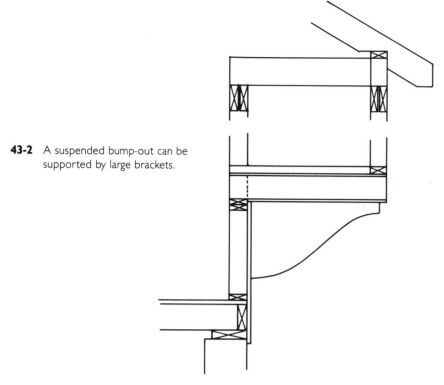

43-2 A suspended bump-out can be supported by large brackets.

BAY WINDOW

A bay, more commonly called a bay window, is constructed in essentially the same way. The appearance, though, is considerably different. Bays typically look more formal, are likely to have their own roofs, often project from the main wall above floor level, and usually are built at the first or ground floor level. (Bump-outs are often constructed at split or upper levels.) Note, though, that such a blanket description does not always hold; there are plenty of exceptions. The major difference in appearance and construction is that most bays have either a pair of walls at 45 degrees to the main wall and a parallel front wall, or two at 90 degrees, two at 45 degrees to those, and then the parallel front wall. Some, in fact, have seven sections, all symmetrically angled.

Construction is the same as for a bump-out, except for the angled corners. Here the easiest solution is simply to make angled corner posts from a pair of 2×4s, using wedge-shaped blocks between them to maintain alignment (FIG. 43-3).

BOW WINDOW

Bow windows are a different matter. They are like a bay in many respects, but they contain at least five and often several more relatively narrow sec-

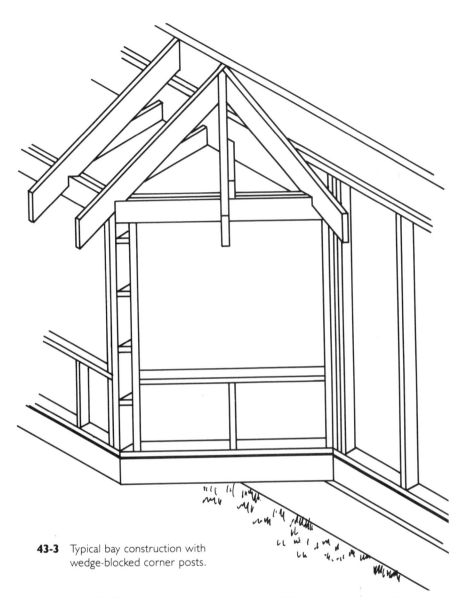

43-3 Typical bay construction with wedge-blocked corner posts.

tions set at shallow angles to one another. This presents a gently curved appearance rather than an abruptly angular one. Typically they extend from floor to ceiling—often the glazing does as well—and they do not project outward very far.

The easiest way to construct a bow window, especially a large one, is to let someone else do it at a factory. Purchase a prefabricated or kit-type bow window assembly (bays are also available) and frame the required rough opening for it. Then the assembly and installation should be a matter of following directions very carefully.

Chapter **44**

Roof sheathing

Once the roof frame has been completed it should be sheathed as soon as possible. This will minimize the potential for warping, splitting, racking, and similar damage to the frame from being left open to the deleterious effects of sun, moisture, and wind. And, of course, the remainder of the structure interior, not to mention the workers, should also be protected from the elements in timely fashion. There are several materials that can be employed for this purpose, and four common roof sheathing methods.

BOARD SHEATHING

The old traditional sheathing material is boards, and this system of sheathing is still used today. Although application is time-consuming, boards can be readily handled by one person working alone, and in some areas this might be the least expensive option, especially for a do-it-yourselfer.

Closed system

In most installations the sheathing should present an unbroken, smooth surface; this is called a *closed* or *solid* sheathing. You can lay square-edged boards but they are not recommended; a better roof deck uses tongue-and-groove or shiplap boards. Nominal 1×6 is the largest size that should be laid. The boards should be straight and well seasoned; if they have more than 12 to 15 percent moisture in them, problems with the weather surface materials are likely to occur later on. Board sheathing is suitable for rafter spacings up to 24 inches on centers.

On a conventional rafter or truss frame, start at the eave edge and lay the boards tight together at right angles to the rafters. Work your way up-roof (FIG. 44-1). Face nail at each bearing with a pair of 8d nails, and make sure all end joints fall on the centerline of a rafter or truss. On a purlin or hip cripple frame, where the bearing surfaces run across the roof instead of up and down, obviously you must lay the boards lengthwise instead of crosswise. An alternative that is advantageous on a flat or shallow-pitch roof (about 3-in-12 or less) is to lay the boards diagonally, which minimizes racking and adds strength to the frame.

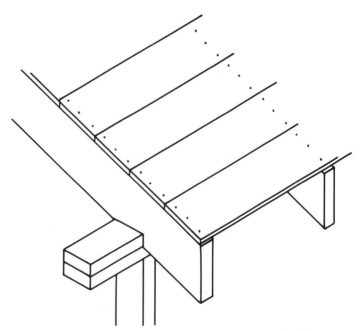

44-1   Tight or closed board roof sheathing on a rafter frame.

Open system

In some areas of the country another system of board sheathing is sometimes used, called *open* or *spaced* sheathing. This arrangement works well where there is no wind-driven snow to cope with. It is highly recommended where the relative humidity is constantly high and dampness is a continual problem, and the weather surface is wood shingles or shakes. The system could also be used in snow country if the roof pitch is at least 8-in-12.

Typically, square-edged 1×3s or 1×4s are used, with the first three or four starting at the eave edge laid tight together. Subsequent boards are spaced apart on centers the same distance that the shingles or shakes will be laid to the weather (FIG. 44-2). Thus, if the shingles are coursed with 6 inches exposed, the nailers must be set on 6-inch centers.

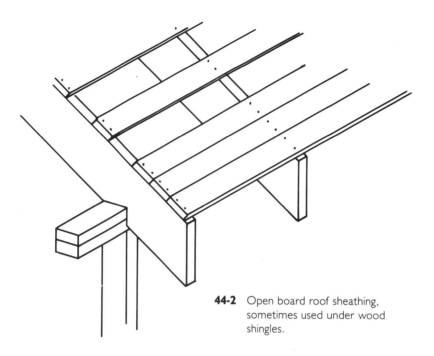

44-2 Open board roof sheathing, sometimes used under wood shingles.

PLYWOOD SHEATHING

By far the most universal roof sheathing today is plywood. It has the advantages of easy and rapid application, high strength, and a smooth, tight nailing surface for the finish roofing materials. Plywood also adds a great deal of rigidity to the roof assembly. The sheet size most commonly selected is 4×8 feet, but the thickness depends upon several factors. These include rafter span, whether or not there is edge blocking at intermediate panel edges, the kind of finish roofing to be applied and its dead load, the degree of stiffness desired, and particularly the live load factor in pounds per square inch.

For conventional residential roof applications, APA rated sheathing, Exposure 1 grade is a suitable material. This can be used to cover the entire roof, but costs can be cut a bit by installing Exposure 1 panels at the eaves and rakes only, and filling in the field of the roof with Exposure 2 panels. In any case, the exposed outer edges at the eaves and rakes of either one should be protected from the weather by sealing off or covering them. An alternative is to use a starter strip, or full panels, of Exterior exposure classification around the border of the roof. Where the soffit will remain open, those panels covering the open eave/rake area should be either Exposure 1 or Exterior classification, because they will be susceptible to moisture damage.

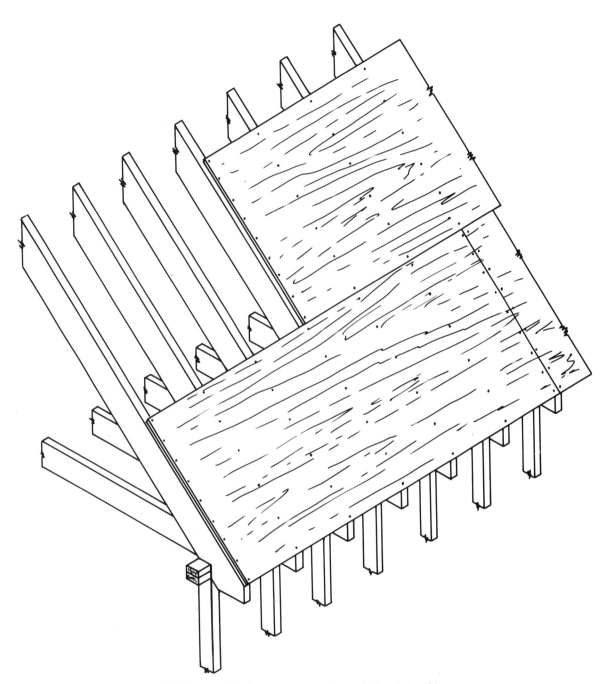

44-3 Plywood is the most commonly applied roof sheathing.

Plywood roof sheathing is laid in much the same way as subflooring (FIG. 44-3). Start with a full panel at one corner of the roof, with the face grain perpendicular to the rafters or trusses. Fasten the panel using 6d common or deformed-shank nails for 1/2-inch thickness or less, 8d for greater thicknesses. Space the nails 6 inches apart all around the edges and 12 inches apart at intermediate bearing points. Don't skimp on this detail; solid nailing is crucial to the strength and longevity of the roof assembly.

Finish out the row of panels and start the next one with a trimmed panel, so the joints are staggered from row to row. Any partial panel should span at least two bays and bear on three rafters. Separate all panels at ends and edges by 1/8 inch for expansion. For added support at intermediate panel edges, install blocking under them, fastened from rafter to rafter, or install panel clips. One clip per bay is sufficient, use two if it is over 48 inches.

DECKING PLANK SHEATHING

Another method of sheathing a roof frame, which actually is a decking process, is used on flat or very low-slope roofs, and also sometimes on roofs of any pitch that remain open to view from beneath and require a finish on the exposed lower surface. This method involves installing nominal 2-×-6 tongue-and-groove decking planks, or some similar material, on the rafters or beams. The exterior surface is then covered with a finish weather surface as usual, and the interior with a decorative applied finish like stain or varnish.

UNDERLAYMENT

The open-sheathing arrangement for wood shingle and shake installation usually does not receive a covering of underlayment, because this would negate the ventilating capability of the open strips. All solid sheathing, however, should be covered with an underlayment—as recommended by the manufacturer of the finish roof covering—as soon as the roof is complete (refer to Chapter 47). This will protect the wood from sun and rain, and also make the roof weathertight for better and safer working conditions beneath it.

OTHER SHEATHING OPTIONS

There are several other considerably more sophisticated (and expensive) roof sheathing/decking systems that can be used in special circumstances, with the roof frame designed specifically for each particular system. These include preframed plywood panels, plywood stressed-skin panels, overlay substrates for special coatings, diaphragm systems, and fire-resistant construction. These specialized systems are beyond the scope of this book, but if you have an unusual design and roofing requirements that are out of the ordinary, the alternatives might be worth investigating.

Chapter **45**

Roof
cornices

Definitions vary a bit, but the eaves of a building are the rafter-end edges of a roof of any style, whether they terminate at the building line (flush with the exterior wall surfaces) or extend beyond. A hip or mansard roof has rafter ends all the way around, and so all the edges are eaves. A gable or gambrel roof, however, has rafter ends only on the lower edges. The edges along the endwalls under pitched roofs, parallel with the rafters, are called rakes because of their upward slant from the horizontal plane. The finish and trimwork at the eaves joint between walls and roof is the cornice, and at the wall/rake joint it is a rake cornice. There was a time when roof cornices displayed all manner of intricate and often fanciful trimwork, including carvings, but nowadays they are largely plain. Even so, cornice fabrication tends to cause a lot of tricky carpentry problems, especially for amateur builders.

There are dozens of possibilities and variations in cornice construction. Wide overhangs with substantial cornices are generally favored, because they add to the appearance of a structure, give the lines some architectural emphasis, provide a drainage gutter installation surface, and help to shield the walls from the weather. In solar designs the angle and extent of the overhangs play a part in the overall heating/cooling plan. Wide cornices of this sort do add to the costs and take time and effort to construct, especially if fully closed and trimmed out at all roof edges. Narrow cornices, on the other hand, are easier and cheaper to build, especially if simple or open, and particularly on unequal-pitch roofs. In all cornice constructions, any of the components that are exteriorly exposed, like the soffit, frieze board, or fascia, must be fastened with rust-resistant hardware. The most common and all-around best choices are hot-dipped galvanized or aluminum nails.

CLOSE CORNICE

The so-called simple or close cornice (FIG. 45-1) is practically no cornice at all. At eaves the rafters terminate in a heel that is cut flush with the edge of the wall top plate. Extend the wall sheathing over the rafter heels with the

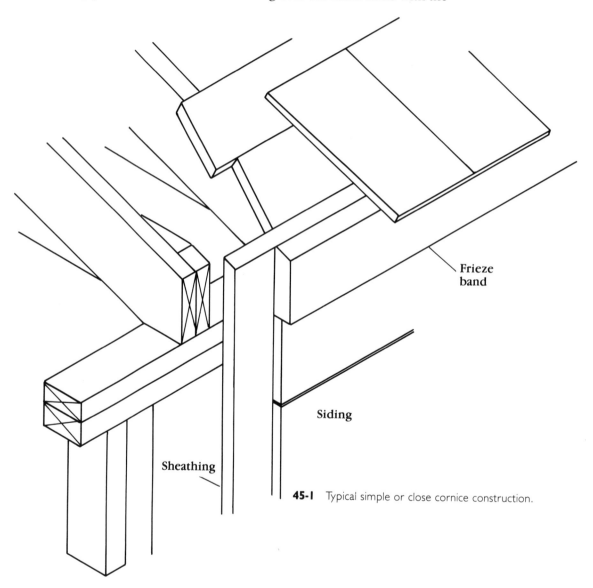

Frieze band

Siding

Sheathing

45-1   Typical simple or close cornice construction.

top edge beveled to the cut of the roof. At rakes, the sheathing extends upward flush with the top of the end rafters. Apply a frieze band all the way around, also beveled flush to the cut of the roof at the eaves and flush along the rakes. Apply the roof sheathing over this, extending it outward just a bit—perhaps 1/2 inch.

For a modestly fancier version apply a molding, typically crown or bed, all around the upper edge of the frieze band, either butted to the roof sheathing edge or beneath, with the sheathing overhanging slightly (FIG. 45-2). This is a marginally better arrangement, because the molding increases the projection of the finish roof covering and thus acts as a drip edge to help keep moisture away from the joint, frieze band, and wall.

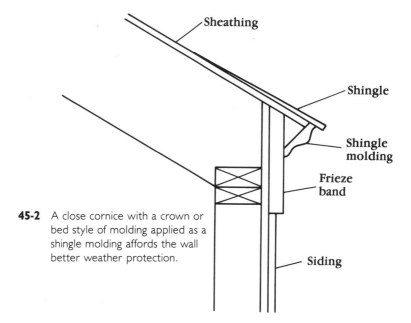

Sheathing

Shingle

Shingle molding

Frieze band

Siding

45-2 A close cornice with a crown or bed style of molding applied as a shingle molding affords the wall better weather protection.

OPEN CORNICE

An open cornice (FIG. 45-3) is the easiest approach where a substantial overhang is desired, and is the method used when the rafter tails are scroll cut or otherwise decoratively finished. Less material is needed than with a closed cornice, but there is a lot of cutting, trimming, and fitting involved.

At the eaves, block in the sheathing between the rafter ends, or cut around them. Extend it upward, flush with the rafter tops, and bevel it to the cut of the roof. Follow suit with the exterior siding or a frieze board and fit the roof sheathing tightly over them, extending slightly beyond the rafter ends. Where attic ventilation is required, inset screened vents close up under the sheathing in sufficient number to provide ample air flow. Finally, install lengths of bed molding to cover the joint between the frieze and the roof sheathing.

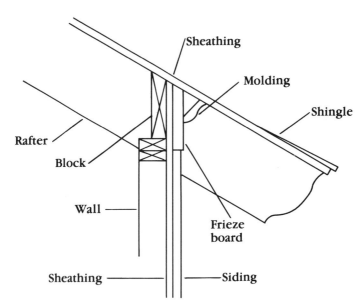

45-3 An open cornice is sometimes used on a wide overhang or where the rafter tails are decoratively trimmed and meant to be left exposed.

This treatment can be cut off flush at the endwall lines and blended into a simple cornice at the rakes. Continue the frieze and bed molding along the endwall/rake joint, beneath a slight roof sheathing overhang, as described earlier (refer to FIG. 45-1). An alternative, if a rake overhang is desired, is to construct a simple return (FIG. 45-4). Install a fly or outrigger rafter along the rakes. This can be anchored by the ridgeboard and a nailing block, or be attached to a lookout ladder (see earlier roof framing details). Carry the frieze board across the open bay to the outer corner of the rafter, then continue it along the upper and outer edge of the rafter to the ridge. Extend the bed molding in the same way, beneath a slight roof sheathing overhang. Then run another frieze board up the rakes and over the endwall sheathing, closing the wall/roof rake joint with more bed molding.

NARROW BOX CORNICE

Despite its greater complexity, the closed or box cornice continues to be the most popular arrangement. A narrow box cornice (FIG. 45-5) is typically anywhere from 4 to 12 inches wide, with the bottom edges of the rafter tails cut level. The heel cut can be plumb or square. The wall sheathing goes on first, snugged up to the rafter bottoms—or flush with the top of the cap plate if the walls are sheathed before the rafters are put on. Extend the roof sheathing to the rafter ends (or a bit shy if the heel is plumb), and apply a soffit to the underside of the rafters. Cover the rafter heels with a fascia board, which usually overhangs the soffit a little and is fitted with whatever screened vent ports are required.

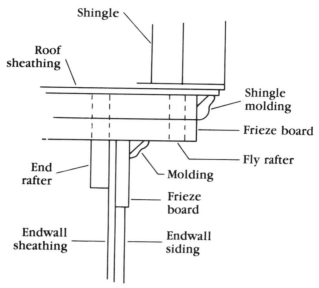

45-4   An open cornice can be returned into a rake overhang by adding a fly rafter and extending and continuing the frieze and molding.

Sometimes a shingle molding is applied along the upper edge of the fascia, but it is often omitted. Depending upon the kind of exterior siding used, a frieze board may be mounted directly below the soffit, or the siding may run up directly to the soffit. A frieze molding may be applied at the siding/soffit joint, but this is often omitted as well.

WIDE BOX CORNICE

A wide box cornice (FIG. 45-6), from 12 inches up, requires more soffit support, which in turn entails installing lookouts that extend from the rafter ends back to the wall on a level line. These are most easily installed after the wall sheathing has been applied. The inner ends can be toenailed through the siding to the wall plate. If the lookouts lie lower than the plate, install a lookout ledger across and fastened to the wall studs, to which the lookout ends can be toenailed. The lookout stock is usually 2×4s, but 1×4s can be successfully used, too. Attach the soffit material, fitted with vents as necessary, to the bottom edges of the lookouts, and install a fascia across the rafter and lookout ends. An alternative is to cap the ends of the rafters with a nailing header, also called a fascia backer. This provides plenty of bearing and nailing surface for the edge of the soffit—which is especially helpful if that is a thin, limber material—and the fascia.

There are several materials that are suitable for soffits, such as plywood, hardboard, exterior plasterboard, waferboard, tongue-and-groove boards, and prefabricated steel or aluminum soffit panels. A frieze board

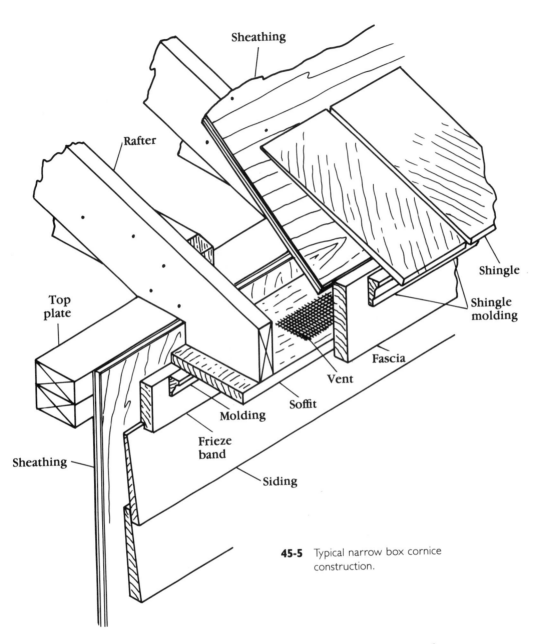

45-5 Typical narrow box cornice construction.

and molding can be added or not, as you wish, and the same is true of a shingle molding. The latter, though, serves to extend the edge of the finish roofing well beyond the fascia, forcing an effective and protective drip edge. Square-cutting the rafter tails also serves to keep runoff moisture well away from the fascia, especially if the roof is steeply pitched (FIG. 45-7).

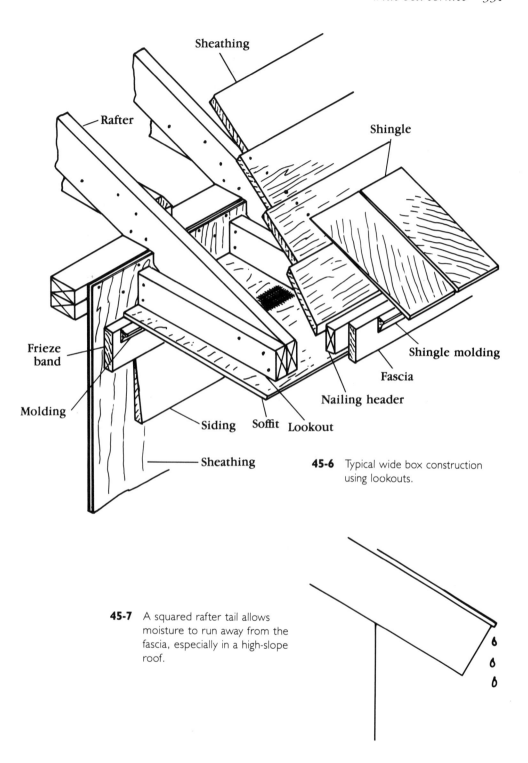

45-6 Typical wide box construction using lookouts.

45-7 A squared rafter tail allows moisture to run away from the fascia, especially in a high-slope roof.

A closed cornice can also be made without bothering with lookouts. In fact, this is sometimes necessary if the window tops are too close to a horizontal soffit line. This involves installing the soffit material directly to the underside of the rafters (FIG. 45-8). Bevel the outer edge to the cut of the roof, and snug the inner edge tight against the wall sheathing. Then run the exterior siding, or a frieze board, up tight to the soffit, and add a molding at that point too, if you wish. Attach a fascia board to the rafter ends, overhanging the soffit by at least 1/2 inch. If the soffit material is thin and tends to bow downward between rafters, you can make the fascia wider and install a stiff molding along the backside of the fascia at the soffit joint, secured through the soffit to the rafters.

CORNICE RETURN

A cornice return is the construction where the cornice turns a corner. If the corner is at another eave, the two cornices merely meet at right angles

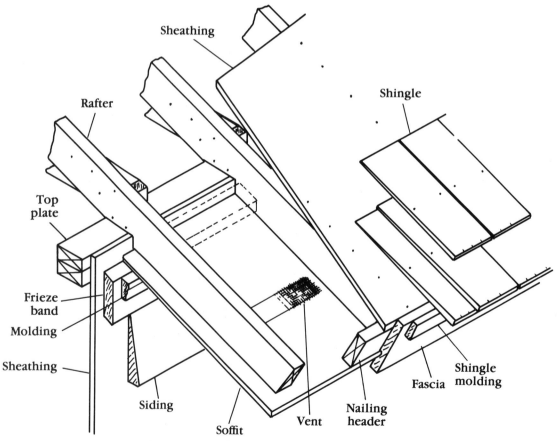

45-8 A typical wide closed cornice construction, where no lookouts are installed and the soffit is fastened to the rafters.

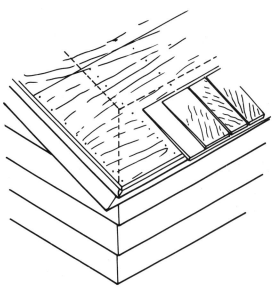

45-9 With proper planning and dimensioning a simple cornice return can be a straightforward right angle.

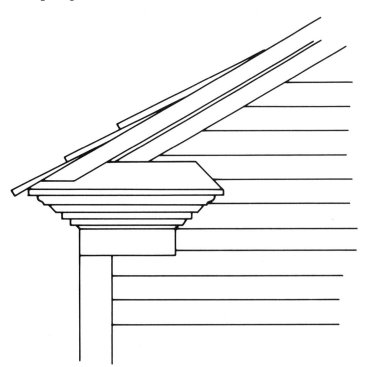

45-10 This formal, ornate cornice return extends only a short distance at right angles, and is met by rake trim.

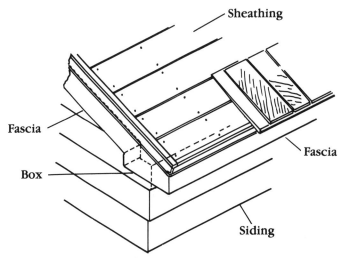

45-11   Wide, dissimilar cornices at rakes and eaves generally require construction of a cornice box at each return.

in conventional fashion. If the corner is to a rake, and if the rake cornice framing has been properly dimensioned and aligned and the rafter tails cut square, construction is also a straightforward right angle (FIG. 45-9). However, disparate dimensions or treatments, unequal-pitch roof sections, and odd meeting angles can create a substantial mismatch. There are any number of ways around this problem, and the details depend entirely upon construction specifics.

One general method for a close or simple cornice arrangement is to make the return a horizontal one that extends for a short distance on the endwall and caps off. A close rake cornice is then brought down to meet it angularly (FIG. 45-10); the two treatments can be the same or different. For wide, dissimilar cornices, usual practice is to build a cornice box (FIG. 45-11). This extends the eaves cornice to match the rake overhang, and by closing off the backside, creates a transition box. The rake cornice can then be built to it. Fascia overhang, moldings, and bits of decorative trimwork can be employed as necessary (or desirable) to cover joints and enhance appearance.

Chapter **46**

Roof drainage systems

*I*n many parts of the country a roof drainage system is a recommended installation that helps protect the exterior siding, maintain a relatively dry foundation, protect foundation plantings, and forestall the incessant dripping of rainwater and snowmelt over windows and doorways and onto people passing beneath. In some circumstances these installations are less important, such as on a house that has exceptionally large roof overhangs and that is built upon a tall pier foundation. With certain buildings, however, a complete, efficient system can be crucial, such as those built on a permanent wood foundation (PWF). In some deep-winter locales, roof drainage systems can actually be detrimental because of constant freezing and thawing and subsequent damage; many builders and architects will often recommend against them in such areas. There can be other problems, too. The system must be properly sized and installed if it is to be effective, and that doesn't always happen. Furthermore, it must be kept cleaned out and well maintained, as well as cared for during freezing weather, or it can cause more problems than it solves.

SYSTEM COMPONENTS

A roof drainage system consists primarily of gutters or eaves troughs and downspouts or leaders. The gutters collect all the runoff from the roof and channel it into the downspouts. These may terminate slightly above ground level, where the water exits onto a splash block and dissipates into the immediately surrounding soil. A better alternative is for the runoff to leave the downspout through an outward-facing elbow, onto a splash block and into a trough that carries the water away from the house to a natural drainage area. Another alternative is any one of several different water dispersion accessories like a canvas soaker hose that unrolls as it fills with water and gently distributes the water onto the lawn. Or, the runoff water may be channeled directly into underground pipes that carry it to a drywell, a ravine or natural runoff watercourse, or into a storm sewer system.

To properly size a roof drainage system, determine the actual square footage of each discrete pitched roof section or individual drainage area. For a roof area of 700 to 800 square feet, install 4-inch gutters; for an area up to 1500 square feet, install 5-inch gutters; over 1500 square feet, install 6-inch gutters. You can use 3-inch downspouts with 4-inch gutters, but otherwise install 4-inch downspouts. To be on the safe side, figure one downspout for every 750 square feet of drained area, and a maximum gutter run of 25 to 30 feet per downspout. Use common sense in choosing these sizes: In locales where torrential rains are ordinary events, or where the roof pitch is steep and water will rush off the roof in a spate, opt for larger gutters and/or more downspouts. Local standard practice is often a good guide, but should be carefully checked for effectiveness.

There are numerous suitable materials for gutters and downspouts, which often are part of complete systems that include matching fittings and hardware. Galvanized steel is common, inexpensive, and sturdy, but subject to rusting. Aluminum is popular but dents and deforms easily and will corrode in salt air. Copper is an excellent choice but expensive. Wood has long been used and still is used occasionally; the advantage is that the gutters can be integrated right into the eaves construction and completely hidden. Although this could be done by incorporating a steel or plastic liner, too, cypress, heartwood redwood, or treated wood is the choice here. An increasingly popular choice is plastic, typically polyvinyl chloride (PVC).

Each drainage system is usually made up of 10-foot gutter lengths, 10-foot downspouts, short and long downspout elbows, downspout extensions, inside and outside gutter corners, strainers or screens, gutter slip connectors, outlet connectors, and assorted mounting straps and hangers (FIG. 46-1). Most systems today are also factory prepainted, or at least primed, usually white or brown.

INSTALLATION

The point during construction at which the drainage system should be installed depends upon the makeup of the system. The gutters might best be hung before the finish roofing is applied, but after the fascia has been primed and painted. Downspouts have to wait until the exterior siding and trim is finished. Underground drainpipes might be installed early in the construction.

The gutters are installed just below the roof edge and spaced out slightly from the fascia (FIG. 46-2). There are several common methods of installation: spikes through sleeves into the fascia, fascia brackets, straps that secure to the roof sheathing, and integral roof-edge flanges supple-

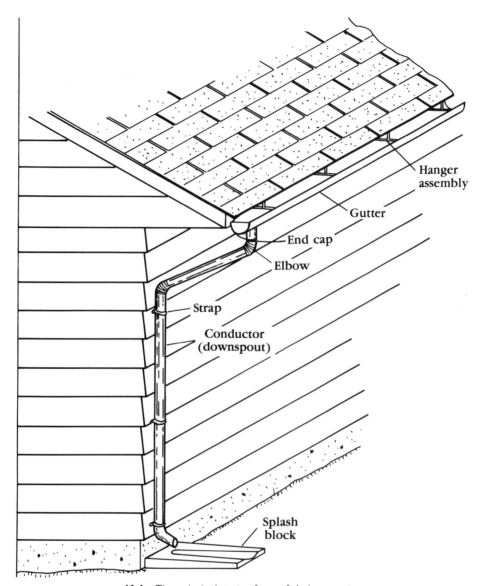

Hanger
assembly

Gutter

End cap

Elbow

Strap

Conductor
(downspout)

Splash
block

46-1   The principal parts of a roof drainage system.

mented with special cross hangers are a few examples. Follow the manufacturer's instructions for installation. The gutters will drain well if they
are dead level. The problem is that they don't always stay level, and so
may lose some of their efficiency over time. Most installers prefer to set
the gutters off level. A fall toward the outlet of about $1/4$ inch for every 5
feet of run provides decent drainage, but the slant can be obvious and visually distracting. Even more slant is better, but frequently unacceptable to
the homeowner in terms of appearance.

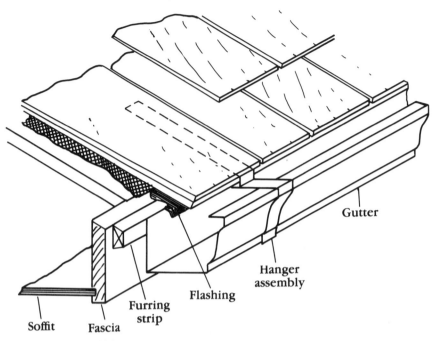

46-2   A general method of installing roof guttering.

As you set the gutters, lock the lengths solidly together and caulk them well. It's an excellent idea to drill and pop-rivet metal slip connectors and end caps. Plastic sections are attached using a solvent that fuses the parts together. Make all the joints as smooth as possible on the inside, for good flow. Make sure the downspouts are solidly attached to the outlets and to the building wall. Set fasteners at top and bottom, and space intermediate fasteners no more than 4 feet apart if they are steel. Set them 2¹/₂ feet apart if they are aluminum, copper, or plastic. Use aluminum, brass, copper, or stainless steel fasteners (or hot-dipped galvanized steel as a second choice). However, make sure the fasteners and the metals being secured are compatible, to avoid deterioration by electrolytic action. There are several accessory items in the way of continuous screening for the gutters, which merit investigation if your system does not include screens.

It is important to arrange some means to carry off the water from the downspouts as soon as the system is installed and operating, even if it is only a temporary measure. Otherwise the new foundation might get an unnecessary soaking, and certainly some soil erosion will occur. Even a chute made of scrap boards will serve. If the downspouts drop directly into buried drainpipes, the installation can be completed; transition fittings to adapt various shapes and sizes of downspouts to standard plastic drainpipe are readily available.

In cold country, roof drainage systems are best fitted with a means to prevent them from freezing solid. That condition, as well as freeze-thaw cycles, formation of ice dams above the gutters, and the dependent weight of gutter ice and icicles, can cause all manner of damage to both the system and the building. The usual preventive is to attach lead-covered heating cables to the roof surface in a zigzag pattern just above the eaves to prevent buildup of ice and snow there. Heating cables must also be installed in the gutters and downspouts to keep them clear. This entails installing suitable electrical outlets at strategic points as the house is being wired. The cables can be operated manually by switches, but attaching them to thermostats with overriding manual switches (the circuit breakers can serve that function) is a more foolproof arrangement. In any case, the fairly substantial added electrical circuitry and load must be programmed into the house electrical system, preferably during the planning stages.

Chapter **47**

Roof underlayment and flashing

With the exception of roofs sheathed with the spaced board arrangement for coverage with wood shingles, normal practice is to cover the roof with an underlayment as soon as the sheathing has been applied. In addition to being required, or at least recommended, beneath most kinds of weather surfaces, the waterproof and reasonably weatherproof underlayment provides easy, cheap, and immediate protection for the roof deck and frame as well as the structure below. In addition, it later acts as a second line of defense against moisture in the event of damage to the weather surface. This installation also allows whatever time is necessary for other work to continue and some schedule flexibility before the finish roofing is installed.

Often as not, the other work includes installing flashing, which must lie atop the underlayment and beneath (or partly under and partly over), the finish roofing material. The flashing is the principal weather seal at roof valleys, roof/vertical wall joints, eaves and rakes—and around vent pipes, chimneys, skylights, or anything else that protrudes through the roof deck.

UNDERLAYMENT

The underlayment most often used in residential roofing applications is roofing felt, an asphalt-impregnated dry felt. This material comes in rolls 3 feet wide and varying lengths, and is available in several thicknesses. The relative thickness is designated by the weight of the material per 100 square feet. The two weights most commonly employed are 15- and 30-pound felt. The 15-pound weight is more popular; 30-pound felt lacks good breathability and can act as a vapor barrier in a position where there should not be one. The inner surfaces of the roof components are not good places for an accumulation of moisture or frost.

High-slope roofs

In the absence of manufacturer's instructions to the contrary, apply a 15-pound felt underlayment on the roof sheathing (FIG. 47-1) as soon as it is completed. Start by installing a metal drip edge along the eaves edge. Use 4d galvanized nails spaced about 24 inches apart and placed at the upper edge of the flange. Then, on a roof with a slope of 4-in-12 or more, start at the eaves edges and roll the material out flat, flush and parallel with the sheathing edge. Fasten it with short roofing barbs spaced about 12 to 16 inches apart along the lower edge, and use just a few barbs to hold the upper edge in place. Alternatively, in place of barbs you can staple the felt. A hammer stapler works fast and easily, and if you don't mind dragging the power cord around, so does an electric staple gun. Immediately roll out the second strip of felt with a 2-inch toplap over the first, covering the fasteners. Most felt has a white line on it to indicate the lap, and this also helps with strip alignment. Run a few inches of felt up vertical walls, such as dormer sides, and fold a flap over the ridge as well. Wherever you must continue a strip with a new piece, make a sidelap of at least 4 inches.

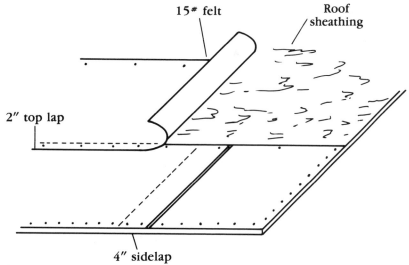

47-1 Single-coverage 15-pound roofing felt applied in this fashion is common practice on a high-slope roof.

Low-slope roofs

If the roof has a slope of less than 4-in-12, the situation is different. The felt must be applied in double coverage (FIG. 47-2). Start the installation by

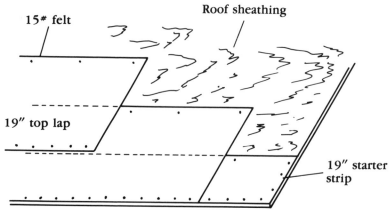

47-2 The underlayment on low-slope roofs should be double-coverage 15-pound felt, applied in this way.

laying a starter strip of 15-pound felt along the eaves edge; this strip is 19 inches wide. Then cover the starter strip with a full-width strip of felt. Lay successive strips with a 19-inch toplap, leaving 17 inches of each strip exposed and a double thickness of felt over the sheathing. Again, most roofing felts have white lines or other indicators on them for you to guide overlaps and trim cuts on. If the felt will not be covered with the finish roofing material within a few days at most, temporarily tack-nail some 1-×-2 furring strips or scrap boards across the felt to keep the wind from ripping it off.

FLASHING

There are numerous bits and pieces of flashing that must be added to a roof, in any order that seems logical. In cold country, especially on wide eaves overhangs, the entire eaves edge of the roof may be flashed as protection against ice dams. This is typically done by laying out one or more strips of 90-pound smooth or mineral-surfaced roll roofing, toplapped 2 inches and sealed at the laps with roofing cement (FIG. 47-3). Lay with the mineral surface up; the outer edge should project past the drip edge about 1/4 inch. The strips should extend up a low-slope roof at least 2 feet past the inside of the exterior wall, and at least 1 foot past if it is a high-slope roof. Fasten the material with 3/4-inch roofing barbs spaced wide apart, just enough to keep it in position until the finish roofing is applied.

Valley flashing

If asphalt/fiberglass shingles are to be applied, valley flashing can also be done with 90-pound smooth or mineral-surfaced roll roofing (FIG. 47-4). Start with a strip 18 inches wide, preferably full-length. If it must be

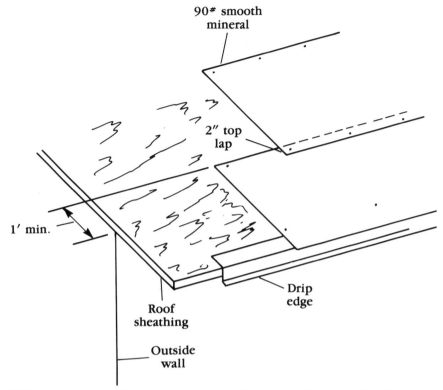

90# smooth mineral

2" top lap

1' min.

Roof sheathing

Outside wall

Drip edge

47-3 In snow country the roof eaves are often flashed with 90-pound roll roofing for ice dam protection.

spliced, toplap at least 12 inches and seal the lap with roofing cement. Lay the strip, mineral surface down, centered on the valley centerline. It helps to gently and only partially fold the strip down the center first—take care that it doesn't break—and then set it in place. Nail one side down with $3/4$-inch roofing barbs along the whole length, press the center down tight into the valley, and nail the opposite edge. Set the nail lines 1 inch in from the edges, and nail 4 inches on centers.

Cut off another strip of roll roofing, full width, and crease it along its centerline. Fold it gently so that the mineral surface will face up. Paint a band of roofing cement along each edge of the starter strip, over the nail heads. Lay the top strip in place, and nail one side first, then the other, pressing the roofing firmly down into the valley and the cement. It should be flush with the ridge at the top and overhang the metal drip edge by $1/4$ inch at the bottom. Again, set the nails 4 inches apart and 1 inch in from the edges, using $3/4$-inch barbs. Then run a second row on each side, also 4 inches apart but staggered from the first row and 4 inches in from the edges.

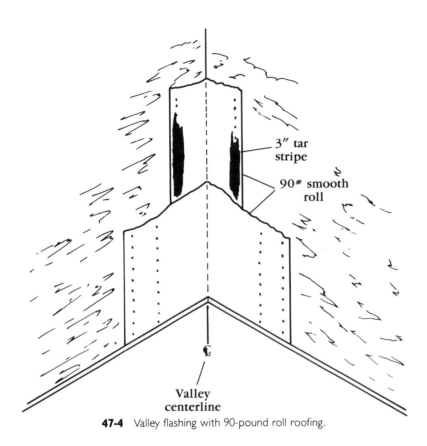

47-4 Valley flashing with 90-pound roll roofing.

And last, gently scribe a line down each side of the flashing, about 2 to 4 inches out from the valley centerline, to mark the point where the shingles will end. The gap that is caused serves to diminish any visual distraction when the shingle courses don't line up from roof to roof. This also marks the free-flow channel for the runoff water, and it should be made wider at the bottom than at the top at a rate of about 1/8 inch per foot of valley run.

Flashing closed valleys

Not everyone likes the appearance of an open valley. There are two easy solutions, which work well if the roof sections are of equal pitch and the shingle courses can be aligned. The first is to install woven flashing, where first one course and then the next is run across the valley and cocked up the opposite roof at least 12 inches past the centerline (FIG. 47-5). Drive one extra nail at the uppermost corner of each shingle. The other solution is to use closed valley flashing. All the courses on one roof are creased at the valley centerline, run up onto the opposite roof, and nailed at the uppermost corner (FIG. 47-6). The courses of the second roof

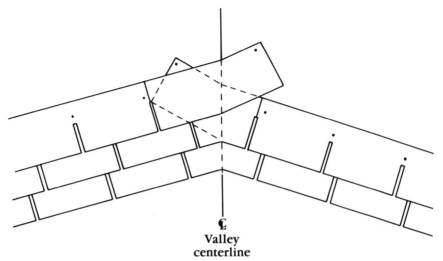

47-5 Woven flashing consists of interleaving the shingles across the valley as each course is applied.

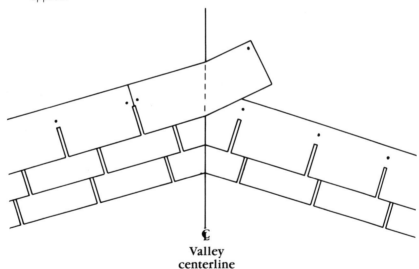

47-6 In closed valley flashing all the courses on one side of the valley extend onto the opposite side, and the opposing shingles are trimmed off along the valley centerline.

are cut off on an angle at the valley centerline and the free end sealed down with roofing cement.

Metal flashing

You can also flash valleys with metal, and should do so for any kind of roofing other than asphalt/fiberglass shingles. Copper is the premier metal in most applications, and stainless steel is used for oceanside houses. Aluminum is popular these days, and galvanized steel, zinc, and terne (steel coated with a lead-tin alloy) are other possibilities. You can also purchase standing seam valley flashing, which has a center rib about 1 inch high. This prevents water from washing off one roof, across the valley, and driving up under the finish roofing on the opposite side.

Best practice calls for a subflashing strip of 15- or sometimes 30-pound roofing felt to be laid first, and the metal to be prepainted (unless purposely left to weather naturally) on both sides. Make the installation by prebending the metal to approximately match the vee of the valley, and nail in place with a row of roofing barbs at each edge. Full lengths of flashing are preferable; any joints should be toplapped at least 8 inches and cemented. Coat the nail heads with a band of roofing cement. Scribe or otherwise mark the lines that delineate the ends of the finish roofing material.

Flashing boots

The simplest of all the flashing chores involves sealing up vent and any other small-diameter pipes. Flashing boots are readily available in a range of sizes. There are several variations, but one popular type has a flat sheet metal base surmounted by a metal bubblelike protrusion that contains a flexible neoprene collar. Pull the whole affair down over the pipe. Seat the base plate on the underlayment, fasten the top two-thirds with two or three perimeter nails and roofing cement, and the job is done. The collar is self-sealing, and the finish roofing slips up beneath the lower third of the base plate (FIG. 47-7). The installation can be made as the finish roofing is applied, or beforehand.

Chimney flashing

Flashing around chimneys is a must. Round metal appliance chimneys, often installed with wood stoves, some fireplaces, and certain appliances such as gas-fired water heaters, are flashed with prefabricated metal cones (FIG. 47-8). Follow the manufacturer's instructions for installation. Typically this consists of slipping the cone over the stack and cementing and nailing the upper half or two-thirds of the bottom flange to the underlayment. The lower half or third is left permanently free so the finish roofing can be slipped up underneath it. Often a storm collar is fitted around the pipe directly above the top of the cone, and that is usually caulked as well. As with pipe flashing, this job can be done during application of the finish roof covering, or beforehand.

Flashing for a masonry chimney is a different matter, and can be a tricky business. Not only are there angles and joints to cope with, but the chimney is also freestanding. Therefore, it moves (by expansion and contraction) independently of and at a different rate than the house, and particularly the surrounding roof structure. There are many different

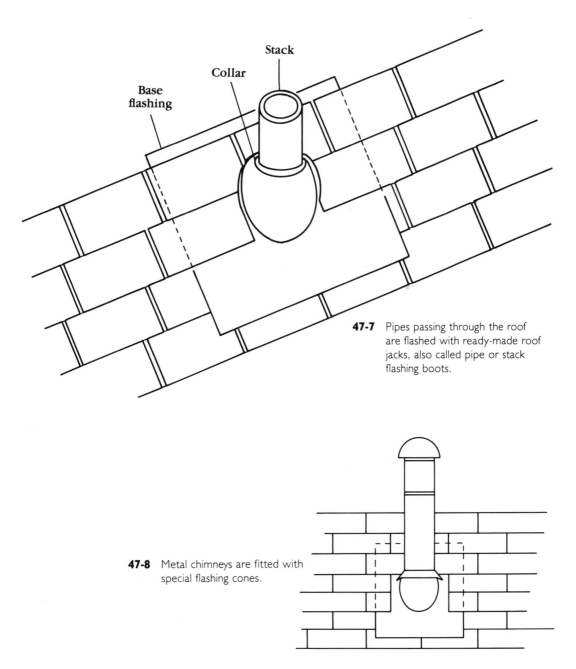

47-7 Pipes passing through the roof are flashed with ready-made roof jacks, also called pipe or stack flashing boots.

47-8 Metal chimneys are fitted with special flashing cones.

techniques and the details depend on the specifics of the chimney construction and the kind of finish roofing involved. In most instances there are two main parts, the base flashing and the cap or counter flashing. Sometimes a third element, step flashing, is included. All of the flashing work is best done as the chimney is being built. The work cannot be done beforehand, and doing it afterward—while possible—makes the job more difficult and the results less satisfactory.

The first step is the base flashing. This band may be either heavy roll roofing (50-pound minimum) that is precreased to fold properly, nailed to the roof sheathing, and cemented with roofing compound at all joints. The flashing may also be metal. Sometimes, especially if step flashing is installed, the metal base is applied only across the front (down-roof face) of the chimney (FIG. 47-9).

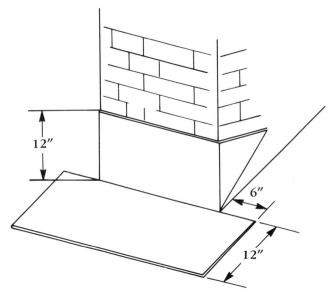

47-9   Base flashing for a masonry chimney.

If step flashing is used, that comes next. The first piece toplaps the base flashing and part of it wraps around the chimney corner (FIG. 47-10). Each subsequent piece of step flashing is bent at a right angle, about 2 to 4 inches vertical and 4 to 6 flat, depending upon chimney size and roof pitch. The height is equal to the shingle exposure plus about 2 inches. Each piece is interwoven with the shingles and held in place by the last shingle nail. In better-quality jobs it is also sealed to the roofing with cement. The flashing is not, however, attached to the chimney.

Cap flashing

Finally, the cap flashing is installed whether the step flashing is used or not. The front piece goes on first, with the top flange bent at right angles and inserted about 1 inch into the mortar joint of the chimney. The bottom straight edge rests upon the flange of the base flashing, but is in no

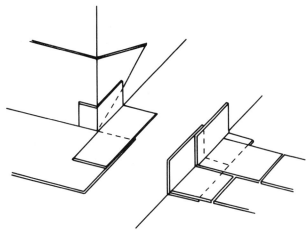

47-10 Step flashing for a masonry chimney, which is interleaved with the shingles as they are laid.

way attached or sealed to it. The side pieces are sometimes made up in several overlapping sections, but really should each be one piece, cut and formed to fit. They must be fashioned to step up one brick course for however many steps are needed to provide several inches of metal above the roof surface at all points (FIG. 47-11). The top flanges insert into the mortar joints just as with the front cap. The down-roof ends wrap around

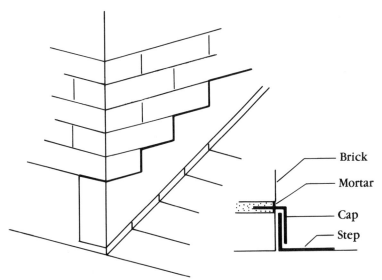

47-11 Cap flashing for a masonry chimney fits over the step and base flashing and is mortared into the joints as the masonry units are laid up; or it is sealed into raked joints afterward.

the chimney corners over the ends of the front cap piece. The back cap piece goes on last, installed in the same way as the front cap. Its free ends wrap around the chimney corners and point down-roof, over the side caps.

If the chimney is built first, the procedure is a bit different, with respect only to the cap flashing. The appropriate mortar joints in the chimney have to be left free of mortar to a depth of 1 inch, to accommodate the flashing flanges. If during layup they are not, they must be carefully raked clean of mortar. Then insert the cap flashing flanges and wedge them tight by driving lead plugs into the joints. Fill the open joints with a top-grade elastomeric caulking compound, which must periodically be replaced. The joints must be absolutely clean and dry for the compound to adhere properly. Mortar is sometimes used instead, but it must be very "fat." Even so, it seems not to bond well in many instances.

Woven flashing

The joint between the roof sheathing and a vertical wall—a dormer side, for example—must be flashed. One common method is to install a strip of 15- or 30-pound roofing felt along the joint, half on the roof and half up the wall, stapled just enough to hold it in place. Then, as each course of shingles is laid a metal "shingle" is interwoven, just as for the chimney step flashing (FIG. 47-12). Secure each shingle by driving one nail through it and the upper outside corner of the shingle beneath; it is not attached to the wall. Actual size of the flashing pieces doesn't much matter, so long as they extend at least 2 inches onto the roof sheathing and 4 up the wall, and extend a couple of inches beyond the top of each shingle course. When applying the exterior siding to the wall, leave a gap of at least 1 inch but no more than 2 between the shingles and the bottom edge of the siding.

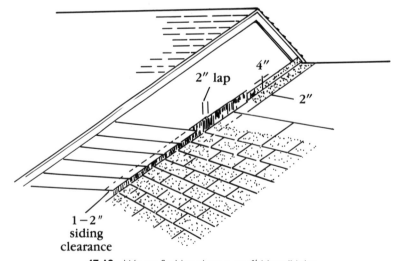

47-12 Woven flashing along a roof/sidewall joint.

Base and cap flashing

Some roof installations, such as for a skylight or an exit hatch, are built with a surrounding curb. The curb/roof joint must be flashed, and in the absence of special flashing (or specifications for same) supplied with whatever is to be installed on the curb. A base and cap arrangement is effective (FIG. 47-13). Surround the curb with an angled base flashing that extends up-roof about 6 inches, at least 2 inches to the sides, down-roof 8 inches or more, and up onto the curb sides at least 2 inches (or full height, whichever is less). Seal it in place with roofing cement and secure it with small roofing barbs around the perimeter, to both roof sheathing and curb. Then install a cap flashing that covers the top of the curb (and preferably extends down the inside a bit) and comes down over the outside faces of the curb to the base flashing flange. Leave a slight gap between the two; provide an upward and inward lip all around the lower edge. Seal the cap in place at the curb top and fasten it with nails. The corners can be soldered together or a wraparound sealed type may be used.

Flashing rake edges

As a matter of course, drip cap is (or always should be) placed along eaves edges, or a narrow strip of flashing laid to bridge the slight gap between

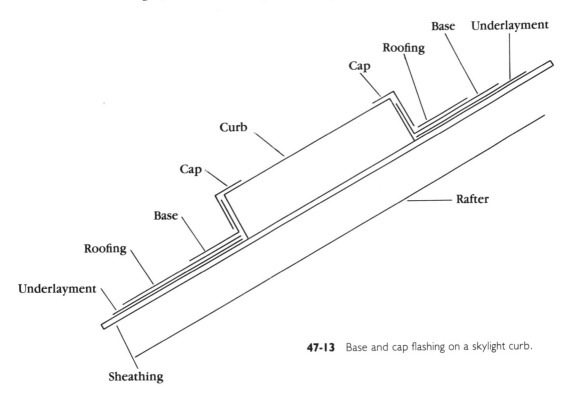

47-13 Base and cap flashing on a skylight curb.

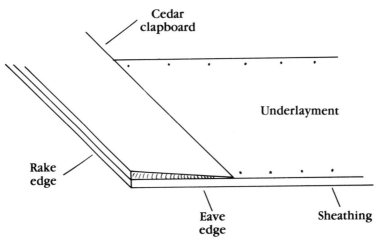

47-14 A length of beveled siding (clapboard) fastened along the rake makes a good drip edge.

the eaves edges and the inner lip of a drainage gutter. Rake edges, however, are frequently ignored. Good building practice suggests that these edges should be flashed as well, to protect the edges of the roof sheathing and help channel moisture away from the rake fascia and trimwork. The same metal drip edge that is installed at the eaves can be used at the rake, but with less effectiveness. Another old-time method works much better. Install a continuous strip of 6- or 8-inch redwood or cedar beveled siding (clapboard) up each rake. Face the thick edge outward overhanging the sheathing edge about 1/4 inch, on top of the underlayment (FIG. 47-14). Lay the shingles on top of that, overhanging the strip by about 1/4 inch.

Chapter **48**

Asphalt shingles

Asphalt shingles in one form or another undoubtedly have for decades been the most popular of all finish roof coverings or weather surfaces. Although that popularity has diminished somewhat in recent years, with the considerable increase in availability of other kinds of roofing, they remain a leading choice. These shingles used to be composed of asphalt-impregnated organic felt covered with fine mineral granules. They had a life span of about 15 years, sometimes 20, before they dried out, curled up, and lost their effectiveness.

TYPES OF SHINGLES

Today the appearance of asphalt shingles is the same, but the shingle base is inorganic fiberglass, asphalt impregnated and mineral-surfaced, and, depending on the weight per 100 square feet, the useful life has been extended toward 30 years. Although there are numerous other shingle choices, some perhaps a little more stylish, asphalt/fiberglass shingles in the laminated heavyweight version continue to be the most cost-effective finish roofing by a considerable margin, with the single-layer lighter-weight types taking a strong second place. As a group, they also offer the greatest variety of color, texture, and pattern.

The standard square-butt three-tab strip shingle style continues to be the most prevalent. Other shapes (FIG. 48-1) include Dutch lap, locking, square-butt one- and two-tab strip, square-butt architectural strip, and one- and two-tab hexagonal. Longevity usually depends upon shingle weight, which is denoted in pounds per square, or 100 square feet; the heavier the better. Strip shingles run anywhere from 220 to 390 pounds

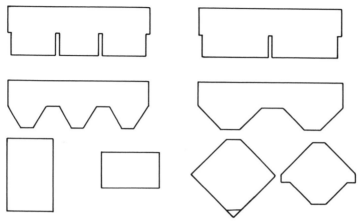

48-I   Asphalt/fiberglass shingles come in a variety of shapes and sizes, of which these are just a few.

per square, with 235 being a favorite weight for the single-layer three-tabs. Architectural strips (also called laminated fiberglass) are the heaviest, have the most dramatic and deeply textured appearance, and are the longest-lived—also most expensive. Most asphalt shingles have a UL (Underwriters Laboratories) fire rating of Class C, which is moderate fire resistance. A few, mostly heavy and including the laminated fiberglass variety, have a Class A rating; these will withstand severe exposure to fire.

APPLICATION

Much has been written about the proper way to apply asphalt shingles, and a lot of it has served to make a relatively simple job appear considerably more difficult than it really is. Professional roofers have all sorts of techniques, tricks of the trade, and opinions about the best approaches, but the fundamental keys to a successful job are to maintain precise alignment, fit with care, nail properly, and exercise patience. And, of course, don't step back to admire your work.

You can apply asphalt shingles to roof slopes as low as 3-in-12—2-in-12 over porches—with a double coverage underlayment. A 4-in-12 slope is the lowest for shingles over single-coverage underlayment. Up to about 5-in-12 you can walk and work on the roof without much trouble. Above that, things start to slip and slide around, including the roofers; install roof jacks and planks to work safely. From around 8- or 9-in-12 slope on up you would be well advised to secure yourself with safety ropes and a harness, or hire a professional.

Preserving symmetry

Common practice is to start laying the first course by aligning the first shingle end at one rake edge of the roof and continuing from there. This means a certain unevenness or asymmetry in the pattern, which some folks find objectionable. This doesn't show much on small roofs, or high low-slopes, but does on larger, lower, or more steeply pitched ones. The solution: Find the vertical centerline of the roof section and snap a chalkline. Start at the line and work left and right, and symmetry will be preserved. There are also several patterns you can arrange when laying the slotted strip shingles, determined by the amount of offset from course to course and the number of courses per set. Other types, like locking or hexagonal shingles, have a predetermined pattern that can only be centered, not varied.

Patterns

The patterns are determined by shifting successive courses by a half tab followed by one tab (6-inch shifts), a third of a tab followed by two-thirds followed by a full tab (4-inch shifts), or by shifting 2 inches on each successive course. A 2-inch shift should be the minimum, and the shingle slots should never align in adjacent courses. You can also lay an irregular or random pattern by cutting varying amounts from the starting shingle end; a suggested pattern of amounts to trim, in inches, is: 0, 3, 9, 4, 7, 0, 3, 9, 6, 0, 9, 4, 7, 3, and repeat. Lay out a few courses in a dry run on the roof, or on a floor, to get an idea of the appearance before you start to apply the shingles. This will also show you if a slot is going to fall at some awkward point.

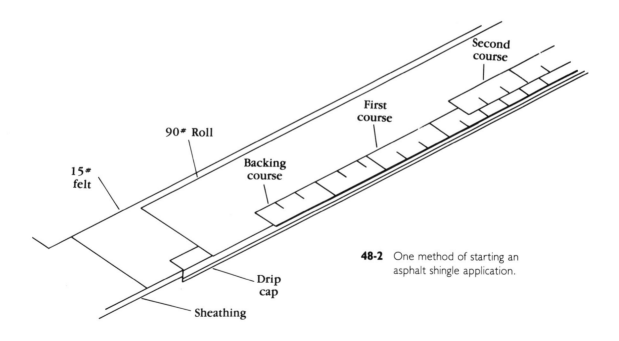

48-2 One method of starting an asphalt shingle application.

Three-tab installation

Figure 48-2 shows the first phase of a three-tab installation. To begin, trim the unmineralized portion (the head) off a number of shingles, or cut a starter strip from 90-pound roll roofing. Lay the mineralized portion (the butts) of the shingles along the eaves edge, overhanging about 1/4 inch. They should be face up, with the slots pointing up-roof. The self-sealing dots must be near the eaves edge; if there are none, make your own with roofing cement.

Start from a centerline or a rake edge with a full strip. Fasten each shingle with one 1 1/4-inch roofing barb just below each slot. Use four nails in all for full three-tab strips. In windy country, drive two nails at each of the full slots, one to each side, for added security (FIG. 48-3). Drive the nails straight and set the heads just flush with the shingle surface, so they don't cut into or deform the shingle. Always start nailing at the end of the shingle butts against the one that has already been fastened. This

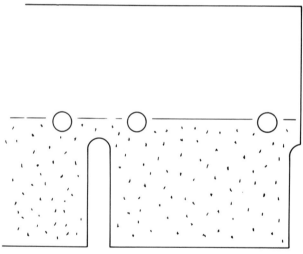

48-3 In windy country, nail two- or three-tab asphalt shingles like this for extra holding power.

keeps the right alignment and avoids overriding or bunching at the ends—which can happen easily, especially if the roof is hot and the shingles limp.

Lay the first course directly over the starter course, tabs and slots pointing down-roof. Begin at the roof centerline, or one rake edge, according to your chosen pattern. For a half-tab shift starting at a centerline, for example, the first shingle would be a full one centered on the centerline. Nail as before, with one barb (two for windy conditions) just above each slot. Work outward, then upward, continuing to add to the courses pyramid fashion. This distributes the shingles in a random coloration pattern and avoids color streaks or patches.

Set the second course to provide the proper exposure to the weather of the first course, typically 5 inches. Continue working uproof in semi-pyramids, until you reach the last course. Keep a sharp eye on the course alignment, which can wander all too easily; even a small misalignment is obvious and hard to correct once made. It's a good idea to snap some chalklines as a guide, once you've got the first couple of courses set.

When you reach the ridge, you might be able to fold the heads of the last course over onto the opposite roof section, or up a wall as flashing, or you might have to trim to get a smooth fit. At a ridge, whether ridgepole or hip, the last step is to apply a ridge trim. This can be a continuous strip of matching roll roofing or a special metal cap, but more often consists of cut pieces of the same shingles used on the roof. To make a Boston ridge, slice a number of three-tabs into three equal one-tabs. Start at one end of the ridge and fold a tab centered over the ridge, with the mineral surface at the rake or eaves edge. Fasten it with one nail, placed about 1 inch in and 5½ inches back on each side (FIG. 48-4).

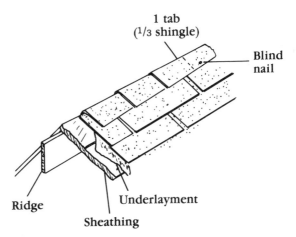

48-4 A Boston ridge made with asphalt shingles.

Continue laying the tabs with a 5-inch exposure; the last one must be trimmed so that there is only mineralized surface exposed. If possible, set the ridgepole cap so that the prevailing wind flows over the shingles, not toward them. An alternative is to lay the tabs from each end toward the middle. Cap the center joint using a mineralized piece secured with a nail at each corner. Hip ridge caps, of course, are always oriented with the butt edge down-roof.

Chapter **49**

Other finish roof coverings

*I*n addition to the considerable variety of asphalt/fiberglass finish roofing products available, today's home builder can select a finish covering from a menu of at least a dozen other excellent weather surfaces. Standard asphalt shingles are the easiest to apply; this is a job that even a completely inexperienced do-it-yourselfer can undertake. However, application of all the other materials is more difficult and complex. None could be considered ordinary home projects. On the other hand, any capable craftsman, amateur or otherwise, who cares to take the time and trouble to study the subject and perhaps work for a while with a roofer or builder can learn just how to install any of these weather surfaces. After all, that's how roofers get to be roofers. But whether professionally applied or not, these other roofing materials deserve consideration. All cost factors should be investigated on a local basis, as installed, for both initial cost and cost per year of expectable service life. Up-to-date product details and specifications can be obtained from manufacturers or suppliers.

ASPHALT ROLL ROOFING

Asphalt roll roofing is mentioned here only because it is widely available and valuable for use as flashing, and is frequently applied as the weather surface on roofs of outbuildings, camps, and vacation cottages. Although cheap and as easy to apply as felt underlayment, it is also short-lived and really not suitable by today's standards for a residence roof.

WOOD SHINGLES

Commercial wood shingles, probably second to asphalt shingles in popularity, are made of redcedar. They are regular in size and shape and smooth-sawn. Of the several grades available, only the premium No. 1 Blue Label should be considered for roofing. No. 2 Red Label shingles might be used in some applications, while No. 3 Black Label are used only in special circumstances. No. 4 undercoursing grade is meant to be used only for that purpose. Three shingle lengths are available: 16 inch (Fivex), 18 inch (Perfections), and 24 inch (Royals). The different lengths allow different standard exposures to the weather—depending upon preference, whether double- or triple-coursing is used, and also upon the roof slope.

Redcedar shingles are packed four bundles to the square (100 square feet), but actual coverage depends upon the weather exposure selected. In any case the maximum recommended exposures on a roof are 5, $5^1/2$, and $7^1/2$ inches respectively. A roof slope of 4-in-12 is usually considered a practical minimum, but 3-in-12 slopes can be successfully covered in some locales. Plain shingles do not have a UL fire rating; they are fully combustible and therefore outlawed in some communities. Some shingles are available with a special fire-retardant chemical treatment, resulting in a Class C fire rating (moderate resistance). The effectiveness of the treatment, however, diminishes over the years as the chemicals leach out of the wood.

Installation is not technically difficult, but does require some knowledge and experience, especially in forming valleys, hips, ridges, and small but complex constructions like chimney crickets. A reasonable degree of patience and craftsmanship, along with some skill with a shingler's hatchet, is needed for good results. The job has to be done with care and should never be rushed, even though it does get rather tedious.

WOOD SHAKES

Wood shakes are also fashioned from redcedar, but present a much more rustic, heavily textured, and varied appearance than the smooth shingles. They can be installed on any roof slope from 4-in-12 up. Depending upon which types are used and the way they are laid, they can convey a unique hand-hewn effect.

Shakes are made in straight-split, tapersplit, handsplit-and-resawn mediums and heavies, handsplit, and tapersawn versions, all of which are fashioned a bit differently and present a different appearance. Lengths are 18 and 24 inches, widths are random, and the butt thicknesses are $3/8$, $1/2$, $5/8$, and $3/4$ inch. In most cases the recommended weather exposure is 10 inches, in which case five bundles will cover one square. Lesser exposures can be used, requiring a greater number of shingles but providing a more rugged and weathertight three-ply coverage roof. Shake roofs are typically somewhat longer-lived than redcedar shingle roofs—30 years average, and more than that in some locales.

Installation procedures and techniques for these shakes are much the same as for redcedar shingles, though the job is somewhat more demanding and takes longer. Because shakes do not lie flat, an 18-inch-wide strip of 15-pound roofing felt underlayment (called *interlayment* in this usage) should be interwoven with each course if the shakes are applied over open sheathing. It might also be applied when the sheathing is closed, if blowing snow is a likelihood. Often rosin-sized building paper is used instead of roofing felt, to allow water vapor transpiration. Ridge and hip caps must be beveled and fitted with alternate crown joints, and all flashing requires special attention.

PANELIZED WOOD SHINGLES

Some manufacturers supply redcedar shingles already affixed to a frame in panel form, 2 feet wide by 8 feet long. Other sizes or variations might be available at any given time. They can be laid over a roof sheathing, but are intended to serve as both sheathing and finish roofing all in one application. They are attached directly to the rafters or trusses. General requirements and characteristics are about the same as for other redcedar shingle products.

WOOD FIBER SHEETS

Wood fiber sheets are made in 12-×-48-inch panels of bonded and compressed wood fibers, called hardboard, that have been textured to have the striated appearance of hand-split wood shakes. The weight is 260 pounds per square for untreated strips, 280 for those treated for Class C flame resistance. There are 6 bundles to the square. Because the weather exposure is 9 by 46 inches, application is rapid and alignment is simple because of the fixed headlap. Hip and ridge installations require cutting and beveling, but are no great chore. The material is intended for use on slopes of 4-in-12 or greater, but can be applied to a 3½-in-12 slope under some circumstances. Life expectancy is in the 25-year range.

METAL SHEETS

Over the past few years, metal sheet roofing has gained a lot of attention and is being installed on houses with increasing frequency. There was a time when corrugated iron and copper were frequently used, then metal went out of favor for many years. Now it is back, but in distinctly different forms.

Metal sheet roofing is not easy to apply, especially in its more complex fabrications or on complicated roofs. It can be noisy in heavy rains and deafening in hailstorms, depending upon how the roof and the house is constructed. Metal roofing installations can be quite expensive, although products vary. However, if properly applied it is exceptionally weatherproof. The useful life of metal roofing can be anywhere from 50 years to well over a century, depending on the product and the conditions. Metal roofing sheds snow and water particularly well, and withstands mechnical abuse better than most roofings. Metal roofings are typically lighter weight than almost all other roofings, so can be applied safely to any standard roof deck. They all have a Class A fire rating.

The most popular material currently used is steel sheet with a factory applied paint finish. Other possibilities include galvanized steel, painted or plain aluminum, copper, stainless steel, and terne—which is steel coated with a tin/lead alloy. Of them all, copper is the most durable and easily worked, while steel is the most rugged. There are also numerous styles available, which present subtly different appearances. The corrugated pattern is probably the most familiar and easily recognizable. Standing seam roofing, with its interlocked vertical seams, is the most weathertight style, and in some constructions can be used successfully on slopes as low as $1/4$-in-12. There are several varieties of seam fabrication, such as swaged single-lock or double-lock, soldered, or welded.

Ribbed seam roofing is suitable for slopes of 6-in-12 or more, and the distinctive squared ribs can be set over battens anywhere from 12 to 48 inches apart. The 5V-crimp panel roofing is less commonly used today, and has been largely superseded by V-beam panels. In these beams, instead of being inverted vees, are vees with the points lopped off to form slant-sided beams. This is the style, in several variations, that has recently become so popular in painted steel; four or five major vees and six minor ones is a typical pattern. These panels are suitable for 3-in-12 and greater slopes, and can be used on 2-in-12 slopes if special weatherproofing precautions are taken. Panels come in lengths up to 40 feet, and in many instances all the panels for a particular installation can be factory-cut to exact size and shape.

METAL UNITS

Most metal unit roofings are made of steel and some of aluminum. They are made in the form of simulated asphalt, or wood shingles or shakes, or simulated tiles. Various finishes are used, such as paint, aggregate, or porcelain. These products come and go in the marketplace, and each must be assessed on the basis of its individual characteristics and specifications. Installation is usually a bit tricky; the units can be hard to work with. In many cases the units must be custom shaped before they are coated, to fit a particular application. Cost is relatively high, but the products typically are long-lived (50 or more years) and very weatherproof. They are low in weight and have a Class A fire rating. A roof with a slope of 4-in-12 is the minimum that should be covered without special precautions being taken, and 6-in-12 can be a minimum for some products.

CLAY TILE

Vitrified clay tile in the familiar terra cotta color is an ancient roofing material usually associated with the Spanish mission type of bulding. In its thickest version it is the heaviest of the finish roofing mattertials; sometimes upwards of 1500 pounds per square. It is an expensive material to buy and to install; a nearby source is almost mandatory because of shipping and handling costs. Installation must be made with great care, and the roof frame, load-bearing supports, and house foundation must all be sized and built to bear the great weight. Also, the roof must be planned to accept the tile layout exactly. A slope of 3-in-12 is minumum. Tile is very weatherproof and has an expectable life of a half century or more, barring mechanical damage. The fire rating is Class A.

CONCRETE TILE

Concrete roofing tile is a fairly recent development. It is also a heavy roofing material that approaches the weight of clay tile and is heavier than some slates. There is a lighter-weight version in the form of thick shingles that look like medium-weight slates. Both types have a useful life of at least 40 to 50 years, and should be applied to roofs with a 4-in-12 or greater slope. The cost of both material and installation is little different than for clay tile. Fire rating for concrete tile is Class A, and weatherproofing qualities are excellent. There is a fair range of colors and textures available.

SLATE

Slate is another old, traditional roofing material that requires special structural support because of its weight, which can be 700 pounds per square and up. The 3/16-inch thickness is now considered standard, but others are available, and there are several sizes as well. Most slates are factory prepunched with nail holes. Installation is difficult, time consuming, and requires expertise and special tools. Slates are susceptible to mechanical damage. This is an expensive roofing, with the cost depending to some extent on the color. Common gray is the least costly and red the most— up to $1500 a square. Other colors are available as well, such as black and green. Slate has a long life; 100 years is not unusual. It is very weatherproof, but must be applied to a minumum 4-in-12 slope and preferably steeper.

MINERAL FIBER SHINGLES

Mineral fiber shingles have been around in one form or another for many years. Once predominently composed of asbestos and portland cement, now they are made up with other kinds of mineral fibers. They are available in a variety of shapes, sizes, and colors, some with their own distinctive characteristics and others in imitation of tiles, shingles, or slates. These shingles were out of favor for some time, but are now gaining renewed acceptance. The cost, however, remains quite high for both materials and installation. They have a Class A fire rating and are suitable for application on roofs with a 3-in-12 or greater slope. Life expectancy is at least 50 years and can extend to 75 or more, barring mechanical damage. In the 1/4-inch thickness, the weight can be less than heavy asphalt shingles, and these can be laid on an ordinary roof deck of 1/2-inch plywood. Thicker versions, however can run to 500 or more pounds per square, necessitating roof frame construction somewhat sturdier than normal.

BUILT-UP ROOFING

Built-up roofing is an old standby, still used for covering flat to slightly sloping (2-in-12) roofs of all kinds. The finish roof covering is actually built up in successive permanent layers on the roof deck, hence the name. Typically the procedure calls for laying or cross laying anywhere from three to a dozen layers of asphalt-saturated roofing felt, each covered with a thick layer of mopped-on hot tar. The whole affair is finally covered with a thick, partly embedded topcoat of uniformly graded stone that may be granules, chips, or small gravel, supplied in assorted natural colors. These roofs are sometimes called 10-year, 15-year, or 20-year bonded roofs—depending upon the thickness, materials used, and the warranty and referring to the projected useful, leakfree life. Installation requires certain skills and knowledge, muscle, a tolerance for heat and the stench of boiling tar, and special tools and equipment.

MEMBRANE ROOFING

Although technically the built-up roofing just described is membrane roofing, this term usually connotes a special installation of a single, seamless, or specially sealed-seam elastomeric membrane. The most durable membrane developed to date is EPDM (ethylene propyolene diene monomer), which is seemingly impervious to practically everything but a sharp blade. Hypalon is another such material, but this is more expensive and difficult to work with, and requires that the seams be welded.

In a typical installation an EPDM membrane is thoroughly bonded to a plywood roof deck with special contact cement, or through a mechanically fastened system. The membrane is then covered with a layer of fine gravel or mineral chips to protect it from sunlight and other damage.

Previously installed almost entirely on commercial and industrial roofs, this system is now becoming available for residences, and even from some manufacturers as do-it-yourself supplies. None of these systems are intended for high-slope roofs, but rather for low-slope, flat, and problem roofs. Membrane roofing can be especially advantageous for application on decked-over flat roof areas. Scraps and leftovers are marvelous for use as flashings, waterproof covers, leakproof liners for shower stall pans, darkroom sinks, and reflecting pools.

Chapter **50**

Roof/ceiling
constructions

One of the more interesting interior arrange-
ments that has become increasingly popular over the past few years—
especially in houses of contemporary design—is the open or cathedral
ceiling. Instead of each room or area being capped in traditional fashion
with an expanse of flat ceiling parallel with the floor, the ceiling area is
pitched. The ceiling itself may be the underside of the roof, or may be set
to a different angle and attached to its own framework. Usually this is carried out in living, dining, and kitchen areas, but it can be done in any
room.

The construction details often are little different than would be
encountered in finishing an attic into a habitable half-story. The visual
impact is far different, however, because of the large volume of empty
space and the impression of loftiness and open airiness the design produces—especially when the ceiling surface is a full 20 or 30 feet above the
floor. Structurally the biggest concern lies in engineering correctly for the
open span.

GRAFTING THE CEILING TO THE ROOF

There are several ways to graft a ceiling to a roof. The simplest is to cover
the underside of the roof rafters with gypsum wallboard, as is done with
most conventional ceilings or walls. This must be done after the roof is
sheathed and the weather surface has been applied, and thermal insulation installed as necessary. The roof frame is designed as usual, and any of
the standard construction techniques can be used. This can be done easily with a truss roof, too, by installing scissors, cambered, three-hinged
arch, or other specially designed trusses.

Once the interior is sheathed, the resulting ceiling surface can be painted or papered as usual. Other finishing possibilities include covering the rafters/trusses or the sheathing with paneling, planking, or acoustic tile plank, or creating geometric designs with applied wood moldings on painted sheathing. This sort of arrangement is the way to go when all of the structural elements of a cathedral ceiling are to be concealed.

FALSE BEAM CEILINGS

If a beamed ceiling is desired, there are numerous ways to achieve the effect. One is to install false beams.

When installing false beams, first put up a gypsum wallboard ceiling before the walls are sheathed. Finish the ceiling, then install beams tight to the ceiling surface and set in beam pockets constructed in the walls (FIG. 50-1). Finish the beams and trim the joint between the ceiling and the upper edges of the beams with a prefinished molding. Touch up as necessary after installation. With a plain ceiling the beams could be set horizontally, at right angles to the rafters, or vertically, parallel with them.

You can also plank the ceiling, with the boards attached at right angles or diagonally to the rafters. Run hefty false beams vertically, spaced 4 to 8 feet apart. You could also first attach 2-×-4 furring strips at right angles to the rafters, then set the boards at right angles to the furring and set the false beams horizontally, as purlins. The beams themselves could be actual full timbers, or timbers sawn in half lengthwise so that when installed the ceiling appears to be attached to the midpoint of heavy beams. Or you can build box beams from boards, dimension stock and

50-1 Two methods of making up beam pockets within a wall frame.

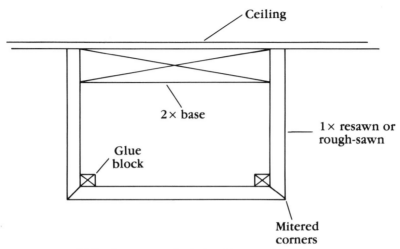

50-2   One easy method of making up a false beam.

boards, or plywood in several different ways (FIG. 50-2). The beams serve no structural purpose and so can be lightweight.

REAL BEAM CEILINGS

The alternative to false beams is real beams, those that are load-bearing and a part of the building skeleton. This requires modified post-and-beam construction techniques, and the roof frame is engineered differently. The beams may be solid wood timbers, but custom-made, glue-laminated beams are preferable. (They do have a different look, however.) They are engineered and built exactly to fit the job at hand, can be prefinished at the factory if desired, are very strong, and are much less susceptible to warping or twisting. There are several approaches to this kind of construction.

Method 1

One is to set a ridge beam, flanked by several successively lower purlins. All msut be beveled and set to the cut of the roof. Then heavy tongue-and-groove decking planks are attached to them and to the wall caps, which are also beveled (FIG. 50-3). An alternative is thick tongue-and-grooved plywood panels. A built-up roof may be applied to the roof deck directly, but usually thermal insulation is installed first, then a finish roof covering.

Method 2

Another method is to set a ridge beam, then erect a series of heavy rafter beam pairs several feet apart, notched to the ridge and joined with a metal

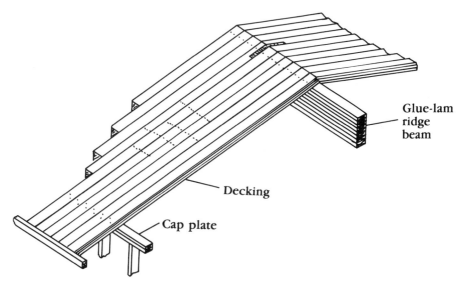

50-3 In this construction, purlins can be introduced as required to support the vertically laid roof decking.

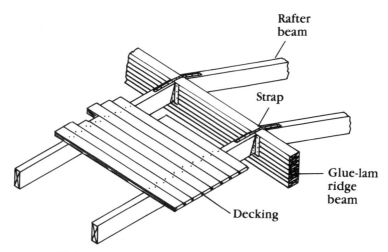

50-4 Roof decking laid horizontally on wide-spaced beams.

plate (FIG. 50-4). Then the roof decking can be applied horizontally, or plywood panels can be installed. If these longitudinal beams are extended well past the building line and ample use is made of glass and load-bearing mullions or other supporting elements, any number of outstanding endwall variations can be designed to lend a distinctive, impressive air to the house.

Method 3

A variation on this theme is to set the ridge beam and rafter pairs as just described, then install a series of purlins perpendicular to the rafters. Then if planks are used, they will be vertical. Whichever way this is done, the beams all must be supported at their ends by columns within the walls, as well as at intermediate points if necessary. If those columns are within interior walls, they in turn must be supported from below by a foundation or a footing and column, so that the load is ultimately supported by the earth.

Exterior wall sheathing and air barrier

*T*here are several materials that can be used for exterior wall sheathing. All of them are effective when employed under the right conditions and correctly applied. There are also preferences as to sheathing application.

SHEATHING METHODS AND MATERIALS

Some builders cover the exterior wall frames as they are being put together on the floor platform and before erecting them. This makes for easier construction, saves a bit of time, avoids having to cut sheathing around rafter ends later on, and provides a little bit of immediate shelter inside the structure. But it also makes the wall sections heavier and harder to erect, more difficult to adjust and anchor in place, and susceptible to wind gusts as the sections are being raised—which can be dangerous.

Other builders prefer to apply the sheathing to the wall frames after they are erected but before the roof is on. This procedure has the advantages mentioned above, and also avoids any problems with wind catching a wall before it is anchored. However, application is more difficult and time consuming, especially on upper levels. In both cases the walls must be strongly braced against possible wind damage later, before the structure is buttoned up.

Yet other builders prefer to wait until the roof is framed and covered before applying any exterior sheathing. Application then is a little more difficult and the roof construction is susceptible to damage from wind gusts swirling through the unsheathed wall frames and catching it like a sail. However, the wall frames and building interior are covered and pro-

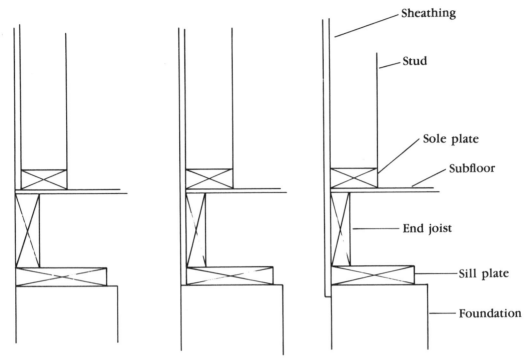

51-1   Wall frames should be placed so that the sheathing covers all the lower framing joints (right). The other two methods are sometimes used but are less desirable.

tected earlier than might otherwise be the case. The exterior sheathing is also partly protected as soon as it is applied, and wind damage to the walls is not a problem. Much depends upon personal preference, the house design, and the dictates of the weather.

Note that in some instances exterior wall sheathing is not required and the exterior siding can be applied directly to the studding. However, this arrangement is not considered premium construction.

The placement of the exterior wall frames relative to the platform floor or the foundation wall determines the position of the exterior wall sheathing at the sill (FIG. 51-1). Sometimes the wall frames are set back from the edge of the floor platform a distance equal to the thickness of the sheathing, so the sheathing face lies flush with the sill and foundation faces. Thus, there is no cross tie from wall to floor frame and there are four uncovered joints. Alternatively, the floor frame can be set back from the foundation face to the extent of the sheathing thickness. Here the wall and floor frames are tied together but there is no protective overlap of the sheathing over the sill/foundation joint. The most satisfactory solution is to set the sill flush with the outer foundation face and allow the exterior sheathing to extend down past the joist by an inch or two. A double bead of top-grade roofing cement or compound or an elastomeric caulk run along the bottom edge of the sheathing is a good low-cost idea that takes little time but is seldom done.

Board sheathing

The traditional method of sheathing the exterior wall frames with boards is still a useful one, resulting in adequately strong construction. In some areas this might be the most cost-effective method, and is an easy technique for a single worker to manage. The biggest drawback to this method has always been the large aggregate area of crackage that can allow substantial air infiltration and consequent heat loss from the building. In the few areas where the climate is perennially benign this doesn't much matter, and in areas where it does matter a new product can be installed that will mitigate the problem.

The sheathing should be nominal 1-inch boards, either tongue-and-groove or shiplap (preferably the former), in a nominal 6- or 8-inch width. You can attach the boards horizontally. Start the first one groove down, with bottom edge about 1 inch below the sill/foundation joint, and work upward. For extra strength, try to span the sill/joist joint and the joist/wall sole plate joint with one board each, and nail into all of those members for a good cross tie. Fasten each board with a pair of 8d common or ring-shank nails at each bearing point. All end joints must be centered over a stud centerline, and always stagger the joints by three studs or more. With this arrangement, the wall frames must be braced at all corners (see Chapter 28).

A better technique, which does not require bracing, is to run the boards diagonally. The directions of the boards should oppose one another at adjacent corners (FIG. 51-2). This requires a little more material; other details remain the same.

Plywood sheathing

The premier exterior sheathing material is plywood. This material goes on rapidly—4-×-8-foot sheets are most often used but other sizes are available—and adds considerable strength and rigidity to the framework. It also obviates the need for any additional wall frame bracing, and makes a solid tie across the wall to the floor frame. And, there are few joints to admit air. In many installations plywood is applied to the entire framework. This is required for a stucco exterior finish; the added stiffness and excellent stability help prevent cracking. Plywood provides a continuous nailing base for wood shingles or shakes. It also makes a solid bearing surface for some other exterior sidings without having to install furring strips or additional blocking, like vertical metal panels, board and batten, or board on board arrangements. It is advisable to install plywood behind masonry veneers.

You can use $5/16$- or $3/8$-inch-thick plywood panels, but $1/2$-inch is the most common size and meshes well with other building materials. APA

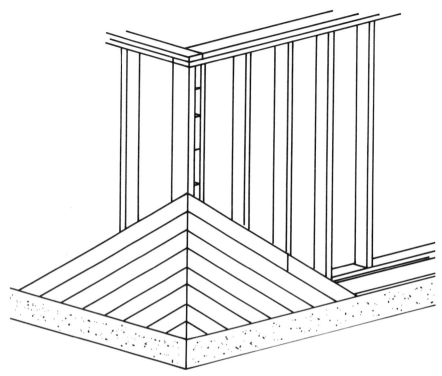

51-2 Diagonal board wall sheathing does not require added bracing and should be applied in opposing directions on adjacent walls.

rated sheathing is suitable, in Wall-16 or Wall-24 grade (or equivalent) as appropriate, Exposure 1. You can apply the panels vertically with at least a 6-inch clearance from the ground (local codes might require 8, 9, or 12 inches), or horizontally with blocking at the open edges between wall studs. Either way, leave 1/8-inch expansion gaps all around; in no case should any vertical joints be unsupported. Any trimmed panel should bear on a minimum of three studs, except for filler strips attached at the sill. Fasten the panels with 6d common, galvanized box, or ring-shank nails. Space them 6 inches on centers on all supported edges, 12 inches along intermediate bearing surfaces (FIG. 51-3).

A common arrangement, which saves some expense but results in an adequate construction, is to install plywood panels only at the building corners to serve as combination bracing and sheathing. Typically 1/2-inch-thick panels are used, on either 16- or 24-inch spaced wall studs. Set them vertically using standard nailing. The panels should be a full 4 feet wide. Then the remaining area is covered with another kind of sheathing of equal thickness, usually fiberboard, but sometimes gypsum sheathing board, waferboard, particle board, or rigid thermal insulation sheathing panels.

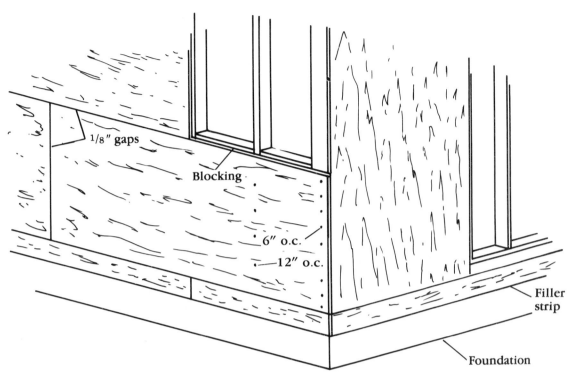

1/8" gaps

Blocking

6" o.c.

12" o.c.

Filler strip

Foundation

51-3 Plywood sheathing panels can be applied vertically, or horizontally if edge blocking is installed.

Other sheathing materials

All of these products can also be used to entirely sheath the wall frame-work. Orientation of the sheets does not matter because they have equal strength in all directions. Nailing, however, does matter and is different for the various products. Local codes should always be checked for specific requirements, not only for nailing but also bracing, edge blocking, and general usage requirements.

Fiberboard is usually fastened with 11-gauge 1 1/2-inch galvanized roofing barbs for the 1/2-inch thickness, and 1 3/4-inch for the 25/32-inch panels. These are spaced 3 inches apart around the edges and 6 inches apart at intermediate bearing surfaces. This is also typical of gypsum sheathing requirements. Particle board and waferboard should be fastened with 6d common nails on 6-inch centers at the edges, 12-inch centers at the intermediate points.

Details for rigid insulation vary, so follow the specific manufacturer's instructions. Roofing barbs long enough to penetrate at least 3/4 inch into the support and spaced about every 8 inches at all bearings would do the job nicely, in the absence of other specifications. The joints between insulation panels, especially if foil faced, are often taped over with a special tape. Again, follow installation instructions.

AIR BARRIER

There was a time when all wall sheathing consisted of boards, and they were usually covered with building paper or sheathing paper. The two products most often applied were red rosin paper and 15-pound roofing felt, both of which are breathable: They do not admit passage of water or moisture, but do transpire water vapor. This interface also helps to cut down air infiltration through the myriad of cracks in the sheathing. Both products are still available, and you can still use them over exterior board (or other) sheathing. However, there is a new product that is much better, even though a bit more expensive. It is a sheet air infiltration barrier product often called *housewrap*.

Housewrap

Housewrap is made of woven synthetic fibers and is very strong. It looks like paper but is not, will never rot or shrink, and if properly installed will last and retain its full effectiveness indefinitely. It will pass water vapor, but keep cold air from getting into the walls and thermal insulation by sealing off all the cracks. At the same time it cuts down the entrance of cool air into the interior of the house, reducing the air-change rate substantially. This very lightweight material comes in rolls ranging from 3 to 9 feet wide and 111 to 222 feet long, and ranges from 6 to 10 mils in thickness, depending upon the manufacturer.

Installation is simple enough. As the name implies, you wrap the house in it, as tightly as you can. Apply it directly over the sheathing (or the studs if no sheathing is installed), including door, window, and all other openings. Staple it carefully; ordinary 1/4-inch staples will do the job. Slit the material at openings and wrap it around so that it seals by being sandwiched beneath other material to be added later, like window or door trim. Then cut away the excess. Overlap seams by 4 to 6 inches; you can tape these off if you wish, for an even tighter seal.

Chapter **52**

Exterior siding

Exterior wall siding can be structural—that is, it can be an integral part of and essential to the overall strength and rigidity of the structure. It may also be nonstructural—not meant to contribute anything but a finished appearance. Siding applied as a decorative skin usually does add to the total integrity of the structure, although that function is often secondary and not even considered. A wide array of exterior siding products are available. Most of them are easy to apply, even for inexperienced do-it-yourselfers, but you will find a few that are best left to experienced professionals.

LUMBER SIDING

Lumber siding of one sort or another is the old standby and is still very popular today. It consits of plain boards, which may be square-edged S4S or S3S, rough-sawn, resawn, tongue-and-groove, shiplap, or any of several patterned lumbers. Pine and fir are often used, especially where a painted or stained finish is to be applied, and both cedar and redwood are popular for a natural finish.

Square-edged boards

Square-edged boards can be applied vertically in any of three ways (FIG. 52-1)—provided that solid, nailable sheathing is applied first or two or three horizontal runs of cross blocking are installed in the wall frame as nailers. The board-and-batten arrangement is the most common, where wide boards (typically 8- or 10-inch nominal) are applied first, with a gap

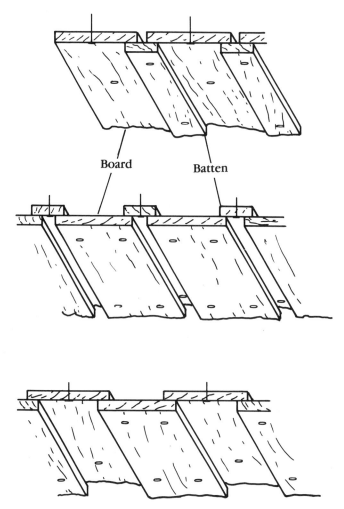

Board   Batten

52-1 Three popular methods of applying square-edged boards as exterior siding are board-and-batten (top), batten-and-board (center), and board-and-board.

of about 1 inch between them. Battens of 1×2 are nailed over the gaps. The board-and-board method is made up of wide boards spaced well apart, with more boards of the same width covering the gaps. The batten-and-board variation is the reverse of the board-and-batten.

Square-edged boards can also be applied horizontally in a lap siding arrangement (FIG. 52-2). This requires a 1-×-2 starter strip all around the bottom of the house. The boards should be set to overlap one another by at least 1 inch. Lap siding is also made in a pattern called bevel siding or clapboard. This material is available in several widths and is also laid in an overlap, such that anywhere from 4 to 8 inches of wood remains exposed to the weather. Another siding that exhibits a similar appearance but fits

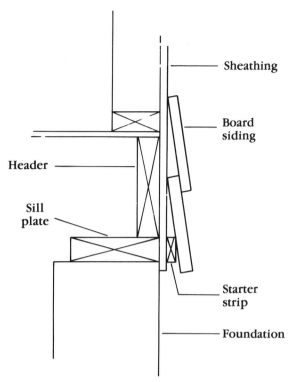

52-2 Square-edged board lap siding begins with a 1-×-2 starter strip under the bottom course.

up differently is Dolly Varden pattern lumber. This relatively thick beveled material has a rabbeted edge that interlocks the strips.

Drop siding

Although seldom done these days, you can use either plain tongue-and-groove or plain shiplap boards placed horizontally, with the tongue or lap facing downward. The result is a flat, blank, shadowless surface like that favored many years ago on some colonial style houses.

There are numerous alternatives in the category called *drop* siding (FIG. 52-3). These boards are smooth milled to several standard configurations that have acquired any number of pet names, mostly localized, like "novelty siding," or "channel-lap," "pickwick," "bevel-edge," "barn board," "vee-groove," and a dozen others. All of these sidings, however, are designated by a pattern number, and that is the only way to be sure of what you are ordering or working with. Patterns are also available in several different faces (exposure to the weather) and overall widths. Log cabin siding is another possibility, and it also appears in several somewhat different profiles, depending upon who is doing the milling.

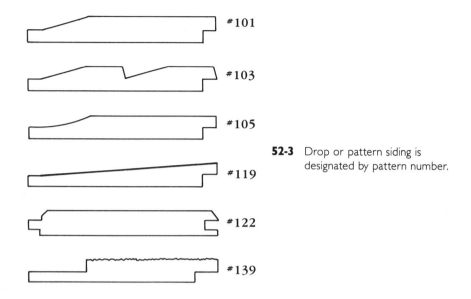

#101

#103

#105

#119

#122

#139

52-3 Drop or pattern siding is designated by pattern number.

All of these sidings are usually applied horizontally, but with some types, especially natural cedar sidings, a diagonal lay or combinations of angular, vertical, and horizontal layouts are popular.

Installation

Installation of any of these sidings is not a difficult chore. Use fasteners that will neither rust nor corrode under local conditions: aluminum, stainless steel, and copper work well. As a last choice, use hot-dipped galvanized nails. Face nailing is necessary in many instances, but whenever there is an opportunity to blind nail—hiding the nail head within a joint or under a lap—do so. In many instances 6d or 8d nails will do the job, but there must be at least ³/4 inch penetration into the bearing surface when fastening relatively thin, lightweight siding, and at least 1 inch for heavier materials. There are cases when 12d nails are barely sufficient. Narrow boards with a locking joint are often secured with only one nail at the top of each board, but if the exposure is over 5 inches two nails should be used, and sometimes three if cupping appears to be a problem. Secure the siding at every stud, or every 16 inches to nailable sheathing.

All end joints should occur over a stud, regardless of whether or not the sheathing is a nailable type. These are usually butt joints, and must be sawn exactly at right angles with a fine-toothed blade to present a tight joint. A plain scarf makes a better joint (FIG. 52-4). When joining pieces, smear a coating of paintable elastomeric caulk—silicone, for example—onto both boards ends. Press them tightly together and immediately wipe away the excess that squeezes out. Cut and trim with care when mating up to casings, sills, trimwork or moldings, and any other openings or protrusions

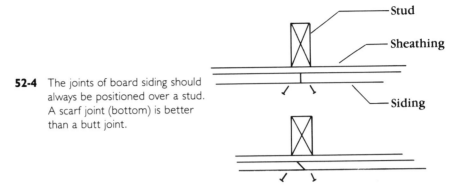

52-4 The joints of board siding should always be positioned over a stud. A scarf joint (bottom) is better than a butt joint.

in the wall surface, so the joints will be clean and tight. Flashings and/or drip caps might be needed at some points, such as above windows.

Where sidings change directions, types or styles, a joint occurs that requires special treatment (FIG. 52-5). For example, vertical siding on a gable can be arranged to overhang the top strip of horizontal siding on the wall below. Or, a break can be installed in the form of a band molding with flashing.

Corners require special treatment, too (FIG. 52-6). In some cases it is possible to install commercially available metal corners that lock or nail into place on the siding. The most common arrangement, though, is to install corner boards. These are typically 1-×-4 or 1-×-6 plain S4S boards,

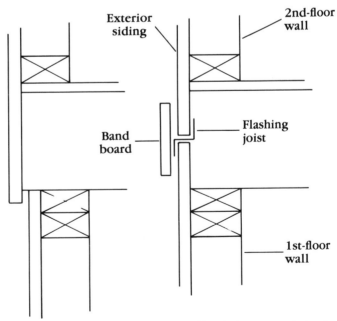

52-5 Two common methods of treating horizontal breaks between exterior siding panels.

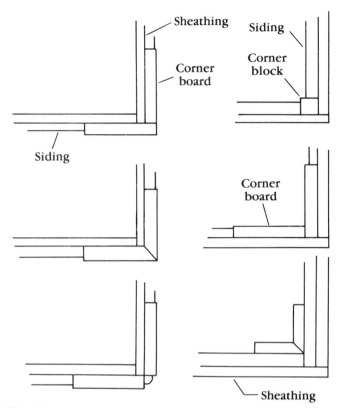

52-6 Common arrangements for outside corners (left) and inside corners.

which on outside corners you can overlap, miter, or set flush with the corner. At inside corners, one method is to fill the corner with a strip of 1×1. The alternative is to install a pair of boards of any desired width in a miter joint, so the boards' widths will be equal. Or, you could use a butt joint but rip a lengthwise strip off one board equal to the thickness, to equalize the widths. Another solution that is sometimes satisfactory, depending upon the configuration of the siding material, is to butt the siding at the corners, then apply corner boards over the siding. Effectiveness depends upon how many gaps occur; they should all be caulked shut, but are often ignored.

PLYWOOD SIDING

Although plywood has neither the flexibility nor the variety of design of lumber siding, it has become very popular over the past decade or so. There is a considerable variety from which to choose, the material is strong and weatherable and installs rapidly, the various grades accept different kinds of applied finishes, and the cost is moderate.

Styles

APA rated siding in the 303 Series is available in several styles. Medium Density Overlay (MDO) wood is treated with a smooth, relatively hard overlay on one side, suitable for painting. COM-PLY® is a composite panel with a solid core and rough-sawn veneer faces. Brushed has a mechanically grained face in deep relief that looks weather-worn. APA Texture 1-11 has shiplapped edges and parallel grooves, and is perhaps one of the most popular plywood sidings ever. Rough-Sawn plywood has a machine-made rough-sawn texture that runs across the face grain at right angles to the length of the panel. Channel Groove has shiplapped edges and shallow vertical grooves, usually on 4- or 8-inch centers. Reverse Board-And-Batten has deep, wide grooves typically on 8- or 12-inch centers and shiplapped long edges.

All of these styles are available at various times and in various locations with different groove patterns and dimensions, surface textures, wood species, and panel thicknesses. Availability and specifications change from time to time. Consult with your building supplies dealer, builder, or architect to find out which style best suits your purposes.

Installation

Panels may be installed vertically or horizontally. This will depend upon whether or not blocking has been installed in the wall frame (necessary for horizontal applications), the kind of bracing needed by the frame (if any), the design of the panels, and the layout of the pattern. For example, where long edges are shiplapped, the pattern can be carried either way. For horizontal application, the overlap should be downward to shed moisture. Set the panels so there is at least 6 inches of ground clearance (more might be required by local code), and leave a $1/8$-inch expansion gap at all edges.

Fasten the panels with nonstaining box, siding, or casing nails spaced 6 inches apart on all edges, 12 inches on intermediate bearings. Use 6d nails for $1/2$-inch or thinner plywood, 8d for thicker—if there is no sheathing or the sheathing is $1/2$ inch thick or less. If the sheathing is more than $1/2$ inch thick, step up to the next regular nail size for every thickness increment. Use box nails over rigid foam insulation sheathing. For example, 10d nails through $1/2$-inch plywood over 1-inch insulation would give you a satisfactory $11/2$ inches of penetration into studs. A penetration of $11/4$ inch is a good working minimum to observe; more is better.

The APA recommends that all panel edges be sealed before the panels are put up. You can do this by applying a transparent, paintable sealer if the final finish will be natural or an oil stain. If the final finish will be paint, you can use this for the priming as well. Vertical panel joints in the field should fall over a stud; although this isn't always possible when nailable sheathing is present. They should also be caulked with an elastomeric caulk. This is best accomplished by running a bead along the panel edge first, then installing it. Always nail both adjoining panel edges, even if they are shiplapped. Vertical joints may be left open, or covered with a batten or a strip of molding.

Vertical corner joints can be butted and caulked only, covered with corner boards, abutted to a corner block, or butted to corner boards, as with lumber siding. Horizontal panel joints should be backed with blocking. Square-edged panels can meet flush and be butted (with a slight gap) and protected with flashing, or the upper panel can be lapped over the bottom one. Shiplap joints automatically overlap. Any of these joints can also be trimmed with a horizontal band molding or board.

RED CEDAR SHINGLES

Lumber and plywood sidings might be the mainstays, but there are a good many more possibilities. One favorite, which has enjoyed a recent resurgence in popularity, is redcedar shingles. Interest has been sparked because of the increased availability of fancy butt shingles (FIG. 52-7) that were common in the Victorian times. Now, in addition to the ordinary shakes and shingles discussed in Chapter 49, you can also find such butt patterns as octagonal, fish scale, hexagonal, arrow, rounded, and acorn, and others. Siding shingles can also be obtained prestained or prepainted, and most come with complete instructions for application.

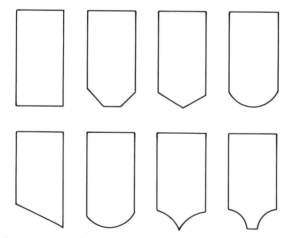

52-7 A few fancy butt wood shingle patterns: (top left to right) standard square butt, octagonal, hexagonal, round; (bottom left to right) diagonal, fish scale, arrow, and half-cove.

Installation

Siding with shingles is a job that can be done piecemeal over a period of time, by a single worker if need be. Because application is neither quite as difficult nor as exacting as wood shingle roofing, it can be successfully done by an inexperienced owner-builder. The shingles are most easily applied over a nailable sheathing such as plywood. Otherwise, horizontal 1-×-4 nailing strips must be secured to the studs on centers equal to the selected weather exposure of the shingles. Either way there should be an interface of building paper or housewrap, stapled just enough to hold it in place while the shingles are applied.

The shingles may be put up in a single-course arrangement, or can be doubled for far better weather protection. To determine the appropriate exposure for single coursing, halve the length of the shingles and subtract 1 inch for No. 1 grade, 2 inches for No. 2, and 3 inches for No. 3. Number 2 18-inch shingles would thus be laid with 7 inches to the weather. For double coursing you can lay up with greater exposure; subtract 4, 5, and 6 inches respectively from the total length of the three grades of shingles. This system allows you to install less expensive No. 4 grade undercoursing shingles as the bottom layer. The outer course should always overhang the inner by about 1/2 inch.

To apply the shingles, guide on the bottom of the sheathing or the sill joint and nail up a row of shingles. Space them approximately 1/8 inch apart, and drive two stain-proof shingle nails about 3/4 inch in from each edge and about midway of the shingle length. Then apply another course right over the first, overhanging about 1/2 inch and with all joints staggered. Nail these shingles about 3/4 inch in from each side and about 1 inch above the line of the butt ends of the next course. If you are double coursing (FIG. 52-8), add yet another layer of shingles to the first course. To

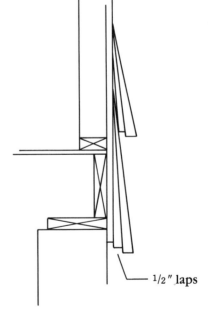

52-8 Double coursing wood shingles require a triple layer of shingles in the first course.

1/2" laps

align the next course, snap a chalkline or tack-nail a straight length of board to the wall. Set the butt ends of the next course to the line or board edge, nailed in the same way, and continue upwards. Secure any shingles wider than 8 inches with a third nail, and centered. The nails should be long enough to penetrate through the sheathing or nailer strips.

Corners can be handled in the same ways as for lumber or plywood sidings. They can also consist of shingles woven together in alternate overlaps on the two adjacent walls, or the meeting shingles can be mitered together.

OTHER SIDINGS

Although the foregoing sidings are about the most popular in one version or another, there are still others from which you can choose. Lap siding, for example, in straight, square-edged or sometimes rabbeted form, can be obtained in plywood, hardboard, and particle board, both prefinished and unfinished. The material can be professionally applied, but the task is not difficult and can be handled by a competent amateur builder.

Masonry and simulated masonry

Masonry veneer siding is a different matter; unless you have some experience in this field, application is best left to the pros. Brick is probably the most popular masonry material, but stone in various forms is also commonly used. In most applications the veneer extends only partway up the walls, with some other siding material installed above.

There is an exception to the professional construction rule: Various simulated masonry materials are available that are specifically designed for do-it-yourself application. Artificial brick and stone patterns are manufactured in thin individual pieces or small sheets. These are attached to a smooth substrate like plywood sheathing with a special adhesive. Joint lines are typically grouted with the same adhesive, and after a curing period the whole surface is treated with one or more coats of clear sealer. The pieces are fully weatherproof, lightweight, easy to trim and fit, and look good.

Stucco

Another traditional material enjoying something of a resurgence these days is stucco. This is a cement-plaster material that is usually applied over a special wire mesh, or sometimes directly on rigid thermal insulation panels, in two or three coats. Virtually any color can be mixed into the material. The surface can be troweled smooth, and is usually textured. Application requires experience and is physically demanding; this is another job for the pros.

Aluminum, steel, and vinyl

Aluminum, steel, and vinyl sidings are also popular, although they are more frequently employed for re-siding purposes than new installations. Some of these materials are smooth surfaced, others are textured in a wood grain, and most of them present either a clapboard or a channel-lap appearance. They are factory finished in numerous colors, and matching accessory items such as formed corners, door and window surrounds, gutters and downspouts, and soffit materials are available. They have the advantage of requiring virtually no maintenance.

Installation

Aluminum, steel, and vinyl installations should be left to the professionals. There is an exception, however. Many of the factory finished metal sheet panels that are currently in vogue for finish roofing can also be employed as siding. They can be installed either vertically or horizontally and make a weatherproof, maintenance-free installation. The biggest problem lies in the trimming and fitting around windows, doors, and similar items; this must be carefully done for tight fits everywhere. Liberal use must be made of caulking and flashing strips, and depending upon the underlying construction, full surrounds at windows, doors, and other openings might be advisable. These metal sheet panels also have the advantages of low cost and rapid application.

Chapter **53**

Window
installation

Proper installation is the key to trouble-free window operation, as well as minimum infiltration of outside air or exfiltration of inside air—both of which are important factors in energy consumption. Installing window units, whether factory-made, locally custom-made, or home shop-built, and whether fixed or operable, is not a difficult job. It does need to be done with care, not only for the sake of appearance but also to help ensure longevity of the unit. In most cases a helper is needed to act as gofer while the installer hangs onto everything, or to boost the window in place and hold it there while the installer makes the final adjustments and fastens the unit in place.

There is an extensive array of commercially available window units, and specific installation details will vary from product to product. The sash may be fixed, operational in the double-hung, single-hung, casement, awning, hopper, horizontal sliding, or jalousie styles. Or, the units may be combinations of these styles. The glazing may be window or heavy sheet glass, regular or heavy float glass, tinted, tempered, laminated, insulating, reflective coated, low-emissivity, low iron, or patterned glass, or plastic. The frames may be made of solid aluminum, thermal-break aluminum, vinyl, wood, aluminum-clad wood, vinyl-clad wood, or fiberglass. And of course there is a myriad of different sizes. Some of these units are supplied with installation instructions and/or recommendations, but many are not. Thus, common sense and sometimes a bit of ingenuity often play a part.

CHECKING FOR SQUARE

Many commercial window units are fitted with temporary cross braces to protect and hold the unit in square during shipping and installation; this is particularly true of units that are partly or wholly framed with wood. Never take them for granted. Before installing any window, check to make sure that it is in square. Use a carpenter's framing or other square, or by measuring the diagonals: If the diagonals are unequal the unit is not in square.

If the unit is not square and there are braces, remove them, and square the unit up by placing it sill down on a flat surface and pushing against a top corner until it racks back into square. Then reattach the braces in different locations. If the units are metal framed and out of square, check first for damage to the frame. If there is something amiss, or you cannot square the frame by gently racking it, return it to the supplier. Also, when possible check the unit for proper operation before you install it. In some cases you can't because of the packing, bracing, or shipping fasteners that stay put until installation is finished.

INSTALLING VAPOR BARRIER

Next, measure the unit and the rough opening to make sure that the window will indeed fit into its designated hole. With that minor detail ascertained, install an air infiltration/vapor barrier around the rough opening (FIG. 53-1). This step is almost universally ignored, but if you want a tight, draft-free installation—especially if the exterior wall sheathing is comprised of boards—this is an essential step in achieving it.

There are two useful choices for materials: 6-mil polyethylene sheet or the spun synthetic fiber sheet known as housewrap. The former will block both air and water vapor, the latter primarily air. Cut a wide strip and wrap it around the rough opening frame like a collar, so you can pull it back over the exterior sheathing about 6 inches and across the inside sheathing at least 4 inches. Staple the barrier to the exterior sheathing (or the framing), fold it through the opening. Tape or staple the excess back along the inside wall out of the way for the moment. Make overlaps of at least 6 inches at all joints, and see that there are no gaps at the corners.

PLACING THE UNIT

Most windows are installed from the outside. The first step is to set the unit on the rough sill and have a helper hold it in place. From the inside, check the height of the window frame header relative to the rough opening header. If necessary, insert shims under the bottom of the unit to approximately center it in the opening. Check for level and plumb using a spirit level, and make whatever adjustments are needed.

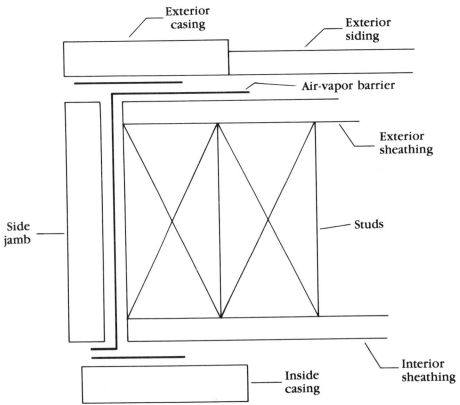

53-1   Windows should be completely and tightly sealed against air and moisture vapor migration through the joints by installing a suitable barrier arranged along these lines.

MOUNTING AND NAILING THE UNIT

Some units are made with an exterior mounting flange, complete with prepunched holes, while others must be nailed or screwed through the side jambs to secure them. With the unit held firmly in position and snug against the exterior wall, drive one nail in each bottom corner. For mounting flanges use roofing barbs, and for wood casings use finish or casing nails; either should be long enough to penetrate at least 1 inch into the nailable sheathing and/or studs. For wood frames, drive the nails only partway in. For flanges, drive the nails almost fully home but make sure they are positioned at the top of oversized factory-punched flange holes. If the frames are designed to be attached with screws through holes provided in the side jambs, drive a pair partly home in two of the lowest holes.

Have a helper continue to hold the unit snug against the wall, especially at the unsecured top. Go back to the inside and check the side jambs for plumb and the sill for level. If anything is out of line, correct as necessary; the unit itself should be in square, as explained earlier. Back outside, drive two more nails or screws nearly home at the top corners of the unit. Check again for level and plumb. If the window is more than about 30 inches wide, tap one or more wedge shims (wood shingles work fine, with small blocks if needed) under the sill. They should be just snug; take care to not drive the sill upward in a bow. The purpose is to keep the sill from sagging over a long period of time.

With the unit still snugged against the wall, pull the braces or other shipping hardware off the unit and operate the sash to make sure it functions smoothly and opens fully. If not, reset shims or make other adjustments until it does. Then finish fastening the unit. Space fasteners 10 to 12 inches apart unless instructed otherwise. If the window is tall and has relatively limber side jambs, many installers prefer to insert a series of snug shims between the jambs and studs at each attachment point. This will keep them rigid and properly aligned. During all of this, try not to damage the air infiltration barrier material.

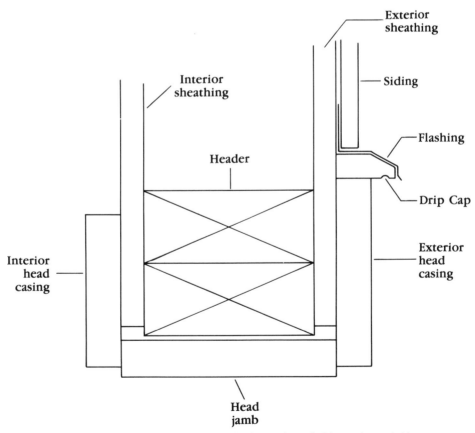

53-2 This window installation includes both metal cap flashing and wood drip cap.

ATTACHING DRIP CAP AND METAL FLASHING

Attach the wood drip cap or metal flashing—some windows have both—to the exterior sheathing. Never attach these to the window unit itself (FIG. 53-2). A narrow, thin bead of caulking might be in order here, depending upon the window/flashing design. From the inside, stuff the crack all around the unit with fiberglass or mineral wool thermal insulation, packed in tight. Fold the inner edge of the infiltration barrier over the window frame edges and staple or tape it in place. Trim it so that it will not show when the interior trim is applied. Cut strips of vapor barrier material—6-mil polyethylene sheet is most commonly used—and staple or tape them over the insulation-filled cracks on the inside, and on the outside as well if the unit does not have factory-installed exterior trim. However you manipulate the barrier material, the object is to create an impenetrable double seal by sandwiching the pieces into the construction elements.

Chapter 54

Site-built windows

*F*ixed window units that match the general appearance of other operable units in a house can be obtained from the same maker. However, there is often a need for units of a special size or shape. Depending upon the design, these can usually be built right on the job site and completed at appropriate points in the construction schedule.

TERMINOLOGY

Before beginning to build these units, it is necessary to become familiar with window terminology. *Glazing* is the transparent part of the window, whether glass or plastic. A piece of glass cut for installation is the *pane*, a piece of plastic is a *sheet*. A *light* is a single pane or sheet installed in the window. The glazing is retained in a framework composed of vertical *stiles* and horizontal *rails*, with lights separated by *muntins*. This assembly is called the *sash*. The sash is mounted in a *window frame* or *back*, which is made up of a *side jamb* at each side, a *sill* at the bottom, and a *head jamb* at the top.

FIXED SINGLE-LIGHT WINDOWS

Fixed single lights are not difficult to make, and there are two approaches. One is to install the glazing directly into a frame that is actually part of the house framework: a finished opening in the wall frame. The second is to install the glazing directly in a finish frame and then install the unit in the rough opening. Two variations are to install a single- or multiple-light sash—instead of the raw-edged glazing—in either a built-in finished opening, or first in a finish frame and then into the rough opening.

Constructing the frame

The first step in making a fixed single-light window is to construct a window frame. This can be built separately and then installed in the rough opening with or without glazing, or built right into the wall framework piece by piece and glazed in place. In either case, when the assembly is complete, make sure the sill is level and the frame dead square at all corners. The frame is usually made up of top-grade, kiln-dried, clear, nominal 2-inch-thick stock (FIG. 54-1). Rip the stock to a width equal to the total

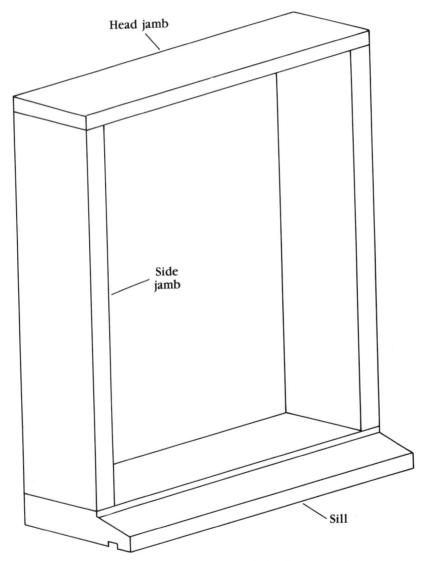

54-1   A typical simple four-piece window frame or buck.

thickness of the wall in which the frame will be installed. This includes inside sheathing, studs, and exterior sheathing—plus exterior siding if it is flat-surfaced and the exterior window casing will lie flat upon it rather than against the exterior sheathing.

Glazing

If the glazing is to be window, plate or float glass, patterned glass, or plastic, the frame size and shape can be whatever you wish because the glass can be cut and shaped to suit. For tempered, insulating, and other specialty glass or already complete sash units, the frame must be made to fit the sash or whatever stock glazing size is available. In some instances glazing can be custom-manufactured for you, for a price. In any event, the inside dimensions of the frame should be sized to allow a $1/4$-inch expansion and setting gap all around.

Back stop

When the frame is complete, check it for correct alignment, then add the back stop, which holds the glass from the inside. The stop edge against the glass is usually positioned about in the center of the jamb faces, but that is variable. The sill back stop may be a narrow strip that is wider and set flush with the inner edge of the sill, or it may actually be a stool that serves as a back stop and extends beyond the interior wall surface. The back stops can be made of any kind of molding with a face about $7/16$ to $3/4$ inch thick, such as square, glass bead, cove, quarter-round, base shoe set flat, or any of several varieties of stops. Butt joints are generally fashioned at the corners if they are right-angled, but mitering is more satisfactory. If the angles are other than 90 degrees, mitered or coped joints will be needed.

Setting the glass in the frame

To set free (no sash) glass, lay a full bed of glazing compound—not putty—all around the outer edge of the back stop. If the glazing is other than insulating glass, tilt the bottom edge of the glass into the compound so that some remains beneath it, and press the glass firmly and evenly against the compound along the side and head back stops. The bed should flatten and curl up and out on the outside, squeeze around the glass edges to the outside, and partly fill the gap between the glass edges and the frame (FIG. 54-2). If you are glazing with the frame upright, keep the glass in place by inserting a few glazier's points. These will not be required if the unit is flat on a benchtop.

If the glazing is insulating glass, fit neoprene setting blocks at the bottom edge of the glass. Then tilt the glass into place bottom first until the inner edges of the blocks come up against the bottom back stop. Press the glass against the rest of the compound bed; there should be a thin layer of

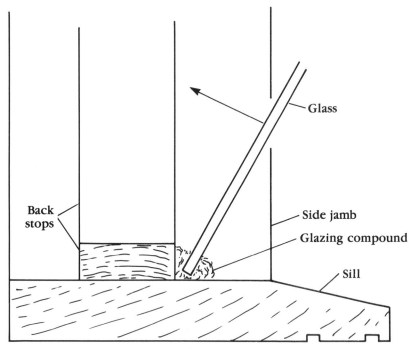

Back stops

Glass

Side jamb

Glazing compound

Sill

54-2 Setting glass in a window frame.

compound beneath the setting blocks and a curl of it around the glass edges (FIG. 54-3). Do not use glazing points to restrain insulating or tempered glass; temporarily tack in a scrap or two of stop on the outside instead.

Next, knife on another full but fairly thin bed of glazing compound around the exterior edges of the glass. Fit face stops around the exterior. Again, you can use any kind of molding that appeals, but it should be angle-surfaced for moisture runoff. Press the pieces flat against the jambs and back into the compound, but not against the glass. Leave a 1/16-inch or wider layer of compound between the two. Nail the face stop to the sill and jambs with galvanized finish nails. Then trim away the excess compound and fill any gaps, leaving a slightly outward-beveled finished edge. Figure 54-4 shows a completed assembly.

FIXED MULTIPLE-LIGHT WINDOWS

If you want to make up a window unit with multiple fixed lights, the general procedure is the same. Instead of a simple box frame, construct an egg crate frame. This can be built right into the house framework during construction, or as a discrete unit to be installed later in a rough opening in the framing. You can use butt joints throughout, if you are working with 90-degree corners. However, double rabbetting the frame corners

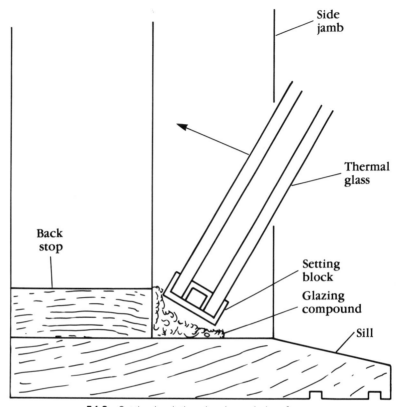

54-3 Setting insulating glass in a window frame.

and fitting the interior members with dado joints (FIG. 54-5) makes a much stronger construction. Set the lights as for single-light windows.

Large lights

When several large lights are to be installed adjacent to one another, the arrangement is somewhat different. An example of such an installation is a row of insulating glass lights of the kind used to glaze patio doors, set to front a sunspace or greenhouse room. The framework that holds lights of this sort is a part of the structural framework of the house as well. The frame is typically built of vertical 4×4s or 4×6s that serve as both window mullions and wall studs. Set other members horizontally between the mullions as sills and headers. Solidly fasten all of these parts together, especially if they are to bear the considerable weight of large insulating glass panels. Mount the glazing on setting blocks and bed it directly against back stops that are attached to the framework. The entire framework may be trimmed out and finished as desired. Redwood and cedar are often used for the entire construction, especially if the finish is to be a natural one.

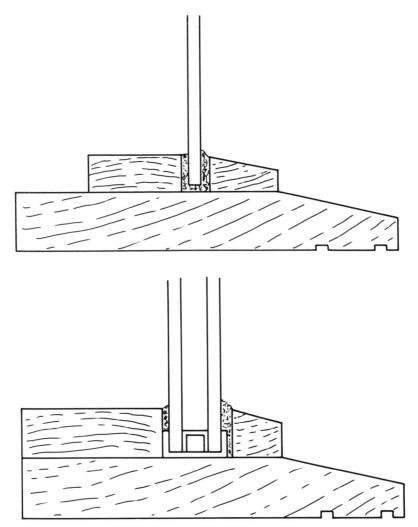

54-4 Completed fixed-light assemblies.

SASH UNITS

If sash units rather than unframed glass are to be installed as fixed units, the procedures are much the same. Each window, whether single- or multiple-light, can be bought or made up as a unit and then installed in a rough opening like any other window. Alternatively, the frame can be built in or installed first, and the sash put in afterward.

Leave a ¼-inch expansion gap between the sash and frame on all sides. Do not use glazing compound or putty. Instead, run a fairly thick bead of elastomeric caulk along the sill about ¼ inch from the sill back stop. Set the bottom of the sash on the caulk and against the back stop,

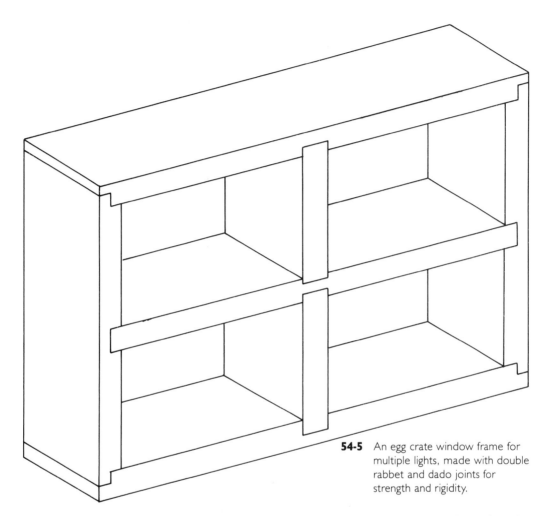

54-5 An egg crate window frame for multiple lights, made with double rabbet and dado joints for strength and rigidity.

squash the caulk down just a bit, and push the sash into place directly against the back stop all around. Hold the sash in place with a pair of 6d nails that are set against the sash stiles about halfway up from the bottom and driven about 1/2 inch into the side jambs of the frame. Then run a bead of caulk all around the sash/frame joint, driving it well into the gap. Fasten the head face stop in place, tight against the sash. Wipe a thin coat of caulk onto the inner edge of the sill face stop and nail it in place. Remove the two temporary nails and fit the side face stops. Figure 54-6 shows this arrangement.

Note: A number of builders, amateur and otherwise, have had excellent success using silicone rubber caulk as a bedding and sealing material for glazing rather than glazing compound, especially where there are no large gaps to be filled. Though a bit trickier to use, this material has the advantage of providing a superior expansion cushion. It adheres and seals

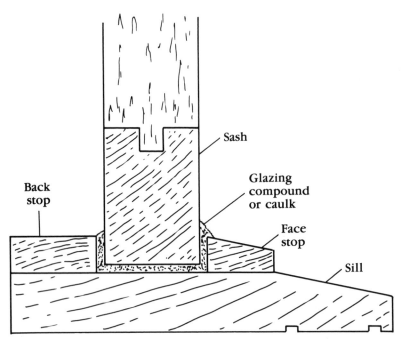

54-6   A complete window sash unit sealed into a window frame.

well, it is long-lived and never hardens, and it is very weather-resistant. Several colors are available. Be aware, though, that many varieties cannot be painted over, because the paint will not stick. Select a paintable type if this is of consequence.

Chapter **55**

Exterior door installation

*E*xterior entrance door installations can be done in several ways, depending upon the type of door and frame used. Doors can be trimmed in many different ways, from plain and simple to complex and ornate. The doors themselves, unless custom-made, come in a standard thickness of 1³/₄ inches. Standard heights are: 6 feet and 8 inches (called a 6-8), and 7 feet (designated 7-0). A width of 3 feet is generally considered minimum for a front entryway door. A 2-8 width is commonly used as well, especially for side and rear entrances. Other less common widths are 2-6—which are not recommended singly but are sometimes installed in front entry pairs (as are other widths)—and 3-6.

Steel-clad exterior doors are becoming more popular because the core (and thus the door) is thermally efficient; little or no maintenance is required; and they are not susceptible to damage, warping, splitting, and similar problems. However, wood remains the favorite material, and there are several kinds of wood doors available. Flush hollow-core doors are composed of wood veneers over a honeycomb interior. These are lightweight and smooth-faced. Flush solid-core doors are made up of veneers over a solid lumber or composition interior, much heavier and sturdier, and also smooth-faced. Solid wood doors are less common, and are available in a limited range of styles. Wood panel doors are the most commonly installed. They consist of a thick frame surrounding thinner inset panels. Dozens of styles are available, with and without lights.

TWO METHODS OF INSTALLATION

There are two approaches to exterior door installations. One is to purchase a prehung unit, which consists of the door already hung within a preassembled door frame, all hardware installed, and with a bundle of unattached trim optional in many cases. Installation involves placing the entire assembly into the rough opening and securing it, then removing the temporary shipping braces and applying the trimwork at the proper time in the construction process. The range of available hardware and door styles is comparatively limited with prehung units, but installation is somewhat faster and easier.

The alternative approach is to select a door—all the hardware elements (hinges, lockset, security lock, knocker, weatherstripping), frame parts, and trim pieces—and install the whole affair from scratch. This is the method preferred by many, and it is necessary if none of the prehung combinations appeal to you. The installation process for a prehung follows the same pattern as for a scratch installation, except that some of the steps have already been completed at the factory.

THE FRAME

The first step is to build and install the door frame. A basic frame consists of ten parts: two side jambs, head jamb, four side casings, two head casings, and a sill. The starting point is an exterior jamb set, which includes the material for the head and side jambs, and a length of sill stock. The former is generally pine, anywhere from 1¼ to 1¾ inches thick, with a single rabbet (sometimes double) to form the stop. This is a more weathertight arrangement than adding a separate stop molding to the jambs. Oak is the preferred wood for the sill. The casings can be any of numerous moldings, or plain S4S 1×4 or 1×6. Or, the entry design might call for added fancy trimwork like pilasters, columns, pediment, side lights, or a transom.

Sill

The exact procedure for assembling and installing the exterior door frame depends upon the sill. Some are thin and flat-bottomed, with a squared or rabbetted inner edge and a tapered nose. They are meant to be set flat on the subfloor and to abut or slightly overlap the finish flooring. They may overhang the building line on the outside by about 1 inch past the exterior siding (FIG. 55-1). In this case, cut both ends of the side jambs square and trim their height so that the distance between the sill top and the header bottom will equal the door height. Trim the sill so that, when assembled, the width from jamb face to jamb face equals the door width. You can include the door and/or sill cap clearance allowances in these measurements if you wish, but many installers prefer to make the frame a little tight and trim the door to fit the installed frame. The idea is that while you can easily trim the door a bit, you can't add to a frame that is too wide or tall.

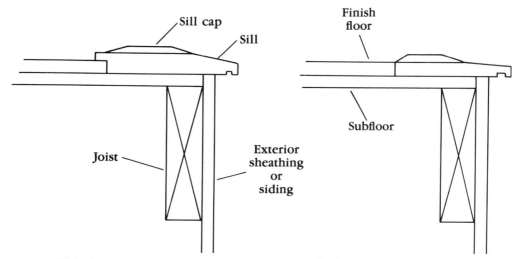

55-1 Some exterior door sills overlap the finish floor (left), while others abut it (right).

Side and head jambs

Lay the side jambs on edge on the floor. Set the head jamb between them, and nail and glue the top corners together. Aliphatic resin (yellow or carpenter's glue) and 6d or 8d ring-shank nails will do the job, or you can use extruded thread or drywall screws. Sometimes the joints are simple butts, but rabbet or dado joints are preferable. The sill fits between the side jamps with butt joints. Attach this with nails or screws only, or add a thin coat of construction adhesive, silicone caulk, or waterproof glue.

Thick slanted sills

An exterior door frame with a thick, wide, slanted sill is handled differently. The subflooring must be cut back and reinforced at the cut edges if the sill lies parallel to the joists, to accommodate the inner edge of the threshold (FIG. 55-2). The header or end joist must also be notched to bear along the lengthwise centerline of the sill. The side jambs are typically trimmed to abut the sill surface, but can abut the sill ends. The sill itself is often trimmed with "ears," depending upon the nature of the finish trim—the inner edges of which lie flat against the exterior sheathing. The ears extend to each side so that their ends align with the outer edges of the exterior casing (FIG. 55-3). The sill may be installed separately, followed by the assembled jambs, or the jambs and sill may be put together and installed as a unit.

Aligning and shimming

To install a frame, stand it up in the rough opening and center it. Wedge it in place at the sides just below the top corners, with shim shingles run in

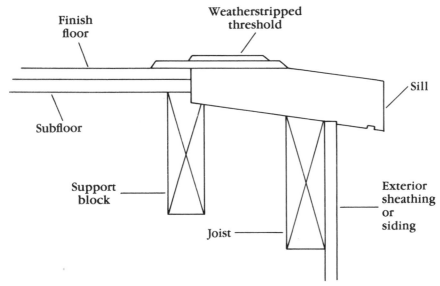

55-2 A let-in exterior door sill requires notching the joist and installing a support block.

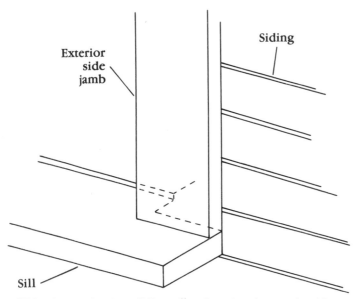

55-3 An exterior door sill "eared" to fit against the exterior siding.

over one another from opposite sides. Drive a pair of hot-dipped galvanized 8d finish nails (sometimes 10d or even 12d are needed) partway in, through each side jamb and shim set into the rough frame. Make sure that the top frame corners stay in square and that the edges are flush with the wall surfaces both inside and out. Then shim and nail the same way about 4 inches above the floor. Make sure that the bottom corners align exactly with the top ones; check with a plumb bob and line along the jamb edges. Space three or more sets of shims at intermediate points along each side jamb. Use a plumb line or long straightedge and adjust the shims until both jambs are straight up and down and don't bow in or out anywhere. Secure the jambs at each shim set with a pair of nails. This will tend to bow the jamb slightly toward the rough frame, so make allowances (FIG. 55-4).

Casings

Drive the nails almost home and check again for plumb, straight lines, and square corners. Make any necessary adjustments and finish driving the nails; countersink them about $1/16$ inch. Place one or two more sets of shims between the rough and frame headers, and fasten the frame top the same way. Once the wall sheathing has been put on, the door casings can be installed on both sides of the frame. The casing edges can be set flush with the jamb faces, but most often they are set back anywhere from $1/8$ to $3/8$ inch (FIG. 55-5). The bottom ends of the side casings are cut square across, but the exterior ends can be bevel-cut if necessary to conform to the slope of the threshold. The upper corner joints can be butt joints, but usually are mitered; complex trim will require more complex joining. The last step is to install a threshold or sill cap or auxiliary weatherstripping threshold, if required.

HANGING THE DOOR

The first step in hanging the door is to size it. Check the door opening width and determine the necessary door height. When the installation is finished, you should have a clearance gap of $1/32$ to $1/16$ inch on the hinged side, $1/16$ to $1/8$ inch on the latch side, and at least $1/16$ at the top of the door. The bottom clearance depends upon the type of weatherstrip that will be applied, if any. If there is none, or if a sweep or surface-mounted type will be installed, allow about $1/8$ to $3/16$ inch above the highest point on the finish floor along the arc of the door swing. Also, if the door will be painted or varnished make allowance for the coating thickness. Three coats of primer and enamel can easily add another $1/32$ inch to the door dimensions in all directions.

Trimming

When you trim, try to remove an equal amount from each side edge, and always remove any major length from the door bottom. Trim large amounts away with a power saw and small amounts with a power plane for best and easiest results. A hand plane may also be used. Remove material gradually and check your progress often by standing the door in the

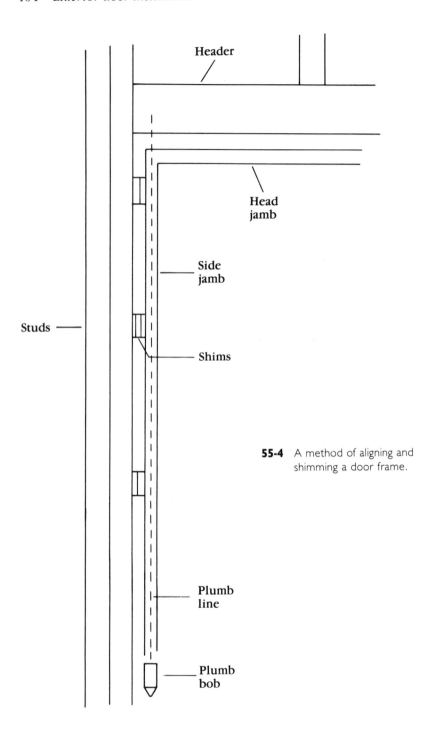

55-4 A method of aligning and shimming a door frame.

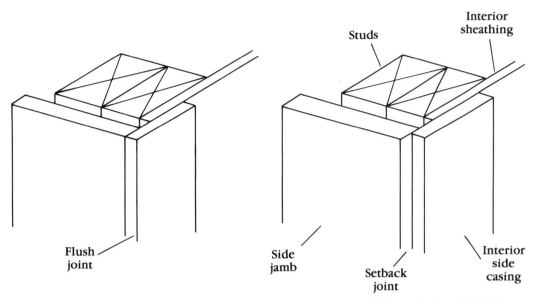

Studs

Interior
sheathing

Flush
joint

Side
jamb

Setback
joint

Interior
side
casing

55-5 Door or window casing edges can be set flush with the jambs (left) or set back a bit (right).

frame. You can compensate for minor bowing of the jambs during this process as well. Once you have a good fit, remove all the sharp edges by easing them to a $1/32$- to $1/16$-inch radius with sandpaper, a small block plane, or an easing tool.

Attaching the hinges

Next, stand the door on edge and clamp it to a sawhorse or similar apparatus and lay out the hinge outlines. Use two hinges for a light/narrow door, three for a heavy/wide one. The most commonly used sizes are 4×4, $4^{1}/2\times4^{1}/2$, and 5×5 inches, in the loose-pin butt type hinge. Typically the top edge of the upper hinge is placed 5 to 8 inches down from the door top, the bottom edge of the lower one 10 to 11 inches up from the door bottom. A third hinge is installed midway between the first two. Although expensive, ball-bearing hinges are definitely recommended for exterior doors, especially for heavy and frequently used ones. Whatever measurements you select, use them for all doors, in the house inside and out.

Separate the hinge leaves by pulling the pins out of the barrels. Use a leaf to trace around at each hinge location; usually the straight edge will align flush with the door face. With a router or a hammer and sharp wood chisel, cut mortises as deep as the thickness of the hinge leaf. Set a leaf with two barrel knuckles in each mortise and locate the screw holes with a centering punch. Make sure of the hinge barrel orientation first, so you don't get them backwards. Drill pilot holes, and drive the mounting screws straight in and centered. If these holes are off center or crooked, the leaf will be cocked and you'll have a terrible time hanging the door.

Follow the same procedures to mount the opposing hinge leaves on the door jamb. The leaves must be set so that when the door is closed its outer face is flush with the outer edges of the jambs. Your measurements have to be exact; remember the top clearance, too. If the top door leaf is 7 inches down from the door top, the top of the upper jamb leaf (which has three knuckles) must be 7 inches plus a minimum $1/16$ inch down from the face of the head jamb. The distances between the hinges must be exactly the same on both jamb and door.

Installing the lockset

Next, install the lockset. These are usually centered about 36 to 38 inches above the finish floor. However, this measurement is variable and not crucial, except that you must stay within the confines of the solid lock block in a hollow-core door. If the door has a single cross rail, usual practice is to vertically center the lockset in it. Again, set all locksets at or near the chosen height, for the sake of appearance. Specific installation details vary considerably for different kinds of locksets and security locks; follow the manufacturer's instructions and templates.

Fitting the door

To hang the door, put the hinge pins where you can easily reach them, stand the door up, and work it into the opening. Align the hinge knuckles; if your measuring, mortising, and fastening were all accurate, the knuckles will mesh together. Hold the door in place with one hand and slip the top pin into the barrel with the other, then do the same for the bottom pin. Gently tap the pins home with a hammer, if necessary. If the knuckles will not fit up, remove the door and back off the screws in the bottom jamb leaf until it is just a bit loose in the mortise. Try again to hang the door. If the knuckles mesh, install the pins, carefully open the door partway, and retighten the screws. If they do not, loosen the top jamb leaf a bit. If that doesn't work something is very wrong, and you will have to check your measurements and reset the hinges as necessary. You might also find, whether the hinge leaves fit together immediately or not, that the door still needs further trimming. This is not unusual. Note the sticking points with a pencil and shave them down with a small plane; remember the extra clearance for paint.

Presumably the door frame is rabbetted and so requires no stop molding. If it is not rabbetted, follow the procedures for installation of an interior door frame, Chapter 63.

Installing the striker plate

All that remains to be installed is the striker plate, and striker box if supplied. Follow the manufacturer's instructions for this. Try for a snug fit of the spring latch against the striker plate edge, and of the door edge against the stop, so that the door doesn't rattle in and out. The fit must not be too snug, however; allow for paint clearance and expansion.

Install any accessory items, such as a knocker, threshold cap, or weatherstripping last. Then remove the door, strip off all the hardware, and apply a finish immediately, before the door has a chance to become damaged by the weather. Be sure to thoroughly seal the top and bottom edges to keep moisture out.

PATIO DOORS

Patio or atrium doors typically consist of two or three door-sized lights in a single frame, with one movable either as a slider or an outswinging entry door. There are other variations as well. Some patio doors are delivered all assembled and ready to plug into a waiting rough opening, while others are knocked down for assembly at the job site. In either case they are basically prehung doors.

Common practice is to install the door frame alone, after either assembling it or removing all the lights. This makes the job a lot easier and also avoids the possibility of broken glass (all of which is tempered). Stand the flat-silled frame in the opening and plumb the sides, square the corners, and shim in place as necessary, following the manufacturer's instructions. Then the lights can be replaced and adjusted for smooth and easy operation, and the trimwork installed.

GARAGE DOORS

Garage doors of the overhead slide-up variety come in knocked-down fashion, ready for assembly and installation at the job site. The procedure usually is to assemble the door piecemeal while the installation is being made. Follow the instructions that come with the door faithfully for smooth and easy door operation; there are numerous variations in installation details.

In general, the installation procedure consists of placing the rails, mounting the hardware on the door panels, stacking the panels in the opening, and tying the panels to one another while locking them into place. The final steps consist of making operational adjustments, attaching counterbalance springs, perhaps installing an automatic opener, cinching down the hardware, and adding weatherstripping. Door trimming is seldom needed, because the whole unit fits over the door opening rather than within it, and the rails are mounted at the sides to suit the width. The job is not difficult, but does require some time and some mechanical ability.

Chapter 56

Utility and auxiliary systems

At about this stage of the construction process, if not earlier, installation of the utilities and any desired auxiliary systems should be getting under way. This is a variable; some builders like to get started as soon as the structure is "dried in"—or relatively weatherproof, with exterior sheathing and roof underlayment installed. Other builders like to wait until the shell is almost finished.

Few general contractors become involved in installing these systems. They subcontract the major work to specialists in each trade and leave the minor details to the owner. Owner-builders and do-it-yourselfers also hire out the utilities installations, unless they have an interest and some expertise in the particular field. However, many of the auxiliary systems can be classed as do-it-yourself projects, and owner-builders can take a part in their installation. In any case, homeowner input is needed in the planning, layout, and selection of the end-use elements of all the utilities and auxiliary systems if they are to be effective and fulfill the needs and desires of the house occupants. Oddly enough, many and sometimes all of the possible auxiliary systems are ignored during construction, when they could so easily be added, and thereby not only increase the value of the property but also substantially enhance the convenience and livability of the house.

ELECTRICAL SYSTEM

The three utility systems are the electrical, plumbing, and heating/cooling. The electrical system should have a 200-ampere capacity; anything less in this modern electrical age is hardly worth considering, especially given the miniscule extra cost over a 100- or 150-ampere service. Installation should follow the National Electrical Code, whether that is in force for the particular building project or not. About twice the code-required minimum number of convenience outlets (wall receptacles) should be considered practical for all rooms. Input from owners/occupants is essential when planning outlet locations; types, brands and siting of both major and minor appliances; special electrical equipment or machinery; and specific kinds and locations of lighting fixtures. Special consideration should be given to new, innovative, energy-efficient, or unusual electrical equipment, such as low-energy lamps and appliances or the extraordinarily versatile low-voltage switching control system for lighting.

PLUMBING SYSTEM

The plumbing system consists of the water supply line, hot and cold domestic water system, and the drain-waste-vent (DWV) system. A water well and/or septic system may be involved in lieu of municipal hookups. The homeowner need not be concerned about the intricacies of the piping. Many other details that do have to be pinned down include the kind and location of fixtures, including sinks, toilets, lavatories, bidets, tubs and showers, water heaters, and outside hose bibs or hydrants. Because there is a vast array of end-use products in a wide range of cost and quality levels that can be connected to a plumbing system, selections and final specifications take a lot of time and thought. Also remember that changes in these installations are difficult and expensive to make after the fact.

HEATING/COOLING SYSTEM

Early in the planning stage the decision must be made as to what kind of heating will be installed: hydronic, forced air, solar. And how will it be fueled: bottled gas, electricity, wood/coal, natural gas, or oil? The kind of equipment to be used, such as heat pump, standard furnace, wall furnaces, radiant ceiling cables, piping in the floor, or various kinds of ductwork, must be determined so that it can be accommodated properly in the construction. Also a back-up system is worth considering.

The preferences of the homeowner are important to all these decisions, though they might be tempered by what is or is not possible given the facts of house design, equipment or fuel availability, and local costs. In some cases, where electric heating equipment is involved, the electrical contractor can make the installation. Otherwise, a heating, ventilating, and air conditioning (HVAC) contractor will take care of all those chores.

All of the details and planning of the utilities installation will be taken care of by the various contractors. In most cases, though, it is up to the homeowner or owner-builder to plan what, if any, auxiliary systems will be installed, to select the equipment, and to either install the systems or supervise their installation. There are several systems to be considered.

DOORBELL

The doorbell system is sometimes part of the electrical contractor's job, sometimes not. You can select from ordinary buzzers or bells, chimes, musical greetings, programmable electronic units that will play several dozen tunes, and a number of various fancy accessories. Except for the line side of the supply transformer, these systems typically operate on 12-18 volts and are easy to install.

TELEPHONE

The days when only the telephone company could supply and install telephones are gone. Now you can purchase your own plug-in telephones and select from a host of other products, ranging from plain and simple to ultra-sophisticated. You can do the internal wiring from the telephone company's incoming line junction box all through the house, and set up whatever kind of system you desire. Many homes now have two lines entering, and some a business and/or FAX line as well. You can also have an electrician, or a telephone installer, or the telephone company itself install the telephone, depending upon local regulations. Installing a system is simple, and there is no longer any reason not to have a telephone outlet in nearly every room in the house—two or more in some of them—and in outbuildings, if you wish.

In some cases a telephone system can be made to serve as a limited intercom system as well, but the best arrangement is to install a discrete intercommunications system throughout the house. This can be easily done by installing suitable multiconductor cable in the framework, running it to outlets in most of the rooms, and installing the intercom units during the finishing process. Radio/tape playback can be incorporated in the system, too.

STEREO

Prewiring the entire house for a stereo music system is likewise an easy chore. Because of the long runs typically involved, No. 16 or even No. 14 stranded wire (lamp cord works fine) should be used to avoid line loss. Speaker lines can be run from a central location where the stereo system will be located—along with a loudspeaker selection switching arrangement—to however many rooms are desired, then terminated in speaker jacks in the walls. The jacks can be placed near the floor, near the ceiling, or paralleled to both locations, depending upon the nature of the room and the kind of speakers that are likely to be used in them.

TELEVISION

Prewiring for television is also an excellent idea, and there are several considerations here. Where cable TV is available, or expected to be in the near future, wiring should be installed for cable hookups in each room where it might be needed. Also prepare for any necessary equipment. Hookup is done by the local cable TV company. Where cable is not available, consider prewiring for a satellite dish and its associated equipment. Alternatively, run television antenna cable from an outside point or in an attic where an aerial will be located, to every room where a television set might be used. Some rooms might have more than one outlet. Each can terminate in a wall-mounted jack with a decorative cover plate.

Also consider installing the wiring for an antenna rotor assembly; this too can be run to as many locations as seem reasonable and terminated in wall jacks. The jacks can be parallel-wired, but if two or more television sets are likely to be in use at the same time, signal splitters, one or more amplifiers, or other auxiliary equipment might be needed. Consult with your local electronics supplies dealer.

RADIO

For those who have an interest in radio, consider prewiring the antenna systems/outlets. This could be used for AM, FM (which can be combined with TV), CB sending and receiving, SWL (shortwave listening), or an amateur radio installation. The requirements differ for these activities, but much of the wiring and outlet equipment can be preinstalled.

FIRE DETECTION

Fire warning and detection equipment is a must nowadays, and is regulated by code requirements in many areas. Failure to have some sort of device in a new home is inexcusable. Battery-operated smoke detectors of one sort of another are the simplest, and can be installed quickly anywhere in the house after it is completed. Follow the manufacturer's instructions to the letter, particularly as to placement. Line voltage smoke detectors, with and without battery backup, are also easy to install; this can be a part of the electrical system. Another good possibility is a low-voltage fire detection system, set up in zones with multiple rate-of-rise heat detectors, smoke detectors, or both, and including internal and external audible warning devices. Another excellent system is the relatively new residential sprinkler system, which is effective, unobtrusive, relatively inexpensive, and particularly suited for suburban and rural homes. The best source of up-to-date information on all of these systems, if you cannot find any locally is: The National Fire Protection Association, Inc., Batterymarch Park, Quincy, MA 02269.

SECURITY SYSTEM

Everyone is security conscious these days, and there are many products from which to choose in the way of security devices and intrusion alarm systems. Some can be installed by the homeowner, but many people prefer to have complete systems installed by a professional. Complex systems definitely should be prewired as the house is being constructed.

OTHER SYSTEMS

Electronic and electromechanical control, detection, and warning systems for many other purposes are now coming into their own, and probably will be commonplace in the coming decades. Examples are computer operated programs for regulating heating and cooling, or automatic/manual systems that control lamps and appliances. Sensors that warn of rain, loss of cooling in a freezer, excess heat or cold in a greenhouse, overflowing drainage sump, or well pump failure, or that turn lights on and off, operate draperies, or perform a hundred other functions can be connected to a master control/telltale panel. All such systems must be preplanned for best effect, and installed during the construction process.

Other specialty devices or systems might have to be prewired and/or installed in appropriate steps as construction goes along. Examples are dumbwaiters, moving stairs or elevators, darkrooms, projection rooms, and complete electronic home weather stations.

Chapter **57**

Insulation installation

Almost all houses require at least some thermal insulation. The amount depends upon local heating/cooling demands, and to some extent upon local building codes as well. There are several types of insulants, all with differing properties and characteristics, that can serve in diverse applications. The type and amount of insulation must be determined as the house is planned. Calculate the comparative heat loss/gain for various installations and combinations of materials, then choose the most cost-effective and thermally efficient. You will have to take into consideration many factors, including not only climatic conditions but house design, insulant properties, availability, installed cost, and your own preferences.

FOUNDATION INSULATION

Insulating the exterior of foundations was covered separately in an earlier chapter, where it was stated that this is the most efficient and effective way to provide maximum thermal protection. However, the job can be done from the inside, too.

Concrete slab

Insulating over a concrete slab requires that a wood subfloor be installed as well. If there is no danger of free moisture accumulating on the slab, first lay down a vapor barrier of 6-mil polyethylene sheet, overlapped at all seams by about 1 foot and lapping up the walls several inches. Nail 2-×-4 screeds face down to the concrete with masonry nails, on 16-inch centers. Level as necessary. Fill between the screeds with fiberglass or mineral wool blanket insulation, or rigid foamed plastic board insulation that is closely fitted. Then lay a plywood subfloor and whatever finish flooring is desired (FIG. 57-1).

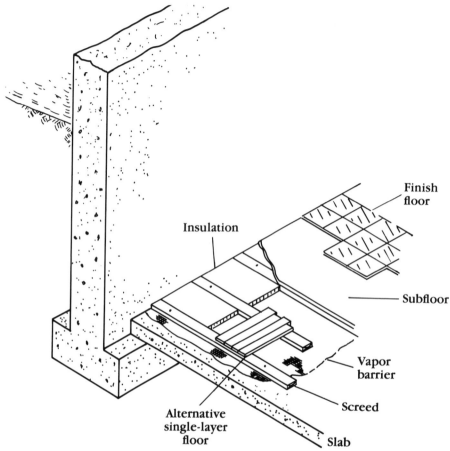

57-1 Insulation installed over a dry concrete floor slab. The system can be used on or below grade.

If moisture might be a problem, coat the concrete floor with a water-proof mastic such as roofing compound. Note that the floor must be clean and dust-free—and also dry, depending upon the material. Lay 1-×-4 screeds in the mastic and cover with a vapor barrier. Then nail down another set of 1-×-4 or 2-×-4 screeds on top of the first ones, and add the insulation and subfloor (FIG. 57-2).

Concrete full basement walls

There are two common methods of insulating poured concrete or concrete block full-basement walls. First coat the walls with a waterproofing.

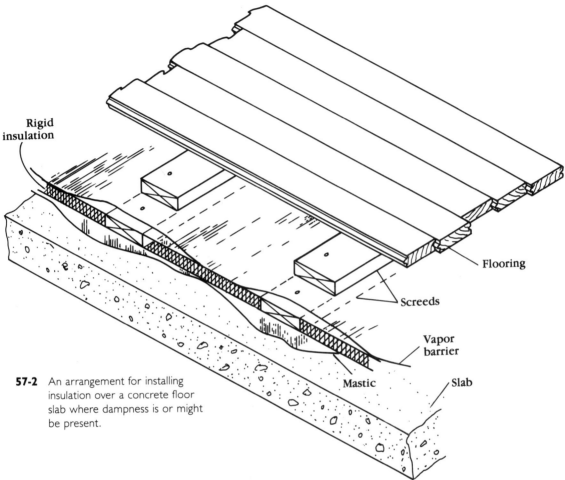

Rigid
insulation

Flooring

Screeds

Vapor
barrier

Mastic

Slab

57-2 An arrangement for installing insulation over a concrete floor slab where dampness is or might be present.

Install a 2-×-2 or 2-×-4 sole plate, a top plate, and furring strips set like wall studs, centered 16 inches apart. Staple fiberglass or mineral wool blanket insulation to the furring, or tightly fit rigid insulation panels between them. Cover the whole thing with a 6-mil sheet of polyethylene vapor barrier, followed by wall sheathing (FIG. 57-3). Or, attach rigid insulation sheets horizontally to the wall with an appropriate adhesive applied in ribbons with a caulking gun. Then glue vertical sheathing panels directly to the insulation, using the same method.

Crawl space foundation walls

The easiest way to insulate an unventilated crawl space from within is to first lay down a double vapor barrier of 6-mil polyethylene sheet. Overlap it well and lap it up the walls several inches. Secure it with construction adhesive and cover with about 2 inches of sand. Then secure lengths of

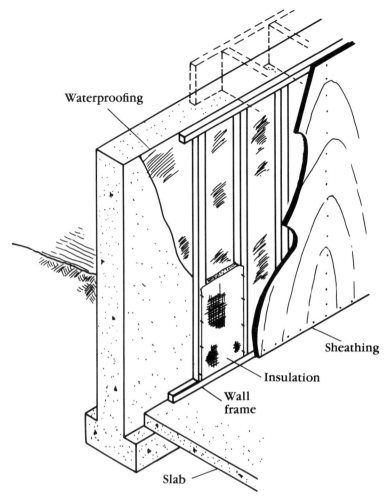

Waterproofing

Sheathing

Insulation

Wall
frame

Slab

57-3 A concrete basement wall can be insulated in this manner.

mineral wool or fiberglass blanket insulation to the end or header joists, tight to the underside of the subfloor. Fold them out over the sill and drape them down to the vapor barrier. An alternative is to install short sections of blanket to cover the end and header joist face and sill, and glue rigid insulation panels to the foundation walls. These panels can extend well below grade level, and capture the free edges of the vapor barrier as well (FIG. 57-4).

Permanent wood foundations

Unlike other kinds of foundations, permanent wood foundations are always insulated on the inside. This is done in exactly the same way as for any wood frame wall construction; consult with that section.

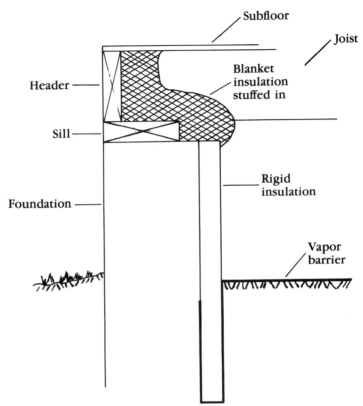

Subfloor

Joist

Blanket
insulation
stuffed in

Header

Sill

Rigid
insulation

Foundation

Vapor
barrier

57-4 An effective method of insulating crawl space foundation walls on the inside.

FLOOR INSULATION

Any living-space floor over an unheated area like a crawl space, or over
any space that is regularly kept a lower temperature than the rest of the
house (by 10–15 degrees) is a cold floor. In most such cases the minimum insulation R-value—the measure of the material's insulating capability—is usually pegged at R-11. The exception is floors over open pier
foundation crawl spaces, which should be insulated to a minimum R-19.
Lesser values are sometimes used, however, as local conditions warrant.
Floors separating heated areas need no insulation at all, except as might
be installed for sound damping purposes. In locales where heat gain into
the house from outside is the concern, insulating can be done in the same
way as for protection against cold, unless local successful practice suggests other methods.

The usual choice for floor insulation is mineral wool or fiberglass
blanket in roll or batt form, available in several standard widths, thicknesses, and R-values. It can be obtained without any facing, or with a kraft
paper or a foil facing and integral fold-out mounting flanges. The facing

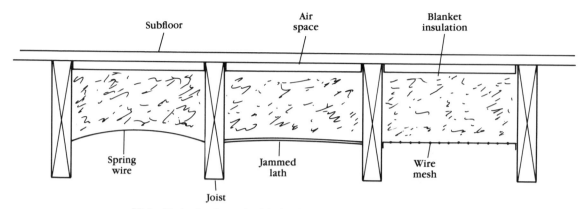

57-5 Methods of securing blanket insulation between open floor joists.

also acts as a vapor barrier, and should be placed closest to the subfloor.

The insulation is installed from below—facing uppermost—in a platform-framed floor, after the subfloor has been laid and the building is weathertight. Thus there is no convenient way to staple the flanges to the joists. Friction and fibers catching on the wood will hold the insulation in place reasonably well, but to hold it firmly and indefinitely, a mechanical restraint must be installed below the material. Furring strips or chicken wire fastened across the joist edges will do the job. You can also jam short pieces of lath between the joists, or lengths of spring wire that are made for just this purpose (FIG. 57-5). To fill spaces of odd shapes or dimensions, trim the material about 1/2 inch wider all around for a snug fit.

WALL INSULATION

There are several ways to insulate exterior walls. These same treatments should be given to cold walls that face an unheated or periodically heated space. In any locale where insulation is required, an R-11 value should be considered minimum. In cold country the insulation value should be R-19, and in deep winter areas, R-24.

Blanket insulation

The most common wall insulation continues to be fiberglass or mineral wool blanket. Either batt or roll form material is suitable, but roll is slightly better because fewer end joints occur between pieces. Either unfaced or faced (kraft paper or foil) insulation can be used. Place faced insulation with the facing toward the interior. In locales where heating demands are high, many houses are now being built with wall frames studded with 2×6s, which allows installation of thicker blanket insulation.

To install the insulation, push it into the bays between studs and smooth it into place, fully fluffed out. Run your hands along the edges to make sure it extends into the back corners against the exterior sheathing. Some installers fold the mounting flanges out over the exposed stud edges, but this is not good practice. Instead, fold the flanges along the inner faces of the studs to allow a 1/2-inch air space between the facing and the inner surface of the wall covering (FIG. 57-6). This avoids creases and bunches in the flanges that can cause problems with drywall installation, and also affords a bit of extra R-value if the facing is foil. Staple about every 12 inches and at all corners, and overlap the facing where cut pieces join. Slide the insulation behind wires and pipes (which should not be in outside walls in cold country. In some cases it might be best to slit the material around these components, or add another layer over them. Make sure that every space is adequately filled. Do not, however, compress the material too much in the hope of gaining greater insulating value; it actually results in less.

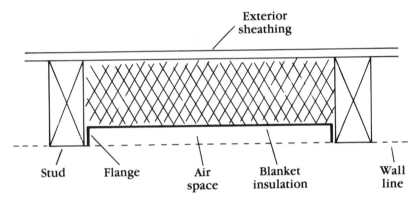

57-6   Blanket insulation installed between wall studs.

Blanket plus rigid foam plastic insulation

Another method of installing wall insulation involves installing the fiberglass or mineral wool as usual, and also applying sheets of rigid foam plastic insulation on the exterior of the walls as sheathing (FIG. 57-7). There are several materials available for this purpose, some foil faced and some not, with several different R-values per inch of thickness. Thus, a material can be selected that will most beneficially fill any requirement. Although thin sheets, such as 1/2 inch, are widely used, thicker material or double applications can also be used. Another layer can also be installed on the inside for even greater protection. If this is done, the exterior walls must usually be sheathed with fire-resistant gypsum wallboard, because most of the foamed plastic materials are flammable.

Other insulation

There are still other methods of insulating walls. For a while, spraying the walls full of urea-formaldehyde cellular foam plastic was a popular

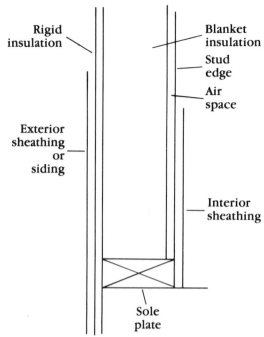

57-7 Rigid insulation applied on the exterior of the walls can supplement blanket insulation between the studs.

method. There were problems with toxicity, however, and the product was banned. Now this method is making a comeback, but a different nontoxic material is used. Wall cavities can be filled with other blown-in materials: mineral or fiberglass blowing wool, vermiculite, perlite, foam plastic pellets, or chopped cellulose. All of these materials are typically installed by professionals using special equipment.

CEILING INSULATION

Sometimes called *cap* insulation, ceiling insulation is essential because heat rises, and thus a large percentage of the heat loss of a house is through the ceilings. Where a traditional flat ceiling is installed below an unheated attic or attic crawlway, the insulation is placed just above the finish ceiling to avoid heating the useless space above. Insulation here is equally important where mechanical cooling is a daily necessity, because ceilings can account for a great deal of heat gain in a house.

Blanket insulation

There are several approaches to cap insulation. Again, the most common in new construction is to install mineral wool or fiberglass blanket in either batt or roll form, and again, roll is slightly more advantageous. The thickness, of course, depends upon the thermal requirements as dictated by the local climate. Make the installation from below. If a facing is present, it should always be downward. Unfaced material will stay in place well enough by friction, and will later be restrained by the ceiling. Push faced material up about 1/2 inch past the lower edges of the ceiling joists, fold the flanges down, and staple about every 12 inches. Fold the corners and ends down and seal them by stapling; overlap all end joints about 1/2 inch.

Allowing for air circulation

Take special precautions at recessed ceiling light fixtures. Unless the fixture is clearly stamped as being approved for installation within thermal insulation, you must allow a minimum of 3 inches of open space (as well as 1/2 inch from any combustible materials) all around the fixture to allow free air circulation and heat dissipation from the lamp (FIG. 57-8).

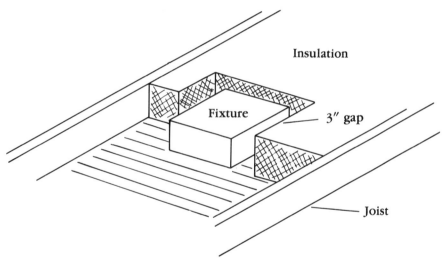

57-8 Allow 3 inches of clearance at all points between recessed lighting fixtures and thermal insulation, unless the fixtures are approved for direct installation.

Leave open any required ventilating airways at the eaves ends of the joists, so that air can enter through the soffit vents and flow upward through the attic space. A small slanted block or baffle is usually all that is needed, leaving at least 1 inch of free space between it and the underside of the roof sheathing. Make sure, however, that the insulation extends out over the wall top plate as far as possible, to minimize heat loss at that critical point (FIG. 57-9).

If a single thickness of blanket between the joists is insufficient, as is often the case, it can easily be augmented. One way of doing so is to add another layer of blanket. Use unfaced material (or strip the facing off faced

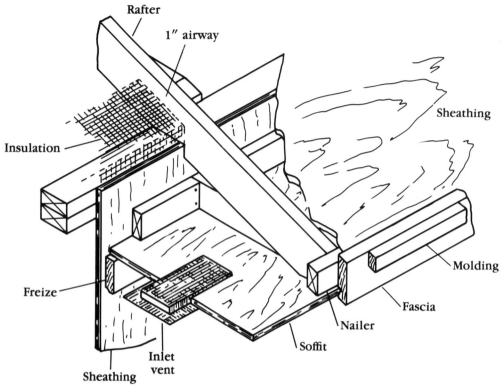

57-9   A ventilating airway should be left at the eaves between the insulation and the under-side of the roof sheathing.

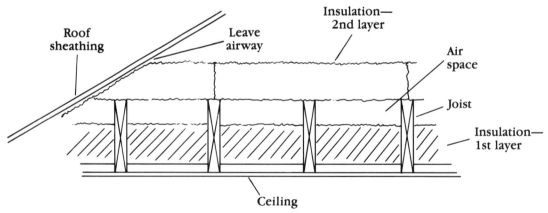

57-10   A second layer of blanket cap insulation can be laid at right angles to the joists and over the first layer.

insulation), because a double vapor barrier can cause problems. Lay the insulation out in rows nestled snugly together at right angles to the joists (FIG. 57-10). Remember to leave airways open and recessed lighting fixtures uncovered. If there is plenty of room in the attic, the installation can be made from above at any time. If not, this "second layer" should be put in first, by passing the batts up between the joists and settling the insulation in place.

Loose-fill or poured insulation

Another method of insulating over a ceiling is to install the ceiling first, then fill the bays between the joists with any loose-fill or poured insulation like fiberglass or mineral wool, chopped cellulose, perlite, or vermiculite. This can easily be done with a rake or a homemade leveler that rides on and fits between the joists (FIG. 57-11). If there is no working space, any of these materials can be blown into place with special equipment. Roll or batt type blanket insulation can also be augmented this way.

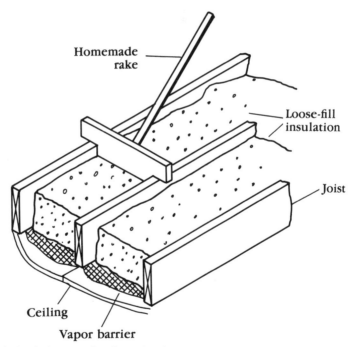

57-11 A simple homemade rake makes short work of leveling loose-fill insulation between joists.

There is one circumstance where use of loose-fill material requires a modification. If the finish ceiling is acoustic tile attached to furring strips, this type of insulation should never be allowed to rest directly upon the ceiling. The solution is to stretch a double layer of 6-mil polyethylene sheet, well overlapped, across the joist bottoms. Then put up the furring and the tile; the insulation will be supported well above the tile by the sheeting.

Chimney protection

Where either masonry or metal chimneys come through a ceiling frame, there should be no combustible materials within a minimum of 2 inches from the chimneys at any point. The chimney opening should be framed as a box. Fill the space between the frame and the chimney walls with noncombustible insulating material such as fiberglass (with no facing), never with foam plastic or cellulose—even if they have been treated with a fire-retardant chemical.

ROOF INSULATION

When all or part of the roof framework is also the ceiling framework—as is the case with a cathedral ceiling design or a finished upper half-story—the inclusion of proper insulation is a must in all climates. Just as with flat cold ceilings, it is usually sufficient to install a single layer of fiberglass or mineral wool batt or roll insulation of appropriate R-value between the rafters, facing down. (Refer to FIG. 57-6.) As much as 12 inches (nominal) of thickness can be installed in this way. More can be added either atop or beneath the rafters by installing furring strips at right angles and adding another layer of insulation.

If there are no rafters and the roof construction is composed of heavy decking on exposed rafter beams or purlins, the insulation must be installed on the outside of the roof deck. This entails installing a rim of appropriate thickness around the perimeter of the deck, and laying sheets of rigid foam insulation. If the thickness is not too great, perhaps 2 to 3 inches, the weather surface can be secured directly to the deck with long nails driven through the insulation.

For greater thicknesses, secure a grid of nailing strips to the roof deck with the insulating panels between them. Top the insulation with a skin of $5/16$ or thicker plywood, depending upon what is needed as a nailable surface for the finish roofing material, and fasten to the nailing strips (FIG. 57-12). On some low-slope or flat roofs, the finish roofing may be a built-up type laid directly on the insulation. There are several kinds of insulation that can be used for this purpose, depending upon thermal requirements. These include extruded polystyrene, foamed cellular glass, polyisocyanurate, phenolic, or polyurethane.

OTHER CONSIDERATIONS

There are a few other items to consider that are often overlooked. Any place where heat can be lost during the heating season, or gained during the cooling season, should be treated with thermal insulation. For example, all ductwork, whether employed for heating, cooling, or both,

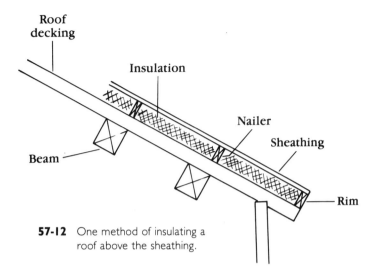

57-12 One method of insulating a roof above the sheathing.

should be thoroughly insulated. This can be accomplished by purchasing factory-insulated ductwork, or by wrapping it with a product made for the purpose. All piping, whether water supply or drain, that is subject to potential freezing should be wrapped with an insulating material, perhaps after being protected with an electric heating tape. All hot water supply pipes or tubing should be insulated with special wrap or sleeves from the heater onward, regardless of the ambient temperature range.

Cold water supply pipes can be similarly wrapped in locations where they may sweat and drip water. Such condensation on the exterior of toilet tanks can be prevented by lining the inside walls of the tank with 1/2-inch thick foam plastic insulation, glued on with daubs of mastic when the walls are clean and dry. All large cracks around windows, doors, and other openings should be stuffed full of fiberglass or foamed shut. All small cracks can be further reduced by means of appropriate weather-stripping on doors, windows, dryer vents, fan vent outlet doors, and window air conditioners. Crawl space vent doors, attic access hatches, and similar items should be insulated with glued-on rigid insulation.

In some parts of the country mechanical cooling is more of a concern than heating. In these cases, homeowners often install special insulation that reflect radiant heat outward. There are several types of this material; be guided by local successful practice in their use. In addition, new kinds of window glazing are available that reflect much of the sun's heat from direct rays back outside. Although these are not insulants in the usual sense, they still accomplish the same purpose. By the same token, in certain parts of the country double, triple, and even quadruple glazing can add a great deal to the overall effectiveness of the thermal efficiency of a house. Both of these energy-conserving installations should be considered in the thermal design of any house not located in a perpetually benign climate.

Chapter **58**

Sound control

Although common enough in modern, high-quality, multiple-family dwellings, sound control measures are seldom undertaken in single-family residences. Practically the only consideration given to sound control is to design the floor plan so that bedrooms are as far away as possible from the activity centers. This does lessen bothersome noise for some of the occupants at least part of the time, but it hardly addresses the overall problem. Furthermore, in many designs—especially small houses—significant spatial separation is not possible. This ignoring of control measures is unfortunate, because for a minor outlay in added cost, time, and effort, reasonable and effective constructions can be included in planning that will add measureably to the livability and value of the house.

Building sections are rated and ranked according to three factors: sound transmission class (STC), impact noise rating (INR), and impact insulation class (IIC). The latter two are essentially interchangeable, with INR being the older system, IIC the newer. In all of these ratings, the higher the number, the better the construction in inhibiting noise transmission.

FLOOR/CEILING SOUND CONTROL

Sound control measures in the floors of a residence need only be built into those that separate upper and lower living quarters. However, the future should be considered: If there is a possibility that a presently unoccupied attic or unfinished basement could be converted to living quarters later on, those floor structures should get the treatment.

Sources of noise

Much of the sound transmitted down through a floor and ceiling to the space below is noise caused by impact. This includes footsteps; objects being dropped or dragged along the floor; vibrations from a refrigerator, washer, or other equipment in operation; the bass thump from a stereo or television set; or water rushing through pipes in the ceiling/floor framework. Some of this noise is airborne, sound emanating from something that causes objects and materials in the vicinity to vibrate. The vibration then radiates in all directions, including down through the ceiling/floor construction and into the space below. Conversely, very little of this noise travels upward from a lower space through the ceiling/floor frame to an upper space, and what does is generally unnoticeable. Therefore, preventative measures can be undertaken in the construction of the pertinent floor and ceiling.

Gypsum wallboard

An example that falls near the bottom of the scale is a floor-ceiling arrangement of ¹/₂-inch gypsum wallboard ceiling, attached directly to 2-×-8 joists with a ³/₄-inch wood floor above (FIG. 58-1). The STC rating is 30 and the INR, -18. Each layer of material added to this improves performance.

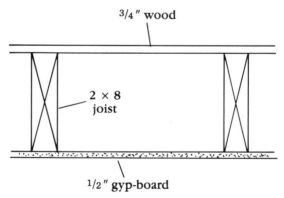

3/4″ wood

2 × 8 joist

1/2″ gyp-board

58-1 This is about the least soundproof of all floor/ceiling constructions.

Carpet

The easiest sound deadener to provide—and one especially good against impact noise—is wall-to-wall carpeting over the entire floor. Even cheap ³/₈-inch nylon carpeting over thin foam padding raises the ratings to about STC 45 and INR +5 (IIC 56). But this is an impermanent solution.

Subflooring and soundboard

For permanent sound damping measures, there are several constructions to consider. For example, lay a ⁵/₈- or ³/₄-inch plywood subfloor. Cover that with 1/2-inch soundboard, a fibrous composition board made for the purpose. (An alternative is fiberboard wall sheathing such as Celotex.) Cover this with a layer of 1/2-inch plywood underlayment, and follow with a finish floor covering. Sheet vinyl and tile (ceramic or otherwise) will add no sound control, wood flooring will add a bit, and carpet and pad will add a lot—increasing as total thickness increases. For greater sound control, separate the soundboard from the underlayment with 1-×-3 or 1-×-4 furring strips laid on 16-inch centers. Install 1/2-inch plywood underlayment for 3/4-inch wood finish flooring, 3/4-inch plywood for all other floorings.

Insulation

To further increase sound-deadening properties, install a layer of 3 1/2-inch-thick fiberglass or mineral wool thermal insulation about 1 inch down from the underside of the subfloor. Staple faced insulation in place by the flanges, but slash the facing open with a razor knife to prevent its acting as a vapor barrier. Restrain unfaced insulation with lengths of lath jammed in place, or use spring wires. To go another step, attach the gypsum wallboard ceiling to the joists—not directly, but to special resilient channels made for this purpose (FIG. 58-2). Alternatively, install a dropped or suspended ceiling. Or, install a separate set of ceiling joists midway between the floor joists and at least 1 inch lower, and secure the ceiling directly to them. Then, the only connection and sound transmission path between the ceiling and the floor is at the walls.

WALL SOUND CONTROL

Given construction methods of frame houses and the need to keep costs reasonable (even in top-quality structures), total soundproofing of the walls is impractical and probably pointless as well. Nonetheless, there are steps that can be taken, ranging from simple to complex, that will minimize sound transmission without going to construction extremes.

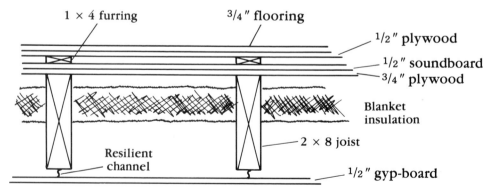

58-2   This complex arrangement is about as soundproof a floor/ceiling construction as is practically possible in a house.

Sources of noise

Most sound transmission through walls is from airborne sound vibrations that strike the wall sheathing. The vibrations pass through the wall space to the opposite wall sheathing and into the adjacent room or area. Some sound transmission stems from impact noise, but this is generally incidental and infrequent. Structure-borne sound adds to the overall noise level, too. This can occur as a result of piping touching the structure somewhere, and from equipment or appliances operating in the vicinity. The vibrations are picked up by the building components and transmitted throughout, including the wall frame, where the sheathing acts as a sounding diaphragm. The pathways followed by these vibrations are often unsuspected, and in frame construction they are impossible to eliminate, practically speaking.

Gypsum wallboard

One simple way to dampen sound vibrations in walls is to install thicker than normal sheathing. In houses, 1/2-inch-thick gypsum wallboard (drywall) is the most common sheathing nowadays. A 2-×-4 stud frame so sheathed on each side has an STC of about 33. But 5/8-inch wallboard, which is only occasionally installed in houses, will damp sound better (STC 37), and 3/4-inch wallboard will do even better than that (STC 40). To achieve the same approximate rating, you could also install a double layer of 1/2-inch wallboard on each side. Adding 3/4-inch-thick planking to one or both sides will add more. Thin wood or hardboard paneling, however, doesn't do much.

Soundboard

Another approach is to sheath the walls with soundboard, a fibrous, low-density material. This can be nailed to the studs, but a better method is to glue it with construction adhesive. Then laminate 1/2-inch or preferably 5/8-inch gypsum wallboard to the soundboard with glue, fastening only across the top and bottom at 12-inch intervals. An alternative is to bond planking or paneling either directly to the soundboard or in a third layer over the wallboard. A 2-×-4 stud wall frame so treated on each side has an STC of about 48, depending upon just how the job is done.

Blanket insulation

Insulating fiberglass or mineral wool blanket insulation in a standard stud and plasterboard wall cavity does not reduce sound transmission, especially if the facing is left intact—as it usually is. However, when installed without facing in a thickness of 2 to 3 inches (more thickness does no good), and in combination with other wall sound control measures, sound reduction qualities are raised by about STC 6 or 7. The material must be well fitted and snug at all corners, edges, and joints, and held in place only by friction.

Party wall

Where greater sound reduction is desired, the starting point is a party wall, of which there are several construction variations. The simplest consists of a double row of staggered studs, 2×3s on a 2-×-4 plate or 2×4s on a 2-×-6 plate, sheathed on each side with ¹/₂-inch gypsum wallboard. The STC in this case is about 45. Using thicker wallboard or doubling the layers on each side, does not increase the STC rating in this construction. Installing a layer of soundboard first and laminating ¹/₂-inch wallboard increases the STC rating to about 50. Weaving long strips of unfaced fiberglass or mineral wool thermal insulation horizontally between the studs and sheathing each side with ¹/₂-inch wallboard gives about the same result.

Maximum sound control

For maximum reduction in sound transmission and a construction of upwards of STC 60, build as shown in FIG. 58-3. Every step not taken reduces the effectiveness by a small amount. The least effective method of sound control is a double stud frame sheathed with ¹/₂-inch wallboard in conventional fashion, nothing else. Either 2×3s or 2×4s can be used for the two wall frames, separated by 1 inch or more and on matching plates. The insulation is 1¹/₂- to 2¹/₂-inch-thick unfaced fiberglass or mineral wool, friction-fitted. The soundboard is glued to the studs, and the wallboard is laminated to the soundboard and held with a few nails or screws, top and bottom. The sole plate is set on sill seal, and the caulk should be an elastomeric type, such as butyl or silicone rubber. This construction could be improved upon a bit by mounting the sheathing on resilient channels secured to the studs, and by making the subflooring discontinuous along the centerline between the two walls.

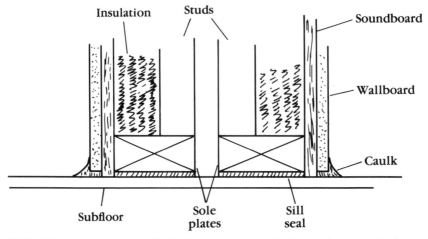

58-3 This wall construction will afford maximum reduction in sound transmission between rooms.

GENERAL SOUND CONTROL MEASURES

Apart from the specific sound control measures that can be taken during construction, there are some general steps to consider. For example, isolating vibration from all equipment helps greatly in reducing noise that can travel throughout a frame structure. This can be done by setting or mounting appliances and machinery on vibration absorbing pads. Equipment installed in cabinetry, like dishwashers or trash compactors, can rest on shock mounts, be surrounded by foam or fiberglass insulation, and be positioned so they do not touch any cabinetry. Audio speakers, music systems, and television sets should be placed on pads, kept off the floor or walls, and set on stands.

Sound-absorbing materials in a room or area also helps dampen sound. Carpeting and rugs, heavy drapes, plants, upholstered furniture, wall hangings, acoustic ceiling tile, and any such soft materials absorb and/or disperse sound waves and cancel reverberations. Doors should be thick and solid-core, well fitted and weatherstripped for best results. Windows transmit less sound (in either direction) if they are at least double glazed and well sealed with weatherstripping. All water piping should be isolated from the house framework by caulking or shock mounting them wherever they pass through either structural members or sheathing. Vent and drain pipes, especially the big stacks, should be kept away from the framing, too; isolating mounts and hangers can be used to secure them. All ductwork should likewise be isolated by mounting all the parts in or on insulation and vibration-proof hangers or supports, with no direct structure contact anywhere.

In short, isolate everything possible that produces noise and vibrations, and introduce as many elements as is practical that will absorb or break up sound waves.

Chapter **59**

Stair construction

Some houses require no stairs or steps at all, but these are in the minority. Houses with basements need stairs; these can be plain but serviceable and inexpensively made if the basement is unfinished. Houses with second stories need main stairways—at least one— and these are typically a feature of the interior design. Split-level houses need abbreviated stair sets on multiple levels for access. Houses with attics large enough for storage need stairs; these can be folding, pull-down or disappearing ladder-like stairs that nest in the ceiling framework, or enclosed stairways. Also, most houses need step sets leading from ground level into the building or onto porches or decks. All of these stair designs, while differing greatly in appearance, have to be built with convenience, sturdiness, and safety as the primary construction factors.

Main or finish staircases are sometimes built from scratch on the job site. However, many stock varieties are available from specialty companies, and they can also be custom-made. These units are occasionally shipped complete, such as some steel spiral staircases, but more often arrive knocked down for on-site assembly. Utility stairways, outside steps, and split-level access stairs are typically site-built as construction proceeds, and the same is usually true of platforms framed for stairway landings. The openings in the floor framing required for stairways are boxed out during the basic framing process, as explained earlier.

FUNDAMENTAL RULES OF CONSTRUCTION

When you build stairways on-site, there are several fundamental rules that should be followed and some points to be observed, and these are frequently mandated by local building codes as well. They apply to all stair sets, whatever their location or usage:

- Straight stairways are the easiest and most convenient to use and also to build. The long L, short L, wide L, double L, narrow U, broad U, curved, winder, circular, and spiral types are progressively harder. The spiral and winder are the most difficult and dangerous to use.

- If there are more than 15 steps in a set, the stairway should be broken at some point with a landing.

- Landings should be at least as long as the width of the stairway between walls or railings. If meeting a doorway, the landing must be longer than the door width.

- The ideal angle of a stairway is from 30 to 35 degrees from the level. The minimum angle is 20 degrees and the maximum 50; the practical extremes for often-used stairs are 25 degrees minimum and 45 degrees maximum.

- The minimum vertical headroom is 6 feet 8 inches for main stairs and 6 feet 6 inches for service stairs, at all points.

- The minimum width for main stairs is 3 feet, and for service stairs, 2 feet 6 inches. However, neither dimension is adequate, especially for furniture moving. A practical minimum for main stairs is 42 inches inside the rails, 48 is better. Allow at least 3 feet for service stairs.

- Handrails should be continuous from floor to floor. Optimum height is from 34 to 36 inches along the stairs and 30 to 32 on landings.

- All risers must be of equal height; variations pose a serious safety hazard.

- All treads should preferably be of the same depth front to back (have the same unit run). However, pie-shaped treads are sometimes necessary, and other slight variations are sometimes acceptable.

- The tread nose or nosing—that part of the tread which projects forward beyond the face of the riser—should extend no more than 1³/4 inches; 1 to 1¹/4 inches is typical and less is also common.

RISER HEIGHT

The *treads* are the part of the stairs on which people step; the *risers* are the vertical back board placed between the treads. The optimum ratio range of riser height to tread depth has long been established. This has to do not with arbitrary regulations, but rather with how the human body can handle stairs without tumbling into a heap. There are three rules: Two risers plus one tread should equal between 24 and 25 inches; one riser

Table 59-1   Typical Stair Tread /Riser Combinations

Floor-to-Floor Height	Unit Rise	Unit Run	Number of Risers	Number of Treads	Total Run
9'	7³/4"	10¹/4"	14	13	11'
9'	7¹/4"	10³/4"	15	14	12'6"
9'	6³/4"	10³/4"	16	15	13'
9'	6"	11"	18	17	15'8"
8'6"	7¹/4"	10¹/2"	14	13	11'4"
8'6"	7¹/4"	11¹/2"	14	13	12'6"
8'6"	6³/8"	10³/8"	16	15	13'
8'6"	6³/8"	11"	16	15	13'9"
8'	7³/8"	10"	13	12	10'
8'	7³/8"	11"	13	12	11'
8'	6"	10³/8"	16	15	13'
8'	6"	12"	16	15	15'

plus one tread should equal 17 to 18 inches; tread depth multiplied by riser height (unit run times unit rise) should equal 72 to 75 inches. TABLE 59-1 shows some typical combinations.

BUILDING A BASIC, UTILITY STAIRWAY

To build a basic or utility stair set, start by cutting the *stringers*, or *carriages*, the long running planks that support the treads and risers.

Stringers

Stringers are usually made from 2×12s. The stock must be of good quality, kiln-dried, and free of warps, cupping, twists, or other defects. Use two stringers for treads 2 feet 6 inches wide and three for wider stairs. Allow for a top bearing against the opening header of 4 inches minimum; at least 3¹/2 inches of stock must remain below the notches after cutting them. Determine the unit run/unit rise figures; the total of the risers must match the floor-to-floor height.

Stair layout

To make the stair layout on the stringer (FIG. 59-1), set a piece of masking tape on the blade of a framing square at the mark representing tread depth (*unit run*), and another on the tongue at the riser height figure (*unit rise*). Set the square on the stringer plank near one end and mark the first notch, then extend the tread line to the back edge of the plank. This is the floor cut line. Reset the square and mark off the next notch, and so on for the total number of steps. Extend the last riser line to the back edge of the plank; this marks the header cut line. Then draw a line parallel to the floor

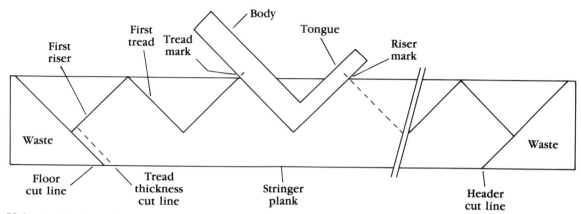

59-1 A stair stringer layout can be made by "stepping off" with a framing square, much like laying out a roof rafter.

cut line, and inside it a distance equal to the thickness of the tread stock. This is the tread drop cut line. Start all the notch cuts, making outboard cuts first to provide maximum saw support. Use a portable electric circular saw and finish with a handsaw or saber saw. Work carefully and make square, even cuts to the lines.

There are a couple of alternative methods of making stringers when only two are needed (FIG. 59-2). One is to cut dados into the inside faces of the stringers, into which the treads can be slotted. The dado depth should be 1/2 inch for nominal 2× stock, and the width should be just a tiny bit greater than the thickness of the tread stock. Make the cuts so that they lie below the layout lines; the top of each tread will lie on the line. Fasten the

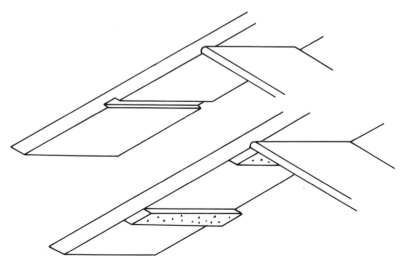

59-2 Stair treads can be set into dados in the stringers (left) or fastened to cleats attached to the stringers (right).

treads by driving nails (or screws) through the stringer faces into the tread ends. Another possibility is to secure cleats to the inside faces of the stringers, then attach the treads not to the cleats, but with fasteners through the stringers into the tread ends. Screws are the preferred fasteners.

The completed stringers can be installed in several different ways. At the top, the stringers must be set so that the top tread surface is flush with the finish flooring. They can be nailed directly to the header, or better, notched over a ledger attached to the header and fastened to both (FIG. 59-3). At the bottom, if the stringers rest upon a wood floor, they can be fastened directly to the flooring/floor frame. However, a better arrangement, especially if the floor is concrete, is to notch the stringer ends over a kicker plate anchored to the floor (FIG. 59-4).

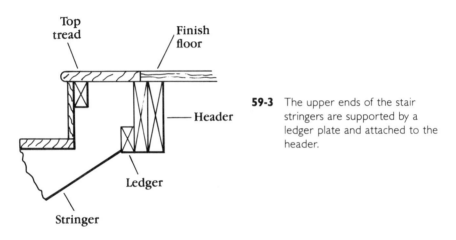

59-3 The upper ends of the stair stringers are supported by a ledger plate and attached to the header.

Treads

The treads on utility stairs should *not* be made of nominal 1× stock, even though they often are. They break too easily, or split off along the nose, which can be dangerous. Ordinary 2× construction material works fine. It looks plain, but is plenty rugged. Attach the treads directly to the stringers from above with decking screws. For a better appearance, install ready-made hardwood stair treads; these are typically $1^{1}/_{16}$ or $1^{1}/_{8}$ inches thick and already nosed. Or, make up treads from similar stock and nose them in any one of the several common patterns (FIG. 59-5). Fasten them to the stringers with three finish nails at each bearing.

Risers

Risers are often dispensed with on utility stairs. When they are installed, the material usually used is pine 1× stock; a No. 2 grade works well. If hardward treads are installed, $3/4$-inch stock of the same species is used. Install them before the treads and fasten them to the stringers with screws at top and bottom, where appearance doesn't matter but sturdiness does.

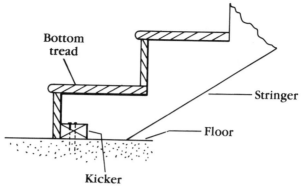

59-4 The bottom ends of the stair stringers are best restrained by a kicker plate fastened to the floor.

After the treads are installed, fasten the bottom edges of the risers to the back edges of the treads from behind (FIG. 59-6).

BUILDING AN ENCLOSED STAIRWAY

The essentials of building enclosed stairways and main or finish stairways are the same as for utility stairs. The differences lie in the grade and kind of materials, the higher degree of finish, the addition of ornamental aspects and trimwork, the added craftsmanship, and the higher degree of polish and sophistication. For example, you can construct a finish enclosed stairway with semihoused stringers (FIG. 59-7), which requires very little additional work beyond that needed for a utility stairway.

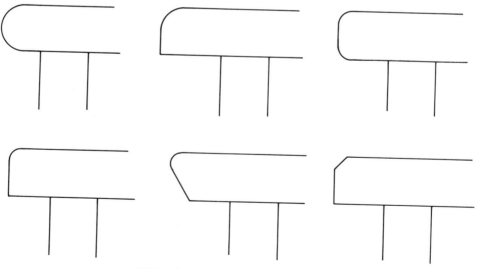

59-5 Commonly used stair tread nosing patterns.

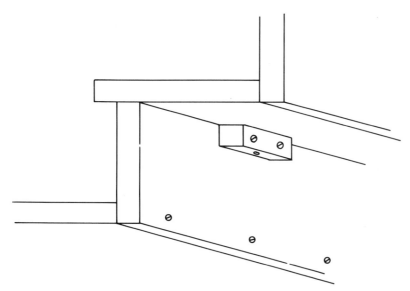

59-6 The riser backs are attached to the rear edges of the treads from behind, and the treads and risers are secured at the upper and outer joint with glue blocks and screws.

The first step is to fasten a pair of finish stringers to the walls. These are wide, top-quality, kiln-dried, unnotched boards or planks suitable for taking a fine finish. Next, install three stringers just as for a utility stairway—and made the same way, of the same stock. Install high-quality risers, fitted tightly against the finish stringers at the ends. Follow with high-quality treads, also fitted closely, with an appropriate nosing pattern. Fasten the risers to the treads from behind, and also install glue blocks centered on each side of the center stringer at the upper joint. (Note: If the stairs are to be covered with carpeting, a lesser grade of softwood treads can be installed and fastened with unconcealed screws.)

An alternative construction is to secure the outside notched or rough stringers to the wall first, then install a notched finish stringer over them before installing the treads and risers. The only advantage is that narrower stock can be used for the finish stringers.

BUILDING A TOP-GRADE STAIRWAY

A top-grade stairway is made with an ordinary notched stringer to support the center, but with fully housed and mitered stringers at the sides (or one side, or parts of the sides, for partly open or half-open stairways). These stringers are generally mill-made, but an experienced craftsman with a router and templates can do the job on-site. The stringers are high-quality finish lumber, routed to accept wedges at both treads and risers (FIG. 59-8). The wedges should be fitted size and made of seasoned hardwood. The hardwood treads and risers are rabbeted to lock into one another. All the

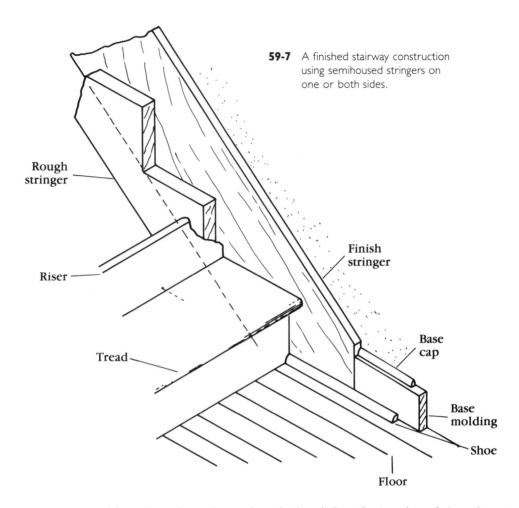

59-7 A finished stairway construction using semihoused stringers on one or both sides.

Rough stringer

Riser

Tread

Finish stringer

Base cap

Base molding

Shoe

Floor

assembly is done from the underside, by sliding the treads and risers into place with glue-coated grooves, followed by the glue-coated wedges. A few finish nails are driven through the back bottom edges of the risers into the treads to hold everything solid.

BUILDING AN OPEN STAIRWAY

There are many treatments that can be given to the exposed side of a open stairway. The stringer may be made of finish material, with the treads extending beyond about 1½ inches. The nosing is carried across the edge in a single or double return (FIG. 59-9), depending upon its con-figuration and size and the extent of tread projection. This can be done by trimming the tread end and adding a short length of matching molding with mitered joints. Often a decorative molding such as a small cove or

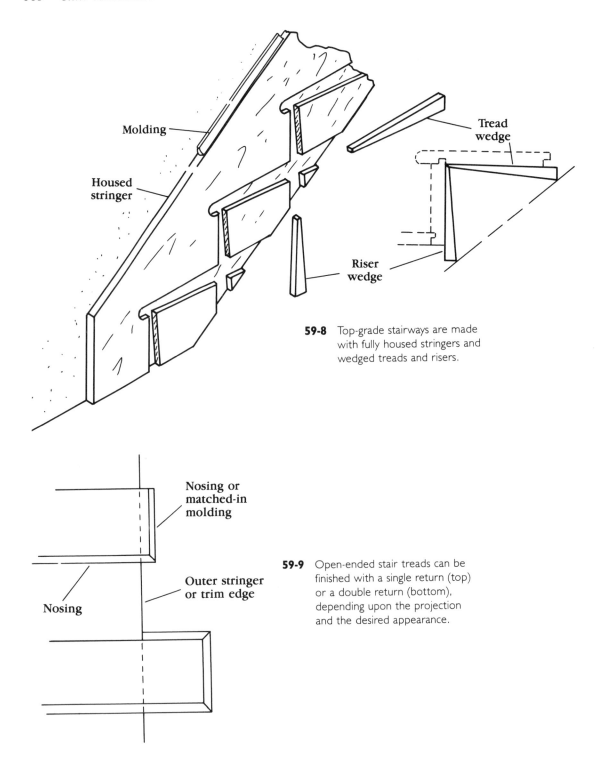

Molding

Housed stringer

Tread wedge

Riser wedge

59-8 Top-grade stairways are made with fully housed stringers and wedged treads and risers.

Nosing or matched-in molding

Outer stringer or trim edge

Nosing

59-9 Open-ended stair treads can be finished with a single return (top) or a double return (bottom), depending upon the projection and the desired appearance.

quarter-round is installed at the upper tread/riser joint. The wall below the bottom edge of the stringer may be inset somewhat and join flush-faced with the base molding (FIG. 59-10); a small decorative cap molding is often attached to the stringer bottom edge. Wainscoting is another option, placed below the stringer. Or, the stringer can be completely covered by the wallboard and the stair treads and risers, edged out with moldings.

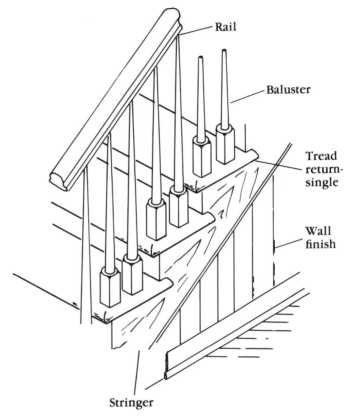

59-10 Typical open stairway construction.

RAILINGS AND BALUSTRADES

Wall-mounted railings are sufficient and satisfactory if there are walls to which they can be attached. There are numerous kinds of railings available, along with the requisite matching mounting hardware. If there is no wall, however, a *balustrade* or *banister* is in order. These can be bought piecemeal in any number of different ready-made patterns, with matching newel posts, intermediate posts as needed, balusters, handrail, and decorative stair end caps or brackets. All that is required of the builder is to assemble and install the parts, then apply a finish. The balustrade can be plain, simple, and strictly utilitarian, but it can also be highly decorative, ornate, or unique—an architectural or interior design focal point. It is an excellent place for a woodsmith owner-builder who enjoys wood turning and crafting to indulge in a bit of self-expression.

Assembling a balustrade is not a difficult job. The key is in solidly anchoring the newel posts, as well as any intermediate posts. This is what gives the entire assembly its solidity and thereby its effectiveness as a safety device. In effect, the newel post—whether at top or bottom of the stairs, or both—is a structural member. As such, one of the best ways to install it is to cut a hole through the flooring and bolt it to a floor joist. If there is no immediately adjacent joist (its position would have to be perfect, which is unlikely), another method is to install a separated double header between the two most conveniently positioned joists, insert the newel post between them, and through-bolt all three together. Failing that, the newel post can be notched to fit up to the outside of a stringer, or to fit down over it. Then it can be bolted to the stringer. Either method, however, weakens the newel post.

Another method is to install a newel post with an oversized bottom end that can be notched without excessive weakening. Bolt it to the stringer, drive one or two substantial lag screws up through the flooring into the newel base, and extend a portion of the bottom step beyond and across the front of the post. Intermediate posts should also be ruggedly anchored. Balusters typically are dowel-ended and set, like pegs, in holes bored in the tread ends and the underside of the handrail. They are then glued in place. The handrail must be securely attached to the newel posts, intermediate posts, and sometimes to a starting point at a wall frame. On utility staircases or exterior porches, decks, or balcony installations, the entire assembly is often lag-screwed, bolted, or attached with steel framing anchors in the sturdiest way possible, with all hardware visible. Criteria for finish and appearance are different here.

Chapter **60**

Fireplaces, wood stoves, and chimneys

*A*s of early 1990, a fireplace ranked in the top ten in every region of the United States as a feature desired by buyers of both new and older homes. It was also one of the top ten items included in remodeling programs. The popularity of fireplaces is unlikely to diminish in the future, and probably will remain a plus factor in the value of any house. Woodburning stoves—some of which burn coal as well—are also very popular, more so in rural areas and localities where firewood is readily available. However, fireplaces and wood stoves are coming under increasing scrutiny by various official agencies, and are being increasingly regulated from the standpoints of potentially hazardous emissions, safe installation practices, and energy conservation. A growing number of municipalities require installation permits, specify the brand and model that can be installed, limit the number of units per household, and disallow the use of wood as fuel (electric or gas units only) and might impose various other regulations as well.

Construction or installation of fireplaces and wood stoves must be assessed and evaluated for each individual house project, and the details often must be worked out in concert with local building authorities. You can get full information from your local building, health, or fire department, any or all of which might have something to do with the subject. Also, most fire departments are usually good sources for the latest information regarding approved products and safe installation procedures.

The details of building masonry fireplaces or masonry stoves is beyond the scope of this book, but there is plenty of good information available on the subject. The fundamentals of all-masonry fireplace and stove construction have been developed over many decades, and their design, sizing, and dimensioning factors, as well as excellence of workmanship, are crucial to efficient and safe operation. This is not a project for a novice; a competent mason can get the job done by following an existing, proven design.

There are some alternatives that make the job easier. One is a steel fireplace shell; there are numerous models available in a wide range of sizes, many of which have warm air recirculating systems included. They are designed to be set in place on an appropriate pad or hearth, and the masonry surround and chimney is then built up around the unit. In some cases a metal chimney is installed. Another possibility is a zero-clearance fireplace unit, which is designed to be installed directly into a framed cavity and requires no masonry; a metal appliance chimney is used.

Yet another possibility is a freestanding metal fireplace unit, which is designed to stand in the open away from walls, on a hearth or integral pedestal. As far as installation is concerned, these differ little from wood stoves, which are also freestanding. Some wood stoves also feature the visible fire attribute of a fireplace without sacrificing the benefits of a stove. In all cases, from scratch-built masonry fireplaces to full-sized, discrete wood/coal burning stoves, there is a huge array of designs, models, features, heating capacities, and sizes available for consideration.

MASONRY FIREPLACE INSTALLATION

All-masonry or masonry with steel insert fireplaces are the only truly freestanding units, in that they must rest entirely independent from the house structure. The masonry mass is extremely heavy, especially for a huge Russian or Finnish heater, but also for a small fireplace. The whole pile must sit on its own footing and foundation base, which typically is made of poured concrete or block and concrete, and is built up right along with the house foundation. All of the pertinent dimensions for this kind of installation must be determined as the house is being planned, so that proper dimensioning can be followed as construction proceeds.

Once the foundation has been completed and framing begins, the next step is to box the first-floor frame out around it; no framing should rest upon or be attached to any part of the fireplace masonry at any point. All combustible materials must be kept at least 2 inches away from the masonry—except at the fireplace opening, where the clearance is 6 inches. Wall framing must be built around the masonry in the usual fashion, with double studding at the sides of the opening and bracing as necessary and full headers above. The opening required in the ceiling/floor frame above is smaller than in the floor at the base, and it is also boxed out in the usual way. From that point upward, rough openings in the framing are sized for the chimney. In some instances the chimney is enlarged just before passing through the roof frame, for visual emphasis on the outside.

PREFABRICATED FIREPLACE INSTALLATION

Installing a zero-clearance prefabricated fireplace, which can be substantial in size and appear every bit as impressive as an all-masonry fireplace, is an entirely different matter. Units vary and all come with complete installation instructions, but the general procedure is to erect a secondary partition wall to house the unit. This entails framing a box-like affair and covering it with gypsum wallboard to enclose the firebox, and framing in chases for an outside air duct, for wiring or gas piping if those are used, and sometimes for warm air recirculating ducts. A facing wall must be framed right around the fireplace unit and attached to it; this is covered with a wall sheathing and supports the mantel, wood surround, ceramic tile facing, masonry, or whatever interior finishes are used. A framed-up, elevated hearth may be installed, with the entire unit raised above floor level, or the hearth may be set directly on a metal safety strip on the sub-flooring. A chimney chase must also be framed and sheathed with gypsum wallboard, and a metal firestop and chimney retainer/support installed in a framed opening in the ceiling/floor framework above. Standard framing materials and techniques are used throughout, and no structural framing is needed. The relatively light weight of the unit is amply supported by any conventional floor frame.

PRECAUTIONS FOR INSTALLING
FREESTANDING FIREPLACES AND STOVES

Installing a freestanding fireplace or a wood stove is a simple matter. So simple, in fact, that often the proper installation procedures and precautions go unobserved. Whether this occurs through ignorance, carelessness or corner-cutting is immaterial; a house can burn down just as fast for any of those reasons. The following are pertinent facts and should always be followed in the absence of any other instructions or regulations to the contrary. They are valid for all noncirculating wood/coal stoves and ranges and freestanding fireplaces, except zero-clearance units:

- The clearance from the bottom of the stove to the finish floor must be 18 inches or more. The floor must be protected from sparks or coals with a noncombustible covering, typically 24-gauge or thicker sheet metal, which should extend 18 inches minimum in front of the unit and 6 inches to both sides and the rear.

- If the clearance from the bottom of the stove to the finish floor is between 6 and 18 inches, the floor must be protected by a non-combustible layer of 1/4-inch-thick mineral-fiber rigid board covered with 24-gauge or thicker metal, or an equivalent protection, extending beyond the stove as just noted.

- If the clearance between the bottom of the stove and the floor is less than 6 inches, the stove must be set upon a noncombustible platform of approved construction, elevated above the floor.

- The distance between the nearest heated surface of a stove and an unprotected combustible wall must be 36 inches minimum. If the wall is covered with a sheet of 1/4-inch rigid mineral fiberboard spaced out 1 inch or more from the wall, the distance can be reduced to 18 inches. If the wall is covered with a sheet of metal spaced out 1 inch or more, the clearance distance can be reduced to 12 inches.

- In the case of circulating stoves, which are designed to see constant duty as space heaters, these dimensions are 12 inches, 6 inches, and 4 inches respectively.

- Stovepipe clearances from an unprotected combustible wall, fiberboard-covered wall, and metal-covered wall are 18 inches, 12 inches, and 9 inches respectively.

Many different methods have been used to fulfill these requirements in the way of protective installations equivalent to the mineral fiberboard or sheet metal, neither of which do much for the decor. Unfortunately, many are useless. Worse, because the occupants of the house don't realize this, they have a false sense of security. A brick or tile veneer pasted to a wood frame and gypsum wallboard wall does not change its combustible status one bit. No noncombustible material applied directly to a frame wall will render the wall noncombustible. Over time, heat will pass through all the noncombustible materials and pyrolize the combustible portions, until one day the wall will erupt in spontaneous combustion.

METHODS OF FIREPROOFING

There are numerous ways to avoid such disasters, and unless considerable use will be made of heavy masonry materials, special framing or structural work isn't required. If there will be unusual weight at any point, simply double the joists and/or add columnar or other support as necessary, in the usual manner. You can surface-mount any of a great number of factory-made, approved, protective backer or floor panels to wall sheathing, and to either subflooring or finish flooring.

If a custom design and installation is preferable, in communities where fireplace and stove installations are regulated and inspected, clear your plans with the proper authorities ahead of time and work with them to develop a safe, attractive installation that will blend with your intended decor. If you are not constrained as to design, bear in mind that the idea is to keep any appreciable amount of heat from reaching any combustible surface, and interpose a shield of some sort between it and the stove. Here are some of the basic possibilities:

- Install a full sheet of metal, 28-gauge or thicker, perhaps copper or brass, with hand-hammered designs or patterns. Stand it at least 1 inch clear of the wall and mount it on porcelain insulators of the type used for stringing electric fence wire. Leave at least 1 inch of open space above and below for air circulation.

- Mount a full sheet of metal in the manner just noted, perhaps painted with heat resistant paint, on the wall. Mount another sheet to the first, also spaced out 1 inch or more. This could be plain, formed or shaped, or have cutouts in patterns to expose portions of the back panel, perhaps in contrasting colors (FIG. 60-1).

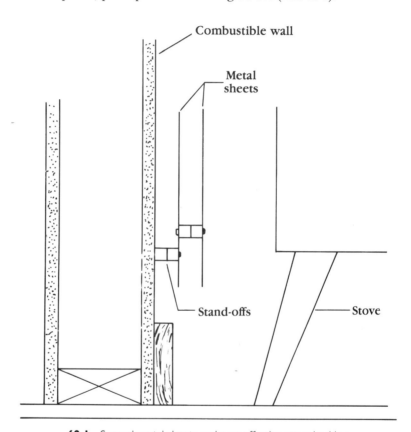

60-1 Spaced metal sheets make an effective stove backing.

- Build a solid brick stem wall set out at least 1 inch from the house wall, or perhaps 6 inches or more to allow for cleaning in behind (FIG. 60-2). Omit every third brick in the bottom course to allow air circulation behind the wall. Alternatively, install a noncombustible panel made up of artificial brick or stone or ceramic tile, and attach it to a backing with a heat-proof cement.
- To gain protection at the stovepipe, mount a curved sheet metal panel to the stovepipe itself with 1-inch or longer stand-offs.

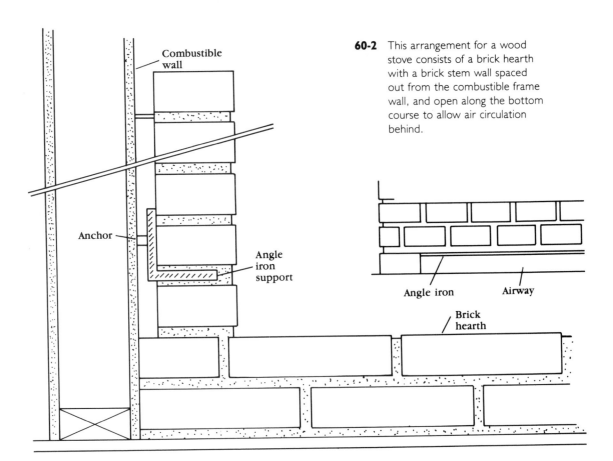

60-2 This arrangement for a wood stove consists of a brick hearth with a brick stem wall spaced out from the combustible frame wall, and open along the bottom course to allow air circulation behind.

(These are commercially available screw eyes with a long shaft and an insulated disk in the eye.) The arc of the metal should cover the back of the pipe (FIG. 60-3), reflecting heat back into the room and allowing cooling air circulation between it and the pipe.

- Construct a built-up masonry hearth using open-cored masonry units that will allow free air circulation beneath and around the hearth (FIG. 60-4).

- Build a simple wood-framed hearth like the one in FIG. 60-5, using fiberglass blanket insulation, 20-gauge galvanized steel sheet, bricks, and decorative garden stone or ordinary gravel.

CHIMNEY INSTALLATION

There are certain precautions that must be taken in chimney installations, too. Masonry chimneys can be built up ahead of the framing, or built up through the framing. Either way, there must be a clearance of 2 inches between chimney and framing. The same clearance must be maintained

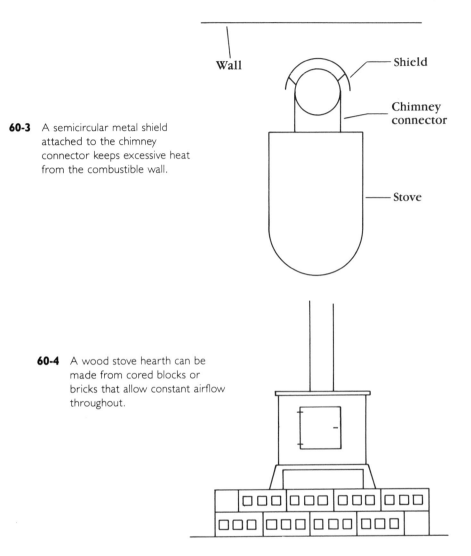

60-3 A semicircular metal shield attached to the chimney connector keeps excessive heat from the combustible wall.

60-4 A wood stove hearth can be made from cored blocks or bricks that allow constant airflow throughout.

with metal appliance chimneys that are used with prefabricated fireplaces, wood stoves and ranges, and freestanding fireplaces. Rough openings must be framed for both types where they pass through floor/ceiling and roof sections. Metal chimneys are simple enough to assemble and install by following the manufacturer's instructions. There are certain code requirements governing masonry flue construction, height of chimney termination above the roof, and similar items that should be checked on a local basis.

One popular course is to disguise the part of a metal chimney that extends above the roof, in the interest of appearance. This is done by building a *chase*, the framed and sheathed shaft through which the metal

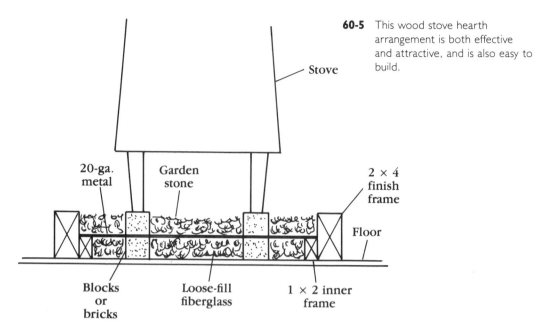

60-5 This wood stove hearth arrangement is both effective and attractive, and is also easy to build.

chimney passes. One of the most common methods is to frame side and end walls of 2×4s, just as any wall is framed, with a single sole plate and a double top plate. The sole plate must be bolted or lag-screwed to the roof frame as solidly as can be managed. The chase is basically freestanding and must withstand a great deal of wind pressure, which comes to bear on the mounting area. The framework should be sheathed with 3/4-inch plywood, preferably screwed on. Any conventional exterior siding can be used, to either match or contrast the rest of the house: clapboards, wood shingles, artificial brick or stone, tile, channel-lap, stucco, etc. The top is also covered with 3/4-inch plywood, trimmed with edge flashing, then covered entirely with cap flashing. The metal chimney extends up through the cap, is flashed to the cap flashing, and ends in a standard termination. The height above the chase cap is typically about 1 foot, but that can vary.

A variation on this theme is to bring the chimney out through a wall, into a chase that starts at the wall base and is framed upward as part of the exterior wall structure. This is an especially popular arrangement where a furnace, fireplace or stove, or water heater flue or a second floor fireplace flue, can be brought out into the same chase, all hidden from view and terminated above the roof line in an easy and inexpensive way.

Another variation is to frame a heavy-duty base in the attic using 4×4s bolted to doubled floor-ceiling joists, cross braced and secured to the rafters as well, to form a platform just below the rafters. Then a brick chimney is based on the platform and built up through the roof, surrounding the metal chimney and terminating in a cast concrete chase cap and a separate chimney cap.

Chapter 61

Vapor barriers and ventilation

Vapor barrier installation has been mentioned in several earlier chapters as a part of the foundation construction. In that application, the barrier primarily serves to prevent free moisture and water vapor from migrating into and through poured concrete slabs or other foundation parts, and to reduce excess dampness in earth floor crawl spaces. A vapor barrier is usually required in all other parts of a frame house, but the purpose there is to prevent migration of water vapor, which is a gas, from the interior of the building out into the building sections. Ventilation is another facet of housebuilding that is often slighted or ignored, but it is as important as vapor barrier installation. This is especially true in many of today's tightly constructed, thermally-efficient houses.

VAPOR BARRIERS

Water vapor, which is generated in considerable quantities within a house as a result of cooking, bathing, respiration, and other daily functions, tends to continually move from warmer to cooler areas. Whenever the outside atmosphere is cooler than the inside house temperature, it is impelled by a pressure differential between the interior and the exterior to travel outward. As it does so, its temperature gradually declines, approaching a closer match with the temperatures of the materials through which it passes. Those temperatures become progressively cooler from inside to outside. In a wall, for example, the wallpaper surface might be 72° Fahrenheit, the backside of the drywall 55°, the middle of the fiberglass insulation 40°, the interior of the exterior sheathing 32°, and the outside of the exterior siding 20°.

At some point in its passage, the water vapor will reach the crucial dewpoint temperature (a complex and highly variable condition), whereupon it will immediately condense into water droplets or frost feathers. Most building materials, especially many of the most commonly used thermal insulants, readily permit the passage of water vapor. The potential result is obvious: Moisture within the building sections causes mildew, fungus growth, rot, breakdown of insulation effectiveness, peeling paint and paper, lifting drywall, and eventual structural damage. The danger of this is greater in houses that are tight, well insulated, and that have a low air change rate.

The preventive for this misery is simple: a vapor barrier, which affords complete, practical condensation control at minimum cost. An effective vapor barrier is also of substantial value in locales where heat and high humidity combine to make mechanical cooling a necessity. This is because in the absence of a barrier the water vapor migrates into the house from the humid exterior, imposing an added load on the cooling system by increasing latent heat.

A discussion of the dynamics of water vapor migration might be interesting to some, but would be largely an academic exercise. The practical fact is this: You should install, or ensure that your contractor installs, a vapor barrier of 4- or 6-mil polyethylene sheet that wraps the entire inhabitable interior space in the house in a plastic envelope. Other materials can be used—anything that has a permeance rating of less than 1.0 will do—but they seldom are because the plastic sheeting is so inexpensive, easy to work with, and universally available.

The facing of fiberglass and mineral wool blanket insulation qualifies as a vapor barrier, but should not be relied upon because of slits, tears and other damage that inevitably takes place, and because of gaps and bulges that occur during even careful installation. Foil-faced rigid insulation or gypsum wallboard panels do provide a good vapor barrier if properly installed and if all seams and joints are foil-taped; these materials can serve well in lieu of poly sheet. The same is true of a few kinds of rigid thermal insulation panels that are made with an impermeable skin. However, installing poly sheet everywhere is the best all-around answer.

Installation on cold floors
Installing a vapor barrier is easy, but should be done with care. On cold floors, application details depend upon what flooring materials are used (FIG. 61-1). The vapor barrier should be installed between a subfloor and solid underlayment, nailed finish wood flooring, or mortar-bedded tile or flagstones. It should be installed between the joists and subflooring or combination subflooring/underlayment when carpet, sheet vinyl, glued wood parquet tile, vinyl tile, or glued ceramic tile will be laid as a finish covering.

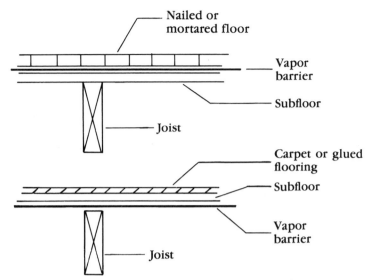

61-1   Placement of the vapor barrier in a cold floor.

Lay the poly sheet out flat and smooth, overlap all edges by about 12 inches, and lap it up all walls about 6 inches. Staple the ends and edges just enough to hold the material in place until it is covered with another flooring layer, which should be done immediately in order to avoid damage to the barrier. If damage does occur, seal it off with vinyl or metalized tape or cover the damage with a patch. No barrier is laid in a warm floor.

Installation on cold walls

A vapor barrier should be applied to the inside of all exterior wall frames just before the wall covering is installed (FIG. 61-2). Hang the poly sheet from the top of the top plate and staple it, leaving a 6-inch or wider strip free to lap onto the ceiling. Smooth it down over the studs and staple it to the sole plate of the subfloor. Lap vertical seams by a full stud bay. Overlap the floor vapor barrier and/or arrange it to be sandwiched into building components as they are installed, to make a sealed joint. At intersections with interior partition walls, lap the sheet through the wall frame over the end stud and back onto the exterior wall. Stretch the sheet across window, door, and other openings, and staple to the edges of the openings. Then cut the extra away, leaving a 6-inch or greater free strip all around the edges that can be sealed in later. Cover electrical outlet boxes. Slit the plastic in an X, and fold the flaps into the boxes. Repair any damage that might occur to the poly sheet before the wall covering is applied.

Installation on ceilings

The procedure is much the same for insulated ceilings (FIG. 61-3). The vapor barrier should be positioned between the ceiling joists and furring

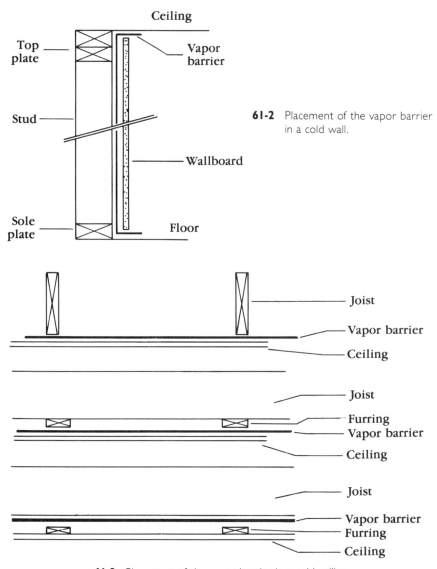

Ceiling

Top plate

Vapor barrier

Stud

61-2 Placement of the vapor barrier in a cold wall.

Wallboard

Sole plate

Floor

Joist

Vapor barrier

Ceiling

Joist

Furring

Vapor barrier

Ceiling

Joist

Vapor barrier

Furring

Ceiling

61-3 Placement of the vapor barrier in a cold ceiling.

strips or the finish ceiling material, or between furring strips and the finish ceiling material. The thermal insulation should always be above the barrier. Carry the sheeting right over openings and electrical boxes and cut them out later, just as with walls. Lap the edges by a full joist bay, and let 6 inches or so hang down the walls to make a seal with the wall vapor barrier.

In a roof/ceiling construction, the position of the vapor barrier, or whether or not it is even installed, depends upon the materials used.

Where the construction consists of insulation between the rafters and wallboard sheathing on the interior, the vapor barrier installation procedure is exactly the same as for a conventional flat ceiling or a wall. If built-up tar and felt roofing is applied over a roof deck, a separate vapor barrier is unnecessary. If sheathing or decking is laid over an exposed framework and thermal insulation installed on top of that, with another layer of sheathing covering all, a vapor barrier might be needed between the first layer of sheathing and the insulation, depending upon its properties.

VENTILATION

There are several aspects of ventilation in residential construction. One was mentioned earlier: crawl spaces must be thoroughly ventilated, with suitable intake and exhaust ports, in order to reduce moisture that could cause damage to the underside of the house.

Natural ventilation

If no moisture barrier covers the earth floor of the crawl space, the net free ventilating area (which is the actual open space not taken up by louver slats, mesh wires, etc.) of the vents should equal a minimum of $1/160$ of the total ground area. A 1000-square-foot crawl space would thus require $6^{1}/4$ square feet of net vent area. If a moisture barrier is in place, that figure reduces to $1/1600$ of the crawl space area, or about $5/8$ square foot. There must be two vents at least, one inlet and one outlet, but more can be installed. They should be roughly opposite one another, preferably facing prevailing wind directions, for good cross ventilation.

Another aspect of ventilation lies in providing ample means of admitting outside air through strategically placed windows and doors, especially windows. By making sure that all rooms have adequate cross ventilation and by preventing "dead" areas, you can make use of natural ventilation to change the air in the house and aid in cooling it in hot weather.

Mechanical ventilation

Mechanical ventilation is the opposite of natural ventilation, and it has taken on new and important meaning in the past few years. In most houses, mechanical ventilation includes vent fans in bathrooms (which are required by code in bathrooms that do not have an operable window or skylight) and usually wall fans, range hood fans, or vent fans on the kitchen stove. Special-purpose exhaust fans might also be installed, as in a photography darkroom or in a gable to exhaust trapped heat. Whole-house vent fans have also become popular in some areas where mechanical refrigeration cooling (air conditioning) is not warranted, but some cooling is occasionally desirable. These units are designed to be permanently installed in attic doorways or access hatches, or in special openings, and draw air from outside up through the house and out through large gable exhaust vents. Small window-mounted fans or air conditioning units can be installed for the same purpose, but are not regarded as permanent installations.

One of the most important applications of mechanical ventilation today is to move air throughout the new superinsulated, highly thermally efficient, practically airtight houses. All of the air in an average new house might be expected to replace itself at a rate of about 1.0 to 0.75 air change per hour (ACH). At this rate, the air remains relatively fresh and free of contaminants under normal circumstances. However, some new houses are built so tight that the ACH may be 0.25 or less, which can be decidedly unhealthy over time, even if no large quantities of contaminants such as cigarette smoke are introduced. Yet, freely ventilating with fans or by opening doors and windows defeats the very purpose of building such a house. Enter the heat exchanger, an old principle in a sophisticated new package, designed for residential applications. These units automatically exchange fresh for stale air, while at the same time retaining most of the interior heat, regardless of the inside-outside temperature differential. They are a must in any ultra-energy-conservative house.

Ventilating attics and roofs

The final aspect of ventilation in residential construction involves providing adequate air flow through unoccupied attics and in certain kinds of roof construction. Though often skimped or bypassed entirely, such ventilation is important in voiding water vapor and eliminating condensation year-round, which reduces attic heat. This consequently reduces cooling loads and discomfort below stairs, and helps prevent roofing deterioration in summer and roof ice-dam formation in winter.

There are many approaches to installing ventilation. In gable-roofed houses the usual procedure is to provide a louvered vent at each peak. If the roof is low pitched and if the attic is small, this might be sufficient, but air flow is usually slight. In this situation, the combined inlet-outlet net free vent area should equal $1/300$ of the attic floor area, minimum. Better results can be obtained by cutting numerous openings in the soffits; this must be done in large attics with tall roofs. The soffit inlets and the gable outlets should each equal at least $1/900$ of the area. This ratio is also sufficient as a minimum for most hip-roof designs.

Flat-roof venting is more difficult, and where airways between the roof and the ceiling must be relied upon, the venting ratio should be reduced to $1/250$ or less. In all cases it is also possible to install wind-operated or even power turbine ventilators or exhaust fans at the higher parts of the roof, with air inlets at the lowest points. The sizes of the units and the inlet vents should be determined by formula for each individual application; local conditions might indicate a need for greater air volume.

Ventilating a roof is a matter of leaving unrestricted airways under all parts of the finish roof covering or sheathing. Inlet vents are cut into the

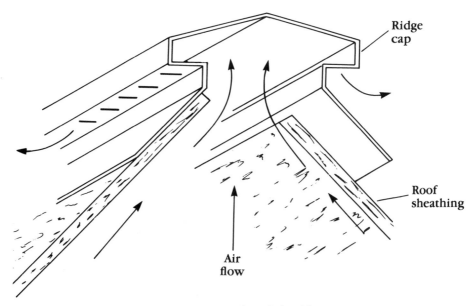

61-4 A special metal ventilating ridge cap.

soffits between each pair of rafters. Baffles should be installed if necessary over the exterior wall top plates to restrain the insulation from shifting out into the eaves area or filling up against the underside of the roof sheathing or decking. The minimum airway here should be 1 inch, and more is preferable if it can be arranged (refer to FIG. 57-9).

The insulation must be installed between the rafters in such a way that it does not and will not ride up against the sheathing. If collar ties are set between rafter legs, the closed-off space above them is the collection area for incoming air. Exhaust vents are built into the gable peaks at each end to complete the flow pattern. If the airways are continued all the way to the ridge, a special ridge cap must be installed the full length of the ridgepole, with suitable openings in the sheathing made as necessary to allow the air to exhaust (FIG. 61-4). The exact arrangement depends upon how the roof is put together and with what materials; there are also several different kinds of ridge caps.

Chapter **62**

Interior wall sheathing

The interior wall surfaces of most frame houses built today are sheathed with gypsum wallboard (drywall) before any finish wall covering is added. There are alternatives: Gypsum lath is sometimes installed under a plaster finish; plaster can be applied over metal lath (wood lath is seldom seen anymore); and hardboard, plywood, particle board, waferboard, and chipboard all can be used but seldom are. There are some specialty sheathing products to consider, too. Type X gypsum wallboard has a core specially compounded for fire resistance, and is sometimes required by code in certain locations—as in a wall separating a house from an attached garage. Water-resistant wallboard (blue board) is recommended for use in kitchens, laundries, and bathrooms, or wherever moisture might be present. It is not suitable, however, for high-moisture applications like steam rooms or shower stalls. Backing board, a waterproof rigid board product, is made especially for that purpose, and is installed as a substrate for ceramic tile in wet locations. Predecorated gypsum wallboard is available in several finishes, such as simulated wood grain paneling, and combines sheathing and finish in one product. And finally, sheathing can be dispensed with entirely if the finish material is $3/4$-inch-thick wood planking or paneling.

Although $5/8$-inch-thick gypsum wallboard is preferable, the size most commonly installed in houses is $1/2$ inch, in 4-×-8-foot sheets with tapered edges. The sheets are usually installed vertically (FIG. 62-1), but the same or longer sheets can be installed horizontally as well. By far the easiest way to get this job done is to call a professional drywaller who makes a business of hanging drywall. Installation is not technically difficult but is

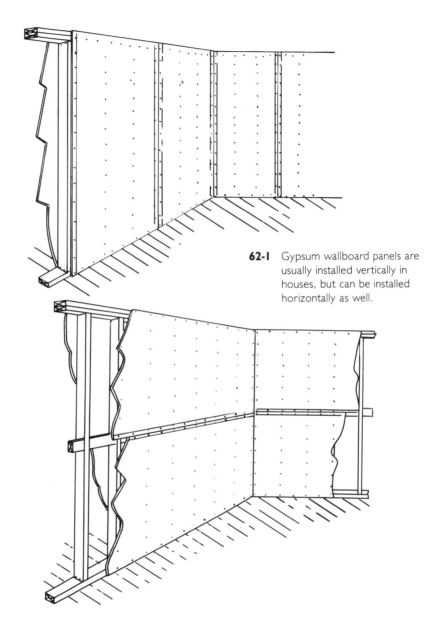

62-1 Gypsum wallboard panels are usually installed vertically in houses, but can be installed horizontally as well.

physically demanding—the sheets are heavy and hard to handle—and can be messy as well.

VERTICAL INSTALLATION OF WALLBOARD

One approach to vertical installation is to pick a room corner and select the first wall stud (in either direction) whose centerline is no more than

48 inches from the corner at any point. With a plumb bob or spirit level, determine a plumb centerline and snap a chalkline down the stud edge. Check all the studs in the room. Use a straightedge or a level, or simply "eyeball" them. Make sure none have bowed in or out excessively, or have knot bulges or any other defects on the edges. This can cause a lot of problems when applying the sheathing, leading to breaks or cracks, pulled fasteners, a wavy wall surface, or other difficulties. Trim the stud edges with a hand or power plane and plan on adding drywall shims during the installation, as necessary, to make the surface as smooth and even as possible.

Trim one end of a full sheet to the wall height if necessary, allowing about 1/4 inch of leeway top and bottom. To trim, score the face of the material by drawing a sharp utility knife along a straightedge, using enough pressure to slice the paper covering and drive into the gypsum a bit. Stand the sheet on edge and snap the waste piece back sharply to break the gypsum. Fold the waste all the way back to make a crease in the backing paper, then slit along the crease from the back with your knife (FIG. 62-2). If the snapped edge is rough with protruding bumps of gypsum, just carve them off by pulling the knife blade back toward yourself along the edge, like peeling an apple.

Stand the sheet in place, working away from the corner, with one edge aligned with the plumb line on the stud. Use a scrap or two to boost it off the floor a bit. Fasten the sheet first to the intermediate studs at about the middle of the sheet, working up and down the studs. Then fasten the outer edges, and across the top and bottom.

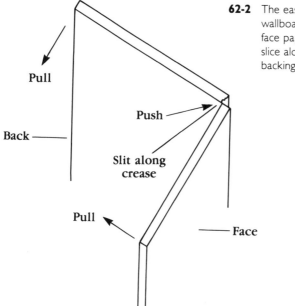

62-2 The easiest way to trim gypsum wallboard is to slice through the face paper, break the core, then slice along the crease of the backing paper.

Fastening methods

The traditional method of fastening is with coated drywall nails, either straight shanked or annular ringed. Use a 1³/₈-length for ¹/₂-inch drywall, 1¹/₂-inch for ⁵/₈-inch material. Space the nails 6 to 8 inches apart, at least ³/₈ inch in from the edges, and set the heads slightly below the drywall surface in a dimple caused by the hammer head.

An alternative method is double nailing. Install each sheet in the usual way, with single nails, but allow a 12-inch spacing at intermediate points. Then go back and add a second nail about 1 inch away from the first at all of those intermediate locations. Another method of securing the sheets is to use adhesive applied from tubes with a caulking gun. Follow the manufacturer's instructions for application; this usually amounts to a zigzag bead about ¹/₄ inch wide down each stud edge.

Yet another method that is gaining in popularity involves driving special screws with a clutch-equipped power driver. This is fast and easy, and does away with the problem of popping nails. It also secures the drywall extremely well. Use 1¹/₄-inch extruded-thread bugle-head drywall screws, which are Phillips slotted and can be either hand or power driven. Set them on 16-inch centers.

Trimming

Continue fitting the panels up edge to edge. At corners, you can install the sheet at the narrow-edged stud first without using fasteners, then jam the adjacent panel tight against it (FIG. 62-3). All corner panels should be edge trimmed to fit up snugly. You could also install drywall clips here, for a floating corner that is less likely to crack along the seam. Make accurate cuts for electrical boxes; have one handy to use as a template. The best device to use for making these and other cutouts or trims that have to be

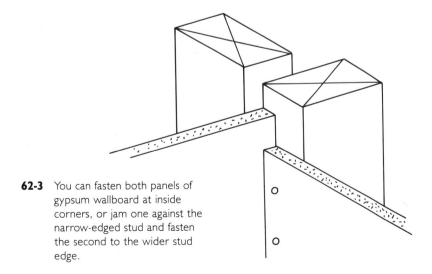

62-3 You can fasten both panels of gypsum wallboard at inside corners, or jam one against the narrow-edged stud and fasten the second to the wider stud edge.

sawed, is a stub-handled, short-bladed saw with coarse, sharp teeth—known, oddly enough, as a drywall saw. Make as much use of the tapered edges as you can when butting edges.   Finish up the installation by nailing metal cornerbead over all outside corners; inside corners stay as is.

FILLING AND FINISHING JOINTS

The next chore is filling and finishing all the joints. It's not a job everyone enjoys; even some professional builders who will cheerfully install the drywall draw the line at this task and call in a professional drywall taper. The job isn't difficult, just long and messy. It does take some practice, and a whole lot of patience. The key is not to fuss repeatedly with the wet compound, trying to get it just so. Work with long, bold strokes, and once the compound is on, let it be. That is, unless the joint is really botched. Then the best bet is to peel the whole mess off and start over.

Use a ready-mixed joint compound, available in 1- and 5-gallon buckets. You'll need three joint knives; a set of 3-, 6-, and 8- or 9-inch sizes works well. The old standby joint tape is perforated paper, but the new self-stick mesh type is easier to use and makes a stronger joint that is less likely to crack.

Don't attempt to tape in a temperature of less than 55° Fahrenheit; at least a bit higher is better. At over 85° you will have trouble with the compound curing too fast, especially if the humidity is low. If the outside relative humidity is below 40 percent or so, keep all windows and outside doors closed against dryness and breezes, and humidify if you can. If the weather is very damp and/or cool, extra curing time will be needed before recoating, somtimes a couple of days or more.

Paper tape

To tape a flat joint with paper tape (FIG. 62-4), butter the joint from top to bottom with your narrow knife, held at an angle of about 15 to 20 degrees. Stay between the edges of the tapers and make the layer smooth and of even thickness, but not too thick—experience will show you the right combination. Thoroughly fill the crack, but don't rework the compound any more than you can help. Then gently press the paper tape into place in the compound, centered on the joint. Smooth it down lightly with your fingers, top to bottom.

Immediately go back to the top, and with your mid-sized knife held at an angle of about 45 degrees, press the tape firmly into the compound, smoothing it as you go along. Work out any air bubbles and watch out for any bumps or ridges in the paper. Make sure the paper edges are down flat and tight, but not so tight as to squeeze all the compound out from under the tape. There has to be about 1/32 inch of compound under the tape to make a solid bond to the drywall. Force out excess compound from under the tape but be wary of tearing or rippling the paper; it gets soft from the moisture in the compound. Before any drying can occur, use the same

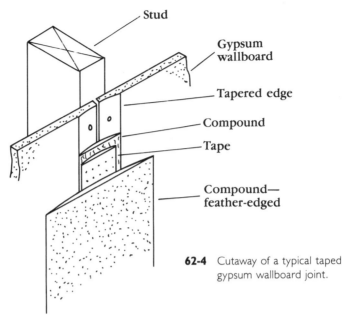

Stud

Gypsum wallboard

Tapered edge

Compound

Tape

Compound— feather-edged

62-4 Cutaway of a typical taped gypsum wallboard joint.

knife to spread a thin layer of compound down over the tape, top to bottom. The tape should be just visible under this skim coat, which should go past the tape edges but still be inside the taper in a band about 3 inches wide.

Allow plenty of time for the compound to dry completely, then apply a second skim coat of compound with the mid-sized knife. Feather this layer out about 1 inch on each side of the first coat, hiding the tape completely. Use long, smooth strokes and don't rework unless absolutely necessary. After a drying period, apply a third coat with the wide knife, feathering it out an inch or more on each side of the second coat. Now the taper should be filled completely, with perhaps a very thin coat feathered out past the taper line.

Mesh tape

The procedure when using mesh tape is similar, but the first step is omitted. Just unroll a few inches of tape and stick it to the wallboard at the top of the joint and align it. Unroll the tape and press it into place along the joint as you do so. Cut it off at the floor line. Apply the first layer of compound so that it fills the joint crack and barely covers the mesh. Apply the second and third coats in the same way as for paper tape.

Taping corners

To tape inside corners, apply a narrow layer of compound down each side of the corner, filling the joint crack in the process. Cut a length of paper tape and fold it in half along the centerline, and set it into the compound. Bed it by smoothing it down alternately on each side. Use your small knife, or use a corner knife that does both sides at once. Either way, take care to keep the tape smooth and even on each side and free of wrinkles, and keep the center from driving into the joint crack. Some workers find it easier to apply the second and third coats one side at a time, allowing drying time between each session. Again, when using mesh tape skip the first buttering step.

Outside corners are easier to do. Just fill across the taper and over the metal edges to the cornerbead in three (or more) successive coats, feathering out a bit further each time to a total extent of 5 or 6 inches. The dimples and fastener heads at all intermediate bearing points also have to be covered with compound. Use your small joint knife at an angle of about 45 degrees and skim over them. After they dry completely, apply second coats—and if necessary, a third.

Sanding

The last step is the final smoothing of the compound. Use 150- or 180-grit sandpaper if the wall will be papered, but 220-grit for a paint finish—which must be very smooth and defect free. Work with a small, inflexible sanding block, up and down the joint line rather than across. Take care not to scuff up the wallboard paper if the walls will be painted, because the marks will show. Inside corners need to be carefully worked so that one side doesn't get gouged out as the other is sanded. Always wear a dust mask while sanding.

Chapter **63**

Interior
door
installation

Once the inside walls are sheathed, the interior doors can all be hung. You will find many more choices for interior than for exterior doors, in both styles and types, and there are different installation arrangements as well. With only a few exceptions, interior doors are made of wood.

TYPES AND SIZES OF DOORS

Flush doors are smooth faced on both sides and consist of a hollow (honeycomb) or a solid (hardboard, wood blocks, composition board) core, covered with a veneer of wood, hardboard, or plastic. Hollow-core doors are characteristically lightweight, flimsy, and subject to warping; they can be easily damaged and are hard to repair. Solid-core doors are much heavier and of better quality. Both kinds are widely used in residential construction.

Panel doors are made of solid wood (sometimes the panels are made of composition board) and consist of heavy vertical stiles and horizontal rails that frame and support one or more thinner inset panels. A wide range of designs is available.

Sash doors are panel doors with lights of glass or clear plastic substituted for one or more panels. Although mostly used as exterior doors, they can be installed inside as well. This is especially true of the type known as *casement* or *French* doors, where all the panels are replaced with lights. If there is only one full-sized light, it is a *rim casement* door, and if multiple lights, a *divided-light casement* door.

465

Louver doors are another popular type, sometimes used as passageway doors in houses but more often on closets. They are made up of a heavy outside frame into which a series of slightly overlapping thin wood slats are mortised. The slats may be *standard*, set at a steep angle and separated by about 1/4 inch; seen from one side of the door they slant upward, from the other, downward. Or, the louvers may be *chevron* style, inverted wood Vs stacked atop one another and facing downward on both sides. These can be set solid or spaced slightly. The entire door can be louvered, generally with a rail at a knob height, or the bottom section can be set with one or more panels. The open louvers should not be installed where sound privacy or noise control are of concern; they do ventilate to some extent.

Batwing or *cafe* doors are designed to fill only the middle part of the door opening, evocative of the saloon doors of the Old West. They can be used singly but are almost always installed as double-swinging, center-meeting pairs. Usually they are used to separate a kitchen from a dining room, but can be used elsewhere.

Accordion folding doors are sometimes installed to close off closets, or in larger form to block off entire living areas. There are several types and numerous styles, but all fold back upon themselves as they close, "stacking" in narrow folds or panels at one or both sides of the opening. They are not suitable where good privacy or sound control are required, but do have numerous decorative and partition uses.

Patio or *atrium* doors, which are intended primarily for exterior applications, are sometimes installed indoors. These units usually consist of a mix of fixed and operable sections; a typical application is a glass-wall divider separating a sunspace or greenhouse from the interior proper.

Except for accordion folding doors, which have no particular standard sizes, interior doors are $1^3/8$ inch thick and come in standard heights of 6 feet 8 inches and, to a limited degree, 6 feet 6 inches and 7 feet. There are numerous standard widths. For passageway use, 2 feet 8 inches is a common size and 3 feet is recommended; 2 feet 6 inches is sometimes used. Common sizes for closets are 2 feet, 2 feet 6 inches, and 2 feet 8 inches. Bifold and multifold doors are installed in sets of two or four to fit 4-, 6-, and 8-foot openings, but many individual sizes are available.

INSTALLATION CHOICES

While exterior doors are installed in only one way—single swinging to the inside (except for sliding patio types)—there are several different possibilities for interior doors. Single swinging, where the door can only swing one way, is the most common, and these usually open into a room or area. A double-swinging door is sometimes installed between a kitchen and dining room; it pivots to swing both ways. Bifold doors are set in one or two pairs that fold in the middle and swing back to either side on the outside of the opening. Multifolding doors have several panels that fold back to one side or the other, much like accordion folding doors but with far fewer panels. All of the folding types are best installed in closets or storage areas. Surface sliding doors cover an opening and are surface mounted on the wall, sliding back to cover a wall area when open. Bypass sliding doors are installed as a pair within a door frame; one covers the other when open, so only half the opening is accessible. These doors are also most suited to closet and storage area applications. Pocket sliding doors may be installed singly or as a center-meeting pair; they slide back to be fully concealed within the walls. They can be used on closets, but their traditional use is as room separators.

SINGLE-SWINGING DOORS

A relatively limited selection of flush and panel single-swinging doors is available in the prehung form—mounted in a completed door frame, hardware and all, ready to install in the rough opening. Accompanying casing trim is an optional extra; casing must be put on after the installation, whether supplied or not. The procedure is much the same as for an exterior door, and usually instructions are included. The general procedure is to stand the unit in the opening on the subfloor, center and plumb it, and insert four or five sets of shims between the studs and jambs on each side, one or two between the header and head jamb. Nail through the jambs and shims into the framing with pairs of 8d casing or finish nails at each set. Remove the factory-installed bracing and shipping/packing materials, check for proper installation, and install the trimwork.

In all other cases, the rough opening has to be fitted with a finish door frame. Make up the frame from interior jamb stock—two side jambs and a head jamb, no sill—in just the same way as for an exterior door (see Chapter 55). Stand it up and install it in the opening in the usual fashion. Assuming the wall sheathing has been put on, the frame can be trimmed with casing at this point (see Chapter 68). Thresholds are often not installed, allowing the finish flooring to go from room to room without a break. In some cases they are made part of the frame and set flat on the subfloor, so that the finish flooring butts each edge. Or, if the finish flooring level is the same from room to room (even though the flooring is of different materials), a thin threshold can be laid after the flooring is installed.

If a single-swinging door will be hung in the frame, a stop will be needed (FIG. 63-1). Attach strips of stop molding—there are several patterns and sizes—to both side jambs and the head jambs, mitering the corner joints. The stop should be set back from the door-mounting side of the frame about $1/32$ inch more than the thickness of the door. This can be done after the door is hung, too; some builders prefer to adjust the stop to the closed door and then fasten it. The bottom of each side stop can be trimmed flush to the floor, but another common procedure is to trim with a 45-degree end bevel about 1 inch more or less above the finish floor line.

To install a single-swinging door, follow the instructions for exterior door. Use the same clearance dimensions, except for the bottom. Interior

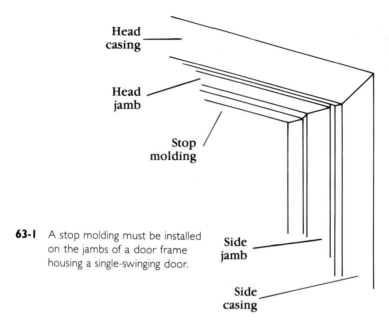

Head casing

Head jamb

Stop molding

Side jamb

Side casing

63-1   A stop molding must be installed on the jambs of a door frame housing a single-swinging door.

doors should clear the highest part of the finish floor by at least ¹/₄ inch, and often 1 inch or more is trimmed away as a clearance allowance for future carpeting. The only other differences lie in the kind of hardware used. Select interior locksets of a type that match the door use—passage-way, closet, or privacy, for example. Only two hinges need be installed; the ball-bearing variety is unnecessary, as are additional security locks and weatherstripping. Be aware that there are many more styles of more attractive appearance and much higher quality levels than are typically found on hardware store shelves; check manufacturer's catalogs.

DOUBLE-SWINGING DOORS

To hang a double-swinging door, first install and case a door frame, making sure that it is perfectly square and plumb. Trim the door as required, including a substantial rounding of the hinge edge and a double bevel or rounding of the unhinged edge. Allow clearance of at least ¹/₈ inch at the top, ¹/₄ inch at the sides, and ¹/₂ inch at the bottom, unless otherwise instructed. Install the pivot hinges according to the manufacturer's instructions. Install a push plate chest-high on each unhinged stile, and a kick plate across the bottom rail, if desired.

For a batwing set, mount a pair of special cafe door pivot hinges in the center of each side jamb at the required heights, and at matching locations top and bottom of the door edges. Hang the doors on the pins (FIG. 63-2). The hinges must be centered plumb and not cocked at all. Side clearance is determined by the hinges. Trim the doors to the opening and also to match and mate properly, bevel or round the meeting edges slightly, and allow at least ³/₁₆ inch between them.

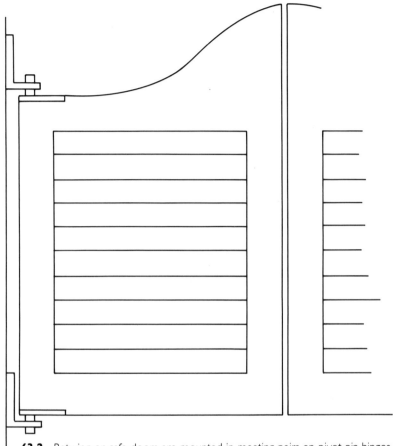

63-2 Batwing or cafe doors are mounted in meeting pairs on pivot-pin hinges.

BIFOLD DOORS

Installing bifold doors can be a bit tricky and confusing. Some variations and instructions are usually included with the door, but the general routine is as follows: Install and case a stopless frame, square and plumb. Trim the doors in equal amounts to fit the opening, allowing the specified top, side, and between-door clearances, and at least $1/2$ inch at the bottom. Mount the hinges on the doors as instructed; this usually results in a $1/16$-inch between-door clearance. Install the upper and lower pivots and the guide rollers in holes that are drilled plumb in the specified locations, usually according to templates, in the door edge corners. Install the track on the head jamb of the opening, the face flush with or set back just slightly from the inner face of the casing. Mount the jamb bracket on the floor against the side jamb, centered beneath the track (FIG. 63-3).

To hang the door set, open the two panels and insert the top pivot into its socket. Life the doors upward and set the bottom pivot into the

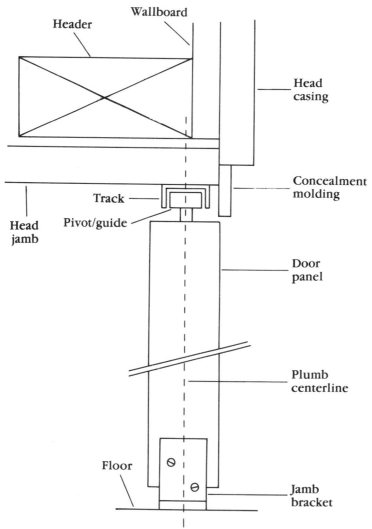

63-3 The jamb bracket of a bifold door is floor-mounted and must be aligned directly under the track.

jamb bracket. Fold the doors in somewhat and push the guide roller or pivot down. Swing the free panel under the track, and let the roller or pin pop up into the track or slider. Make the operating adjustments by shifting the top pivot socket and/or the bottom pivot forward or back, and raising or lowering the bottom pivot on its screw threads.

SLIDING DOORS

Sliding doors are usually simple to install. There are many variations, but surface sliders typically are fitted with rollers at the top. These hang on or

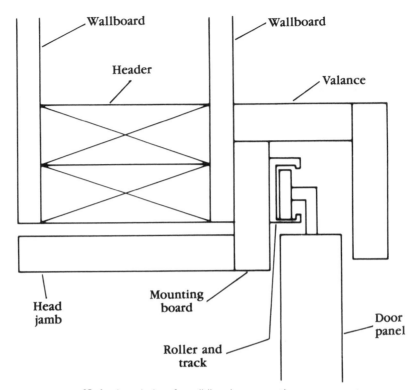

63-4 A typical surface sliding door mounting arrangement.

lock into a track assembly that is surface-mounted on a mounting board installed above the opening. The whole installation is concealed by a valance (FIG. 63-4). Adjustments for floor clearance and door plumb are made at the rollers, and guides restrain the door bottom from moving out of line. Doors may be single or center-meeting double, which are trimmed to cover the opening. Any kind of stopless cased door frame is fine.

Bypass sliding doors

To install bypass sliding doors, first build a stopless cased door frame. Mount an upper track or guide on the head jamb; its face is typically concealed with a trim molding. Mount a lower track on the floor, exactly in line with the upper one. Trim the doors according to the specified clearance requirements, and install the guides, rollers, and/or hangers as instructed, along with your chosen door pulls or knobs. To install the doors, tilt the inner door into the upper rear track, then down into the lower rear track. Check it for proper fit and operation, then install the outer door in the same way. The side and top jambs can be fitted with small concealment moldings to hide any gaps between the doors and the jambs, and also to conceal the hardware (FIG. 63-5).

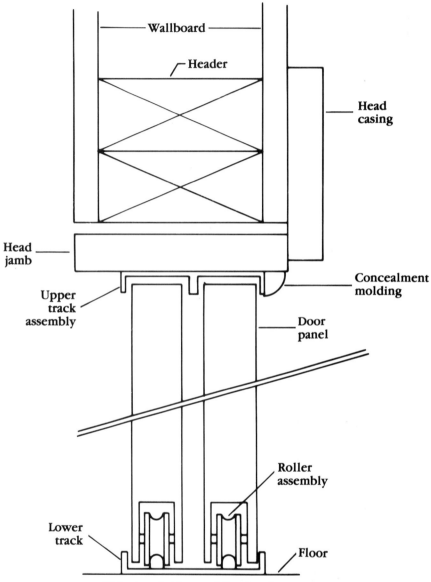

63-5 A typical bypass sliding door installation.

ACCORDION DOORS

Accordion doors are supplied with all necessary tracks and hardware and installation instructions. A stopless cased door frame is needed, along with a door that most closely matches the opening size. Close trimming for fit within the opening is not needed. The usual arrangement has the door hanging on rollers or slides from an overhead track that is trimmed to fit across the head jamb. One side of the door is attached with screws to a side jamb, and a latch assembly is secured to the opposite side jamb. Some doors run along floor tracks or guides as well, others hang free and clear the floor by anywhere from $1/2$ to several inches.

POCKET SLIDING DOOR

Installing a pocket sliding door is a sizable project that starts with the basic framing of the wall itself. An extra-thick assembly that is double studded with a center slot for the door is required. This is essentially a custom fit unit, and installation depends entirely upon the nature of the doors and the specific hardware to be used. The recommended course of action is to obtain a particular manufacturer's specifications during the house planning stage, and perhaps the hardware as well, and make accommodations to suit. Then build the required pockets during the wall framing phase of construction, installing the concealed track and associated hardware at the same time. Then the doors can be fitted and hung during the finishing stages of construction, according to the manufacturer's instructions.

Chapter **64**

Interior wall
finishes

*T*here are several different materials that make
excellent interior finish wall coverings, and of course the number of decorative variations is endless. Making selections often is not easy and
requires some thought, so the basics of interior decorating deserve some
attention. That is beyond the scope of this book, but here we will take a
look at some of the choices, because of the construction and preparation
requirements that must be taken into consideration.

PAINT

One of the most popular and widely applied wall finishes is paint. Gypsum wallboard sheathing accepts paint finishes nicely if properly prepared. There are many brands and kinds of paint available at any given
time; they change frequently, and certainly not all brands are universally
available. Apart from color, the paint you select for specific purposes
depends upon service conditions, the kind of surface being painted, the
desired final appearance, and other factors. Check with your local paint
suppliers and be guided by their and the manufacturers' recommendations as to what might be best for your applications.

The paint most often applied to gypsum wallboard is interior latex,
which is reasonably odorless, nontoxic, nonflammable, easy to use, and
cleans up with water. Usually a flat latex is applied in rooms like the living
or dining room, bedrooms, or dens, where the walls are unlikely to
become soiled and only infrequent cleaning is needed. The recently
introduced ''scrubbable'' flats will hold up much better under periodic
washing than plain flats. In bathrooms, nurseries, kitchens, and other
rooms were moisture, spillage, splatters, and soil are commonplace and

unavoidable, a washable semigloss latex should be applied. They more readily shed staining agents and will stand up to repeated scrubbings. High-gloss coatings are not often applied because they chip and scratch easily and reflect light harshly, and also show up every little defect in the wall. They do clean easily, though. The typical choice is either an oil-base, high-gloss enamel or a polyurethane enamel.

The biggest key to a nice paint job lies in the preparation. The glossier the paint, the more imperfections beneath the paint will be revealed. However, no paint has great defect-hiding power. Inspect all of the taped joints and the covered fasteners. The joint compound should be sanded perfectly flush with the wallboard surface. There should be no ridges or ripples, pinholes, sandpaper scratches, or dimples in the jointing, and the edges should feather onto the wallboard with no scuffing. Shine a strong light right along the wall and sight across the beam to detect imperfections. Do any necessary touchup work—it's tedious but necessary—then vacuum the walls and the rest of the room. Just before you start to paint, wipe the walls down with a cloth or a tack rag.

Apply the paint with a pad, roller, brush—or a combination of these. Painting should be done in a room temperature range of 65° to 75° Fahrenheit, humidity of 40 percent or more, and still air. Follow the manufacturer's application instructions, applying a primer first, if necessary.

TEXTURING

Texture coatings are an interesting alternative to paint. They leave a thick, flat, variable rough finish. The surfaces are not easily cleanable, so texturing should only be done in areas where cleaning is an infrequent necessity. Also, this is a permanent finish that can't be removed; it can only be painted over in a redecorating process, or covered with a new layer of wallboard.

There are several kinds of texture paints or compounds available, mostly in neutral colors like eggshell or white; tinting is possible, however. Specific application details vary, so check specifications and instructions. For thin texture paints, the wallboard should be smooth and clean with well-sanded joints, but minor imperfections don't matter. For thick, troweled-on compounds, rough taping is all that is needed. A wallboard primer might have to be applied before texturing. Application may be made with a brush, broad-bladed putty knife, or a trowel, in thicknesses of anywhere from 1/8 to 3/8 inch. In some cases, nubbly effects can be achieved by spraying the material on. Texturing is done as the material sets up.

Texturing can be done in innumerable patterns or designs, with all sorts of strange tools. You can striate the material with a whisk broom, scrub brush, comb, or similar tool. Stipple with a stippling roller or texturing roller, or pat with a dry sponge, wet sponge, wood block, trowel blade set flat, or a chunk of carpet—all the patterns will be different. Working in crosshatches or arcs will produce other patterns. Impress the bottom or rim of a water glass or bottle, or use a set of cookie cutters, for geometric forms and patterns. There are myriad possibilities, and the results are always unique.

PAPERING

Because not all wallpapers are actually paper, the correct term for these finishes is "wallcoverings." There is a dizzying array of them, in all grades of paper, vinylized paper, vinyls, fabrics, foils, flocks, and even bamboo. Some are very expensive and difficult to apply, and so are best hung by professionals: velvets or metal foils, for example. Others, especially the paper and vinylized paper products that make up the bulk of the offerings, are popular with do-it-yourselfers. Selection of the pattern is up to the homeowner, but required quantities should be discussed with the supplier or left to the paperhanger; estimating can be tricky, and a wrong estimate costly.

The wallboard surface should be as smooth and clean as for painting, because most imperfections will show through to the finished surface. However, this does depend, to some extent, upon the thickness of the wallcovering.

For further information on applying wallcoverings, consult any of the many do-it-yourself interior decorating or remodeling books.

PLANKING AND PANELING

Plank or panel wallcoverings have long been popular, and there are numerous products from which to choose. Panels are usually made in the 4-×-8-foot size, most $1/4$ inch thick and some $3/4$ inch thick. They may be hardboard with a vinyl finish or a baked-on modified melamine finish; many colors and patterns are available. Hardwood plywood panels are composed of three or more layers of wood, including a face veneer made of any of several dozen wood species both domestic and exotic. In fact, there are about 18,000 possible combinations. Wall planking is available in many wood species, several thicknesses, in full-length planks or random-length pieces, edge-matched or square-edged, end-matched or not, some prefinished and many raw.

All thin paneling or planking should be applied over a backing of $3/8$-inch or thicker gypsum wallboard, gypsum sheathing, plywood, or waferboard. These materials are typically secured with a combination of panel adhesive and ring-shanked matching-color panel nails. A backing is best installed behind $3/4$-inch plank or panel too, but is not essential. Panels or either diagonal or horizontal planks can be applied to the wall studs using nails or glue. Vertical planks must be applied to either three or four rows of cross blocking installed in the wall frame, or to a like number of horizontal 1-×-4 furring strips fastened to the wall studs (FIG. 64-1).

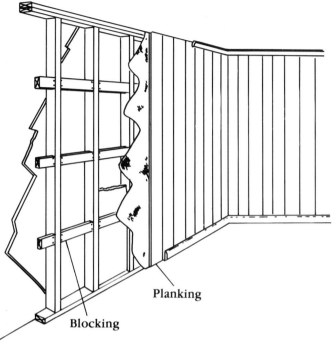

Planking

Blocking

64-1 Two or three rows of blocking or furring are installed to provide bearing and nailing surfaces for vertically applied wood wall planking.

MASONRY VENEER

A masonry veneer can be used to excellent effect as an interior wall-covering, especially on a fireplace wall, behind a wood stove, or in a kitchen. Some of the products to consider are old or new brick; natural random or cut stone; prepared tiles of marble, sandstone, slate, granite, or terrazzo; or any of several synthetic brick, slate, or stone facings.

There are two major considerations when using any of the thick natural masonry veneers. One is weight and the other is space. A single-thickness brick wall 8 by 12 feet would weigh about 4000 pounds, or 330 pounds per linear foot. Even a 3-foot wainscot would run about 125 pounds per linear foot. Stone could easily be heavier. And, such a wall or wainscot would use up about 4 to 5 inches of floor space. But if the space is programmed into the plans and the underpinnings are made substantial enough, there should be no problem. Any kind of veneering can be done if the proper preparations are made.

Stone tiles are another matter. They are typically only 1 inch or less thick, and weigh in at 2 to 6 pounds per square foot. These can be installed, using any one of several standard methods, directly to a wallboard or other suitable backing without any special engineering or structural modifications. The synthetic materials, the best of which have a very realistic appearance, are designed for do-it-yourself (as well as professional) application. Cutting and fitting is not difficult and the pieces are put up on a smooth backing using special mastic adhesive. Grouting joints is done with this same material. The backing most frequently used is gypsum wallboard, which can be left untaped.

CERAMIC TILE

In most modern houses ceramic tile is the wall covering of choice for bathrooms, and is often installed in kitchens as well. There are also other applications for this tile, such as sideboards, counters, server tops, fireplace surrounds, and stove backers. The tiles are available in a huge range of sizes, shapes, colors, and patterns. They are plain, scored, imprinted, raised, textured, hand-painted, and can come in brilliant, matte, crystalline, semimatte, and unglazed finishes. They can be combined or arranged in all kinds of ways.

Wall tiles can be applied to nearly any kind of solid, smooth backing, including gypsum wallboard (which is best taped to fill in the tapered joint areas). However, in areas where moisture might be present, the backer should be water-resistant wallboard (blue board). In high-moisture areas, especially steam rooms and shower enclosures, plan on installing a special waterproof backing board.

As with wallpapers, selection of the tile is up to the homeowner, but estimating the requirements should be done by, or with the help of, the supplier or the installer. Most builders prefer to have a professional tile setter make the installation. However, tiling is also a popular do-it-yourself job, and suppliers have become used to helping out with advice and tips. The job is neither technically nor physically difficult in most residential applications, though some practical experience helps. Only a few tools are needed for most projects, and there are many good sources of printed how-to information available on the subject.

NONCERAMIC TILES

There are several kinds of nonceramic tiles that should not be overlooked as useful wall finishes. The $4^{1}/_{4}$-inch square metal tiles work well as accent and backsplash coverings in kitchens, and can also be used in other applications. They are available in brushed finish copper, aluminum, stainless steel, and coppertone. They are easy to trim and fit, and can be applied either with mastic adhesive or tabs of double-stick foam tape.

Resilient tile flooring, which is available in several sizes and numerous colors and patterns, can be applied equally well on walls, to any smooth, solid backing. Sometimes the floor tile is wrapped right up the wall, over a cove or cant strip at the wall/floor joint, and continued as a sort of wainscot.

Mirror tiles and cork tiles are usually set as accent pieces, but both are sometimes installed to cover entire walls. They can also be inset into wall recesses so the faces are flush with the wall surface, which takes some preplanning and sheathing material surface adjustments.

WAINSCOTING

Wainscot is an ancient architectural feature that is not much seen these days, but can be installed to provide a fine decorative effect. It usually covers the bottom 3 to 4 feet of a wall, and can be installed on one or all walls of any room. Wainscot is typically found in dining, family, recreation, or great rooms, as well as dens and libraries.

There are several ways to wainscot. The most popular method is to glue thin wood wall-plank strips vertically to a gypsum wallboard backing. Base molding is applied over the bottom end of the wainscoting in the usual fashion, and the top edge is capped with a small molding (FIG. 64-2). Sections of hardwood plywood panel can be applied in the same way.

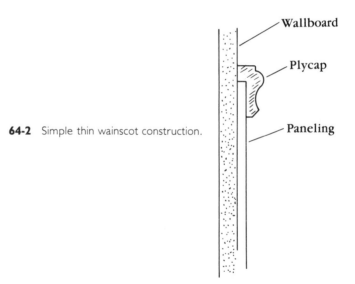

64-2 Simple thin wainscot construction.

For a heavier, more emphatic appearance, fasten 1-×-4 furring strips directly to the wall studs, with the top one at the wainscot top height. Install cross blocking between the studs at this point, and apply gypsum wallboard to the upper portion of the wall. Then blind-nail 3/4-inch boards to the furring. Unusual woods like butternut, bald cypress, tupelo, cherry, black willow, black ash, or teak can provide a rich, elegant appearance in natural finish. If the stock is not a tongue-and-groove pattern, install a thin backing like 1/8-inch hardboard. Paint or stain it to roughly match the color of the wood or applied finish being used. Then, if the joints between pieces widen somewhat, the interior of the wall won't be

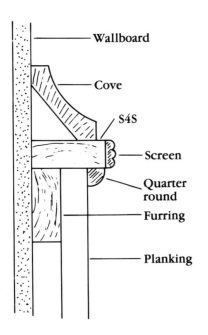

Wallboard

Cove

S4S

Screen

Quarter round

Furring

Planking

64-3 Complex deep wainscot construction.

visible and the cracks will be unobtrusive. Cap the wainscot with molding (FIG. 64-3).

There is another type of wainscot that has been successfully used in many bathrooms over the years. In modern form it consists of a water-resistant or waterproof backing that extends to a height of about 4 feet, and is covered with ceramic tile bedded in an epoxy thinset and finished with epoxy grout. A variation, less expensive and easier to construct, is excellent for a nursery or playroom. This involves nailing relatively thin plywood—1/2-inch is ample—to a gypsum wallboard backing and then bonding a plastic laminate like Formica to plywood with contact cement. A smooth-surfaced plastic in matte finish is best, and many colors and patterns are available. Apply a cap to the top of the wainscot, and a base mold at the bottom. Spills and crayon scribbles will do no harm.

The cap atop a relatively thick wainscot can range from simple to ornate, depending upon how the moldings are arranged. Square or rectangular (in cross section) S4S used alone is the simplest, while ply cap or a similar combination of moldings is a bit more decorative. As many as four or five different molding patterns can be combined in a ledge, skirt, and cover for an ornate arrangement.

Chapter **65**

Finish ceilings

*T*he most common finish ceiling continues to be painted or textured gypsum wallboard. But there are several other possibilities as well, including tile, wood plank, suspended grid, wallpaper, and beams. Ceilings don't have to be blank white expanses, although there's nothing wrong with that. They can also be an integral part of the overall interior decorating scheme, rather than just something that has to be covered over and never looked up to.

FINISHED GYPSUM WALLBOARD

The same materials that are installed on walls also serve for ceilings, and the techniques and procedures are about the same. Professionals often use long panels to reduce the number of joints, especially if doing so spans a room and avoids end joints. However, standard 4-×-8-foot panels are just as widely installed. They should be positioned with the long axis at right angles to the joists for direct attachment. Often—especially if the joist edges are uneven—the ceiling is furred or strapped with 1×4s on 16-inch centers. The furring strips can be shimmed or slightly notched into the joists so that the ceiling will be level and smooth, with no ripples.

Installation

To start the installation, trim the first sheet (if necessary) to fit snugly into a corner. Tack-nail a temporary 1-×-2 cleat to the wall just below the joists or furring to hold one end of the sheet. Tilt one end of the sheet up and lay it against the cleat, then boost the other end up and push the sheet forward onto the cleat at the same time. Hold the sheet in place with one or more T-braces made up of 1-×-4 stock (FIG. 65-1). Adjust as necessary; all joints should fall on a joist or furring strip centerline. Secure the sheet, preferably with 1¹/₄-inch extruded-thread, bugle-head wallboard screws spaced about 12 inches apart along all bearing surfaces.

The joint taping and fastener covering process is the same as for walls. It is just a little more difficult because of the overhead location.

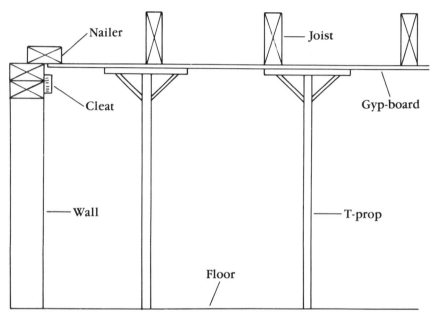

65-1   To install a gypsum wallboard panel on a ceiling, support one end on a temporary wall cleat, swing the other end up, and jam the panel in place with temporary T-props while fastening.

Painted finish

To accept a paint finish, the ceiling must be as smooth as possible. By far the most commonly applied paint is flat latex in a neutral color, but there is a myriad of shades and tones available. Neither semigloss nor high-gloss paint are usually recommended for ceilings. Some exceptions include bathrooms, laundry areas, or other locations where moisture might condense on the ceiling surface. Application can be made by brush, pad, or roller.

Textured finish

For a textured finish, the wallboard should be taped to close the joints and fill the tapered areas level, but fine smoothness is not critical. The heavier the texturing compound, the more defects and unevenness it will cover— including fastener heads and dimples. Often ceilings are spray-textured for a nubbly effect. Otherwise, application can be made as described earlier for walls.

Wallpaper

Although not a common practice, ceilings can be wallpapered. The job is not as difficult as it sounds for anyone with some paperhanging experience. Follow the same procedures as for papering walls. The wallboard must be well finished with smooth joints and coated with a suitable wallboard primer, followed by a coat of glue sizing. Some tips to help make the job easier: Set up a suitable low but wide staging for comfortable working, or wear drywaller's stilts. Select a wallcovering that lies and smooths well and is not awfully heavy. Use the correct adhesive, and work in favorable atmospheric conditions.

ACOUSTIC TILE AND PLANKING

There are many new and attractive acoustic tile patterns that are suitable for installation in any room in the house, except for steam rooms, saunas, and high-moisture bathrooms. Most tile comes in 12-inch squares $1/2$ inch thick. Some are washable. Ceiling plank has a simulated wood-grain appearance, and comes in 4-foot lengths of assorted widths. Both are usually sold by the case, although a few dealers will sell singles or broken cases. Quantities needed depend upon the room configuration and the way the tile is to be oriented; consult with the supplier.

Installation

Installation of acoustic tile can be made in several ways. One is to first install a gypsum wallboard or other backing, then glue the tiles to the backing with dots of mastic adhesive. Another is to install a series of 1-×-2 or better yet, 1-×-4 furring strips to the joist bottoms. These are shimmed or notched in as necessary for a level surface, on 12-inch centers. Tiles are then stapled to the furring strips (FIG. 65-2). A third method is to install special steel runners or tracks at right angles to the joists. The tiles clip to the tracks with special hardware. This last procedure is probably the simplest for most applications. Complete installation instructions for all of these arrangements are included with each case of tile.

SUSPENDED CEILINGS

A suspended ceiling is a complete system consisting of an interlocking, metal-channel, grid-type framework; ceiling panels that fit within the grid; and associated hardware (FIG. 65-3). Several panel patterns are available in both 2-×-2-foot and 2-×-4-foot sizes, and in two styles. In the regular style, tiles are flush with the gridwork; in the recessed style, the tile face drops slightly below the gridwork. Recessed fluorescent lighting fixtures, called *troffers*, are also available, along with several different kinds

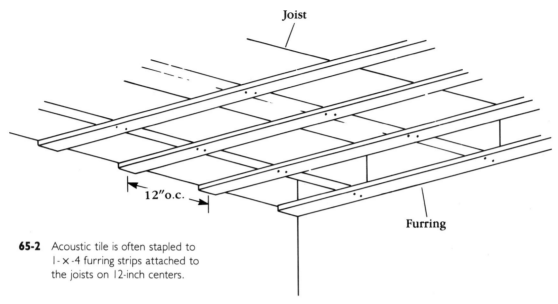

Joist

12"o.c.

Furring

65-2 Acoustic tile is often stapled to
1-×-4 furring strips attached to
the joists on 12-inch centers.

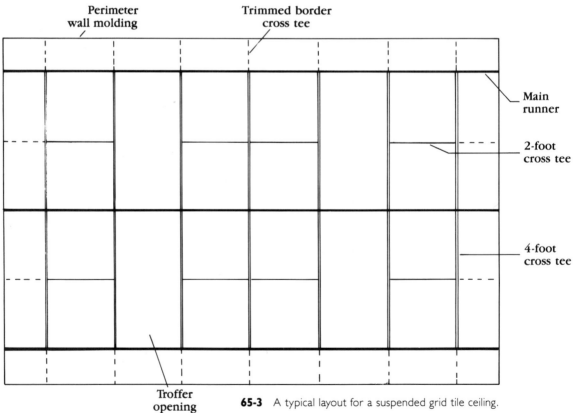

Perimeter
wall molding

Trimmed border
cross tee

Main
runner

2-foot
cross tee

4-foot
cross tee

Troffer
opening

65-3 A typical layout for a suspended grid tile ceiling.

of diffuser panels, that fit into the grid. Recessed incandescent fixtures can also be installed in the panels. These are frequently installed in kitchens, and are also applicable to some bathrooms, recreation rooms, basements, and family rooms.

Installation

Although the system seems complex, installation is not difficult and complete instructions are supplied. Enlist the help of the supplier in determining material requirements if you are unfamiliar with the process. It is a good idea to have a detailed and dimensioned outline, preferably to scale, to work with. Also, the grid can be laid out in several ways depending upon the room configuration, so a decision sometimes has to be made as to which is best, especially if integral lighting is desired. An essential requirement is several inches of working room everywhere between the grid and the joist bottoms. About 6 inches minimum is typical, but this can vary. Only hand tools and a lot of patience and climbing up and down stepladders is needed to make the installation. This is a good do-it-yourself project.

WOOD PLANK

Wood planking has been used as a finish ceiling material for centuries. In many modern designs featuring open or cathedral ceilings, where the ceiling is the underside of the roof section, decking plank or some similar stock forms the finish surface. Often it is treated with a clear finish for a natural look, sometimes it is stained, occasionally it is painted.

Installation

Wood planking can be easily attached to a conventional flat ceiling. Nominal 1-inch tongue-and-groove, end-matched boards in 4- or 6-inch widths work well, and can be applied directly to the joists by blind-nailing (FIG. 65-4). Square-edged stock should be applied over a thin backer sheathing such as 1/4-inch hardboard or plywood, so the cracks will not be overly noticeable and to keep dust from filtering through from above. Any available wood species can be applied as a finish ceiling, but softwoods are considerably easier to work than most hardwoods and generally lighter in weight as well.

Thin stock can be glued to a gypsum wallboard, waferboard, or plywood backing, along with a few nails here and there to help out. (Hardboard is too hard to nail into easily with thin panel nails.) The keys for successful installation are: Use a high-tack adhesive, do not cover too much area at one time, and support installed sections with T-props made from 1×4s until the adhesive cures. There are many different packaged wall-planking products, in various wood species and patterns, that are excellent for this purpose.

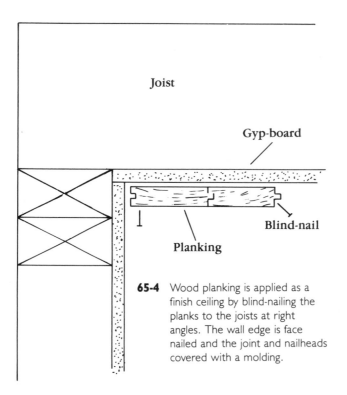

65-4 Wood planking is applied as a finish ceiling by blind-nailing the planks to the joists at right angles. The wall edge is face nailed and the joint and nailheads covered with a molding.

CERAMIC AND STONE TILE

Tile is seldom used on ceilings, but can be very effective from a decorating standpoint. Nearly any of the ceramic tiles are suitable for this purpose. Marble is the usual choice for stone, although granite or limestone may also be used. The smaller the tiles, the easier they are to put up, but nearly any size is suitable. Typical applications are bathrooms, exercise rooms, shower enclosures, steam rooms, and similar areas. However, tile is at home anywhere, as a full surface or as accent. This is a job for an experienced tile setter, and not recommended as a do-it-yourself project.

COVES AND CORNICES

Coves and cornices can be easily constructed and serve to break up and add interest to an otherwise plain, flat, dull ceiling area. They are installed at one or more wall/ceiling junctures, usually in living or dining rooms, but are found in other rooms as well. The manner of framing and the materials used depend upon the size and complexity of the cove or cornice. Large installations may be built right after completion and as a part of the wall and ceiling frameworks, or later when the framework has been sheathed.

There are several different ways to build a cornice, but basically it is a box built in place against the wall and ceiling. One method, good for a relatively small, lightweight cornice, is to mount a horizontal nailing strip to the wall for fastening the inner edge of the soffit, and another to the ceiling for the upper edge of the fascia. The soffit and fascia can be fastened together in an ell and lifted into place, then secured to the nailers as a unit (FIG. 65-5).

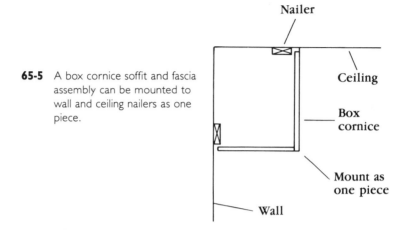

65-5 A box cornice soffit and fascia assembly can be mounted to wall and ceiling nailers as one piece.

Larger cornices can be built by constructing a number of box frames from 1×4s or strips of plywood (FIG. 65-6) and mounting them individually to the wall and ceiling. They are then covered with plywood or wallboard and trimmed out with moldings. Large cornices can also be framed with 2×4s attached directly to the studs and joists, then sheathed as the walls and ceiling are covered.

A cove, in this use, is merely a shelf with a vertical or slightly outward-angled fascia attached to the outer edge. Construction proceeds in much the same way as for a cornice. Some coves are small and strictly decorative, others are substantial and can hold plants or other objects. With a properly slanted fascia, they can also be used for indirect lighting. A combined cornice and lighting cove extending into the room for 2 feet or more is excellent for this purpose (FIG. 65-7).

BEAMS

Beams can be installed to visually break up an expanse of flat ceiling, and to add interest, and often a rustic air, in a different manner than coves and cornices. The beams may be full-sized real timbers set beneath the ceiling, or full timbers sawn in half lengthwise to appear half-concealed in the ceiling construction. In both cases, the beams are set into beam pockets built into the wall frames before the sheathing goes on. The beams can actually be load-bearing, supporting part of the weight of the floor above, or nonload-bearing and only decorative.

A more common arrangement is to install box or false beams, either

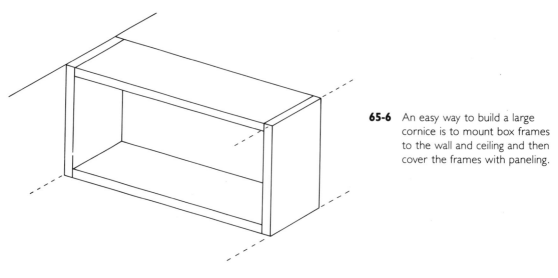

65-6 An easy way to build a large cornice is to mount box frames to the wall and ceiling and then cover the frames with paneling.

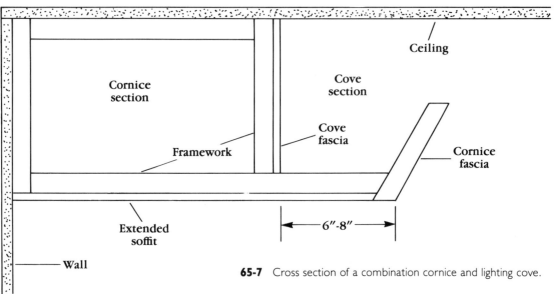

Ceiling

Cornice section

Cove section

Cove fascia

Framework

Cornice fascia

6"-8"

Extended soffit

Wall

65-7 Cross section of a combination cornice and lighting cove.

half or full. There are several ways to build them, but one easy design uses a 2×6 or 2×8 lagged flat to the ceiling joists to form a base. Then a 1×6 or 1×8 is attached to each side, with another between them as a bottom. Moldings can be added as desired, and the beams can also be made to look old by denting, scratching, scarring, making adze marks with a hatchet, and making a few rust-stained nail holes. With concealed glued joints and enough abuse, a false beam can be made to look quite authentic. Refer to Chapter 50 for more information.

Chapter **66**

Finish flooring

*T*he subflooring and finish flooring in a house, or in one part of a house, might be one and the same. Such is the case, for example, with a smooth-finished concrete basement floor. Sometimes 5/4 finish plank flooring is installed with no subfloor, or 2-×-6 tongue-and-groove decking material may be laid over wide-spaced beams to serve as finish floor above and finish ceiling below. However, in most instances any one of several other finish floor coverings are installed over a sub-floor. Often two or more different kinds of floorings are used in the same house, as well as a variety of colors and patterns.

The most common flooring choices include stretched-in carpeting, wood strip, sheet vinyl, vinyl tile, and ceramic tile. Less popular coverings are wood plank, rubber tile, carpet tile, glued carpeting, stone tile, flagstone, brick, terrazzo, and seamless poured plastic. In many cases, installing underlayment before finish flooring is either advisable or necessary. This strengthens and stiffens the floor; adds a bit of insulating value; affords a clean, smooth surface for the finish flooring; and compensates for different thicknesses of materials, so the entire finished floor will be at a uniform level.

UNDERLAYMENT

There are several kinds of underlayment that all accomplish the same purpose, but are not all necessarily suitable under all kinds of finish flooring. Self-stick tile or carpet squares, for example, will not adhere to particle board. Plywood is a common choice, in APA Underlayment INT grade for interior use. There are other grades for various conditions, too, all available in several thicknesses. Particle board, chipboard, and waferboard are useful for underlayment, and also are available in various grades, densities, and thicknesses. All of these materials are usually installed as 4-×-8-foot sheets. Another possibility is hardboard in underlayment grade, which comes in 4-×-4-foot sheets $1/4$ inch thick. Low-density fibrous soundboard is sometimes installed as underlayment where sound control is important.

To lay plywood or other sheet materials except hardboard, start at a corner and lay the sheets best face up (if there's a difference) at right angles to the subflooring. Do not allow joints to coincide. Leave a gap at the wall lines of about $1/4$ inch for plywood, $3/8$ inch for the others. Leave a $1/32$- to $1/16$-inch gap at all end and edge joints. Stagger all joints and make all cuts square and clean so they fit up well. For $1/4$- to $1/2$-inch thicknesses, fasten with 3d ring-shank nails; use 4d nails for $5/8$- and $3/4$-inch thicknesses. Space the nails in about $3/4$ inch from the edges and 6 inches apart, and space intermediate nailing 8 inches apart in all directions for plywood, 10 inches for the other boards. If you can determine the locations of the floor joists and are able to align some of the nailing with them, do so with 8d nails.

To lay hardboard, follow the same procedures but lay the pieces rough side up, not smooth. Leave a gap of about $1/8$ inch along the wall lines and about $1/16$ inch between panels at all joints. Fasten the panels with 2d or 3d ring-shank nails, $3/8$ inch in from the edges and 3 inches apart, and spaced 6 inches apart in both directions in the field.

CARPETING

Carpeting of one sort or another is suitable for every room in a house, except for a workshop. Special types are available for bathrooms and kitchens. These are usually fitted and laid in place loose over another, water- and stain-resistant finish flooring like sheet vinyl, and can be easily taken up for washing or cleaning.

Carpeting that is stretched in over a pad, wall to wall, should be laid over a smooth subfloor or underlayment. The floor height should be adjusted as desired to compensate for the thickness of the selected type of pad and carpet; the combination can be well over 1 inch in some cases. Roughness, gaps, holes and other defects will eventually telegraph through to the carpet surface. Carpet installation is usually done by professionals, but the equipment can be rented and many do-it-yourselfers have successfully laid carpet.

Carpeting can also be glued directly to the subfloor or underlayment, and here it is essential that the surface be smooth and clean. A special mastic adhesive is used, and a plywood surface is usually considered best. Installation is a matter of trimming the carpet to closely fit the room, spreading the adhesive section by section and smoothing the rolled-back carpeting out onto it, and making sure there are no dry spots, wrinkles, bulges, trapped air bubbles, or glue gobs. The last step is to fasten a shoe molding to the baseboard to cover the carpet edge. This carpeting is installed without a pad and is typically thin, so matching the level to adjoining floorings of a different kind can usually be done with special carpet-edge molding.

WOOD STRIP AND PLANK

A wide variety of manufactured wood strip and plank flooring is available in numerous wood species. It can be prefinished but is mostly unfinished, in thicknesses ranging from 5/16 inch up and random lengths, usually edge- and end-matched. There is also a substantial array of plain wood boards or planks that can be employed for this purpose, in all manner of sizes and wood species. Strip flooring usually refers to widths of 3 1/2 inches or less in width. Plank flooring is wider than that; to most people the term ''plank flooring'' means boards at least 6 inches wide and preferably more.

The details of estimating requirements and installing and finishing various kinds of wood plank or strip flooring are outside the scope of this book; the subject is extensive. In general, materials 3/4 to 1 1/4 inches thick are usually laid directly on a subfloor. Those less than 3/4 inch require either a thicker-than-usual subflooring or an underlayment. Materials over 1 1/2 inch thick can be attached directly to joists or beams. When the floor frame is designed, thought must be given to the kind of subflooring/finish flooring combination that will eventually be installed.

WOOD PARQUET

Wood parquet or pattern flooring, also called block flooring, is an old method of installing finish wood floorings that can bear handsome results. Today a variety of readily available, fairly inexpensive parquet block products are available that are suitable for do-it-yourself installation. For this reason, parquet flooring has gained rapidly in popularity. Slat or finger blocks, factory prefinished in 12-inch square interlocking tiles, usually about 5/16 or 3/8 inch thick, are probably the most commonly used materials.

Installation consists of making a tile layout pattern in the same way as for any tile installation, then setting the pieces in a special mastic adhesive. Trimming can be done with nearly any kind of saw fitted with a fine-toothed blade, including handsaws. The substrate can be plywood or any of the solid wood-product composition boards; parquet tile or slat should not be set directly on concrete. The thin tile is generally installed over an underlayment that suitably adjusts the height of the finish surface. Heavy tile—in the 1/2- to 3/4-inch range—can be set directly on 1/2-inch or thicker plywood subflooring. Use thin underlayment as an interface over board subflooring.

CERAMIC TILE

Ceramic tile has long been a favorite finish flooring, and today there is a wider than ever variety of products from which you can make selections.

The most common usage of tile is in bathrooms, but it is often installed in kitchens, nurseries, foyers and entryways, mud rooms, some halls and interior stairs. Many people also use tile for smaller accent areas, such as a fireplace hearth or a small floor section in front of a built-in sideboard or bar. It is also a popular material for countertops, kitchen and otherwise, and for counter backsplashes and lavatory surrounds.

Thick-bed method

There are two general processes for ceramic tile installation (FIG. 66-1): thin-set or thick-bed. There are variations on each. Thick-bed setting results in the longest-lived, most durable flooring and involves laying the tile in a mortar bed spread over a layer of concrete. The thickness of the section, which can be substantial, must be compensated for so that the various floorings are level with one another. This is usually accomplished by building the tile-designated floor frames lower than the other, or by elevating the nontile floor sections, depending upon which is the more complex and costly procedure. Also, in some cases the substantial weight of the flooring, especially if it covers a large area, must be considered when an underlying wood frame floor construction is designed. The thick-bed method can be readily used on a concrete slab floor on or below grade. (Figure 25-4 in Chapter 25 shows one method of providing a concrete surface on a suspended frame floor.)

Thin-set method

In residential applications, a thin-set method is usually considered adequate. Professionals prefer to lay floor tile in either a dry-set mortar or a

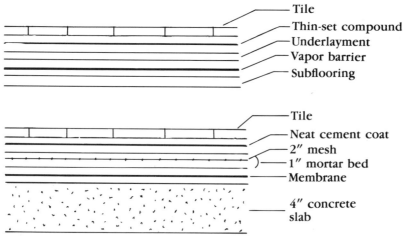

66-1   The thin-set method of ceramic tile laying (above) uses any of several adhesive compounds. The thick-bed method (below) can be used on a sturdy wood substrate as well as on a concrete slab.

latex-portland cement mortar, both of which give excellent results. The organic adhesive or mastic method is suitable for most residential applications, and is ideal for do-it-yourself projects. It can be used over all wood substrates and also small areas of moisture- and alkali-free concrete. An epoxy thin-set, best handled by a professional, is most suitable for large areas of concrete slab.

In all of these methods, the minimum thickness of the subfloor should be 5/8 inch. A good arrangement is 1/2-inch plywood subflooring topped with cross-laid 1/2-inch underlayment plywood. The key is to reduce deflection of the flooring to practically zero, to obviate cracking and loosening of both tiles and grout lines. Thus, the overall thickness of floor sections tiled with a thin-set method must also be considered as construction proceeds.

STONE AND BRICK

Stone or brick are sometimes laid as finish floors, especially in greenhouse or sunspace rooms, but often in dining areas, kitchens, and rec rooms as well. Both of these are often seen as fireplace or wood-stove area floorings. Brick is usually laid flat, sometimes on edge, either in a mortar bed or sand bed, and the joints can be filled with either. Natural random stone must be well bedded in mortar, and the joints are grouted with mortar. These constructions are heavy; a full bed 6 inches thick overall can run 75 pounds or more per square foot. Installation on a concrete slab, the surface height of which must be set to suit the thickness of the finish floor, is the best bet because it can easily support the weight. If the installation is made on a suspended wood-framed subfloor, the construction must be engineered to suit, rugged and well made.

Stone tile or flagstones 1 inch thick or less are a different matter. Granite, sandstone, limestone, marble, and slate are often used for this purpose, either as random-shaped flags or regular cut pieces. If they are cut or ground smooth on the backside, they can be laid with one of the thin-set methods, in some cases even with an organic adhesive. If they are rough-faced, a mortar bed works best. Either way the overall weight is light, anywhere from 2 to 7 pounds per square foot, and the overall thickness is not exceptional either. The floor frame should be stiff and sturdy, but special construction or added support is usually not needed. Consider 5/8-inch plywood as a minimum thickness for the subflooring. Thicker is better, and subflooring plus cross-laid plywood underlayment is better yet. Adjoining floor areas will probably have to be height-adjusted to some degree.

VINYL SHEET AND TILE

Both of these products are available in an endless array of colors and patterns, and also in several sizes, thicknesses, and quality levels. As a rule their use is restricted to kitchens, bathrooms, entryways and mud rooms, laundries, and sometimes nurseries and rec rooms, but they actually can be laid anywhere. These materials are all thin, typically about 5/32 inch or less, and have varying degrees of resiliency. All are flexible and cushiony to some degree—some include a layer of foam cushion—and they must be applied over a smooth, even, defect-free surface. This usually means that underlayment must be installed, both for the clean surface and to build the finish level up to match other floorings, in compensation for the thinness of the vinyl.

Some of the sheet floorings are manufactured with the do-it-your-selfer in mind. Most, however, are best installed by a professional crew, especially if the room configuration is complex. The tile, which is available in several sizes—with 12-×-12-inch and 9-×-9-inch being common—is easy to work and an owner-builder can do the job readily. Written how-to information on installing these floorings abounds; no special preparation is needed except as noted for the sheet vinyl products.

Chapter **67**

Cabinetry
and built-ins

One of the construction elements that separates ordinary "cookie-cutter" houses from those with greater flair, livability, convenience, and value, is the quality and scope of the cabinetry and other built-in storage or furnishing items. Better homes do not consist of a series of barren cubicles like the cloisters of a monastery, but rather are extensively fitted with integral facilities throughout for the enhancement of daily living. These constructions include the following:

- Capacious kitchen cabinetry with various built-in appointments, stationary appliances and aids, ample storage space for small appliances and cookware, pantry-type storage for foodstuffs, and closet storage for household cleaning and maintenance supplies and equipment.

- In dining areas, substantial storage area both closed and glass-fronted or open to house china, tableware, glassware and crystal, table linens, and assorted dining and party specialty items. Also, space enough for wine and liquor storage and associated items, even if the house owners are totally abstinent.

- In living, family, great, and recreation rooms, ample storage space in the form of cabinets or cupboards, drawer units, and bookshelves, for books, papers, magazines, games, hobby equipment, stereo and video equipment, and all such family entertainment paraphernalia. Also, open or closed shelving, window seats, closets, and built-in furnishings such as a wall-hung couch, a conversation pit, or fireplace seating.

- In a den or library, bookshelves, built-in desks or a worktable, perhaps built-in stereo or video equipment, a gun cabinet or other display cabinetry, or file cabinets.

- In bedroom closets, sets of special drawers and/or bins for sweaters, socks, and other articles, full-sized bureau-type drawers in stacks, open and closed shelving, shoe or boot racks or drawers, necktie racks, and so on. Also beds that include storage headboards and footboards, as well as drawer units beneath, and cabinets or drawer sections that can be separately built right into a wall face.

- In bathrooms, storage cabinetry for a plethora of medicants and health aids, personal grooming items, sickroom gear, and possibly physical fitness equipment. Ample medicine-chest space can be built in between wall studs, and custom cabinetry can support the lavatories and provide a great deal of general storage area, as can an over-toilet arrangement. At least one full-sized closet fitted with shelves above and drawers below should be built in for storage of linens, bedding, and towels (this kind of storage is often located in a convenient hallway, too).

- In entryways, foyers, mud rooms, vestibules and similar entry points, built-in storage space for winter clothing, outerwear, and sometimes assorted equipment as well, like a snowshovel. Also, drying racks for clothing and boots, and in the front entry a closet to hold dressy outerwear and the coats and hats of guests.

- Closet and other storage space for all of the odds and ends that any family accumulates over time: toys, yard and garden equipment and supplies, tools, suitcases and trunks, sporting goods, trash barrels, etc.

There are a thousand and one ways to construct various kinds of cabinetry and built-ins. This large but fascinating subject includes the niceties of joinery, drawer and door construction, and the details of casework; numerous books are available on the subject. Insofar as the framing of the house is concerned, not a great deal needs to be done to accommodate these constructions. Closets and any other elements that will be recessed into a wall must be made a part of the framing plans early on, and they are built up as construction proceeds, using the standard framing methods. In most instances the spaces, which are really nothing more than tiny rooms, are also sheathed in the usual fashion before anything else is done. Then whatever added construction is required, such as installing shelves or drawer sets, can be done as each item demands, and the finishing and trimwork coordinated with that of the rest of the house.

Kitchen cabinets of all kinds are readily available from numerous manufacturers and also can be custom-made at dozens of shops throughout the country, in both standard and special sizes. Many of the styles are suitable for use in other parts of the house, such as a rec room, workshop, walk-in storage closet, or dining room. Bathroom cabinets of various sorts are also readily available. In the smaller sizes, these units can be surface-mounted on the walls with no prior preparation. For a large, multiple-unit installation like a row of kitchen wall or base cabinets, however, it is a good idea to install blocking and/or nailing strips in the wall frame as it is being constructed. This affords ample rugged support for the cabinetry—which when filled can be very heavy—with a minimum of struggle. In most cases installation is made after the walls and ceilings are sheathed, but before trim has been installed and finish work started.

Other built-ins may be framed as the pertinent parts of the structure are framed, then completed after the wall sheathing has been put on, but before finish and trimwork takes place. Items that need no integral framing can be built later. At least a general idea of what is required should be determined during the house planning stages, so that enough space in the proper locations can be allowed for the various installations. Then the finish and trimwork on these items can be coordinated with the rest of the work in the area, in a logical sequence and with compatible materials.

For example, a full-height built-in bookshelf would be started after the wall and ceiling has been sheathed, at about the time the room is ready for trimming out. The sides and shelves can be put together as the mopboards and door and window casings are fitted, tying the bottom of the bookcase in with the mopboard. Then as the wall/ceiling molding is installed it can be run right along the sides and face of the bookcase. Just before or just after this, the ceiling can be painted. Then all the woodwork including the bookcase is filled, sanded, and painted in the same operation. Finally, the wallpaper is hung, the finish flooring is laid, and a shoe molding is installed.

Chapter **68**

Interior trim

*T*he interior trim of a house, as far as the carpentry is concerned, consists of the various moldings that are applied as part of the finish work. Some houses, especially inexpensive tract homes, have little or nothing in the way of trimwork. In many expensive custom-built houses the trimwork is skimpy, insubstantial, and appears not to have been coordinated with the house design at all. For the most part, the quality, design, and coordination of the interior trimwork in a house can make or break its finished appearance. Although the job can be overdone, a lack of good trimwork creates a pedestrian appearance that can do little to complement the decor. The total cost and effort involved even in extensive trimwork represents only a small fraction of the overall cost of the house. Why pinch pennies here? This is an area where, if you want to, you can add much for very little.

The trimwork is composed of moldings, which can be a single element or a composite made up of two or more different moldings. One problem is that most lumberyards, especially small ones, only stock a few molding patterns, yet there are dozens of commercial styles and sizes in standard patterns. Dozens more can be turned out by custom milling or woodworking shops. With the aid of a planer-molder, a spindle shaper, or even a router/shaper, moldings may even be made up on the job site.

FLOOR/WALL TRIM

There are three areas in a house where most of the trim is installed. The first is at the floor/wall joints, with the moldings being fastened to the wall (FIG. 68-1). Often this joint is gapped purposely to allow for expan-

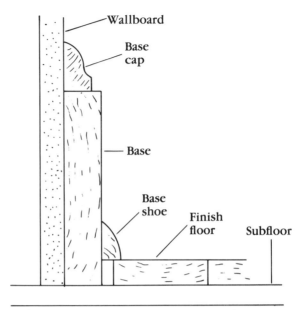

Wallboard

Base cap

Base

Base shoe

Finish floor

Subfloor

68-1 A typical molding installation at a floor/wall joint.

sion of the underlayment and/or finish flooring. A wide baseboard (or mopboard) is a good choice here, and the bigger the room and the higher the ceiling, the taller the baseboard can be. Plain S4S is one possibility, and it can be used as a starting point and further trimmed with other, smaller moldings along the face or upper edge. That upper edge molding is the base cap, and there are several stock patterns. There are also several stock patterns of baseboard. When the baseboard does not cover a flooring expansion gap, shoe molding can be attached to the lower face of the baseboard (not to the flooring) to accomplish that purpose. Again, numerous patterns are available.

WALL/CEILING TRIM

The second area of consideration is the wall/ceiling joint. This sometimes is not treated with a molding at all, because there is no need to leave the joint open, and it can be taped and coated with compound just like all the other wall and ceiling joints. Unless a characterless pencil-line transition from wall to ceiling is desired, this is a favorite spot to install at least a simple cove molding, and often a more decorative crown or bed molding, all of which are available in several standard sizes and patterns (FIG. 68-2). In high-ceilinged rooms, more complex and ornate moldings can be installed, either by concocting a composite of several stock or custom patterns, or by installing a commercially manufactured architectural molding in a classical pattern such as Georgian, egg and dart, or ivy leaves.

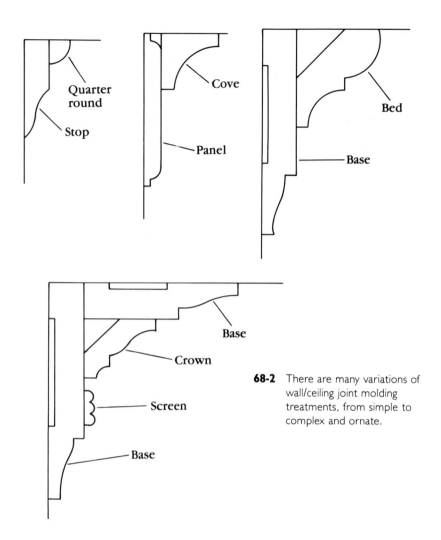

68-2 There are many variations of wall/ceiling joint molding treatments, from simple to complex and ornate.

DOOR AND WINDOW TRIM

The third major area of consideration is the door and window trim. Usually these keep the same pattern or motif, although the sizes might differ between the two. At the least, a narrow, plain molding must be installed as side and head casings around both doors and windows to conceal and seal off the open joint between the rough framing and wall sheathing and the finish frame. But there are many other possibilities, too. S4S works fine, and is a good base for a composite arrangement; you can add screen, half-round, quarter-round, flat astragal, base cap, or panel moldings to it (FIG. 68-3). There are stock casing patterns, that can also be used and mullion or chair rail makes an interesting trim.

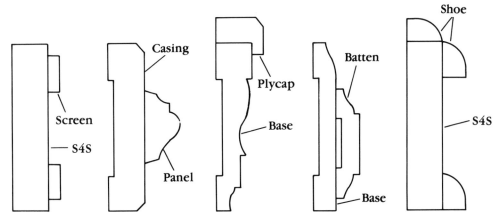

68-3 A few of the many different molding combinations that can be used to trim doors and windows.

OTHER TRIMWORK

In addition to these areas, there are usually other points in a house where trimwork is needed: surrounds around built-in items like a woodbox or an open cabinet, for example. Bookshelves and other cabinetry often are fitted with trim to match other nearby trimwork. Flush doors, either full-sized or cabinet, can be trimmed with various kinds of flat-backed moldings to form patterns. The same can be done on walls. Often a chair rail is set horizontally about 3 to 4 feet above the floor, then moldings can be used to form geometrics above or below the rail, or both. Ceilings can be trimmed this way, and so can stairways, stairwells, and step sets. Plain, flat lattice is a favorite for trimwork of this sort. In fact, there is no end of things you can do in the way of trimming out with moldings, and the effects can be handsome indeed.

Chapter **69**

Decks and porches

Up until fairly recent times, a porch was considered a necessity on almost every house. Today, porches are not as popular as they once were; in fact porches on many houses have been remodeled into enclosed sunspaces or greenhouses. Some house designs do include a small porch or roofed entrance as a convenience, and a few large porches are still being built.

Outdoor living—complete with barbecue, landscaping, and often a pool of some sort is today's watchword, especially in the West and Southwest, and this involves decks and patios. A patio is usually a grade-level masonry construction, often of brick, flagstones, concrete, or tile, that is independent of the house structure. Decks and porches, however, are usually built of wood, and in most cases depend upon the house structure for part of their support. Both can be added as afterthoughts to any house, but in the interests of construction ease and economy, they should be designed and incorporated during the house planning stage, then built in logical sequence along with the rest of the structure.

PORCHES

The fundamentals of porch construction are not difficult. Often porches are built using the same materials and methods as used in the house construction process. There are many design variations. A porch floor can be made by extending a portion of the first-floor frame beyond the house sill as though it were being cantilevered (see Chapter 24). A series of pier supports are then provided at the outer end, as well as at intermediate points as necessary. Or, the joists can be attached to a ledger plate fastened

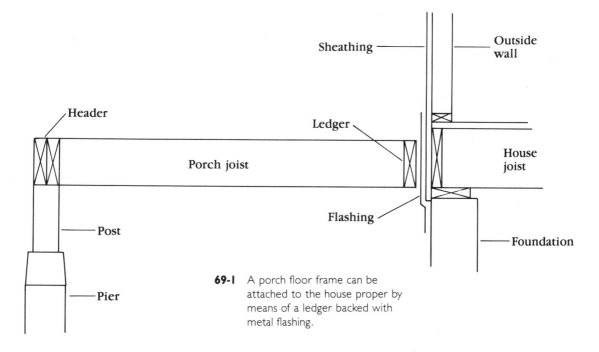

69-1 A porch floor frame can be attached to the house proper by means of a ledger backed with metal flashing.

through the exterior sheathing to the house sill, with flashing between the ledger and the sheathing (FIG. 69-1).

Another alternative is to pour a concrete foundation stem wall along the porch perimeter and raise the grade level inside the resulting box with compacted gravel. Then pour a 4-inch-thick reinforced concrete slab whose inner edge rests atop the house foundation wall and against a set-back sill and header or end joist. Install flashing in between. The outer edges all lie atop the porch foundation wall, keyed to it with reinforcing rod, and the surface is a few inches below the inside finished floor level (FIG. 69-2).

The outer edge of the porch roof is supported by columns of wood or metal. There is one at each corner, one on each side of the steps, and the required number of intermediate posts to carry the roof load and securely anchor the roof against the wind. Remember, the roof is a big sail, or wing, depending upon how the wind hits it. The posts are anchored to the foundation piers or slab with hardware made for the purpose. A beam, usually made up of two 2×6s or 2×8s on edge with a 1×4 fastened to their bottom edges, surmounts the posts and is attached with mounting hardware.

The house ends of the rafters can be anchored in any of several ways. One is to nail them to the wall studs before the exterior sheathing is installed; this makes a solid arrangement. Another more common method is to attach a ledger plate to the studs after the sheathing has been put on, then secure the rafter ends to the ledger with steel framing anchors. A

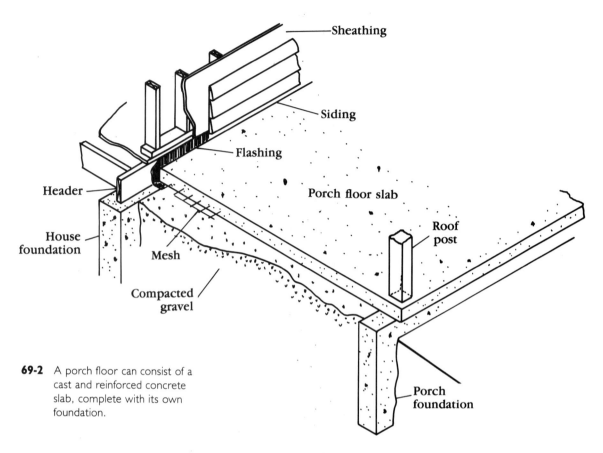

69-2 A porch floor can consist of a cast and reinforced concrete slab, complete with its own foundation.

third method is to fasten the rafters directly to the wall cap plate and the outer ends of the main roof rafters, just as any shed roof would be installed. Then the roof sheathing blends smoothly from one pitch to the other. The other ends of the rafters lie atop the beam and extend a short distance so that a soffit and fascia can be installed, along with face trim for the beam. The porch can have a ceiling; boards or exterior gypsum wallboard are often used. In this case the soffit should be well vented. Ordinary roof sheathing is then installed. The finish roofing usually matches the main roof, although it sometimes is a different material. Figure 69-3 shows a typical porch roof construction.

DECKS

A deck is essentially a porch without a roof, although it is generally easier and less expensive to construct on a per-square-foot basis. Because decks have no protection from the weather, they are almost always built of redwood and/or pressure preservative-treated stock. Some are considerably more extensive and complex than porches, if they are on several levels

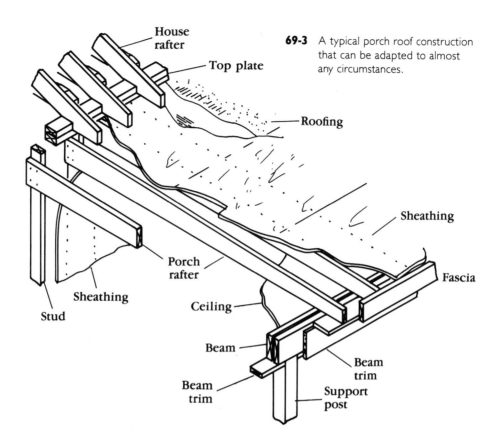

69-3 A typical porch roof construction that can be adapted to almost any circumstances.

House rafter

Top plate

Roofing

Sheathing

Porch rafter

Fascia

Sheathing

Ceiling

Stud

Beam

Beam trim

Beam trim

Support post

and include attached walkways, planters, retaining walls, benches, and other amenities. In this case, the eventual cost of the deck is likely to be more.

The methods of building a deck, and the designs and ideas for them, seem to be endless. One of the most popular methods, useful for decks

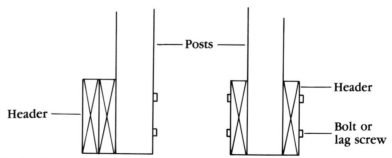

Posts

Header

Header

Bolt or lag screw

69-4 A deck post can be bolted or lagged to a doubled header or rim joist, or set between a pair of rim joists separated for just that purpose.

up to about 4 feet above grade level, is as follows: At the outer end, as well as intermediate points, cast small (6- to 10-inch) piers in tube forms. Space 6 to 8 feet apart. Mount single or double headers (depending upon size, deck loading, and pier spacing) on the piers using steel anchoring hardware made for the purpose. The deck joists can rest atop these members, or be fastened between them with steel framing anchors.

The decking is typically 2-×-4 or 2-×-6 stock laid at right angles to the joists. These are usually on 16-inch centers—or on 24-inch centers for the 6-inch-wide decking. A rim of the same material is often added around the perimeter. Nailing is not a good idea, especially in winter country, because the nails will inevitably pop up from freeze-thaw cycles. This makes snow shoveling an exasperating chore. Use long, annular-threaded, Phillips-slotted, bugle-headed deck screws. Drive them with a heavy-duty, clutch-equipped or variable-torque power driver (rentable) until the heads countersink slightly. Penetration into the joists should be at least $1^{1/4}$ inches.

Any portion of a deck that is more than an average step above grade— 8 to 10 inches, 12 maximum—should be fitted with a railing, if not edged with attached benches or planters. Spacing of 4 feet is satisfactory for posts. Bolt or lag-screw these to the rim or header joists (FIG. 69-4). The main support posts can also be brought up through the deck planking to serve as part of the railing assembly. Then attach two or three horizontal rails to the posts with bolts or lag screws, and add a cap to the top (FIG. 69-5).

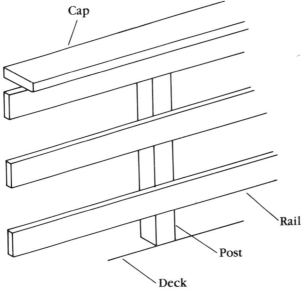

Cap

Rail

Post

Deck

69-5 A deck railing can be easily built much like a fence, with two or three rails surmounted by a flat cap.

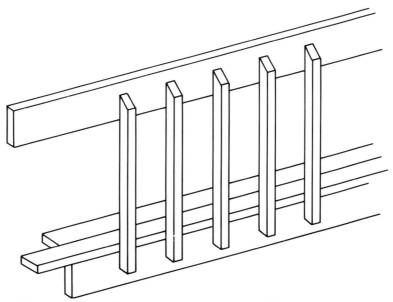

69-6 This arrangement of 2-×-2 balusters bolted to the rim joist and a cap rail is popular for both decks and balconies.

There are innumerable other designs. One popular arrangement has no large posts but a continuous row of 2-×-2 balusters lagged or bolted to the outside of the rim, with a 2×6 bolted on edge to their upper ends (FIG. 69-6).

Index